DANCE ME A SONG

Dance Me a Song

ASTAIRE, BALANCHINE, KELLY, AND
THE AMERICAN FILM MUSICAL

Beth Genné

To Sue + Dick
└ the best A² dance critic
Love,
Beth

OXFORD
UNIVERSITY PRESS

Oxford University Press is a department of the University of Oxford. It furthers
the University's objective of excellence in research, scholarship, and education
by publishing worldwide. Oxford is a registered trade mark of Oxford University
Press in the UK and certain other countries.

Published in the United States of America by Oxford University Press
198 Madison Avenue, New York, NY 10016, United States of America.

© Oxford University Press 2018

Library of Congress Cataloging-in-Publication Data
Names: Genné, Beth, author.
Title: Dance me a song : Astaire, Balanchine, Kelly, and the American
Film Musical / Beth Genné.
Description: New York : Oxford University Press, [2018] |
Includes bibliographical references and index.
Identifiers: LCCN 2017011492 (print) | LCCN 2016043882 (ebook) |
ISBN 9780195382181 (cloth : alk. paper) | ISBN 9780199700332 (updf) |
ISBN 9780190624170 (epub)
Subjects: LCSH: Dance in motion pictures, television, etc. | Choreography. |
Astaire, Fred. | Balanchine, George. | Kelly, Gene, 1912–1996.
Classification: LCC GV1779 .G46 2017 (ebook) | LCC GV1779 (print) |
DDC 792.8—dc23
LC record available at https://lccn.loc.gov/2017011492

9 8 7 6 5 4 3 2 1

Printed by Sheridan Books, Inc., United States of America

To Allan with love

Contents

ACKNOWLEDGMENTS ix

Introduction: The Choreographer-Director and the Synergy of Music and Moving Image 1

PART ONE | FROM STAGE TO SCREEN

1. *Astaire's Outlaw Style and Its New World Roots* 15

2. *Astaire's Roots in Ballroom, Ballet, and Other Forms* 35

3. *Old World Meets New World on Broadway: Balanchivadze and Dukelsky Meet the Gershwins and Rodgers and Hart* 63

4. *Balanchine in Hollywood: Jazz Ballet for the Camera* 89

5. *Dancing with the Camera: Introducing Kelly and Donen* 115

PART TWO | FILM-DANCE GENRES

6. *Song and Dance as Courtship* 143

7. *Freedom Incarnate: The Dancing Sailor as an Icon of American Values in World War II* 167

8. *'S Wonderful: Euphoric Street Dances* 179

9. *Dreaming in Dance: Astaire, Minnelli, Kelly, and Donen* 193

PART THREE | MAKING FILM DANCE

10. *Making Film Dance: The Through-Composed, Through-Choreographed Musical* 229

11. *Legacy* 255

APPENDIX: TIMELINE 271
NOTES 287
REFERENCES 323
INDEX 331

Acknowledgments

THIS BOOK IS a culmination of many, many years of research. I am grateful for the archives, and I wish to thank first the archivists, curators, and librarians without whom scholars like me couldn't do our research. The list that follows is necessarily incomplete, as I cannot hope to acknowledge every single one of those who have helped me, some of whose names I do not even know. At the British Film Institute: Elizabeth Heasman, Virginia Hennessy, and John Gillet and Gillian Hartnoll. The National Film Archive, London. At the Victoria and Albert Theatre Museum Archives, the remarkable dance historian Jane Pritchard, along with Jonathan Grey, now editor of *Dancing Times*. Boston University, the Howard Gotlieb Collection and its curators. At the Museum of Modern Art Archives: Charles Silver and Steve Harvey, who shared my interest in Vincente Minnelli and Fred Astaire. The Schaumburg Collection, New York Public Library, and their dedicated librarians and archivists. At the University of Southern California: Ned Comstock and the holdings of the Freed Unit and Roger Edens Collection. The Margaret Herrick Library of the Academy of Motion Picture Arts and Sciences, especially Sandra Archer, who has become a valued friend. At the Library of Congress, I would especially like to thank Elizabeth Aldrich, the founder and curator of the Dance Heritage Coalition, which has contributed so much to the history of dance, as well as the curator of their film archive. The Columbia University Oral History Archive. The archives on World War II in Caen, France.

At the Ira and Lenore Gershwin Trust, San Francisco, Mark Trent Goldberg helped me in my research for the Popular Balanchine Project, not only allowing me to see and copy material from Ira Gershwin's work with Vernon Duke and Balanchine on their numbers for Josephine Baker, but providing me with the unpublished score for Ira and

Vernon Duke's music written for Josephine Baker directed by Balanchine. More recently, the Gershwin family member L. J. Strunsky, who now heads the trust, has been extremely helpful in many ways, including with permissions to quote Ira Gershwin's lyrics. The Harvard Theatre Collection at the Houghton Library of Harvard University, holder of Balanchine's personal papers, including his copy of the piano score for *An American in Paris*, which, with George Gershwin's permission, he edited for the "American in Paris" ballet for the film *Goldwyn Follies*, and their wonderful staff. The Jerome Robbins Dance Collection at the New York Public Library for the Performing Arts at Lincoln Center, and many of its librarians, starting with Genevieve Oswald, its founder, and Madeline Nichols, along with Jan Schmidt and Linda Murray, and their wonderful librarians, archivists, and dance historians Susan Au, Tanisha Jones, Charles Perrier, Daisy Pommer, Patricia Rader, and all of the others on its extraordinarily helpful staff, including Eydie Wiggins. At the George Balanchine Foundation: Ellen Sorrin and, most of all, the extraordinary Nancy Reynolds, director of research at the Balanchine Foundation and founder of the Balanchine Interpreter's Archive, who helped me with permissions to publish excerpts. I first met Nancy in a summer seminar run by Selma Jeanne Cohen, and I have benefited enormously both from her encouragement and from her knowledge of Balanchine and willingness to discuss him with me over many years now. It was my involvement with the Popular Balanchine Project, spearheaded by Nancy and Claude Conyers, that led me to research, gather, and then benefit from the treasure trove of material I was able to collect as director of research for the Hollywood films of Balanchine and for *Ziegfeld Follies of 1936*, all of which I have used in the chapters on Balanchine in this book. I have also made use of materials collected by my colleagues who researched other Balanchine Broadway shows, including Lynn Garafola, Camille Hardy, Marilyn Hunt, and Barbara Newman.

My most important informants have been those artists who were directly involved in creating the works discussed in this book. These early encounters, along with close analytical study, sometimes frame by frame, were crucial to how I shaped my approach to this material. Finding out about the actual process of the creation of their work and their own aims and concerns were at the heart of my research.

I wish to thank Vincente Minnelli and Stanley Donen—both of whom read and commented on the dissertation on which this book is in part based. Minnelli's encouragement of my approach to the analysis of his films in my dissertation (and whose marginal comments therein I still cherish) and his appreciation of my first published article on *Meet Me in St. Louis* helped me stay on the path I was taking—the path of using visual and musical analysis as main tools. Minnelli furthered my interest in reconstructing the complex, many-layered work of actual film- and dance-making as it occurs on the ground, so to speak, and connecting that to the historical and cultural context in which it occurs.

I especially acknowledge these further sources: Interviews with the music director and orchestrator Saul Chaplin, who worked closely with Gene Kelly, and with Bill Saracino, a virtuoso musical editor who worked on Kelly and Astaire musicals at Metro-Goldwyn-Mayer (MGM) and who demonstrated the intricate task of wedding music to moving image, opening my eyes to the varied and complex tasks involved in postproduction as well as production. (I still treasure the strip of film he gave me.) Betsy Blair Reisz, Gene Kelly's first wife, who was first hired by Kelly as a dancer, talked to me about his approach to work and his involvement in the dance world around him. Their daughter, Kerry Kelly Novick, also talked to me about her father, as did her son, Benjamin Novick, who shared images of his grandfather and his family doing Irish dance—and who, I'm proud to say, is an alumnus of the University of Michigan Residential College, where I teach.

Claude Bessy, former head of the Paris Opéra Ballet, who danced in Kelly's *Invitation to the Dance*, talked to me about Kelly's knowledge and understanding of ballet, which she greatly respected. Camille and John Chiappuris, former members of the Ballet Russe de Monte Carlo and now Royal Academy of Dance (RAD)-certified ballet teachers with their own school in Ann Arbor, Community Ballet, were also helpful in reconstructing that world. James T. Maher talked to me about the composers of the American songbook and his work with Alex Wilder on his seminal book on American songwriting. With respect to Balanchine: Fredrick Franklin, who first saw Astaire in London and who also worked closely with Balanchine, as did Rosemary Dunleavy, whose photographic memory keeps the Balanchine repertory alive at New York City Ballet, as well as Jacques d'Amboise, Karin von Aroldingen, Suzanne Farrell, Nicole Hlinka, Arthur Mitchell, Violette Verdy, and Bonita Borne, a Balanchine dancer and daughter of Hal Borne, who worked with Astaire. All of them kindly spoke with me about working with Balanchine.

I thank many teachers and colleagues at the University of Michigan, where I studied and am now on the faculty. Thanks to the university's scholarships and fellowships, I was able to attend college and graduate school—which, as the daughter of a single mother, I couldn't possibly have afforded without their considerable support. Ultimately, my work on this book began with my doctoral dissertation in the history of art at the University of Michigan. I thank my adviser, Diane Kirkpatrick, a pioneer in promoting the study of film and digital imagery within art history, who edited the first *Art Journal* devoted to film as well as an important series of film books, and who supported me in my ambitions to write on film—especially musical films, which combined my two favorite subjects: art history and music history (my undergraduate major). I was lucky to benefit from the advice and encouragement of Rudolph Arnheim, who spent his final teaching years in the University of Michigan's art history department. I took hope from Erwin Panofsky's pioneering article, "Style and Medium in the Motion Picture," and his theory of how sound and moving image worked together to "co-express" a narrative in a moving picture. Also on my committee was Judith Becker, who, with William Malm, introduced me to the field of ethnomusicology, which had a profound impact on my intellectual development and has also been a major influence on my approach to this material. I am also grateful to Robbins Burling, who introduced me to the field of anthropology and was also a key influence on my development.

The research in this book has benefited from the help of many other colleagues at the University of Michigan: in particular, Richard Crawford, who kindly read and commented on the first part of the book and whose magisterial biography of George

Gershwin is forthcoming. I audited his course on American music during my year as a Getty postdoctoral fellow, and his articles and books have been of great importance to me. I have been helped by Mark Clague, director of research at the Gershwin Initiative at the University of Michigan, who will serve as editor-in-chief of the George and Ira Gershwin critical edition, and by my colleagues on the faculty advisory board. I also thank Roland John Wiley, whose works on the Tchaikovsky ballets and others have been essential tools. In the Department of Dance, I have benefited from the advice of the choreographer, historian, and now chair Jessica Fogel, who read and commented on this book while it was in progress. Robin Wilson, one of the founding members of Urban Bush Women and a historian of African American and African diasporic dance, was supportive of my research into the Africanist influence on Fred Astaire. Early on she introduced me to her own mentor, Brenda Dixon Gottschild, for which I will always be very grateful. Christian Matjias, who shared my interest in Balanchine and music, was of the greatest assistance in helping to analyze the Vernon Duke scores for *Ziegfeld Follies of 1936* and Balanchine's edited score for *An American in Paris*, which was collected in connection with the Popular Balanchine Project. In the musical-theater department, I thank Linda Goodrich for her insights into dance and for her demonstration of the lexicon of drags and other steps used by the Broadway choreographers with whom she worked, including Jerome Robbins. I also thank Susan Filipiak, our resident tap guru, for discussing her work with the great tap dancers who taught her.

I was pleased to serve on the dissertation committees of Todd Decker and Rebecca Schwartz-Bishir, both of them now my colleagues. Decker's dissertation had a major section on Fred Astaire which he refined into his excellent book *Music Makes Me: Fred Astaire and Jazz*. As he explained in his acknowledgments, I urged him "to think broadly about Astaire's place in American dance." I thank him for taking Astaire seriously as a subject of musicology, and I valued his interest in my own attempts to place Astaire within the history of dance and film. Schwartz-Bishir commented on parts of my book draft, taught my dance history classes when I was relieved from teaching to finish this book, and is currently working on a promising book about *musique dansante*.

I wish also to thank my mentors in the field of dance studies: Mary Clarke, Selma Jeanne Cohen, Ivor Guest, and Anne Hutchinson Guest, all of them pioneers in this still-young field. All of them, in various ways, encouraged me to take the leap into the discipline which they themselves were pioneering, and which, despite great strides, is still struggling to gain a firm foothold in academic life. I am very lucky that the University of Michigan was willing to allow me to create dance history courses and seminars both in the College of Literature, Science, and the Arts and in the School of Music, Theatre, and Dance.

Stephanie Jordan's pioneering work in what is now called choreomusicology has been an inspiration to me, as has Marian Smith's wonderful work in nineteenth-century ballet and opera. We now intend our research collaboration to lead to a book on "hidden Balanchine," starting with our article with Lisa Arkin, "Balanchine and Folk Dance."

My greatest admiration goes to the pioneering work of Jean and Marshall Stearns, whose meticulous research and tireless sleuthing, especially in their great book of 1968, have been foundational in bringing jazz dance into the broader history of dance. I thank my colleague Constance Valis Hill, who, over more than two decades in her indispensable books, articles, and conference papers, has devoted herself to bringing the art of tap dance into the mainstream of dance history. In our conversations over the years, I have been immensely grateful for her expertise and encouragement. (Brian Seibert's book on tap dance came out too recently, unfortunately, for me to take substantial advantage of it.)

I am very grateful to those who read and commented on various sections of the manuscript: Marian Smith, Jane Pritchard, and Stephanie Jordan (all of whom I have mentioned already), along with Judith Becker, Rebecca Schwartz-Bishir, Robbins Burling, Hugh Cohen, and Kendall Walton, who gave me the opportunity to present some of my material at his Aesthetics Discussion Group and benefit from his insightful comments. I am incredibly grateful to Robert Gottlieb and Deborah Jowitt, who plowed through the entire manuscript and took the time to give me many valuable comments, as did my fellow dance-film scholar Mindy Aloff, who helped me as well with fact-checking and editing. I thank all of them for their insightful comments and criticisms. I thank Robert Greskovic, who generously shared the holdings of his remarkable photographic archive. I have benefited also from insights and discussions over many years with my friends and much-valued colleagues: Jack Anderson, Virginia Brooks, George Dorris, Jon Elster, Alastair Macaulay, and John Mueller, whose encyclopedic *Astaire Dancing* is essential to any Astaire research. It was Arlene Croce's brilliant and foundational *The Fred Astaire and Ginger Rogers Book* that originally inspired me to work on this material. My thanks also to Kathleen Riley and Chris Bamberger, who invited me to participate as a keynote speaker in their Astaire conference at Oxford University in 2008, where I first presented my material on Astaire and Balanchine, and where I was able to meet a variety of wonderful Astaire scholars, as well as Astaire's daughter, Ava (and her husband, Richard MacKenzie), who gave me wonderful descriptions of her father. I have particularly benefited from my conversations with the ethnomusicologists Judith Becker and Susan Walton, and from my colleague F. X. Widaryanto, a specialist in Javanese music and dance—all of whom helped me in more ways than they can imagine to look at Astaire from a world perspective. I have benefited too from the many undergraduate and graduate students who participated in my seminars at the University of Michigan on Balanchine and on dance in the film musical. I especially note and thank the student research assistants who have worked with me: Kathryn Dickason, Orit Greenberg, Gillian Jakab, Anne Kouzmanoff, and Lena Leeson. Of course, with all this help, any mistakes and omissions remain my responsibility.

My deepest gratitude, too, to my editors, Norman Hirschy and Helen Nicholson, along with everyone at Oxford University Press, as well as to my copyeditor, Barbara Norton, all of whom were helpful and whose patience I tried many times.

I have been generously supported over the years by substantial grants from the University of Michigan, the J. Paul Getty Foundation, and the Fulbright Foundation.

The University of Michigan also allowed me to take off time from my teaching responsibilities to work on this book.

Most important have been my friends and family: My uncle Ben Goldstein played saxophone in a Navy band stationed in the South Pacific during World War II and took a lively interest in this book; I was grateful to hear his memories of the jazz players whom he worked with and listened to in the 1930s and '40s. My cousin Leon Goldstein, a violinist in the New York City Ballet, told me his memories of working with Balanchine and Balanchine's attitudes toward music. My friends Marge and Larry Sondler and Marilyn Leipziger, who share my love of musicals, have supported me throughout. Especially important have been my close family: my mother, Sara Genné, a painter who first encouraged my interest in music and art; my father, Joseph Genné, a civil-rights activist; and my stepmother, Noma Genné, who as Educational Field Secretary for the NAACP in the 1940s, working with Thurgood Marshall on intercultural education and knowing W. E. B. Dubois, gave me a vivid sense of the climate of race relations in the 1940s in New York City. As a young white woman who lived and worked with African Americans, she gave me my first insight into the incredible barriers, major and minor, in personal and public life faced by her African American friends. I thank my sister, Maria Dubois Genné, founder and choreographer of the intergenerational dance company Kairos Alive; her husband, Cris Anderson; and my nieces, Parker Genné and Elinor Anderson-Genné. My eldest brother, Joe, a Navy air veteran of World War II, gave me important insights into the period and the attitudes, body language, and close relationships of his sailor buddies. His cache of photographs taken during the period are now archived. I thank him; his wife, Joannie; and my nephews, Tom, Matt, and Andy, and their families. Matt helped me with the photos. My sister-in-law Sarah Gibbard Cook, a professional editor and author, has played an important role, especially in the final stages of preparation.

Most important of all are my immediate family: Stephen Gibbard and George Gibbard; Stephen's wife, Harriet Gu, and my grandchildren; Dylan and Maya Gibbard; and my husband, colleague, editor, and best friend, Allan Gibbard. As a philosopher, he dug into my arguments and theories seriously in long discussions over the years as I was writing. As an experienced author himself, he gave me invaluable editorial support, and there isn't a page in this book that he hasn't read and discussed with me. He accompanied me willingly to more dance performances than I can count. I also can't imagine that there is any other philosopher who has willingly seen as much film dance, with the possible exceptions of Ludwig Wittgenstein and Sir A. J. "Freddie" Ayer, who learned to tap dance and adored Fred Astaire. Without Allan's love, help, and support, this book could never have been written. The book is dedicated to him.

Material in this book is drawn, with expansions and modifications, from these previous publications of mine:

"Dance in Film," in *The Living Dance: An Anthology of Essays on Movement and Culture*, ed. Judith Chazin Bennahum and Ninotchka Bennahum, 3rd ed. (Dubuque, IA: Kendall–Hunt, 2012).

"Vincente Minnelli and the Film Ballet," in *Vincente Minnelli: The Art of
    Entertainment*, ed. Joe McElhaney (Detroit, MI: Wayne State University
    Press, 2009), 229–51.
"'They Have Done It All': George Balanchine and Folk Dance," with Lisa C. Arkin
    and Marian Smith, in Society of Dance History Scholars Proceedings,
    Thirty-first Annual Conference, Skidmore College, Saratoga Springs, NY,
    June 12–15, 2008 ([New York]: The Society, 2008), 195–97.
"Collaborating in the Melting Pot: George Balanchine, Vernon Duke and
    George Gershwin," with Christian Matjias, in *Proceedings of Sound Moves: An
    International Conference on Music and Dance, 5th and 6th November 2005*
    (London: Roehampton University, 2006), 53–61.
"Swine Lake: American Satire on Russian Ballet and What It Tells Us," in
    *Proceedings: Twenty-ninth Annual Conference, the Banff Centre, Banff, Alberta,
    15–18 June 2006* (Riverside, CA: Society of Dance History Scholars, 2006).
"Balanchine and the Black Dancing Body" [an essay in the form of a dialogue
    between myself and Constance Valis-Hill], *Discourses in Dance* 3, no. 1
    (2005): 21–28.
"Glorifying the American Woman: Josephine Baker and George Balanchine,"
    Discourses in Dance 3, no. 1 (2005): 31–57.
"Dancin' in the Rain: Gene Kelly's Musical Films," in *Envisioning Dance on
    Film and Video*, ed. Judy Mitoma, Dale Stieber, and Elizabeth Zimmer
    (New York: Routledge, 2003), 71–77.
"'Dancin' in the Street': Street Dancing on Film and Video from Fred Astaire
    to Michael Jackson," in *Re-thinking Dance History: Issues and Methodologies*,
    ed. Geraldine Morris and Larraine Nicholas, 2nd ed. (London and
    New York: Routledge, 2017); an expanded and revised version of "'Dancin'
    in the Street': Dancing on Film and Video from Fred Astaire to Michael
    Jackson," in *Re-thinking Dance History*, ed. Alexandra Carter (London and
    New York: Routledge, 2003), 132–42.
"Freedom Incarnate: Jerome Robbins, Gene Kelly and the Dancing Sailor
    as an Icon of American Values in World War II," *Dance Chronicle* 24, no. 1
    (2001): 83–103.
"Creating a Canon, Creating the 'Classics' in Twentieth-Century British Ballet,"
    Dance Research 18, no. 2 (2000): 132–62.
"The Film Musicals of Vincente Minnelli and the Team of Gene Kelly and
    Stanley Donen, 1944–1958" (Ph.D. diss., University of Michigan, 1984).
"Vincente Minnelli's Style in Microcosm: The Establishing Sequence of *Meet Me
    in St. Louis*," *Art Journal* 43, no. 3 (Fall 1983): 247–54.

INTRODUCTION

The Choreographer-Director and the Synergy of Music and Moving Image

GENE KELLY, DRENCHED and euphoric, walk-dancing down the street in the driving rain, swinging his umbrella and singing of his love for Debbie Reynolds in *Singin' in the Rain* (1952); Fred Astaire and Cyd Charisse strolling through an urban park on a soft summer night in *The Band Wagon* (1953). In both of these films, this simple, everyday movement is gradually transformed into dance, giving us two great moments in American cinema. Why do these movies enthrall us? Young men in love and singing and dancing about it are standard fare in Hollywood musicals. The music and dance are key. If you take the song and dance out of *Singin' in the Rain* or *The Band Wagon*, what's left is a bloodless parody of silent-film techniques or a rehash of the let's-put-on-a-show genre.

Singin' in the Rain and the "Dancing in the Dark" sequence in *The Band Wagon* are late examples of a new, modern style, iconography, and group of film-dance genres developed first by Fred Astaire in the 1930s and continuing with Gene Kelly and others, including Astaire himself, working with such directors as Vincente Minnelli and Stanley Donen. They were choreographed specifically for the film medium and for the songs of the so-called Golden Age of musical-theater and film musicals (roughly from the Gershwins' *Lady Be Good* with the Astaires on Broadway to the rise of rock and roll).

Astaire and Kelly were also part of the wider dance world outside of Hollywood, and the interaction of these dance worlds is a key part of the tradition I trace. In this book I place their film dances within the history of dance as well as film. The films *Singin' in the Rain* and *The Band Wagon* include not only shorter songs and dances but also more extended storytelling dance sequences, sometimes called "film ballets." One of the most influential figures in developing this genre was the young Russian ballet master George Balanchine, part of the Diaghilev diaspora.

Drawing on his own tradition and influenced by Astaire and George Gershwin, Balanchine would follow them on Broadway to work with Rodgers and Hart and with his compatriot Vernon Duke to expand the movement repertory of Broadway dance, making dance as important as song and kick-starting the ascent of the dancer-actor and choreographer as a prominent force in the 1940s and '50s—and would make a brief but pioneering contribution to musical films. All this would in turn benefit his own work in ballet.

Astaire, followed by Balanchine, Kelly, and others, each in his own way, recognized the importance of jazz music and dance, not just as a popular fad, but as essential nourishment for the development of American theatrical dance. They grappled early with the key aesthetic issue of their era for the nation of immigrants of which they were a part: the genius of African American music and dance, standing alongside and interacting with the genius of Europe and its extension into America. Astaire modeled a dance style for musical theater and films that, like the musical style of George Gershwin, blended black and white, highbrow and lowbrow, and Old World and New World in dance and music to create a unified style. (The endemic racism woven into the fabric of American life would render African Americans invisible in this tradition, except for highly constrained roles. But their essential contribution to the shaping of this style will be a key part of the story I tell.)

Astaire, Balanchine, and Kelly also faced the question of how dance and music could be transformed for the twentieth century's most revolutionary artistic medium, the sound moving picture. Their film dances are not dance as we usually think of it. In their original form, they are actually thousands of pictures, or frames, which make up the strip of film fed through the projector whirring away behind the audience. In the darkness of the theater, projected at many times life size onto the huge screen, these frames create, literally, moving pictures.[1] Each image is arranged with painstaking care, much as a painter might arrange color, light, and objects in a frame. In Kelly's "Singin' in the Rain" dance sequence, for example, lighting turns the rain into shimmering ribbons of silver through which we view the dancer. Warmly lit, orange-yellow shop windows punctuate the space of the screen, and the puddles through which Kelly splashes glimmer with the reflected glow of streetlamps. And this enchanted picture moves—to music. As Kelly shoulders his umbrella and begins to walk down the street, the camera, supported by the gentle, repetitive pattern of the tune he hums and its atmospheric orchestral accompaniment, strolls in front of him, taking us, the audience, along. In the climactic central section, when Kelly uses his open umbrella as a sail and catapults from sidewalk to street, the camera takes us back and up, riding a crescendo of sound over the glistening street.

Kelly's rhythmic movements interact not only with the pulse, shape, color, and texture of the music, but also with the camera, which shapes the space in which he moves. The cuts respond in a kind of visual rhythm to changes in key and orchestral color. And Kelly's steps act as a percussion instrument, embroidering a filigree of sound to underline and enhance his gestures and the simple tune he sings.[2] It is music visualized, or moving image musicalized. The combination is a new art form, film dance, now called by scholars screendance or filmdance.

Film dance, as its creators immediately understood, is far more than dance on film.[3] In dance as it is performed live on a theatrical stage, the dancer controls only his own body, not the space around him. In film dance, the director controls the image—and its movement—in its entirety. He decides what sounds we will hear when we see a particular image. When dialogue is added, it too is enhanced by, and in turn enhances, its companion media. The moving image, the music, and the words of the song work together in a synergy of sound and image that becomes more than just the sum of its parts. It becomes a kind of *Gesamtkunstwerk* possible only in the medium of film.[4]

THE DANCER AS DIRECTOR AND CHOREOGRAPHER

Kelly did not just choreograph and dance in *Singin' in the Rain*; he also, together with Stanley Donen, directed it. *Singin' in the Rain* and *The Band Wagon* are the culmination of a tradition that began soon after the introduction of sound film in the early 1930s, spearheaded by Astaire in *Top Hat, Swing Time,* and other films. Astaire too controlled not only his choreography but the way it was filmed: how he was framed, where the camera moved, where the editing occurred, and how all this was coordinated with the music. He did not direct any of the films in which he appeared, but he did have directorial control over his dance sequences. So did Balanchine.

These director-choreographers took advantage of all the new forces at their disposal—the moving camera, editing, lighting, special effects—to create a dance form that took the fullest possible advantage of the new technology of the twentieth century and its ability to enhance our experience of dance. Blending music and moving image to get the remarkable impact that they achieved took painstaking effort, as they planned, filmed, and performed in film musicals—and in postproduction work that was as important as the performances themselves. These three choreographers participated in all these phases of film-dance creation to hone the final product.

The dance-film tradition that I describe in this book, in which the choreographer-dancer is also his own director, represents the first time in dance history that great dancers have been captured exactly as they themselves wanted to be seen. Dance is the most ephemeral of the arts. Unlike music and drama, it has no universally accepted system of notation. Important systems have been devised and some of them have been adopted to a limited extent, but none has had the kind of near-universal use that standard music notation has among musicians. Choreography has mostly been passed down from one generation of dancers to the next in an oral tradition. It has survived only as interpreted by dancers, who alter works slightly or greatly in accordance with their fallible memories, their particular skills, and changing fashions. The result is like a game of telephone: the farther away the message is from the original source, the more distorted it becomes.

New systems of notation and the advent of film, videotape, and digital recording have begun to ensure that the loss is not as great as it once was, but notation cannot recreate the original dancer's performance, and the camera cannot capture it fully on the proscenium stage from the viewpoint of the audience for whom it was originally created. The dances I discuss in this book were made specifically for the medium of film. They exist just as the dancers for whom they were created meant them to be experienced. Movies, then, for the first time, could make dance as durable across the generations as painting and sculpture. Our great-grandchildren may or may not hear tales of Nijinsky's leap in *Spectre de la rose* or the riveting dramatic power of Martha Graham. But just as they can go to Rome and see the ceiling of the Sistine Chapel, they can watch Fred Astaire and Ginger Rogers dance in a Manhattan ballroom and Gene Kelly splash through the puddles on a Hollywood street.

As choreographers and dancers, Kelly, Balanchine, and Astaire aimed to use dance as a vehicle for the development of a character or plot within the context of an overall film-musical narrative. Both the camera and the choreography participated in telling the story. Astaire pioneered dancer-centered filming as a direct alternative to the style of dance filming introduced in the early 1930s by Busby Berkeley, in which dancers were objects manipulated from various angles by the moving camera and ever more intricate special effects. Astaire made the actor-dancer, the human body shaping space, the focus of the viewer's experience. As the director of his own dance sequences, he usually insisted on framing the whole of the dancer's body, with no close-ups or cutting away to break up the flow of the dance. Like Berkeley, Astaire exploited the new opportunities offered by film by occasionally exploring special effects and striking camera movements, but on the whole his dances were planned on a more intimate and human scale. Later, Balanchine and Kelly would widen the repertoire of camera movements and of the angles from which dancers were filmed, but, like Astaire, they never violated the flow of the dance, nor did they draw attention to their editing, camera movement, or special effects.

The musical drama that Astaire and Kelly most often played out was one of courtship from the perspective of a young American man. In was important, then, for these dance sequences to achieve their intimacy of movement. Astaire began the tradition with his marvelous dances with Rogers, self-contained mini-dramas of seduction and fulfillment embodied in movement and music. Balanchine and Kelly, following Astaire's lead, developed variations of their own on the seduction dance, altering and expanding it with new varieties of camerawork and editing that kept both dance and dancer at the center of the viewing experience.

Astaire also originated—and Kelly fully developed—another film-dance genre, the street dance, which capitalized on the new possibilities of camera movement and editing to take the dance out of the studio and into an ever-widening, ever-lengthening street. Kelly was particularly brilliant in using street dance to express the euphoric high of falling in love. "Singin' in the Rain" is an example, as are "'S Wonderful" in *An American in Paris* and Kelly's extraordinary dance on roller skates in *It's Always Fair Weather*. Sometimes their dances expressed the lows of thwarted love: think of Astaire's despairing, drunken dance in "One for the Road" in *The Sky's the Limit* and the street dance of Kelly's angry alter ego in *Cover Girl*.

The jazz-ballet genre first made popular on Broadway by Balanchine explored more extended stories in music and dance. Film ballets in this tradition developed character and relationships and sometimes explored the complex and conflicted feelings that lurk beneath conscious thought in that dream world that so fascinated psychoanalysts and artists in the 1940s and '50s (as in *Yolanda and the Thief, The Pirate, On the Town,* and, in the mother of all dance dream sequences, *An American in Paris*).

When the United States entered World War II, Kelly and Donen explored the buddy-dance genre, dances that valorized male bonding. They featured the military men on leave who filled the streets of America's port cities, looking for love but ultimately depending, as shown in such film musicals as *Anchors Aweigh, On the Town,* and *It's Always Fair Weather,* on male solidarity—a key relationship on the battlefield.

HOLLYWOOD PLURALISM

Astaire and Kelly sang and danced to the music of the great American composers—notably Irving Berlin, George Gershwin, Jerome Kern, Cole Porter, and Richard Rodgers—who presided over the birth and development of American musical theater and film and made American song one of the most transformative of this country's contributions to music. Balanchine too loved this repertory. These songs were mostly written (and were always orchestrated and arranged) specifically for the dancers—the characters they played and the dances they developed. Astaire, Balanchine, and Kelly worked out their choreographies in tandem with composers, orchestrators, and arrangers to create a score for a dance that used the songs they sang as the foundation of miniature or extended dance sequences or dance dramas—a series of dance variations on the theme (musical and dramatic) of a song.

This style was made to go with the songs they sang and to which they danced, songs whose lyrics poeticized the American English of a generation. The lyrics of Irving Berlin, Cole Porter, and Ira Gershwin employed American English and its rich vocabulary of slang, idiom, and pronunciation ("I Got Rhythm," "'S Wonderful"). Similarly, Astaire's and Kelly's dances were founded on and poeticized the everyday movement, casual posture, gestural language, and sports moves of the young Americans who came of age after World War I. This was a more casual, more relaxed, less hierarchical way of moving than the more formal European style. Astaire and Kelly stuck their hands in their pockets, leaned indecorously against walls, and sprawled with one leg casually draped over the arm of a sofa. They drew on everyday American life by making ordinary objects, from coat racks and umbrellas to mailboxes and streetlamps, extraordinary. To the young Americans of their generation, it all looked completely natural, and to those who saw Astaire and Kelly across the ocean, it signified a new way of moving that was distinctively American.

Astaire's and Kelly's film dance also reflected a unique set of historical and societal events. Their parents and grandparents formed part of the largest and most disparate wave of immigrants to settle in the United States in its history. Just as important was the great movement northward of African Americans. These migrations helped bring about a renaissance of dance as an art form in America and the blossoming of a plethora of dance artists, schools, companies, and styles. In the nineteenth century there were three main dance centers: Paris, Milan, and St. Petersburg. In the twentieth, the centers of dance shifted to London, New York, and Los Angeles.

Like America itself, the ideas about movement found in these cities were pluralist, drawing on elements of dance styles from the many cultures that settled America, unconcerned with keeping to the rules of one or another "pure" style. Astaire and the other artists I write about drew from rhythm jazz tap and flash tap, from the waltz and the Lindy hop, and from the French and Danish tradition of the nineteenth-century *ballet d'action*. They also drew from the Russian Imperial Ballet, the modernist works of Diaghilev's Ballets Russes, sports moves, gymnastics, children's street play, Escuela Bolero and flamenco, vaudeville and street dancing, Appalachian clogging, Irish step dancing, and the Eastern European and Russian squatting jump, all wedded to the choreography of the camera.

Although Astaire and Kelly are most often spoken of as tap dancers, jazz tap was only one of the many and varied elements of movement, from the Old World and the New, that they drew on to create their style. Despite its eclectic roots, the style is not a pastiche. It is a whole, in and of itself. It needs to be recognized alongside other major twentieth-century dance forms such as modern dance, modern ballet, and jazz tap itself.

This style needs a name. Astaire called it his "outlaw style." But that doesn't tell us what the style is. The phrase "Hollywood musical vernacular pluralism" might be close to the mark: it recognizes the origin of this American art form and the way it arose from many roots, celebrating the way it is inextricably linked to the medium for which it was created. But that is a pretentious mouthful, and so, for short, I'll call this style "Hollywood pluralism." To be sure, other styles besides the one I treat in this book could be given this same name, in its short form or long, but when I use the term "Hollywood pluralism," I mean the dance style originated by Astaire and further developed by Balanchine and Kelly first on Broadway and then transformed for cinema, the style that is the subject of this book. I will also keep Astaire's term "outlaw style" for him and for anyone who puts his own stamp on the tradition.

COLLABORATION AND INFLUENCE

One of the first to recognize Astaire's fusion of Old and New World forms was Balanchine, who applied Astaire's ideas in his own way to the Broadway musical and to film. Although his corpus of films was small and the movies in which his dance segments appeared were on the whole undistinguished, he would influence not only Kelly and a second generation of dancers and choreographers, but the film-musical director Vincente Minnelli. On Broadway in the 1930s, Balanchine developed and popularized a modern American form of what the eighteenth-century ballet master J. G. Noverre christened the *ballet d'action*—a story told entirely in dance and music. Shortly afterward Balanchine brought this form to the screen. Minnelli, who had worked with him on Broadway, would go on in the movies to work with both Astaire (*The Band Wagon*) and

Kelly (*The Pirate, An American in Paris*) to build on and expand these techniques and traditions. This was not only for dance: Minnelli took his experience with the synthesis of music, dance, and drama, first with Balanchine and then with Astaire and Kelly, and combined it with careful analysis of early film musicals such as those of Rouben Mamoulian and Ernst Lubitsch. All this shaped his approach to filmmaking as a whole.

Kelly worked with Donen on many of his films, and Donen admired Astaire as well as Mamoulian and Lubitsch. Donen would go on to work as solo director with Astaire (*Royal Wedding, Funny Face*) and other choreographers such as Michael Kidd in *Seven Brides for Seven Brothers*. Eventually Minnelli, Kelly, and Donen would apply their ideas to the direction of an entire motion picture, with most of the movement and dialogue choreographed and linked to music.

These artists worked not only with the eyes of dancers, choreographers, and directors, able to see every inch of the body and how it shapes space, but also with those of painters, who use color and light to control an entire space. As directors, they controlled the dance, the frame through which the dancers move, and the perspective from which movie audiences see the dancers.

These directors could not have achieved their goals without the vast and deep human and technical resources of the Hollywood studio system at its height, from cinematographers to set and costume designers, from editors to gaffers and gofers. In line with common studio practices, many of these people remained buried in the opening credits or went entirely uncredited.[5] André Previn has pointed out the exceptional quality of the musicians who worked at MGM. And as I discuss later in the book, orchestrators and arrangers played a crucial role in determining the sound of the scores written for both small and large movie dances. I try to highlight their work wherever possible—especially those involved in the music—but to mention them all is far beyond my scope.

Then, too, all three choreographers I discuss relied on dance assistants who performed a variety of tasks—helping to test out, discuss, and at times contribute to dance steps. They acted as partners in working out the choreography and helped to teach dancers once the choreography was complete. Astaire's most prominent assistant was Hermes Pan, but he worked with many others as well. Kelly's dance assistant Stanley Donen went on to become his co-director and to have a distinguished career of his own.[6] Kelly also worked with Carol Haney, Jeanne Coyne, and Gwen Verdon. Because Astaire's, Balanchine's, and Kelly's styles remained recognizable and consistent from picture to picture, it is difficult to sort out distinctive personal influences from these dance assistants—even in the case of Pan, who worked so closely with Astaire for so many films.[7] This is also true of Balanchine, who for straight tap-dance sequences worked with Herbie Harper, and unnamed others.[8]

Hollywood pluralism did not arise in isolation from the rest of dance and its history. The makers of film dance were shaped at the outset by the world of theatrical dance onstage, and film dance in turn influenced dance onstage. Kelly's and Astaire's dances grew out of the history of dance as well, from the courtship dances of the Italian and French Renaissance to pas-deux forms of nineteenth-century ballets such as *Giselle*. At the same time, Astaire traded steps at the Hoofers Club in Harlem and danced at the Savoy Ballroom—but also learned from the ballerina Adeline Genée. Gershwin contributed to Astaire's dance vocabulary, and Astaire's manner of delivery and movement affected Gershwin's music. In turn, Astaire's dances thrilled Balanchine, who transformed his own ballet style to blend its Russian origins with the new streamlined and off-balance look he saw in jazz dancers in Harlem and on the stages of London, Paris, and America—and, perhaps most of all, in film musicals. Balanchine worked with Josephine Baker both in France and in America, and also with the Nicholas Brothers. With Katherine Dunham he explored the rich movements of Afro-Caribbean dance. Astaire and Kelly would in turn be influenced by Balanchine's transformation of Broadway dance. They each attended not only Broadway musicals but ballet and modern-dance performances. Modern dance's high priestess, Martha Graham, admired Kelly's work, and Kelly idolized her. Kelly adored ballet: he was one of the original subscribers to the company that became Balanchine's New York City Ballet. This cross-fertilization has continued through several generations of dancers who, from Twyla Tharp to Michael Jackson, have learned from the film dance of Astaire and Kelly.

Film dance is sometimes viewed as a low form of art occupying a world of its own, but any division of dance styles into "high" and "low" is untrue to history. In the literature of dance history, movie dance has too often been ignored or marginalized as "popular." The distinction between high art and low entertainment, however, is artificial and socially constructed. In the nineteenth century, both social circumstances and romantic writers and critics changed the perception of composers and visual artists of certain narrowly defined genres from artisans to artists. Artisans were skillful makers of things; artists were geniuses, prophets, visionaries.[9] In the history of film dance, this has meant until recently that so-called art dance-filmmakers such as Maya Deren and Yvonne Rainer have been factored into the history of dance, but their contemporaries in popular dance forms have not—although the latter have had a much more powerful impact on the history of dance worldwide.

My approach to film dance stems from the thesis I stressed at the outset: critical to what drives our responses to film dance is the way its creators synthesized moving image and sound to create a synergy. To investigate this, I have drawn on methods not only from dance studies, but from disciplines that early on pioneered and refined ways to analyze and articulate visual and aural forms. They include art history's development of visual, iconographical, and iconological analysis of the history of images, and musicology, which combines aural analysis with the history of musical forms.[10] Ethnomusicology is especially important. From its inception, ethnomusicology stressed the analysis of dance and music within a specific cultural context—not limiting its investigation to Western forms, but including all types of music and dance from cultures around the world.[11] My methods are tied as well to the field of choreomusicology pioneered by Stephanie Jordan and Marian Smith, who study the interaction of music and dance.[12] I also look to those in film studies who have examined the synergy of music and moving image in film,[13] and to dance analysts, who examine the human body in motion.[14]

While I cannot hope to explore in the depth and technical detail that specialists in these fields attain when they study one of these arts individually, I can try, by joining visual analysis to musical analysis and dance analysis, to suggest in a more general way how the interaction of these elements may work. I combine and extend them to see how sound and image interact, and how these things are tied to the culture that produces them, the artists that create them, and the audiences for which they are made.

Melanie Bales and Karen Eliot stress the importance of first understanding the "complexity of the dance in situ" before applying theory from outside the field to produce "foregone conclusions."[15] My subject is film dance, and my primary evidence starts with a close analysis of the dance, music, and camerawork itself as well as the choreographer, his training and influences, and the wider world of dance, music, and film in which his work was created. Theory can be useful, but my aim is to theorize in a way that grows out of these elements and out of the cultural and historical situation in which these artists lived and in which these dances were created. I ask how the dances reflect, interact with, and themselves influence that wider culture.

My observation and analysis are supplemented and supported by interviews with dancers, choreographers, directors, and film technicians to find out what they thought and what was important to them, as well as historical records such as production files, contemporary accounts, newspaper criticism, and the like. The primary evidence, though, is the works themselves, which reveal influences that are not necessarily recognized by outside critics and scholars. One case in point is the profound influence of Africanist elements in Balanchine's style, which was ignored until it was articulated recently by the scholars Brenda Dixon-Gottschild and Sally Banes, among others. Another is the way Astaire's style, when broken down, reveals influence from ballet as well as black dance and a variety of other forms from the Old World as well as the New.

Much of the job of an art or music historian consists of articulating nonverbal creations in words and showing how, in form and content, they influence one another. As with all art, sound moving pictures evolve, in significant part, through emulation—which spurs further inventions that are emulated in their turn.[16] The canon that most matters is an invention not of scholars or critics, but of artists judging whom best to look to and emulate, judging whose work to develop with further skill, invention, and elaboration. The artists I study worked in the first three decades of sound cinema, and so they chose their influences unhampered by a canon established by an academy of scholars and critics. I follow one stream or canon of artists from Astaire to Balanchine, who used devices from dance to apply throughout an entire musical, to Kelly, Donen, and Minnelli.

Choreographers and composers develop formal devices, visual and musical, to engage us not only intellectually but, more important, emotionally. The artist's central concern is how to shape those devices to best produce the desired effect on their audiences. For the creators of dance and music in film, as for any artist or craftsperson, "every minor detail is a major decision"—the dictum Stephen Sondheim puts in the mouth of the post-impressionist painter Georges Seurat.[17] This book traces many such decisions and their cumulative result: how to arrange the positions of dancers in relation to one another to tell a story; how to choose the instrumentation and dynamics of a song to achieve an effect; and how to fuse camerawork, editing, lighting, and color with music to create mood as well as meaning . These "minor details" are meant to pass unnoticed in favor of the whole they create. I don't describe these to just to describe them, but rather to draw their significance and purpose to the reader's attention.

The professional jargon that specialists use to describe music and movement does not always work for my purposes, and even technical terms fail to convey what is happening until the artist brings the terms to life. In the end, of course, no descriptive analysis, however perceptive and subtle, could come close to the total impact of the work. But I make every effort to describe and analyze music and dance in plain, nontechnical language. My goal is to develop a more nuanced and evocative descriptive analysis of the myriad ways in which sound and the moving image combine to play upon our minds and emotions. As Martin Scorsese has said, the key to understanding cinema is visual literacy.[18] I would add that aural literacy is needed as well. Furthermore, we need to begin to understand how the synergy of moving image and sound conveys meaning, and how it arises from a long historical tradition in dance as well as film.

WHAT'S TO COME IN THIS BOOK

This book is of necessity not a precisely detailed history. Because film, especially the film musical, is a collaborative medium and, within the Hollywood studio system, poorly documented, with many of its contributors uncredited, many "firsts" are, owing to the destruction of much early footage, lost to us or subject to debate. (We may not be certain, for example, who in the history of film created the very first close-up, but we do know which early filmmakers best and most imaginatively exploited it and imprinted it on the imaginations not only of their colleagues but also of the public.) Astaire, Balanchine, Donen, Kelly, and Minnelli devised and developed dance genres, conventions, and film techniques that are still in use today. I discuss the film techniques that they developed for conveying the theme of the courtship that is played out in most film musicals. Importantly, I also connect these artists with the larger world of dance, of which they were a vital and stimulating part. Music and dance styles and themes, of course, arise in response to the wider spirit of the times, but I look at cultural and historical context chiefly as the times are reflected in the dances themselves.

The book consists of three main parts. Part I, "From Stage to Screen," is organized chronologically. It traces the history of the Hollywood pluralist style by focusing in turn on Astaire, Balanchine, and Kelly. For each, it looks at cultural milieu, dance training, and early films—along with their artistic relationships with each other and the artists with whom they worked on Broadway and in Hollywood. Chapters 1 and 2 survey the development of Astaire's "outlaw" style and its multiple roots in Old and New World dance forms. Chapters 3 and 4 look at Balanchine's development of his own outlaw style for musical theater and films. Chapter 5 looks at the further development of Hollywood pluralism by Kelly and Donen in the late 1930s and early '40s.

Like artists in any realm, including the masters of modern ballet and modern dance, film-dance makers developed a series of genres and conventions that were distinctive, recognizable, and influential. Part II, "Film-Dance Genres," is organized thematically, tracing and comparing the interrelated dance genres that these artists developed, beginning with Astaire. I look at the roots of these genres in the history of dance, music, and film, and their ties to the history and culture of which they were a part. Astaire's and Kelly's dances chronicled the vicissitudes of American courtship and friendship: dances of seduction and courtship (chapter 6); the rise of the dancing military man and buddy dances (chapter 7), which became increasingly important during World War II, when interdependent male relationships were cast in a new light; and street dances (chapter 8), which chronicled the euphoria, despair, and camaraderie of friends as well as lovers. Finally in this part we come to the extended film-dance form that was sometimes called the film ballet (chapter 9), introduced in short form by Astaire, expanded in dance and mime by Balanchine, and extended to its most elaborate length by Kelly and Astaire, working with Minnelli.

Part III, "Making Film Dance," consists of two chapters, one (chapter 10) on the through-choreographed film musical, and a final chapter (chapter 11) on the legacy of Golden Age film musicals. In the through-choreographed film, ideas derived from dance are applied to the film in its entirety. Visual-musical storytelling devices fuse sound, actor movement, and camerawork to give the entire film the feeling and rhythmic momentum of dance. This was developed by Minnelli and by Kelly and Donen under the influence of the film pioneer Rouben Mamoulian, whose work with Rodgers and Hart in *Love Me Tonight* (1932) set a model for the form. So did René Clair's *Le million* (1931) and Ernst Lubitsch's musicals. The formal and iconographic devices they developed—the musical establishing sequence, the musical montage, and the musical finale—influenced other filmmakers, so that these conceptions began to be applied to non-dance films too, musical and otherwise. The final chapter on legacy begins with the advent of rock and roll and the consequent demise of the Golden Age dance-film musical, and it goes on to suggest later influences of classic dance-film musicals on both dance and film, from post–modern dance to Bollywood to video and digital imagery—ending with a quick glance at the movie *La La Land*, which came out just as this book was nearing completion.

From Stage to Screen

1

ASTAIRE'S OUTLAW STYLE AND ITS NEW WORLD ROOTS

IF ANY SINGLE performer-choreographer can be said to be the father of the film-musical dance tradition that is traced in this book, it is Fred Astaire. The roots of almost all the film-dance genres analyzed in this volume can be found in his work. But Astaire's contributions to dance did not begin with the movies. To understand film-musical dance, we need to look at the origin and development of Astaire's style and the Broadway musical-comedy form in which it was forged onstage before sound film arrived. Astaire is most often classified as a "tap dancer," but tap is only one element he used in creating a larger whole. He invented a style of his own, which he called his "outlaw style." This style stands as a peer to modern dance—the style commonly viewed as the central radical dance achievement of the twentieth century—and to jazz tap, an equally modern style. Much of the movie dance tradition discussed in this book traces to this outlaw style of Astaire's.

Astaire's outlaw style was pluralist. It arose in a multifaceted cultural and artistic climate rooted in the great migrations of the time of his birth and the diverse cultures that met and mingled in New York City's theatrical world. The eclectic training, growth, and development experienced by young Fred and his sister Adele could serve as a case study of how American diversity played out in dance education of the time.[1] Like George Gershwin, his closest colleague in musical theater, Astaire embraced this diversity. He looked for quality and inspiration wherever it could be found, lowbrow or highbrow, elite or popular. While early modern dancers mostly looked away from the extraordinarily rich contributions of African Americans to popular dance and music, Astaire and Gershwin drew on these as serious and core elements of their style and fused them with European so-called fine and other art forms to create their own pluralist styles. The Astaires also were influenced by and drew from Old World sources such as ballroom dance and folk dance, not to mention European ballet—both early nineteenth-century romantic ballet and the later innovations of Diaghilev. All of these Astaire adapted to his own purposes in the creation of his outlaw style.

By the time he arrived in Hollywood in 1933, Astaire and his sister, Adele, had already developed a mature performing and choreographic style in the course of nearly a quarter of a century in vaudeville, on Broadway, and in London. The Astaires were internationally identified with what was just beginning to be viewed as a uniquely American art form—modern musical comedy. George and Ira Gershwin's first major musical shows, *Lady Be Good* (1924) and *Funny Face* (1927), were written with the Astaires' distinctive song and dance styles in mind. Brother and sister also worked with the musical innovators Jerome Kern, Arthur Schwartz, and Howard Dietz. Cole Porter composed Fred Astaire's last Broadway effort, his first without Adele. All of these composers and lyricists would go on to write for Astaire in the new medium of musical films. Together they helped to shape not only the Broadway musical, but the songs and dances in the film musicals that grew out of them.

For the young Fred Astaire, musical theater was the ideal format in which to forge his style, first and foremost because of its creative freedom.

> I felt at the beginning that there should be no restrictions. I wanted to do all my dancing my own way, in a sort of *outlaw style*. I always resented that I couldn't point my toe in, or some other rule. . . . I felt I was going to become a musical-comedy performer or bust *and this meant there should be no limitations*.[2]

When Astaire called his an outlaw style, he was defining it by what it wasn't—inside the rules. But we need to define what it was.

Astaire found the label "tap dancer" inadequate:[3] "When I'm called a 'tap dancer' it makes me laugh. Because I am in a way, but that is one of the kinds of dancing I do. It was strictly a sideline. I didn't just hop the buck—I'd move around and do things. I did so many other kinds of dances."[4] As Astaire points out, his style was related to that of such great jazz tap dancers as Bill Robinson and John Bubbles (by whom he was crucially and powerfully influenced), but it was not the same. "*I am a creator*," he insisted,[5] and he was recognized as such by his early critics in New York and in London. As early as 1928 Astaire's outlaw style of musical-theater dance was beginning to be recognized as a new way of moving that was making a real contribution to American arts—distinct from the American avant-garde who were creating "modern dance." Under the headline "Musical Comedy's Contribution as Shown by the Astaires' Current Program," one critic wrote:

> The dancing of Fred and Adele Astaire as exhibited nightly in "Funny Face" is a subject on which might be hung a dissertation on the esthetics of dancing, incongruous though it may seem to some to associate esthetics with popular musical comedy.
>
> We in America, though we flock to the box office month after month, are inclined to underestimate our musical comedies artistically.
>
> Nobody perhaps would be more amused than the Astaires themselves at being measured by any solemn esthetic standard and certainly such is not the intention

here. However all the skill and artistry of the dance is not being exhibited exclusively amid chaste draperies and dim lights at Sunday evening recitals.[6]

The Sunday evening recitalists to whom this critic compares the Astaires were part of the bourgeoning group of young Americans—Martha Graham, Doris Humphrey, and Charles Weidman, among others—whose style would be eventually be labeled "modern dance." But, though the Astaires were just as modern (in the literal sense of that term), critics had no categories in which to place their style. "They belong to no particular school of dancing, yet they have grace and charm,"[7] wrote one American reviewer. The English critic J. T. Grein agreed but went further in the direction of articulating their style. "It is difficult to describe their dances," he wrote;

> they are a smattering of the branches of the jazz and trot family, yet never anything in particular for long. It is like a dish of *fruits panachés*—a distinct (and delicious) flavour of many things, which you know by their taste, but not by their fragments. So surprise follows upon surprise. . . . Jazz gyrates with the pirouette.[8]

As Grein recognized, Astaire's outlaw style was pluralist, the result of a unique blending of many kinds of dancing from many sources.[9] Astaire himself would probably laugh at Grein's fruit-salad analogy, but it is not a bad metaphor. As Grein insists, it had a "delicious flavour" of many things but was nonetheless "distinct."

DANCE IN A NATION OF IMMIGRANTS

Astaire's insistence on "no limitations" and his pluralist approach to dance had everything to do with the artistic and social climate of New York City, where, beginning in January 1905, he and his sister studied from the tender ages of five and eight, respectively.[10] The young Astaires were the beneficiaries of the rich tapestry of music and dance created by the diverse peoples who had settled in the city in one of the largest waves of immigration in U.S. history. In 1910, five years after the Astaires' arrival, almost half of Manhattan's population was foreign-born (Fig. 1.1a). Between 1850 and 1900 the population of Manhattan nearly quadrupled to almost 2 million; the population of the five boroughs of New York City, created in 1898, doubled from 3.4 million in 1900 to 6.9 million in 1930. Neighborhoods of Irish, Italians, Eastern Europeans, Germans, and other nationalities spread across the city. The Jewish refugees from the shtetls of Russia and Poland crowded the tenements on the Lower East Side, and between 1901 and 1925 the city's Jewish population tripled. The White Russians (Russian Orthodox Christians), refugees exiled by the October Revolution, began arriving after 1917.[11]

All of these immigrants brought both their classical and folk music and dance forms with them: the step dances of Ireland, England, and Scotland; the squatting jumps of Russia and Eastern Europe; Sicily's tarantella; the Eastern European

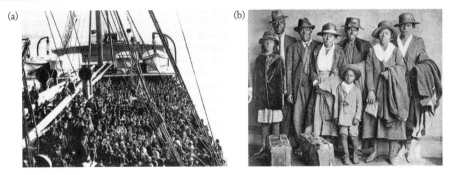

FIGURE 1.1 (a) Immigrants to the United States, c. 1910. (b) African American migrants to the north.

ora (*horah*); the line dances of Greece and the Balkans; and the polkas, ländler, and schuhplattler of Germany, Austria, and Bohemia. On the West Coast, Asian musicians and dancers had brought not only their dance acrobatics but also their extraordinary reed and plucked instruments. The classical European dance and musical forms came too—music and ballet from not only the Russian diaspora fomented by the revolution, but also émigré musicians, composers, and dancers from Italy, France, and Germany.[12]

There were also the internal migrants to New York City. Between 1900 and 1960 an estimated five million African Americans, just one or two generations out of slavery, migrated from the rural south to the industrial north (Fig. 1.1b). Beginning around 1910, they began to make Harlem, in Upper Manhattan, not only their home, but the crucible for new, unprecedented, and extraordinary music and dance. In Manhattan the proportion of residents who were black grew from 3 percent in 1910 to 16 percent in 1940.[13]

African Americans brought with them their own distinctive music and dance—a truly New World form, forged and developed, as Constance Valis Hill has detailed, from the fusion of the music and dance of their African ancestors and the art forms of the many and varied cultures they had encountered in the Americas—especially the step dancing and clog traditions from Ireland and the other British Isles. African American music and dance were distinguished in part by their use of varied and (to European ears) irregular rhythms in the form of syncopation and polyrhythms. Under varying names ("ragtime" and, eventually and finally, "jazz" and "swing"), the music and dance developed by African Americans in the New World would radically alter the nature of American popular music and dance, their key elements becoming its defining characteristics. Jazz was born as dance music, and jazz dance shared the music's intricate syncopations, among other features. Descendants of African slaves in the United States were joined in New York by the descendants of African slaves from the Caribbean and South America, who would bring with them their own Africanist-inspired music and dance, this time melded with the music and dance traditions of the Spanish and French colonizers.[14]

In 1908 the Jewish playwright Israel Zangwill, an immigration officer for the U.S. government, wrote a new play called *The Melting Pot*. Despite mixed reviews, it became wildly popular. The play put forward a new image of America in general and of New York City in particular, and its central metaphor immediately entered the language—used by the public and politicians alike to characterize their place, their times, and their hopes for what America might become. In an uncanny forecast of one of the major artistic themes of the era, a young Russian Jewish immigrant composer, proud to be a new American, is inspired by his new home to write an "American" symphony. (George Gershwin is eerily prefigured: he would later use the title of Zangwill's play to describe his own *Rhapsody in Blue*.) The symphony is a paean to the New World as well as a unique product of it, a world where, as the young composer rhapsodically suggests to anyone who will listen, Christian and Jew, black and white will meet on an equal footing and, most important, mingle in a new kind of society. The young gentile woman who helps him produce it is a settlement worker, the daughter of the Russian officer who led the pogrom that killed the composer's father back in Russia—not an impossibility at the time the play was produced. After the first performance of the new symphony, the two meet on the settlement house rooftop, where, against the skyline of New York on one side and the Statue of Liberty on the other, they finally cast off Old World prejudices of race, class, and religion and unite. Gesturing toward the city spread out around them, the composer rhapsodizes to his wife-to-be:

> Ah, What a stirring and a seething. Celt and Latin, Slav and Teuton, Greek and Syrian, black and yellow, Jew and Gentile, East and West, North and South, the palm and the pine, the pole and the equator, the crescent and the cross—how the great Alchemist melts and fuses them with his purging flame. Here shall they all unite to build the Republic of Man and the Kingdom of God. . . . What is the glory of Rome and Jerusalem where all nations and races come to worship and look back, compared with the glory of America, where all races and nations come to labor and look forward.[15]

As Zangwill explained in the preface to the 1915 edition—which he dedicated to one of its most vocal admirers, Theodore Roosevelt—the melting pot was a new kind of crucible. "The process of American amalgamation is *not assimilation or simple surrender to the dominant type*, as is popularly supposed, but an all-round, give-and-take by which the final type may be enriched or impoverished."[16] Many contemporary scholars use the term "melting pot" in the sense that Zangwill disclaims and debunk the metaphor as meaning assimilation to a dominant white, Anglo-Saxon, Protestant culture, with the consequent erasure and denial of any previous ethnic identity.[17] But it is clear that this was not Zangwill's intent. Furthermore, as evidence that there truly is nothing new under the sun, one of the preferred metaphors for American multiculturalism today is Grein's description of the Astaires: "fruit salad."

At the time, however, Zangwill evidently hit a nerve. The idea of the melting pot, in which a stronger America could be created by the ever-changing interaction and mingling of different backgrounds, became a powerful part of the country's imaginative life during this era. The term itself was used by arts writers, and the mingling and marriage of different cultures and classes, as well as the blending of their various art forms, would be a fertile theme for American music and theater, from *Abie's Irish Rose* to *Showboat* to *West Side Story*.

One of Astaire's teachers, Ned Wayburn, also liked the phrase. In "The Melting Pot of Dance," a chapter in his book *The Art of Stage Dancing* (1925), he applied Zangwill's metaphor to dance in America and pointed to the wide variety of dances brought by immigrants as vital sources with which to forge a new dance in a new kind of society. He condemned the "narrow and unpatriotic" thinking that would dismiss any one form of dance brought by "foreigners," and, like Zangwill's young composer, he enthuses about the possible results of their blending. Enriched and nourished by the dance of all nations, American dance would become a new and superior form.[18] Wayburn's was the second of the two theatrical-arts schools attended by the young Astaires, but their first teacher, Claude Alvienne, was equally open to the blending of a variety of dance forms. As his brochure proclaimed, "Mr. Alvienne's interests are as alive as life itself, as wide as the world; he is not, as many masters are, a recluse in a studio, dormant to new arts and creations. . . . Mr. Alvienne investigates the technique of all masters in all parts of the world, accepting, rejecting, improving, so that his technique is a marvel of progress and efficiency."[19]

The eclectic approach of these two academies could be found in many other dance schools across the United States. Specialist dance academies (such as those that taught only ballet, for example) were rare. "We learned *everything*," remembers Adele. This would continue to be true of most American dancers who studied dance during the first half of the twentieth century, with almost all dance schools offering a variety of styles rather than specializing in one. As the dancer and actress Betsy Blair, Gene Kelly's first wife, described it, there was always "toe (ballet), tap, interpretative dancing, Spanish dancing . . . you name it we did it!"[20] As we shall see, with the establishment of specialist schools of ballet, jazz, and modern dance in the 1930s and '40s, this would gradually change, but it is still not at all unusual even today for young American dancers to start out with an extremely eclectic dance education.

On the small-town vaudeville stages in New Jersey where little Freddie and Adele launched their careers in 1908, their ability to perform in a variety of styles, sometimes in the most unusual and incongruous combinations, was applauded by American audiences who had no rigid preconceptions about proper schools or styles. Claude Alvienne put the act together.

They do two styles of dancing in particular that are positively astounding in performers so young. They change from soft shoes to hard ones and execute a number of waltz clog steps that would be meritorious even if done by adults. The other style is a positive novelty and it is doubtful if it ever was seen in Perth Amboy before. They do a regular buck dance on their toes; a feat that was vociferously applauded by the audience.[21]

But this mixture was not the only way of moving in what the trade paper *Yankee Clipper* announced as an "electrical musical toe-dancing novelty act" performed by "the greatest child toe dancer in the world." Brother and sister appeared as bride and groom figurines on top of two electrically lit wedding cakes, "and with their toes they played the Dreamland waltz on musical bells attached to the cakes." After a "graceful solo" by Adele and Fred's "buck and wing dance on his tip-toes," the two kids, dressed now as a lobster and a glass of champagne, did "an eccentric duet dance" with a "comedy musicale finale" in which they "played popular tunes on novelty stairs, with their hands and feet." They exited the stage doing a cakewalk on their toes.[22] Photos show eight-year-old Adele, swathed in a fluffy white bridal gown and veil, and six-year-old Fred, his tiny body almost overwhelmed by his formal top hat and opera cloak, doing a folk dance step, the *kazatski*—a jumping squat with legs alternately kicking out that appears all over Russia and Eastern Europe and was adapted in all sorts of ways, even in a jazz version called "Russian tap."[23]

This eclecticism, this bumping up of many art forms from many different places, was a completely natural part of the atmosphere in which the Astaires grew and of the vaudeville houses in which they performed. The Astaires were the children and grandchildren of immigrants from different cultures. Their father, Frederic ("Fritz") Austerlitz, came to the United States from Vienna in 1892, and their mother, Joanna Gelius, was the daughter of East Prussian immigrants. Fritz loved Viennese operetta, then at its height, and its signature musical and dance form, the waltz; and he had a healthy respect for the European symphonic repertoire, opera, and ballet. Most of all, he loved musical theater—not just operetta but also the new form it was helping to birth in the United States. Music ran in the Austerlitz family. Fritz's grandfather was a cantor, who sang the liturgical music of Orthodox Judaism. (However, his parents and his two older siblings converted to Catholicism before Fritz's birth, in part to escape the restrictions on employment, settlement, and social mobility resulting from the Austro-Hungarian empire's anti-Semitism.[24] The family members who stayed behind in Germany were labeled *Mischlinge* ["mixed blood"] and suffered during World War II.)

In Tin Pan Alley and on Broadway, the young Astaires encountered other musically talented children of immigrants who would help shape modern musical comedy—Kern, Berlin, the Gershwin brothers, Rodgers, Hart, and Hammerstein. Many of them were, like the Astaires, the first of their family to be born in America and grow up as citizens. As such, their ties to the music of the New World were as close as their bonds to that of the Old. Many were Jewish (with ancestors from Russia, Eastern Europe, and Germany) but, without denying their heritage, identified themselves first and foremost as "Americans."[25]

HIGHBROW, LOWBROW, AND THE JAZZ AGE GENERATION

Astaire and his close friends in musical theater belonged to the American generation that came of age during the teens and twenties. They would forever be identified with the new popular music of their era by F. Scott Fitzgerald in his first collection of short stories, *Tales of the Jazz Age* (1922). Born into a stable and largely agrarian economy—a slower nineteenth-century world—Astaire's generation was transformed by World War I (1914–18) and the dramatic societal and technical transformations that followed it, including women's suffrage, commercial aviation, and especially the development of mass electronic media: records, radio, and sound film. Jazz and jazz-influenced forms would come to dominate twentieth-century American popular entertainment, and it was for jazz that Astaire would fully develop his outlaw style. In music and dance, this generation was enlivened by its encounter with the musical and dance genius of the great black composers, musicians, and dancers who had settled in Harlem and who, along with African American social visionaries, philosophers, and poets, helped to create the Harlem Renaissance. Astaire's generation would forever identify with the new syncopated music they heard as young people, music that would come to be identified with the spirit and character of twentieth-century America and *all* of its citizens, black and white alike. "Jazz" today is a word whose definition is still hotly debated by specialists, with many subcategories, but for Astaire's generation it was a broad, loose, and all-encompassing term. It could stand for new popular music and dance of all kinds, from ragtime to King Oliver to Louis Armstrong, but it could also be associated with those European American Broadway composers who, along with their African American colleagues, helped to develop American musical theater and the songs by Berlin, the Gershwins, and others that grew from it. This broader usage is what I will employ in this book, although I will also use the term "swing," an extension of the jazz tradition that replaced "jazz" in the mid-1930s, when referring to that era. Swing continued in popularity until after World War II, when it was gradually replaced by bebop, which gradually became divorced from dance and evolved into music strictly for listening.

Jazz was first and foremost a popular art form; its originators were from a marginalized and often disdained group. In the popular language of the era it was labeled "lowbrow"—a new and increasingly widespread slang term used at the turn of the twentieth century. It stood in contrast to "highbrow," a term first used in the 1880s in the United States. Both of these terms derived from the nineteenth-century theory of phrenology, which linked head shape to intellectual capacity and was widely used to "prove" the intellectual superiority of "high-browed" (read: "Caucasian") peoples and the associated refinement of their aesthetic tastes. "Highbrow" came to be associated with elite European art forms such as symphonic music, opera, and ballet, which were seen as appealing to a small, select, intellectually superior, and supposedly higher-class group. The lowbrow styles were the popular arts produced and consumed not only by African Americans, but also by the new groups of working-class immigrants from around the world who flooded into the United States at this time, as well as the great mass of native-born Americans. These labels reflected a turning point in America's understanding of the performing arts. For better or worse, they reflected assumptions made almost unconsciously by most American arts critics, audiences, and performers.[26]

In this climate, most of Astaire's contemporaries in modern dance and some in ballet rejected jazz out of hand.[27] But with his policy of no limitations, Astaire did not worry about the distinction between highbrow and lowbrow in either music or dance. Jazz was fundamental to his style. Astaire and his colleagues fit the pre-romantic artisan tradition of Shakespeare and of Bach and Mozart, who didn't see a contradiction in being at once popular, entertaining, and artistic. Their jobs were to enthrall and enchant, to please audiences and their patrons and to make a good living doing it. But although he distrusted artistic pretension and hierarchical thinking, Astaire venerated artistry, which he sought and found in every form of music, dance, and movement. "I do nothing that I don't like," he wrote in his autobiography, "such as inventing 'up' to the arty or 'down' to the corny. Believe me, there is an artistic way to pick up a garbage can."[28] Astaire investigated all kinds of movement:

> He admires good ballet work, for example, and all other types of the dance behind which there is a more or less artistic purpose. He also feels the need of variety for which reason he has made himself expert in soft-shoe dancing, tap dancing, grotesque and comic steps. He has a profound admiration for the art of [the German Expressionist dancer Harold] Kreutzberg whom he considers a great man.[29]

Thus, in Astaire's universe, all genres, from ballet to *Ausdrucktanz*, and any everyday movement, such as lifting a garbage can, could be worth watching and using.

EVERYDAY AMERICAN MOVEMENT AND AMERICAN POPULAR SONG

There can be no adequate summary of Astaire's pluralist style, but if I were to choose just one fundamental and innovative element, it would be Astaire's observation, understanding, and artful adaptation of everyday American movement and gesture. Like the popular songs that used the vernacular, slangy language of jazz-age Americans, and like those American vocalists, including Astaire himself, who, aided by increasingly sophisticated microphones, made those songs sound as natural and casual as the speaking voice, Astaire captured not only the way his generation spoke, but also the way it walked and gestured. Astaire's movement style contrasted powerfully with the remnants of court behavior on which ballet was based and which was still echoed, during Astaire's era, in much European middle- and upper-class behavior—straight-backed, centered, contained, and formal. (Think *Downton Abbey*.)

Even in tuxedo and top hat, Astaire exhibited a manner rooted in New World behavior: relaxed, casual, spontaneous, and loose-limbed. His movement derived not only from the fluidly elegant movement of urban African Americans, but also from the informal ways of young white Americans raised far from the strictures of class-bound Old World behavior: the easy quality seen in such movie midwesterners as Jimmy

Stewart and Henry Fonda, who could sprawl back in a chair, clasp their hands behind their heads, prop their feet on a table, and make it all look attractive.[30]

Astaire's art looked as at home on the sidewalk as it did on the stage. And he made it look right in domestic spaces: among and on sofas, tables, and chairs, patting out rhythms on the fireplace mantle, kicking the wall for punctuation. But although the way he moved looked like a spontaneous and normal extension of everyday American movement and gesture, it was planned, practiced, perfected, and performed as precisely as ballet. And like a ballet dancer, he disguised the effort it took to achieve the effect. Thus, although ordinary Americans could identify with Astaire's movement and aspire to it, they would be genuinely surprised when they discovered that it wasn't as easy as it looked. It was entirely artful.

Astaire shared his eclectic vision with George Gershwin, his first and closest composer colleague in musical theater, and George's brother, Ira. This connected their music and his dancing in a special way. George Gershwin had a no-limitations policy of his own and his own outlaw style. He did not discriminate between high and low art, and, like Astaire, he mingled Old and New World forms to create something unique to him. In Gershwin's work as in Astaire's, jazz was a key and fundamentally transformative element, but he also did not hesitate to make use of other styles. In 1924, at the now-legendary Aeolian Hall concert organized by the bandleader Paul Whiteman, he combined elements of American jazz with the European classical tradition in *Rhapsody in Blue*. Interestingly, he used the melting-pot metaphor to describe it. The *Rhapsody*, Gershwin would later write, was "a sort of musical kaleidoscope of America—of our vast melting pot, of our unduplicated national pep, of our blues, our metropolitan madness."[31]

Astaire never openly acknowledged, analyzed, or articulated, as Gershwin did, his classical sources, but as we will see, he did not hesitate to use them. The same year saw the debut of Fred and Adele Astaire in George and Ira Gershwin's first major musical comedy, *Lady Be Good* (1924). From the beginning Gershwin's music and Astaire's dances were seen as linked, a definitive statement, in song and dance, of the jazz-age generation. As the critic Alexander Woollcott later put it: "I do not know whether George Gershwin was born into this world to write rhythms for Fred Astaire's feet or whether Fred Astaire was born into this world to show how the Gershwin music should be danced. But surely they were written in the same key, those two."[32]

Gershwin and Astaire met when both were in their teens at Remick, the sheet-music publishing house where Gershwin played popular songs for potential buyers and where Astaire often hung out searching for new material. Astaire was not only a dancer but, like Gershwin, an aspiring songwriter. He played the piano, in a stride style similar to Gershwin's, but with his Viennese heritage he was no stranger to classical music. (His mother took him and his sister regularly to concerts). And like Gershwin, Astaire sought to expand his knowledge of the European symphonic tradition. During the long London runs of the Gershwin shows, Astaire took courses in harmony and theory at the Guildhall School of Music with his friend Noel Coward. Gershwin was also, according to his friends and colleagues—including Astaire—a good dancer who actually contributed steps to the Astaires' routines.[33]

Not surprisingly, they hit it off immediately, and Gershwin told Fred that he'd like to write a musical comedy for him someday. *Lady Be Good* (1924) and *Funny Face* (1927) were the eventual results—landmarks in the history of the new American musical form that Astaire, Gershwin, and their colleagues would bring to the stage and later to the screen.

CRAZY FASCINATING RHYTHM: ASTAIRE AND THE JAZZ AGE

Apart from its use of everyday movement, first and foremost in Astaire's dance was a key quality of jazz: syncopated rhythm.[34] In 1928 a London theater critic took a stab at defining the new style of the modern American musical and its particular appeal to young audiences of the 1920s. He held up as his example *Funny Face*, starring the Astaire siblings, and compared it with the equally popular hit of the previous decade in England, *Chu Chin Chow* (1916), the favorite date musical for soldiers on leave from World War I and the longest-running musical in the West End at that time. The single most important distinguishing factor for him was rhythm. Of these two dates, 1916 and 1927, he wrote:

> It is in-between that we have had this incursion of an entirely new element—the all conquering rhythm, to which story music and stars together are just incidental.
>
> Instead of listening to some simple and graceful melody such as contented their fathers and mothers, the truth seems to be that among many of our younger generation a use of rhythm is developing which does not need melody. . . . To the uninitiated, a meaningless sort of Morse code. . . .
>
> Any who imagine that the minds of environing enthusiasts are just vacant while Mr. Fred Astaire, for instance, is doing his concertos seem to be quite wrong. Behind all that tap and skip a regular symphony of rhythm is going in the imaginations of young people who know.
>
> In short, so far from being less intellectual than the old fashioned musical comedy, these nights of rhythm in which the very stage itself has to take its part and make its changes of scene with magical speed so as to keep up the swing are leaving the old fogeys all behind in their simplicities.[35]

Of course, all music has rhythm—regular or irregular, straight or syncopated—but the rhythm that the critic describes was really the "fascinating rhythm" that Ira Gershwin refers to in the song he and George wrote for the Astaires in *Lady Be Good*.[36] He meant the syncopated rhythms of jazz—a key factor in making of American musical comedy modern and new. The song "Fascinating Rhythm" is full of rhythmic surprises, with unexpected accents, starts, and stops. It contained a driving energy that made you want to dance, or, in Ira Gershwin's words, "quiver . . . just like a flivver" (the slang term for shaky jalopies). Richard Crawford points out that rhythm was a new word for the public in 1925 and shows how the Gershwins promoted its common usage through their songs.[37] For the next two decades "rhythm" would become almost synonymous with the jazz-age generation's music, manners, and mores.

Broadway itself was first and foremost identified with "rhythm": "Broadway Rhythm, it's got me, everybody dance!" go the words of the song written by the film-musical pioneers Arthur Freed and Herb Nacio Brown. "Broadway Rhythm" would become a theme song for a new film genre that took off with the advent of talkies. From *The Broadway Melody of 1929*, in which it first played, to its valedictory performance in the "ballet" from the movie *Singin' in the Rain* (1952), it epitomized the new era. "Who could ask for anything more?" asks Ira Gershwin in "I Got Rhythm" (1930). Joan Crawford, cinema's representative dancing flapper, danced to "The Rhythm of the Day" (Rodgers and Hart) in the movie in which Astaire made his film debut, *Dancing Lady* (1933). In another movie, *Shall We Dance* (1937), Astaire praises his beloved, Ginger Rogers, as the epitome of the new and modern dancer. "Now that's rhythm," he says, showing a friend her picture in a flip book. As for Astaire, as one critic praised him, he was "rhythm itself."[38]

But the word "rhythm," like the word "jazz," was also associated with lowbrow taste and wild, uninhibited behavior. In the song "Crazy Rhythm" (1928), the supposedly highbrow singer tries to shake off his infatuation with syncopated rhythm but finds it irresistible: "They say that when a high brow meets a low brow / Walking along Broadway / Soon the high brow, he has no brow / Ain't it a shame and you're to blame. / What's the use of prohibition / you produce the same condition. / Crazy Rhythm, I've gone crazy too."[39]

Whether it was called "fascinating," "crazy," "broken," or "Broadway," the term "rhythm," like "jazz," could also be seen in the 1920s as a kind of code word for black, risqué, and dangerous. "Rhythm is our business / Rhythm is what we do," sang the African American bandleader Jimmie Lunceford.[40] One of his band's big hits is featured in a Vitaphone soundie from 1936 in which Lunceford, dressed as the devil—complete with pitchfork—calls for "hot rhythm."[41] More insidiously, jazz "rhythm," one newspaper reporter wrote in 1918, was "an atrocity in polite society. . . . We should make it a point of civic honor to suppress it."[42]

THE AFRICAN, IRISH, AND BRITISH ROOTS OF ASTAIRE'S RHYTHM DANCES

Though syncopation and intricate rhythmic devices are certainly used in classical music, increasingly complex rhythms came to the New World with enslaved Africans. The rhythmic intricacies of Gershwin's paean to "fascinating rhythm" cannot compare with the virtuosic polyrhythmic and polymetric drumming traditions of the regions (particularly West Africa, home of the most complex rhythms) from which African slaves were taken. In the Americas, white owners tried to prevent slaves from drumming because of the fear that it could be used to send coded messages over long distances—as they were in various regions of Africa, where drumming patterns had developed into a rich and subtle language.

In response to these restrictions, African American slaves employed a variety of tools to use in place of drums, just as their African forebears had augmented and interwoven the sound of drums with that of a variety of other rhythm instruments. First and foremost they had their bodies—clapping, slapping, and stamping sounds—but they also used materials that came to hand: sticks and bones of every size and shape, gourd rattles, and stones. They also drew from the tradition of melismatic singing common in the Middle East and North Africa, in which words and syllables could be stretched out or broken up, rhythmically varied and elaborately ornamented, or used to punctuate and keep time with shouts and vocables of every kind. These were characteristic of Latin American dances as well, the fascinating rhythms of Africa taken to South American and Caribbean countries mingled with the Spanish rhythms of those countries' colonizers, resulting in dances like the rumba, the samba, and the conga.

But in the Americas, complex rhythms and the use of the body as a percussion instrument did not come solely from African culture; they were characteristic of Irish step dancing as well. The Irish had their own intricate step-dancing traditions in which the dancer became a percussionist, using the sound of feet hitting the ground in precise, fast rhythms.[43] (This was also true of the clog-dancing traditions of the British Isles that flourished in the Appalachians.) While the Irish were not as interested as African Americans in the use of polyrhythms (multiple rhythmic patterns played simultaneously), their traditions stressed in particular the sharp, clipped sound of the shoe hitting the ground. In contrast, African step dances were performed barefoot and on soft earth or sand.[44]

In Astaire's youth, the dance that grew out of the fusion of these traditions, which arose as African slaves mingled with Irish indentured servants in the New World, was called "buck" dancing, a term that was eventually expanded to "buck and wing." The rhythms of these dances became even more intricate and varied in the 1920s, when rhythm tap was developed and dancers began attaching metal taps to their shoes to emphasize and amplify the sounds of their feet, using them to interact and improvise with the other instrumentalists in a jazz band.[45]

From his earliest years, Fred Astaire was in "awe" of the "genius" (his words) of the African American dancers he saw in vaudeville and later on Broadway. He watched them with fascination from the wings and asked them to teach him steps between shows in the alleys outside the theaters. Such dancers included Bill "Bojangles" Robinson (1878–1949), whom Astaire met around 1915–16, when he was still a teenager.[46] The Astaires and Robinson appeared on the same bill, and Astaire treasured the encouragement of the older dancer. (Astaire proudly recounted in his autobiography that Robinson had told him admiringly, "Boy, you can dance!").[47] Later in his career Astaire would pay tribute to the dancer in "Bojangles of Harlem" (*Swing Time*, 1936).

Astaire's and Gershwin's careers took off within this context and in response to the flowering of the genius of tap dance on Broadway as well as in Harlem. Three years before *Lady Be Good*, African American dancers, who had been largely confined to performing in clubs in Harlem and off Broadway, invaded the Great White Way with an all-black musical that thrilled Astaire's generation and led to a series of African

American shows and their imitators. Their impact would be definitive, changing the face of American musical theater and dance in musical theater forever. *Shuffle Along*, by Eubie Blake and Noble Sissle, introduced the great dancers Florence Mills and, on tour, Josephine Baker, among others. *Runnin' Wild* and other black musicals followed, including Lew Leslie's *Blackbirds* (1928), featuring Robinson who, at age fifty, at long last became a star in a wider world.

Already influenced by Robinson, Astaire joined the tap revolution while it was happening and in doing so contributed to it. During the 1920s Fred and Adele were regularly going to learn steps from black dancers and choreographers such as Buddy Bradley (1905–72), but for Astaire the most exciting new development was a refinement of tap technique practiced most famously by John W. Sublett (whose stage name was John W. Bubbles), whom Astaire cited in a 1931 interview as the dancer he "most liked to watch." Bubbles was one of the originators and the most masterful developer of what came to be called "rhythm tap" (Fig. 1.2a). Astaire encountered Bubbles at the Hoofers Club in Harlem, where dancers came to learn from and challenge one another. He saw Bubbles perform with Louis Armstrong at Small's Paradise in 1925–26, where Armstrong was inventing musical scat with "Butter and Egg Man."[48] Bubbles began to expand the basic structure within which dancers improvised: he "changed from two-to-a-bar to four-to-a-bar, cutting the tempo in half and giving himself twice as much time to add new inventions."[49] As the dancer Honi Coles explains about Bubbles's technique:

> With two's you just have time to do the traditional steps with as much skill as possible. With fours, a good dancer works just as fast, even though the tempo is slower, but he has to fill in with his own ideas as well as watch his balance. In fact, he has to learn to handle his entire body more gracefully. . . . When he started dropping his heels, he could get an extra thud whenever he wanted it. [Bubbles began] accenting off-beats with the heels and toes in a variety of cramp rolls, which made for greater dynamics. . . . He did new things with his toes, too, adding taps behind and bringing them together for an extra accent in front. At the same time he worked out turns and combinations, or rhythmic patterns, some of which extended beyond the usual eight bars.[50]

Bubbles and others also upped the ante by adding metal taps to their shoes—which, depending upon how they were used, could both increase and vary the volume of the dancer's "drumming" on the floor. Astaire adopted this innovation, and by 1931 he was being regularly consulted by other dancers on how to place and use taps.[51]

ASTAIRE AND THE INTEGRATION OF MUSIC AND DANCE

The tight interlacing of sight and sound that Bubbles accomplished with his feet was to become a hallmark of Astaire's style. But Astaire did not just concentrate on the feet; he expanded his focus to the entire body, each part interplaying with the music—not only its rhythm, but the melodic line, countermelodies, and texture and color of the orchestrations. "He *gives, through feet and legs, hands and arms, head and torso, the physical actuality of the music, warp and woof,*" wrote one critic who tried to capture Astaire's intricate choreographic attentiveness to music's inner workings.[52] Like his African American colleagues, Astaire did not just mimic the physical actuality of the music but interacted with it. A gesture of the arms, hands, or legs, for example, could visually punctuate or counterpoint a rhythmic phrase.

The integration of music and dance extended also to Astaire's collaboration with the composers and orchestrators of his work as well. Writes Alec Wilder: "Every song written for Fred Astaire seems to bear his mark. Every writer, in my opinion, was vitalized by Astaire and wrote in a manner they had never quite written in before: he brought out in them something a little better than their best—a little more subtlety, flair, sophistication, wit, and style."[53]

In creating the shape and style of the music for his dances, Astaire's composers worked with him intimately. Gershwin, for one, loved to watch the Astaires, and Fred enjoyed watching him dance too: "It made me laugh."[54] Gershwin had a strong affinity for interesting off-the-beat rhythms and a gift for picking up complex and multilayered rhythmic patterns.[55] Astaire's account of how he and Gershwin worked together illuminates the dancer's important but often overlooked role in the development of *Lady Be Good*.[56] As can be heard in recordings made at the time, Gershwin and Astaire fanned each other's creativity, their camaraderie and joyous enthusiasm almost palpable. Gershwin would come in on his own time to play the piano for Astaire's rehearsals, from time to time "jumping up from the piano to demonstrate an idea for a step or an extra twist to something I was already experimenting with."[57]

Gershwin's "Fascinating Rhythm" was composed with the Astaires in mind, to be danced as well as sung. The last step of this dance was, as Astaire tells us, a "complicated precision rhythm thing in which we [Fred and Adele] kicked out simultaneously as we crossed back and forth in front of each other with arm pulls and heads back." How could he top it to create more of a "wow" ending? After Astaire had fretted about it for days, Gershwin suggested upping the ante by traveling with the step to the wings. It was, in Astaire's words, "the perfect answer to our problem . . . a knockout applause puller."[58] "Fascinating Rhythm," song and dance alike, was the most exciting thing Broadway had seen in a long time. As one critic enthused, it was the high point of the show:

Fred and Adele we salute you! Last night at the Liberty Theatre this young couple appeared about 8:30 o'clock and from an audience sophisticated and over-theatered received a cordial greeting. At 8:45 they were applauded enthusiastically and when at 9:15 they sang and danced "Fascinating Rhythm" the callous Broadwayites cheered them as if their favorite halfback had planted the ball behind the goal posts after an 80 yard run. Seldom has it been our pleasure to witness so heartfelt, spontaneous and deserved a tribute.[59]

"Fascinating Rhythm" was the first in a long line of other "fascinating rhythm" songs associated with Astaire, including Irving Berlin's "Top Hat" and "Puttin' on the Ritz," with their off-the-beat-accented lyrics; Gershwin's "Shall We Dance"; Jerome Kern's "Bojangles of Harlem"; and Hal Borne's waltz (often, and erroneously, credited to Jerome Kern) in *Swing Time*, to name just a few.

George Gershwin helped to rehearse as well as create Fred Astaire's first major rhythm solo in musical comedy. This was "The Half of It Dearie Blues," which was added to *Lady Be Good* just before the show moved to London. You can hear the results on the record along with the spark and enthusiasm of the interchange between the two performers and the way they loved to play around with different rhythms and musical jokes—including Gershwin interjecting quotes from his *Rhapsody in Blue*. Todd Decker argues that, although twelve-bar blues was a standard basis for jazz compositions, Gershwin and Astaire were the first to use it in musical theater, in "The Half of It Dearie Blues."[60] In a brilliant imitation of jazz musicians, pianist and dancer play call-and-response games: one sets up a pattern and the other reacts as the two artists try to one-up each other in a conversation in dance.

FIGURE 1.2 (a) John W. Bubbles demonstrating rhythm tap. (b) Fred Astaire in *Follow the Fleet* (1936), "I'd Rather Lead a Band," one of his most intricate rhythm tap numbers. (c) Call and response in *Top Hat* (1935), "Isn't It a Lovely Day." Astaire taps forward and Ginger Rogers starts to respond. (d) Challenge dance: Astaire and Powell try to one-up each other in *Broadway Melody of 1940*.

Like the African American dancers he admired, and like Gershwin, Astaire would put intricate rhythms into his dances and use both call-and-response and challenge devices in many of his dances, from *Roberta* ("I'll Be Hard to Handle"), to *Top Hat* ("Top Hat, White Tie, and Tails" and "Isn't It a Lovely Day"), *Follow the Fleet* ("I'd Rather Lead a Band"), and many more. Compare Bubbles and Astaire doing rhythm tap (Figs. 1.2a and b), and in an example of call and response, note how Astaire dances forward (call) as Rogers begins to respond (Fig. 1.2c). When he worked with professional tap dancers, he could really pull out all the stops: his extraordinary tap challenge with Eleanor Powell in *Broadway Melody of 1940*, in which each takes turns calling and responding with their foot sounds, is a highlight (Fig. 1.2d), and so is his dance "The Babbitt and the Bromide" with Gene Kelly in the film *Ziegfeld Follies*, where the two, in Astaire's words, "beat the hell out of the floor."[61]

Like his African American colleagues, Astaire employs not just his feet but his hands and other parts of his body—as well as inanimate objects—as rhythm instruments. His integration of clapping hands and tapping feet is nowhere more obvious than in his tribute to Bill Robinson and John Bubbles in *Swing Time*, when he sets up a complicated series of clapping and patting rhythms. In the *Broadway Melody of 1940* jukebox dance, Astaire and Powell hit their uplifted feet so fast you can barely see the slaps (Fig. 1.3a). In fact, however, any surface that comes in handy can be employed. In "Needle in a Haystack," from *The Gay Divorcee*, Astaire sets up a rhythm with his feet and punctuates it by drumming on the mantel. In *Roberta*, he casually kicks the wall to help start off "I'll Be Hard to Handle." In "No Strings," from *Top Hat*, he pats the top of a sideboard in his friend's London suite (Figs. 1.3b and c). In the same sequence he spies a cigarette urn full of sand, which he sprinkles on the floor in the tradition of such African American sand dancers as Robinson and Sandman Sims, then creates soft, soothing rhythmic sounds to lull his angry beloved to sleep. Two decades later he brushes, glides, and taps on sand in a valedictory song in *The Belle of New York*, "I Want to Be a Dancing Man." Other examples include the drum dances in *Damsel in Distress* and *Easter Parade*, when both hands and feet are used to the hit the drums. It should be noted that making music with hands as well as feet is not just an African American tradition: the clapping, stamping, and slapping-the-body rhythms also come from the schuhplattler dances—although these are not syncopated—of Astaire's own Austro-German heritage.

The most prominent way Astaire exploited objects that come to hand was his use of a walking stick or cane as a rhythm instrument (Fig. 1.3d). During his formative years, canes could be fashionable accessories of able-bodied men on English and American urban streets. Call-and-response techniques for cane and chorus are used in the songs "Top Hat" and "Puttin' on the Ritz," in which the syncopations of his cane are answered and amplified by a chorus of identically dressed men behind him—or duplications of himself. In *You Were Never Lovelier*, Astaire is not afraid to accent a dance by sharply tapping Adolph Menjou's temptingly bald head. He finishes his impromptu audition by deftly launching the cane into a holder at the far end of the room to punctuate his dance with precision. He does the same with an umbrella in the film *Funny Face*. Such use of

FIGURE 1.3 (a) Astaire and Eleanor Powell slapping their uplifted feet in the jukebox dance from *Broadway Melody of 1940*. (b and c) Astaire dancing and patting out rhythms on an Art Deco sideboard in *Top Hat* (1935), "No Strings." (d) Astaire tapping out rhythms with his cane to punctuate the dance in *Top Hat*.

FIGURE 1.4 (a) A drag and (b) a slide, both by John Bubbles in *Cabin in the Sky* (1943). (c) A slide by Astaire in *Top Hat* (1935), "No Strings."

these kinds of props—and, as the century went on, many more—was characteristic not only of Astaire's dancing, but of film-musical dance as a whole.

Astaire draws heavily from African American dancers' use of their feet in various shuffle and sliding and gliding steps, which had been developed to a high level by African American dancers long before Michael Jackson's moonwalk became famous.[62] John Bubbles was a virtuoso at this kind of dancing. The dancer shuffles by brushing back and forth on the floor with the balls of his feet and glides by sliding along its surface, almost like a skater on ice. Tap dancers could also drag one foot—the side of the shoe brushes the floor—or they could "chug" forward or back on two feet, a kind of abrupt, on-the-ground jump. (The dancer looks as though he is preparing to jump by bending the knees, but he actually stays on the floor and "travels" by dragging both feet back or "chugging" forward.) Bubbles demonstrates his skill in *Varsity Show*, interspersing his rhythm tapping with all sorts of nuanced brushing, dragging (Fig. 1.4a), and sliding steps. In the film version of *Cabin in the Sky*, he crosses an entire nightclub floor on one foot by sliding (Fig. 1.4b). Gliding, dragging, and shuffling steps were also part of old style (*sean nos*) step and clog dancing of western Ireland, which contributed to the Afro-Irish fusion that was tap dance.[63]

In "I Ain't Hep to That Step" from *Second Chorus* (1940), Astaire and his partner, Paulette Goddard, use chugging forward and back as a key step. Glorious partnered slides and drags are part of *Roberta*'s exhilarating "I'll Be Hard to Handle," and again the sounds of the shuffles and glides could be amplified by sprinkling sand on the floor, as Astaire does in the reprise of "No Strings" in *Top Hat* (Fig. 1.4c) and in *The Belle of New York*. Later Balanchine, inspired by African American dancers and Astaire, would incorporate dragging feet in pointe shoes into ballets such as *Rubies*, *Agon*, and *Who Cares?*

Forms developed in the New World were only one part of Astaire's arsenal of dance techniques. Astaire was only one generation removed from his European heritage. The next chapter examines forms tied to the Old World that were also foundational influences on his style.

The principle of ballet dancing underlies
everything.
—Fred Astaire, "Dancing as a Profession"
[c. 1923]

2

ASTAIRE'S ROOTS IN BALLROOM, BALLET, AND OTHER FORMS

TAP, MOSTLY A solo performance idiom, was only one element of Astaire's style. European ballroom and social dance forms of all kinds and from every era also influenced Astaire's style profoundly. During his formative years and indeed until his thirties, working mostly as his sister's partner, Astaire logged thousands of hours practicing, refining, and developing dances in which precise coordination and interaction with a female partner was the goal. Especially important in this respect was the influence of the ballroom dancers Vernon and Irene Castle.

Vaudeville, Astaire's training ground, was also key. A typical vaudeville bill was a glorious mix of everything from trained animals acts and acrobatics to actors, singers, dancers, instrumentalists, comedians, and dance of all kinds: "eccentric dancing," tap, clog dancing, Irish step dance, ballroom, "aesthetic" dancers à la Isadora Duncan, the orientalist posturing of Ruth St. Denis, flamenco, Escuela Bolera, and ballet.

Ballet, with its stories told in dance, held particular importance for Astaire. From it he drew the concept of whole-body choreography, especially that of the upper body—the arms and hands in particular. However, he flatly rejected some of ballet's central features: turnout, the stately symmetry and balance of its nineteenth-century expression, and the ethereal upward thrust of male ballet dancers. Instead, Astaire preferred off-balance dancing and into-the-ground movement. Astaire had in common with modern dance the use of so-called naturalistic movement, but his was of a very different kind.

BALLROOM DANCE AND PARTNERING

The Astaires were born into an atmosphere saturated with Viennese music and dance. Their father grew up at the height of Viennese operetta and its signature dance form, the waltz, and with the music of the Strauss family. In 1904, when Astaire was five and his sister was seven, Franz Lehár's *The Merry Widow* not only was the hit of Vienna, but also spread quickly to all of Europe and America, its title waltz played, sung, and danced to by young and old Americans from Los Angeles to New York. The waltz seems sedate now, but in its heyday it was seen, like jazz dance, as the dance form of the young and wild. It even had a fascinating rhythm of its own: the mad Wilis in *Giselle* (1841) dance in three-quarter time in a musical signal of their abnormal, outlier status.[1] The waltz also reflected a loosening of puritanical strictures. Social dances such as the minuet had kept middle- and upper-class men and women at a hand-holding distance, as did quadrilles (also called lancers) and all sorts of country dances wherein the individual interacted with more than one partner. The intimate waltz linked one man to one woman tightly at the waist and shoulders.

The waltz (along with the Ländler, the country cousin from which it grew, and its Eastern European up-tempo relative, the polka) continued its popularity into the 1910s, '20s, '30s, and '40s; it was featured especially in operetta, which thrived alongside modern musical comedy from the 1920s through the 1940s on Broadway. The Astaires' appearance in the Fritz Kreisler and Victor Jacobi operetta *Apple Blossoms* was a fulfillment of sorts of their father's unrealized ambitions, and although Astaire never appeared in the sound films that came out of the operetta tradition, he was certainly aware of them and was a very skilled waltzer.[2] Astaire's mastery of the waltz, as well as his ease with the courtly manners, formal behavior, and uplifted posture associated with this Old World form, can be seen in the dance drama "This Heart of Mine" in the film *Ziegfeld Follies* (Fig. 2.1a), in which the introductory and ending sections are waltzed in a crowded ballroom setting reminiscent of scenes from *Die Fledermaus* and *The Merry Widow*. Astaire also incorporates waltz sections in other dances of his, from "The Continental" in *The Gay Divorcee* and "The Piccolino" in *Top Hat* to "The Wedding Cake Walk" in *You'll Never Get Rich*.

In his films Astaire not only waltzes, but expands and transforms the waltz by melding it with elements of rhythm tap and other forms. One example is the waltz in *Swing Time* (1936). Astaire softens the shotgun sound of tap dancing and counterpoints the syncopated melody in the center section with a whispering filigree of steps. The dancers face each other, linked by their arms in a standard waltz position as, constantly turning, they skim across the floor with the speed and close coordination of a couple used to covering large spaces in a vast ballroom. This hovering effect is related to another popular ballroom dance, the quickstep, still a standard of ballroom competitions today. But most important, this is a jazz waltz, syncopated in rhythm and counterpointed by the dancers' foot sounds.[3] It is the composer's and choreographers' (Astaire's with Hermes Pan) swinging of the standard waltz that makes the difference. Astaire also swings a waltz in a section of his and Rita Hayworth's dance to "I'm Old Fashioned" (Jerome Kern and Johnny Mercer) in *You Were Never Lovelier* (1942). Another use of the soft tap counterpointing appears in the "Begin the Beguine" section of *Broadway Melody of 1940* (Cole Porter), but here the patterns seem to relate to the traditions of flamenco display and the paso doble: chest held high and proud, arms moving up and down in curvilinear gestures. The dancers never link arms; rather, they

FIGURE 2.1 (a) Astaire and Lucille Bremer waltzing in the MGM movie *Ziegfeld Follies* (1945), "This Heart of Mine." (b–c) Astaire and Rogers, *Top Hat* (1935), "The Piccolino," folk-dance steps: (b) arms akimbo, facing each other, (c) unclasped-locket position.

circle each other in a kind of subtle challenge dance. Only in the finale of the sequence will they get down to a serious rhythm-tap challenge.

"The Piccolino" in *Top Hat* shows an even earlier use of four-footed soft-tap "embroidery," but this dance also gives a sense of what the Astaires learned from theatricalized European folk-dance forms: the heel-and-toe motif that begins the dance reveals its origins (Fig. 2.1b). Most distinctively and brilliantly, Astaire often uses his version of a common folk-dance partnering position to vary the face-to-face ballroom position as the couple breaks open like an unclasped locket, arms linked, to face the audience and skim along side by side, forward, backward, or with drags and slides (Fig. 2.1c). An especially exhilarating example of this way of moving appears in the finale of *You Were Never Lovelier*, when Astaire and Hayworth seem almost to levitate, propelling themselves as they skip across the floor, moving from clasped to unclasped positions, riding on Conrad Salinger's exhilarating arrangement of Kern's title melody. Astaire used many creative variants of the unclasped-locket hold in his partner dances, keeping the couple from being locked into a face-to-face position.

VERNON AND IRENE CASTLE

Peoples of African heritage who mingled with Europeans in the Americas brought the next phase of ballroom dancing, helping to change a pattern that had been active since the Renaissance. Astaire saw this as one of the great contributions of jazz to the world of dance:

> There is less grace in the ballroom since the introduction of jazz, but there is no reason for decrying music because it demands different steps from the old-fashioned waltz, polka and lancers. The ballroom of a decade ago had something of the air of a finale to a musical comedy with its interchaining dancers. Jazz has killed all that, but it has made dancing more interesting.
>
> Since the coming of jazz, partners have become more intimately related; their contact is more personal, and they are not continually leaving each other to change partners as in a set of lancers.
>
> Jazz has made dancing a hundred percent more popular. Now it is within the scope of all, and the ballroom has no terrors for the self-conscious dancer who was formerly afraid of a false move spoiling a figure for as many as six or seven other people as in lancers.[4]

Astaire is referring to the kind of dance that was introduced and popularized in middle-class America and Europe by Vernon and Irene Castle, who drew on both the European tradition and that culture but also introduced the brilliant new dances originated by descendants of Africans and others in the Americas. The Castles' rise to fame began at the Café de Paris in Paris in 1912, and it continued after their return to New York later that year. "She and Vernon were idols of my sister and me when we were starting out," Astaire once said. "They were terrific. I don't think anybody in this generation . . . [can] imagine the size of their popularity. . . . They just became world famous."[5]

Astaire's interest in the Castles might have been in part sparked by the Coccias, a famous vaudeville team who in 1913 created a new and more adult act for Fred and Adele in response to their transition from childhood to young adulthood. Grown to his full height, Fred could now be a partner for his older sister, and dances modeled on those of the Castles may have entered their repertoire at this time.[6]

The Castles introduced African American social dance—especially the so-called animal dances, the fox trot and the turkey trot—and Latin American dances such as the Brazilian maxixe and the Argentine tango to white middle-class audiences. Their dances were accompanied by James Reese Europe, an African American bandleader who in 1918 would lead the first ragtime band to tour in Europe during World War I.

In the couple dancing derived and modified from African American and Latin American models and introduced to the white middle and upper classes by the Castles, man and woman were pulled even closer together than in the waltz. For the Castle Walk, for example, the two simply walked in ballroom position; the smoothness of the dance depends on the precise coordination of the two bodies moving as a unit, with hardly any space between them. The pair's chests, torsos, hips, and legs were aligned so that the dancers seemed to move as a single unit (Fig. 2.2a). The man led the woman by varying the pressure of his hand on her back, while she wrapped her left arm around his shoulder and placed her extended right hand in her partner's left.

In dances like the tango, previously sacrosanct spaces (between the legs, for example) could be invaded by kicking in, or the partners could brush their thighs, hips, and breasts as they crossed and recrossed.[7] *The Story of Vernon and Irene Castle* (1939) shows Astaire and Rogers making every effort to duplicate the Castles' dances under Irene's supervision (Fig. 2.2b). Irene Castle admired Astaire, who happened to look very much like her husband, and a few years after Vernon's death in 1918, she employed Astaire to create the choreography for her solo comeback on Broadway.[8]

But the Castles altered the animal dances as performed by their African American originators to make them more acceptable to white middle-class audiences, who

FIGURE 2.2 Couple dancing: (a) Vernon and Irene Castle. Photograph by Moffett, Chicago. (b) Astaire and Rogers performing the Castle Walk in *The Story of Vernon and Irene Castle* (1939). (c) Dancers at Harlem's Savoy Ballroom in the 1930s. (d) Astaire and Rogers in *Roberta* (1935), "I'll Be Hard to Handle."

could still be shocked at seeing these fluid, loose-limbed dancers almost lean into each other, their breasts, hips, and thighs tightly and thrillingly glued together (Fig. 2.2c). The Castles straightened up the torso, kept the head erect, and subdued the open sensuality of the dances. (The Minnesota novelist Maud Hart Lovelace in her autobiographical novel has a "proper" young lady of 1914 justify her passion for social dancing by proclaiming that the Castles "have made the popular dances much less vulgar now.")[9]

After the Castles, however, Astaire would loosen these strictures and follow the lead of African American dancers, like the ones in the Savoy Ballroom shown in Fig. 2.2c. In *Roberta*'s "I'll Be Hard to Handle," Astaire, walking hip to hip with Ginger Rogers, bends her pliant back daringly until the couple begin to slip and slide (Fig. 2.2d).

THE CHARLESTON

The Astaires and the Gershwins helped to further popularize a new dance craze—one originated by African Americans. The Charleston, in which the dancers faced each other or danced side by side without touching, would become *the* dance symbol of the new "jazz generation," not only in America but in Europe. It was introduced in 1923 in the all-black Broadway show *Runnin' Wild*; and two years later Josephine Baker, in the Revue Nègre, had overwhelmed Parisian and later English and other European audiences with her thrilling version—admired not only by the general public but by the artistic avant-garde, including Diaghilev's new young choreographer George Balanchine and the esteemed Russian ballet critic André Levinson. The Astaires, who made it a point to visit Paris regularly to catch up on the latest dances, would also have seen her dance.

Capitalizing on the new dance's popularity, Gershwin and the Astaires put a new song into *Lady Be Good* during its London run. In "I'd Rather Charleston," Astaire, playing Adele's guardian, tries to get his jazz-baby ward to settle down and behave conventionally, but her response to his attempt to educate and enlighten her in more serious matters is the song's title, which could easily be seen as a paean to the new manners and mores of her generation. The English public including the younger members of the royal family, such as the Prince of Wales and his brothers, loved it, but some of the more established English dancing halls and their older-generation managers mounted an effort to ban the dance. However, as one newspaper reported, "Fred and Adele Astaire, the American dancers, are doing much to popularize the Charleston in the West End and popular clamour for it may overcome the objection of the hotel."[10] Adele's spirited defense of the Charleston was published in the paper the next day. She suggested that far from being immoral, the Charleston was a reflection and embodiment of the innocence and playfulness of the African American originators of the form. Her stereotyping of African Americans reflects the attitudes of her day, but her description is nonetheless a sincerely admiring one. As she readily acknowledged, she had much to learn from the African American dancers with whom, like her brother, she studied and whom she tried to emulate:

> As I see it, the Charleston is just like little children at play: it was invented among the colored people of the United States, and it is the perfect expression of their happy-go-lucky, easy going, don't-care-a-hang spirit.
>
> What's harmful in it? People dance it in New York ballrooms, in the most se- lect houses, and nobody thinks anything about it. Why should they here? I never heard such a narrow-minded thing in all my life.
>
> If anybody wants to know what I think of the Charleston, you can tell them that I think it is the finest, happiest, liveliest, most individual dance in the world.[11]

The Charleston was followed by the big apple, the black bottom, and the Lindy hop. Astaire would draw elements from all these popular African American–based social- dance forms as his work progressed. And, following in their tradition, he would go on to present more and more new "named" dances in his films, beginning with "The Carioca" in *Flying Down to Rio*, powerfully influenced by Brazilian dance forms; "The Continental" in *The Gay Divorcee*; "The Piccolino" in *Top Hat*; and "The Yam" in *Carefree*. Even in later years, when the younger generation's new dances were responding not to the music of Astaire's generation but to rock and roll with the stroll, the twist, the frug, and dancing farther and farther apart until finally they barely touched on the dance floor, Astaire was still looking to hook the younger generation with new dances such as "Sluefoot" in *Daddy Long-Legs* and "The Ritz Roll and Rock" in *Silk Stockings*.[12]

Although Astaire's dances drew heavily from popular social dance, his complex and highly dramatized couple dances required skills that were far beyond those seen on an ordinary dance floor. In *Follow the Fleet*, for example, Astaire and Rogers compete with highly accomplished yet nonprofessional social dancers straight from Los Angeles– area public dance floors; the stars' highly stylized, endlessly rehearsed, polished dances are a world away from those of their real-life counterparts. Although simplified printed instructions of Astaire's named dances were prepared for the public by ghostwriters and published in newspapers, complete with illustrations, they were too complex to teach and too difficult to perform.

None of Astaire's dances caught on in the ballroom like the Charleston or the Lindy hop, which, like the black bottom, had originated in popular dance halls, improvised and "grown" by social dancers for their own use and expression. In their films, though, Astaire and Rogers, like the Castles, would revive the craze for popular social dance across the country, and Astaire would eventually open his own chain of ballroom- dance schools. Onscreen, these dances gave the public an idealized reflection of them- selves and of the emotional relationship of lover and beloved that could be expressed in movement. As Gene Kelly would say at Astaire's 1981 tribute by the American Film Institute, "Everyone who goes out dancing on Saturday night owes a debt to Fred Astaire."[13]

Astaire was constantly on the lookout for new ideas and steps. In his autobiography he lists a number of vaudeville acts from which he learned by watching from the wings and getting to know the performers backstage. He became good friends with Zenzo Hashimoto, a young boy who appeared with his family in a famous tumbling and juggling act called the Kita Banzai Japs. Young Fred stood in the wings every night to watch "the older Japanese lie on their backs on a specially built thing and juggle my pal back and forth with their feet." Their feats of juggling and acrobatics, of using ordinary things in extraordinary ways, like "jugs filled with water that were attached to either end of a long rope and swung by Zenzo's parents through the air without ever losing a drop," would give rise to Astaire's love of props—golf clubs, umbrellas, coat racks, even Eleanor Powell's compact—in "marvelous, impossible" ways.[14]

Movies were also featured in vaudeville: as late as the 1930s a film would sometimes conclude the live part of the vaudeville program. And the Astaires were clearly interested in movie dancers, one of whom they actually incorporated into their act with the famous "Chaplin walk"—heels apart and feet splayed out. Astaire even quotes it in the "Looking for a Needle in a Haystack" number in *The Gay Divorcee* (Fig. 2.3a).

It was not unusual for the "lowbrow" forms of eccentric dancing and acrobatics to mingle on the vaudeville stage with items that could be considered "highbrow." Pavlova had appeared in vaudeville, the young Balanchine "Russian State Ballet" dancers would appear on the same bill with a variety of music hall acts shortly after his escape from Russia, and even Diaghilev's company gave in and appeared at London's tony Alhambra music hall.

From the wings the young Astaire also studied the Cansinos, a Spanish dancing family (Fig. 2.3b). Eduardo, his brother Angel, and his sister Elsa had immigrated from Madrid around 1913 and danced in the tradition of the Escuela Bolera. They opened a dancing studio at Carnegie Hall and appeared in the *Ziegfeld Follies of 1915*; they also toured in vaudeville and later appeared in films. Eduardo and his wife (Volga Hayworth, also from Spain) were the parents of Margarita Carmen Cansino (Fig. 2.3c). After she changed her name to Rita Hayworth, she went on to become—according to Astaire's daughter and son-in-law, Ava and Richard McKenzie—his favorite partner. Recalled Astaire: "They were headliners with their magnificent Spanish dancing act. Adele and I were a small act on the bill and occupied the number-two spot. I watched Eduardo at almost every show. He and his sister were exciting performers. We worked with the Cansinos for a number of weeks [and] we became good friends."[15] Gene Kelly, who would later dance with Hayworth in *Cover Girl* (1944), studied at one point with her uncle Angel Cansino.

Both Astaire and Kelly learned from Spanish dancers' proud, uplifted carriage and beautiful, expressive port de bras (literally, "carriage of the arms"), which included undulating arms lifted high in the air to manipulate castanets. (Astaire's dance with Rita Hayworth in *You'll Never Get Rich* to Cole Porter's "So Near and Yet So Far" takes advantage of this lovely quality in her movement.)

The young Astaires also appeared on a vaudeville program with Ruth St. Denis, who, along with Isadora Duncan, was one of the matriarchs of the new style that eventually

FIGURE 2.3 (a) Astaire imitating Charlie Chaplin in *The Gay Divorcee* (1934), "Needle in a Haystack." (b) Eduardo and Elisa Cansino. (c) Margarita Cansino, later known as Rita Hayworth.

would form the foundation of what we now refer to as modern dance. St. Denis worked in what might have been called aesthetic dance, drawing her inspiration from imagined dances of ancient Egypt and, after some serious world travel, elements taken from dances of India, Southeast Asia, Japan, and China. Adele Astaire, who received a *Dance Magazine* award at the same time as St. Denis, remembers watching her in awe from the wings.[16] She may have seen an early solo performance, or perhaps the troupe St. Denis formed in 1915 with her husband, Ted Shawn, called Denishawn. The troupe toured with a more extravagant show that included such dancers from her school as Martha Graham and Doris Humphrey. Adele certainly could have seen both.

BALLET

The European waltz, African American and Irish forms, and acrobatics were for the most part popular dance forms. The general framework for Astaire's style and some of the basic concepts for using those forms, however, came from a theatrical dance tradition and training system that originated in the courts of Europe: the *danse d'école*, more popularly known as ballet.

If jazz dance in America was seen as lowbrow, popular, and New World, ballet was its opposite: highbrow, elitist, and Old World. Both forms were stereotyped in the American public imagination. Astaire, determinedly au courant, did *not* want to look like a ballet dancer. Nonetheless, he was impressed by them and their training methods—and, most important, he drew on some of its most basic principles to shape his style. Astaire "wanted to retain the basic principles of balance and grace, but . . . did not want ballet style to be predominant"[17]—and he was exposed to a wide variety of ballet styles, from the nineteenth-century *ballet d'action* to the modern ballet of Diaghilev's Ballets Russes.

Ballet was one part of the eclectic curriculum offered in the two theatrical schools the Astaire children attended, those of Claude Alvienne and Ned Wayburn. But while the breadth of Alvienne's and Wayburn's advertised offerings was staggering, it is difficult to determine their depth—especially in ballet. They catered to a variety of pre-professional dancer-actors, and their intent was to train their students in a mix of styles for a life in vaudeville and on Broadway. Unlike the strict pre-professional ballet academies in France, Italy, Denmark, and Russia, where students concentrated exclusively on ballet and were trained gradually over many years to build up the strength, flexibility, and turnout demanded by this distinctive and highly stylized form of dance, Astaire and his sister received drastically abbreviated training.[18] The Astaire children studied less than a year at Alvienne's, between January and November 1905, and at Wayburn's for perhaps one or two years (1910–11 or –12). Alvienne sent them to the ballet master Luigi Albertieri (whom both Fred and Adele mistakenly remembered as Albert Chéri) of the Metropolitan Opera Ballet.[19] Wayburn also offered classes in ballet, but how much and with what teachers the Astaires studied is not known.

Wayburn was proud of this speeded-up training in what he called "Americanized ballet," but Alvienne was well aware of its difficulties and dangers.[20] In his detailed article "The Art and Agony of Toe Dancing," published in 1900 in *Metropolitan Magazine*, he makes it clear that the slowly and rigorously trained graduates of European dance academies would always be superior to those Americans forced into abbreviated training. But Alvienne was in America, and most of his dancers would make their careers in vaudeville and musical comedy. The "toe dancing" he described was a kind of novelty trick extracted from the vocabulary of the *danse d'école* (the academic ballet technique first officially codified at the court of Louis XIV, who created the Royal Academy of Dance in 1666) but adapted for a different kind of dancer in a very different context.[21] Although Alvienne would incorporate such novelties into Astaire's early choreography and bill him as "the greatest child toe dancer in the world," he—if not his audiences— was well aware that this was far removed from the world of professional ballet.

Nonetheless, the Astaires were certainly taught the rudiments of European *danse d'école*. "Ballet training is the finest you can get," Astaire wrote. However abbreviated his experience with Albertieri, he was taught in a style that extended from Carlo Blasis (1797–1878) to the famous ballet pedagogue Enrico Cecchetti (1850–1928), Albertieri's mentor and adoptive father. Astaire admired ballet dancers' rigorous technical standards, attention to detail, and stress on the continual maintenance and improvement of their skills through daily class and repeated practice, and he applied their work ethic to his own dancing. "Fred *worked* like a ballet dancer," insisted Adele. "I could never have done that. . . . I was the madcap."[22]

THE FULL RESOURCES: WHOLE-BODY DANCING

Astaire himself insisted that the key lesson he took from ballet training was his attention to the use of his upper body, particularly his arms and hands, in coordination with his legs. This came to be recognized as a distinguishing element of his style. According to Wayburn, "Astaire was the first American tap dancer to consciously employ the full resources of his arms, hands and torso for visual ornamentation."[23] Another critic wrote: "One finds in his dancing a distinguishing feature. It is not only that his legs and feet dance, but his arms and hands have rhythm of their own which is the perfect counterpart of his footwork, and places his dancing on a singularly high plane."[24] Observed Frederick Franklin, who first saw Astaire in London in the 1920s: "Astaire used his *whole body* in his dancing! We had never seen anything like that before in London in the West End."[25]

The tap and other step and clog dancing traditions in which Astaire had grown up focused on footwork: the exciting action took place below the waist. In Irish step dancing, for example, the arms hang quietly at the sides, the torso is held upright, and the head faces forward. Although rhythm-tap dancers like Robinson and Bubbles could extend or raise the arms for balance to punctuate a phrase, or in the popular "trucking" gesture when pointed fingers oscillate in the air, the focus was still on the extraordinary feats of the feet.

In contrast, the *danse d'école* took the entire body into account. A variety of head, neck, shoulder, torso, and arm and hand positions (*épaulement* and port de bras) were coordinated with the placement and movement of the legs to create an overall shape that extended from the tips of the toes to the top of the head. Albertieri, Astaire's first ballet teacher, would have stressed this aspect of ballet from day one of the boy's training.

However, American males of Astaire's generation faced a powerful stigma attached to the stylized use of the arms and hands. Its association with ballet and opera stereotyped it as Old World, elitist, effete—and, above all, "foreign." The flamboyant Italian Rudolpho Tonetti played by Erik Rhodes in *The Gay Divorcee* exemplifies this. Astaire himself exploits the stereotype when, playing the Russian ballet dancer Petrov, his florid gestures bewilder Ginger Rogers in *Shall We Dance*. Despite this stigma, Astaire, in a 1927 interview, made a point of the significance he himself attached to careful attention to the choreographing of arms and hands and upper body—one of the lessons, he explained, that he had learned from ballet. "What you do with your hands is pretty important. . . . It is no good just putting them in your pocket."[26]

The ballet port de bras modeled for Astaire was characteristic of an older style. Nineteenth-century French romantic choreographers, for example, favored softly curved arms with the head tilted demurely, as seen in the pose taken in this lithograph of Carlotta Grisi in the French romantic ballet *Giselle* (Fig. 2.4a). Astaire, by contrast, favored dynamic vectors, lines, and angular shapes to fit in with the modernist, machine-age aesthetic of his era (Fig. 2.4b). His upper-body movement and the overall shape of his body veered away from the positioning of classical ballet, and the streamlined look he would go on to develop would be a model for many others—not only on Broadway and in the movies, but in the work of his ballet-master contemporary George Balanchine.

Ballet dancers' careful attention to the overall design created by the artful placement of the entire body, along with the coordination of that shape in relation both to fellow

(a) (b) (c) (d)

FIGURE 2.4 "What you do with your hands": whole-body dancing and line. (a) Carlotta Grisi in *Giselle*, hand-colored lithograph by John Brandard, 1840s. © Victoria and Albert Museum. (b) Astaire in the air. (c) Alina Coracaju and Johann Kobborg, whole-body line and partnering in *Giselle* (Royal Ballet). (d) Astaire and Rogers, *Swing Time* (1936), "Swing Time" (waltz).

FIGURE 2.5 Streamlining: (a) In decorative design: an art deco vase. (b) Astaire and Rogers, *Roberta* (1935), "Smoke Gets in Your Eyes." (c) A streamlined train. (d) Astaire and Rogers illustrating line and streamlining, *Follow the Fleet* (1936), "Let's Face the Music and Dance."

dancers and to the frame and three-dimensional shape of the stage, was also a key feature of Astaire's art. Ballet dancers call it "line"—the creation by the whole body of a beautiful and expressive shape in space. This was true of partnered as well as solo dances: a male dancing with a female might parallel or complement the line of his partner's body by echoing the line of her body or extending it into space with his own limbs. Astaire pays careful attention in all his dances to line and its interaction with his partner. (See, for example, Fig. 2.4c, a couple dance in the ballet *Giselle*, and Fig. 2.4d, Astaire and Rogers in *Swing Time*.) Furthermore, his choreography carefully integrates his props with the line of his body.

But although his dancing stressed line, Astaire's was radically different from that of any nineteenth-century dancer. Balanchine and his wife, the ballerina Maria Tallchief, called it "streamlined"—a newly popular word in the 1930s associated with the clean, dynamic lines of the streamliner trains and also with art deco. The florid decoration of the Victorian and prewar eras was gone. The year after the Astaires opened in *Lady Be Good*, 1925, the Exposition des Arts Décoratifs et Industriels Modernes opened in Paris, from which art deco took its name (see Figs. 2.5a–d). The clean, dynamic lines of the Chrysler and Empire State Buildings gradually replaced the richly ornamental and sculptural decoration of buildings in old New York. In clothing, sleek, short, straight-falling flapper shifts and close-to-the-head bobbed hairdos and cloche hats replaced the floor- and ankle-length dresses, intricately arranged long hair, and elaborately trimmed bonnets of the preceding era. Heavily carved furniture, intricately patterned wallpaper, and multicolored oriental rugs were thrown out in favor of simple, clean lines and angles with all-white walls and furniture.

TELLING STORIES IN DANCE: ASTAIRE, ADELINE GENÉE, AND
THE *BALLET D'ACTION*

Astaire's use of line and the "full resources" of his arms, hands, and torso had to do with another of Astaire's distinctive dance interests. As an actor-dancer, Astaire made a high art of using his whole body to convey emotional relationships in dance. His models for this almost certainly came from ballet, or at least had their roots in it and its European precursors. He traced the varying stages of courtship in song and dance: pursuit, seduction, euphoria, and occasionally despair. At times he developed a longer plot entirely in extended dance sequences: the ballet of the beggar and the ballerina in the stage version of *The Band Wagon* (1931); "Limehouse Blues" and "This Heart of Mine" in the film *Ziegfeld Follies* (1946); "Shoes with Wings" in *The Barkleys of Broadway* (1949); and "The Girl Hunt Ballet" in the film version of *The Band Wagon* (1953).

The use of stylized gesture and body movement to tell a story has been around for centuries: it was part of Greek and Roman theater and a key aspect of commedia dell'arte,[27] which accumulated a huge vocabulary of gestures that both portrayed character and told stock tales. In ballet, the use of the body to tell a story entirely in movement and music was promoted by the choreographer and dance theorist Jean-Georges Noverre (1727–1810), who called for a ballet in which a narrative was conveyed only by music and movement, combined with costume and set design. His theories about what he called the *ballet d'action* were published in the eighteenth century, and the form reached its apogee in such nineteenth-century romantic ballets as *La sylphide, Giselle*, and *Coppélia*, and later in Russia with, among others, *Swan Lake, Sleeping Beauty*, and *Nutcracker*. Ballet developed a gestural symbol system in which the stylized use of the arms and hands conveyed complete sentences (often in French—the language of ballet, just as Italian is that of music). To convey the sentence "I love you," for example, the ballet dancer will first touch his chest, then point to his partner, then cup his hands over his heart (literally, *Je t'aime*, "I you love"). Strictly speaking, mime is a form of dance—both mimes and dancers use the whole body as well as gestures—but in nineteenth-century ballet the divisions between fairly long mime scenes (which concentrated on gestures of the upper body) and "pure dance" (whole-body dance) were clearly delineated in the way that recitative and aria were in Italian opera.

This distinction was preserved far longer than anywhere else in the Danish school, to which Astaire's first dance model, Adeline Genée, belonged. Fred and his sister never had a formal dance lesson from Genée, but they learned from her. In a tradition not uncommon among young dancers at the time, they would painstakingly study (or "copy," to use Adele's word) her steps and manner of moving.[28] The siblings attended twenty-eight performances of the 1908 musical *The Soul Kiss* (Fig. 2.6a), in which Genée starred, writing down her steps after the performance and experimenting with her moves in the theater aisles at intermission.[29] This was not an unusual way for young dancers to learn. Astaire's contemporary in London, the young Ninette de Valois, who would go on to found the Royal Ballet, expanded her choreographic vocabulary in the same way as, from an upper-balcony seat in London, she painstakingly recorded Anna Pavlova's performances of Mikhail Fokine's *The Dying Swan*, which she later performed herself. This way of learning was still being used by the young Gene Kelly when he watched Clarence "Dancing" Dotson.

Genée made her career in the ballets that were a feature of such famous music halls as London's Empire, and they could be as elaborate as any created by a ballet company attached to an opera house.[30] This tradition was also a part of the variety houses on the Continent, and it was adopted by American entertainment as well. Genée danced in a wide variety of *ballets d'action*, her most famous role being the soubrette Swanhilda in

FIGURE 2.6 Bournonville: (a) Poster for Adeline Genée in *The Soul Kiss* (1908). (b) Valborg Borchsenius and Hans Beck dance the tarantella from the ballet *Napoli*, choreographed by Bournonville (1842), in the Peter Elfelt film (1903). (c) Astaire and Eleanor Powell, *Broadway Melody of 1940*, "Jukebox Dance."

Coppélia (1870), by Arthur Saint-Léon and Léo Delibes. But she also appeared in ballets with contemporary themes: in *The Soul Kiss*, for example, Genée choreographed and appeared in a hunting ballet. As Genée herself explains, it depicted "the chase after the fox, beginning with the meet, the caracoling of the horse, the start, jumping the hedges, and finally the capture of the brush. I have to dance as the horse and the rider at the same time and depict the exhilaration of the rider as well as the nimbleness of the animal."[31] "It was beautiful," remembers Adele, who, seventy-one years later, still had vivid memories. "The men came out in the pink coats. There were no horses, but the hound dogs came out, and then she came out as if she were on the horse . . . [She] wore a riding habit with [a] skirt that comes up on the side . . . and did the most gorgeous dance."[32] The British critic J. Crawford Flitch wrote that her hunt dance went as

> far in the direction of high spirits, of exhilaration unmixed with passion, of sheer delight in the physical fact of life, as it can possibly go. The spirited little horse-woman in black riding-habit that clings to the lines of her gay and lithe figure, has an air at once of fragility and vigour; she is borne through the air on her dashing leaps, she curvets, she caracoles, the slender steely limbs make nothing of the weighty burden of skirt and boots—and yet all is done with such a whirl and wind of enthusiasm that the motive force appears to be not muscular activity, but merely a fever of the blood. All the jollity, all the glorious high spirits, all the high-heartedness, all the intoxication of delight, in all the hunting mornings that ever were, are concentrated in that swaying, swirling, leaping, laughing figure.[33]

Genée was trained by her uncle Alexandre, who had a variety of teachers as a youth but made a point of stressing his connection with Christian Johansson, a pupil of Auguste Bournonville, the great Danish ballet master. Bournonville himself had studied in Paris with Auguste Vestris during the era of romantic ballet and went on to develop his own branch of romantic ballet in Copenhagen. Bournonville style is a very close relative of early nineteenth-century French romantic ballet style. Preserved in a continuous teaching tradition at the Royal Danish Ballet, it is probably the closest approximation we have to what French romantic ballet originally looked like. It followed Noverre's prescription for the *ballet d'action*: telling stories in music and dance. It also stressed quick, intricate, precise footwork; rapid changes of direction and *petit allegro* (small, fast steps) as well as *terre à terre* (literally, ground to ground) movement, in which the dancer seems to skim or hover over the floor. Much closer to baroque dance than was later ballet, it is intimately connected to the jigs, hornpipes, and intricate step dances that would later be blended with Africanist elements, leading eventually to tap dance. This earlier nineteenth-century French style contrasts with the sustained pointe work, higher leg extensions, space-eating jumps, and gravity-defying lifts of the Russian Imperial style. Before settling in England, Genée had danced with Alexandre Genée's company in Copenhagen, and we know that she performed such Bournonville works as the pas de deux from *Flower Festival in Genzano*.

Key to Genée's (and Bournonville's) style was the sense of joyous spontaneity conveyed by movement (*allégresse*). Early dance descriptions of the Astaires suggest that they shared these qualities. Not only did critics compare Adele to Genée but, more important, Genée herself recognized the connection. In 1927, two decades after the Astaire children watched her so intently in *The Soul Kiss*, Genée—along with the Prince of Wales, his brothers, and just about every celebrity who could get in—went to see Fred and Adele, now the toasts of London. The occasion was the final performance of Gershwin's *Lady Be Good* at the Empire Theatre before it was demolished to make way for the new-fangled movie theater that still operates there. Earlier in the century the Empire had been the venue of Genée's greatest triumphs, and Astaire acknowledged her inspiration in his farewell curtain speech. Genée's return note expressed her admiration for them and acknowledged that they did indeed have something distinctive in common: "It was a delight to me to see such lightness and joy in your work which is all too rarely witnessed in dancing as a rule."[34]

Steps from Bournonville ballets actually appear in Astaire's film work, and there is a good chance that Astaire first saw them danced by Genée. One of Astaire's particular favorites was a partnered turn *en attitude* (a ballet position in which the dancer raises one leg in arabesque behind her but, instead of keeping the leg straight, bends it at the knee) that may have come straight from Genée and can also be seen in a dance from Bournonville's ballet *Napoli*.[35] Attitude turns are most often performed by the woman, with the man providing ballast. But Bournonville's step reverses this relationship: the man and woman, linked by arms around each other's waists, turn in place; the male still serves as ballast, but it is he who holds an attitude turn, swiveling in place while she circles him (see Fig. 2.6b).

In a tap number from *Broadway Melody of 1940*, Eleanor Powell counterbalances Astaire as he swings around on a flat foot with his knee angled behind him (see Fig. 2.6c). It becomes one of the perky folk steps in "The Piccolino" from *Top Hat* as well—the angle of the knee visually rhymes it with an arms-akimbo top. But it also appears in the great 5/4 rhythm number "Coffee Time" in *Yolanda and the Thief* (1945), with Lucille Bremer, and Astaire uses it most remarkably, in a gradually slowing tempo, to climax a phrase in the romantic "I'm Old Fashioned" number with Rita Hayworth in *You Were Never Lovelier*.

RUSSIAN IMPERIAL BALLET AND THE BALLETS RUSSES

Genée was of course not the only ballerina whom the Astaires saw, and the early nineteenth-century style was not his only experience with ballet. The children's mother also took them to see and study the Russian ballerina Anna Pavlova. Between 1910 and her death in 1931, she regularly toured the United States, giving many Americans their first glimpse of ballet. Her signature piece, *The Dying Swan*, was choreographed by the young Russian ballet revolutionary Mikhail Fokine (1880–1942), who would make his name with Diaghilev's Ballet Russes (1909–29). This was a kind of reminiscence or encapsulation of one of her most famous roles in the full-length ballet *Swan Lake*, but Fokine's short piece went further in the direction of naturalism, with the dancer's undulating arms and fluttering hands gradually stiffening into dying spasms. Pavlova also toured with a truncated version of the romantic ballets *Coppélia* and *Giselle*—and Astaire, like most of the American public, seemed to equate the standard male ballet persona with the yearning seriousness of her beloved, Albrecht (and others like him), who tries to but never can capture the ethereal spirit that Giselle has become in Act II. Later, in Paris in 1927, Astaire and his mother would see the great Russian ballerina Olga Spessivtseva in *Giselle* ("a sublime artist," as Astaire's mother recorded in her diary; see Fig. 2.7a). And in 1931 Astaire would dance onstage with his friend Tilly Losch in *The Band Wagon* in a dream ballet full of visual references to *Giselle* and *La sylphide*, about a beggar who yearns for a ballerina whom he can never have—a standard romantic ballet trope (Fig. 2. 7b).

FIGURE 2.7 (a) Olga Spessivtseva in *Giselle*. (b) Fred Astaire and Tilly Losch, *The Band Wagon*, Broadway (1931), "The Beggar and the Ballerina"; both Jerome Robbins Dance Division, New York Public Library for the Performing Arts, Astor, Lenox and Tilden Foundation. (c) Astaire, cabriole in *The Gay Divorcee* (1934); compare to (d) Herman Cornejo as the Bluebird in *Sleeping Beauty*, American Ballet Theatre.

But Pavlova had another side, too, and it is this aspect that Adele Astaire particularly remembered. Pavlova incorporated some of the innovations of Isadora Duncan's early modern dancing—a more relaxed and fluid torso, freer and more expressive use of the arms, and the use of flowing draperies—into *Autumn Bacchanal*, which she danced with her partner Mikhail Mordkin, and in the solo *La nuit*. Pavlova was a marvelous actress as well, eventually appearing in a silent film, *The Dumb Girl of Portici* (1916); her eloquent movement created a vivid and compelling character in the truncated version of the story ballet *Giselle* that she took on tour with her small company.

Pavlova's iconic status in America was confirmed when *The Passing Show of 1912* featured the "Bacchanal Rag" and the comedienne Fannie Brice lampooned her *Dying Swan* on Broadway in *Ziegfeld Follies of 1916*. Genée, although never as great a legend as Pavlova in the United States, was also paid homage when, according to Adele Astaire, the sprightly Marilyn Miller used elements of her hunting ballet in one of the Broadway *Ziegfeld Follies*.[36]

Noverre's theories about the *ballet d'action* were altered and expanded by Fokine and his colleagues in Diaghilev's Ballets Russes, which brought ballet into the modern age in London and Paris between 1909 and Diaghilev's death in 1929. Whereas mime in the eighteenth- and nineteenth-century ballet world was a stylized and codified series of gestures, Fokine called for a move away from codified gesture and mime restricted to the hands, arms, and upper body toward the movement of the whole body. Movement should change in style, he asserted, depending upon the period and subject matter depicted in the ballet. The Ballets Russes toured the United States in 1916–17, and if he didn't see them, Astaire would have surely known about them. Later, his several stays in London in the 1920s coincided with some of the Ballets Russes seasons. We know, for example, from her diary that his mother attended several performances—including modern ballets by Léonide Massine (*Parade*) and Balanchine (*The Triumph of Neptune*)—and it is hard to imagine that Astaire and his sister did not see them as well.

Astaire got to know at least one Ballets Russes principal, Patrick Healy-Kay, a young Englishman who performed under the stage name of Anton Dolin. Dolin remembers Astaire consulting him about his technique and taking him to a ballet class taught by Cecchetti.[37] Astaire was so intrigued by Dolin's vocabulary of "beating" steps—entrechats, *brises volés*, cabrioles—that he asked him to model them for him (see Figs. 2.7c and d), and the results can be seen throughout his films. Dolin was also noted for his acrobatic skill, which Bronislava Nijinska incorporated in her ballet *Le train bleu*, where denizens of Côte d'Azur beaches, dressed in the latest Coco Chanel sportswear, perform moves from tennis, swimming, and beach acrobatics. This ballet was itself influenced by the streamlining and angularity of art deco (Fig. 2.8a). *Le train bleu* and other modernist ballets by Nijinska, Massine, and Balanchine were exploring in their own way a new vocabulary for dance that accorded with contemporary manners and mores on the Continent. The Ballets Russes must have confirmed Astaire's interest in a more modern vocabulary of mime. In *Parade*, for example, the Little American Girl mimicked typewriting and parodied melodramatic gestures from such silent films as *The Perils of Pauline* (Fig. 2.8b).

(a)    (b)

FIGURE 2.8 (a) Anton Dolin, star of Diaghilev's Ballets Russes, who taught Astaire ballet moves in London, wearing a Chanel swimsuit in Bronislava Nijinska's *Le train bleu* (1924). (b) Marie Chabelska as the little American girl in Massine's *Parade* (1917). Photo: Lachmann, Victoria and Albert Museum.

PLACEMENT AND OFF-BALANCE DANCING

Although Astaire's perfectionist approach, his whole-body choreography, and his dance storytelling were derived from models he saw in such dancers as Adeline Genée, he overturned ballet's most basic precept: symmetrical and stable body placement, and its attempt to force the human body to conform to a geometric ideal. When Astaire, insisting on "no limitations," declares his independence from the "rules" of "not being able to point the toe in or some such notion,"[38] he is referring to the foundational rule of ballet body placement called turnout, in which the dancer stands erect, shoulders back, chest open, spine straight and centered, while turning the legs out from the hips at almost all times with the feet opened out to form a symmetrical and stable base on which to balance equally between the right and left legs. This position, contrary to the human body's natural parallel stance, displays the inner thighs and calves (rather than the knees) directly to the audience. The rotating of the hips outward with the feet turned out to either side (Fig. 2.9a) is the first position a dancer learns to take at the barre, moving the legs (and arms) through a series of positions from the center to the front and back with pointed foot.

Nineteenth-century ballet dancers also prepared themselves visibly to move from a turned-out position by centering the body and bending the knees in plié before moving from one position to another, after which, at the end of the phrase, they returned to a balanced and stable position. (This sometimes gives ballet a "pose to pose" look rather than the sense of an uninterrupted flow of movement.) The music for these dances

(a)

(b)

(c)
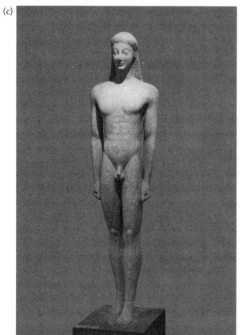

(d)

FIGURE 2.9 (a) First position in ballet, body symmetrical. (b) Astaire in *Top Hat*, slight contrapposto, weight on left foot, right leg relaxed. (c) *Kouros*, Greek (6th c. BCE), weight evenly distributed. © Vanni Archive / Art Resource, NY. (d) Polykleitos, *Doryphoros*, showing contrapposto,weight on right foot, left leg relaxed; Roman copy of Greek original (ca. 440 BCE). Photo credit: Scala / Art Resource

was made to order for this, phrases and cadence patterns punctuating these starts and stops with musical commas, colons, and periods. Ballet dancers maintain their upright posture and balanced shape and line precisely, carving out a balanced picture in space even as they move through the air. Perfection of line is so important that it is not unusual for dancers to move ever so slightly out of coordination with the music to achieve it; dancers who could coordinate their movements with the music in absolute precision were singled out as especially "musical."

Astaire consciously broke those rules of symmetrical placement and preparation. His basic stance, at the beginning of many of his dances and at other points, was a more relaxed and natural position, ankles crossed with the weight on one leg, causing the distribution of the muscles to shift, one hip higher than the other (Fig. 2.9b). It is a variant of what art historians call contrapposto, which you can see in everything from Polykeitos's *Doryphoros* (Fig. 2.9d) to Michelangelo's *David*. It transforms the body from an abstract geometrical ideal, balanced, symmetrical, and presentational ("Attention!"; see Figs. 2.9a and c) to a more everyday, vulnerable, and human stance, asymmetrical, relaxed, and informal ("At ease"; see Figs. 2.9b and d). This was the starting position for Astaire's famous loose-limbed, rhythmic walk, which became a key element in many of his dances (Fig. 2.9b): it was the inspiration for Gershwin's opening of *An American in Paris* and his music for Astaire's "Walking the Dog" sequence in *Shall We Dance*. It looks completely natural, but very few could do it: it was the result of thousands of hours of practice and preparation.[39]

Astaire makes fun of ballet turnout and preparation in the "Slap That Bass" number in *Shall We Dance* (1937), where he finds himself unconsciously reverting to ballet's first position, body precisely placed. He also makes fun of academic ballet's stress on the pointed as opposed to the more natural flexed foot as he extends one leg in a low arabesque and arranges his arms in a typically French romantic port de bras, then ruefully shakes these habits off as he tries to "swing."[40] In the "Tiger Rag" from *Let's Dance* (1950), he starts out by using the piano as an imaginary ballet barre to parody ballet dancers' exercises; another sendup appears in "Stereophonic Sound" in *Silk Stockings*.

Central to Astaire's pluralist style was off-balance dancing. Like jazz and tap dance, with their syncopated, unpredictable, broken rhythms and their performers' love of rubato and risk-taking improvisation, Astaire's movement thrived not just on the unexpected starts and stops of broken rhythm, but on dancing off balance. Instead of returning constantly to an upright center, his preferred line was a diagonal, his body forming a dynamic, streamlined vector in space so that even when he was standing still he seemed to move with an exciting element of risk (see Figs. 2.10a–d; see also Figs. 2.5b and d). Along with his use of drags, glides, and slides (like the clarinet smear at the beginning of *Rhapsody in Blue*), it eliminated the precise boundaries from one movement to the next. This is one reason Astaire's dancing looks so free and spontaneous. Like jazz musicians, Astaire loved tilting and teetering on the edges of the beat rather than coming to full and secure stops. Rather than moving from pose to pose, he flowed from one step to the next. And of course there is the cakewalk, an African

FIGURE 2.10 Off-balance movement: (a) *Top Hat* (1935). (b) With Ginger Rogers, *Shall We Dance* (1934), "They All Laughed." (c) With Rita Hayworth, *You Were Never Lovlier* (1942), "Shorty George." (d) Off-balance on a chair, *The Gay Divorcee* (1934), "Needle in a Haystack."

American dance of which Astaire was very well aware, in which the dancers lean back off-balance and kick their legs forward.

Even when standing still, Astaire wasn't stable and centered. In keeping with the unselfconscious American manners of the Jazz Age and the increasingly informal body language of young flappers and their boyfriends, he leaned against walls, one hand in his pocket, one foot negligently crossed over the other (Fig. 2.11a). Instead of centering himself straight-backed on a living-room couch, he would perch on its side, one leg draped over the upholstered arm, singing to his companion (Fig. 2.11b).

While Astaire drew, consciously or unconsciously, on principles of the *ballet d'action* and Fokine's more modern theories of whole-body mime, developing a fusion of dance and mime, he crucially drew for its look on a more casual, spontaneous-looking American movement, capturing the informal way Americans walked, talked, and interacted. The artistic result was that each dance seemed a natural extension of the dialogue or lyrics preceding it. His movements employed a vocabulary very much of its time and place, full of a dance slang that captured and poeticized the way Americans not only spoke, but stood and moved. Leaning on a fireplace mantle, he drums his fingers idly on its marble surface and taps his feet nervously while he puzzles how to find his beloved (Fig. 2.11c). Although he might touch his heart (in an abbreviated reminiscence of the old *je t'aime* gesture from ballet) while singing

FIGURE 2.11 Everyday American vernacular movement. (a) Leaning against a door and (b) leg draped over a sofa, *Top Hat* (1935), "No Strings." (c) Leaning on a mantel and drumming his fingers, *The Gay Divorcee* (1934), "Needle in a Haystack." (d) Mock fisticuffs with Ginger Rogers, *Roberta* (1935), "I'll Be Hard to Handle."

"Night and Day" to show his love to the reluctant Rogers, he sets the seal on his danced lovemaking in one of the most eloquent of modern gestures by brushing his hands above her to convey satisfaction at his success (see Fig. 6.1g) and then offering his overwhelmed partner a cigarette. He affectionately chucks Rogers under the chin at the beginning of the opening tap duet in *The Barkleys of Broadway*, and they enthusiastically shake hands to conclude the "Isn't It a Lovely Day" sequence in *Top Hat*. He pulls up a chair and straddles it backward to prevent Cyd Charisse from walking away, then uses it as a dance partner to tempt her into dancing in *Silk Stockings*. He catches Roger's wrists and uses her clenched fists against her as she takes a mock swing at him in response to a joking insult in "I'll Be Hard to Handle" in *Roberta* (Fig. 2.11d), then draws her hand down and uses that position as the beginning of a dance. He uses modern mime and call-and-response tap techniques to have a conversation in dance. They conclude the dance by collapsing into two chairs and sprawling back laughing.

He could also build long vernacular mime scenes into his numbers. In the most famous from *Top Hat*, he incorporates a mysterious dance-mime sequence with an invisible partner whom he greets on the street, then crouches low in response to a threat he senses but does not yet see. (It turns out to be the famous line of male dancers that he "shoots" and defeats at the climax of the dance.) In "Let's Face the Music and Dance," from *Follow the Fleet*, he encapsulates in vernacular movement the rise and fall of a gambler who considers suicide but is saved when he rescues a woman (Ginger Rogers) who, having lost her own fortune, is also about to kill herself.

MODERN DANCE

Modern dance, like Astaire's dance, was based on the natural gestures of walking and running, but still, it belonged to another world in which jazz and everyday vernacular movement were not particularly relevant. Though modern dancers saw themselves as distinctively American, the style's roots lay mostly in the heroic and tragic visual gestures of classical and Hellenistic Greek art and in the movement vocabulary of the nineteenth-century teacher François Delsarte, who drew on these artistic models. Isadora Duncan's dancers were nymphs cavorting in a woodland glade or on a sweep of lawn in front of a neoclassical building (Fig. 2.12a; contrast Figs. 2.12b and c). Like the sculptures of American dignitaries in government buildings across the land (think Horatio Greenough's statue of George Washington), Duncan classicized and monumentalized her dancers, just as she would do later when portraying the worker heroines of the new socialist utopia where she settled briefly with her husband, the poet Sergei Esenin, in the newly formed Soviet Union. Modern dancers also took inspiration from the exotically stylized and hieratic gestures of those Near and Far Eastern pictorial and sculptural forms beloved of Ruth St. Denis, whose dancers graced the steps of ancient Babylon in D. W. Griffith's epic *Intolerance* and who toured vaudeville houses with extravaganzas set in ancient Egypt, India, and other exotic lands (Fig. 2.12d). Graham's and Humphrey's heroines, drawing from both these traditions, were conceived as archetypes in what was by then a legendary American frontier and farmland. They were symbolic American stand-ins for humanity: the Man and the Woman in Humphrey's *Day on Earth*, or Graham's Bride, Bridegroom, and Pioneer Woman in *Appalachian Spring*. Graham also drew on archetypes from Greek tragedy. Her heroines Medea, Jocasta, and Phaedra embodied the emotional forces of the unconscious as defined by the psychoanalytic theories of Sigmund Freud and Carl Jung, which were named for Greek archetypes.

To be sure, like Astaire, modern dancers abandoned ballet's strictures, from turnout to the pointe shoe, and explored off-balance movement as developed by Rudolf Laban, Mary Wigman, and the German Expressionists. Angles and diagonals were an important part of their vocabulary, but they were used with a kind of theatrical gravitas and undisguised effort that had less to do with the thrill of speed and dynamism than with expressing powerful angst or heroic bliss. The musical language to which they danced also had roots in the European symphonic tradition—from the atonality and serialism of Arnold Schoenberg, Anton Webern, and Alban Berg to the new harmonies of Claude Debussy and Igor Stravinsky. Modern dancers favored those composers who were the heirs to this European classical-music tradition, such as Aaron Copland and Samuel Barber. When American flavor was called for, as in Copland's scores for Martha

FIGURE 2.12 "Modern dance" and Astaire's relaxed modernity. (a) Isadora Duncan. (b) *The Gay Divorcee* (1934), "Needle in a Haystack," opening. (c) With Cyd Charisse, *The Band Wagon* (1953), "Dancing in the Dark." (d) Ruth St. Denis and Ted Shawn.

Graham, they most often came from the Anglo-Saxon folk-song tradition, which both dancers and composers recognized as part of a mythical American past. For the most part, modern dancers ignored not only the popular music and movement of the Jazz Age in which they lived, profoundly imbued as it was with African American music and dance, but also the many other cultures that made up the New World of New York in the 1920s. In their aspirational world of high art, lowbrow music and dance had no place.

In Astaire's vernacular pluralist style, in his songs and dances, in his casual movement, Jazz Age Americans recognized themselves and their generation. They identified with his love stories in song and dance and the casual movement he developed to convey these tales. Astaire danced to the music of a generation, those popular songs to which young Americans themselves sang along and danced. Americans could recognize in Astaire's songs and dances the values that his dance embodied—departing from Old World values of caste and class and formal behavior, offering a new view of male and female relationships, and taking a pluralist approach to dance making that embraced all movement forms. Audiences could aspire to his dances, although inevitably they were surprised to find it wasn't as easy as it looked. As for the international audiences to whom his films were widely distributed, for them too Astaire's dances created a new dance archetype. The informal body language at the heart of his style came to signify a distinctively American style of music and dance that became for his audiences the epitome of American behavior and values. For both America and the rest of the world, then, Astaire and his partners came to signify a distinctively American style that conveyed pluralist and populist values.

3

OLD WORLD MEETS NEW WORLD ON BROADWAY

Balanchivadze and Dukelsky Meet the Gershwins and Rodgers and Hart

ONE OF THE greatest admirers of Astaire's outlaw style was the young choreographer George Balanchine (born Balanchivadze), who immigrated to the United States in 1933, the same year Astaire left New York for Hollywood and his film career. For Balanchine, Astaire was "the most interesting, the most inventive, the most elegant dancer of our era." He compared Astaire to one of his musical heroes, J. S. Bach: "He has the same concentration of genius; there is so much of the dance in him that it has been distilled."[1]

Influenced by Astaire and Gershwin and by the great African American jazz dancers whom he had encountered in Europe even before he came to America, Balanchine would mingle Old and New World influences to develop his own outlaw style for the "no limitations" context of American musical theater and films in the 1930s and '40s. Working with his compatriot, the composer Vladimir Dukelsky (Vernon Duke), and with Richard Rodgers, he would powerfully influence the trajectory of dance in American musical theater and film and subsequently the film-dance tradition that I discuss in this book. Both Fred Astaire and Gene Kelly were born and raised in the United States. A look at the relationship between Balanchine and Vernon Duke (both classically trained in Russia) shows how quickly American jazz music and dance spread to Europe, and how it seized the imagination of young artists.

Balanchine and Duke, like Astaire and Gershwin, responded powerfully to the artistic importance of jazz music and dance and how it could be used to nourish Old World classical music and dance—and vice versa. The divide between "highbrow" and "lowbrow" meant very little to them, even though many of their colleagues clung to it. Balanchine and Duke loved the jazz they heard and saw, and that was enough. Prevailing and often unconscious assumptions, however, would discourage anything that might undercut the stereotypical divides of black and white and of low and high—especially, as we shall see, for black female dancers.

Balanchine is far better known today, of course, as the founder and choreographer of the New York City Ballet. His involvement with Broadway has been downplayed as moonlighting, a necessary way to make a buck. But Broadway and Hollywood recognized him as one of their own. Even if his contribution to musical theater and films was brief compared to Astaire's and Kelly's long careers there, it would have a long-lasting influence on the shape and style of American musicals and was critical to his development as a ballet choreographer. Balanchine combined jazz and classical elements with vernacular movement and a variety of dance forms, social and folk, to create a model for the miniature dance-drama sequences (or "ballets") that would become almost mandatory in the 1940s and early '50s on Broadway and in musical films. His work would have a direct impact on key figures in the tradition of film musicals that I discuss in this book, and they in turn would influence him. As the Broadway and film-musical dancer Ray Bolger put it, "He opened up a whole new world for the American musical comedy stage." Alan Jay Lerner, himself a musical-theater innovator, wrote, "Into a choreographic world that was a mélange of decorative movement, legs and taps, Balanchine opened the door and ballet leapt on to the popular musical stage, directed by a supreme artist."[2] Gene Kelly summed it up at a memorial organized by the Hollywood community barely two months after the Balanchine's death in 1983: "His contribution to dance will never be surpassed. He was a man of great daring and ingenuity and he influenced every dancer living. . . . He could do anything and everything. . . . His legacy will remain forever, no matter what happens."[3]

Balanchine helped to develop a style of Broadway dance that drew upon the skills and flexibility of ballet training and the dramatic devices in the storytelling ballets of the nineteenth century, as well as the modernist one-act ballet of the Russian impresario Sergei Diaghilev's Ballets Russes, while retaining the rhythmic vitality of jazz tap dance. All this would demand an additional skill set from dancers for musical theater and films, who were now called upon to use their full body to convey dramatic meaning and to convey stories and emotional relationships in movement. Jazz rhythms were still there, but eventually they moved up from the sounds of the feet into the body of the dancer in a new style of jazz dance that would eventually replace tap as a dominant form—and the pounding of multiple tapping feet would gradually diminish on Broadway, although never disappear entirely.

Balanchine was part of the Diaghilev diaspora. In New York he was one of many Russians looking for a new home and work in the wake of the Russian Revolution, Diaghilev's death, and the break-up of the Ballets Russes in Europe. On August 26, 1935, the *New York American* reported on Balanchine's newly formed ballet company's incorporation into the Metropolitan Opera—and the report actually featured Astaire. The headline read, "Metropolitan Ballet: Fred Astaire Likely to Be Seen on Opera Stage, Possibly as Soloist." Like Astaire, Balanchine was interested in a variety of dance forms. The Balanchine's company's spokesman, Edward Warburg, who, along with his Harvard buddy Lincoln Kirstein, was bankrolling the enterprise, enthused: "Ballet isn't just chasing tulle, just toe-dancing. We will introduce other forms. Balanchine is experimenting now with tap dancing. We probably will use it. . . . Take Fred Astaire. He is a great tap dancer, and at the same time a great ballet dancer. Someday, maybe, we will have Astaire as soloist in a ballet at the Metropolitan."

Astaire was probably astonished but flattered when Irving Berlin excitedly sent him this clipping, its headline firmly underscored. But by then he was settled in Hollywood, and he never appeared with the ballet company. Balanchine, however, continued to nurse his ambition to work with Astaire. As Balanchine told Frederick Russell of *Dance Magazine* in 1939, the Astaire-Rogers movies captivated him: "I can watch them dance again and again. They have something no other team has. I hope someday to have an opportunity to work with them."[4]

Not only did Balanchine transform aspects of musical theater, but the influence went both ways: Balanchine's experiences with musical theater and films would also affect his own style of ballet. For Balanchine, as for Gershwin, the relationship between Old and New World forms was a vital aesthetic issue. Ballet was a living, evolving art form with roots in the past but nourished and transformed by the present. For Balanchine, born in 1904, jazz movement was an expression of his generation and of the modern age and American identity in the twentieth century. It was not used simply to spice up a traditional form; rather, it offered principles that became integral to Balanchine's style and vital to his ballet's development into a truly modern art form. Asked to predict the future of dance in 1939 in the journal *Dance*, Balanchine responded: "Tap dance will be brought very close to ballet and both forms will exercise a mutual influence upon each other. Not only will there be an interchange of steps and arms and body movements, *but the very character of ballet movement*, and with it the floor pattern, may acquire new forms."[5]

Balanchine's answer differed drastically from that of any of the other choreographic luminaries polled by *Dance* that year. The founders of modern dance saw themselves as revolutionaries, part of the romantic cult of the artistic genius who sweeps away all before her. They repudiated classical European ballet tradition and training and created new techniques geared to the performance of their idiosyncratic styles. They also rejected popular, commercial entertainment and, with some exceptions, turned their backs on the jazz dance forms that exemplified it. For them, American identity was reflected in a by-then mythical pioneer past and its folk dance forms, as developed by the country's early English settlers.

Balanchine would build on the Euro-Russian ballet tradition and use contemporary movement to grow it. He thought in evolutionary terms. Like Astaire, he had a policy of no limitations, drawing freely from the Old and New Worlds and from both popular and fine-art forms. "Musical comedy," Balanchine wrote, "which I regard as seriously as classic ballet or classic drama, is simply one branch of theatrical art."[6]

ON YOUR TOES

Astaire, Balanchine, and George Gershwin were also on the minds of Richard Rodgers and Lorenz Hart, who around this time envisioned the dancer as the star of their next musical—about "a hoofer who becomes a ballet dancer, with satirical overtones about the Russians and Russian ballet."[7] The stage production of *On Your Toes* (1936) gave a new dance twist to the now-established notion of transforming classical musical traditions with the new rhythms and devices of African American musics. Gershwin's latest—and highly publicized—attempt to do this with opera, *Porgy and Bess*, had premiered in October of 1935. That year the first public performance of Balanchine's newly formed American Ballet included a jazz-influenced, American-themed ballet, *Alma Mater*. Balanchine had wanted Gershwin to write the score, but the composer, busy with *Porgy and Bess*, recommended his close friend and musical assistant Kay Swift. Gershwin went to the premiere of *Alma Mater* with some of the best and brightest from the American musical-theater and classical-music worlds, including Rodgers and Hart, who were enthusiastic. "Once Larry and I had seen his work," writes Rodgers, "Balanchine was the man we wanted."[8]

In *On Your Toes*, instead of creating an American symphonic poem or an opera, like Zangwill's hero in *The Melting Pot*, or a "jazz-concerto," as George Gershwin had once called his *Rhapsody in Blue*, a young American composer sets out to transform the world of classical ballet.[9] Astaire, firmly ensconced in Hollywood, turned the role down, and the young Ray Bolger was cast instead. Balanchine was hired to choreograph not only the ballet, "Slaughter on Tenth Avenue," that concluded the show, but the whole thing. At the end of the season, an article in *Theatre Arts Monthly* by Edith Isaacs hailed Balanchine's contributions to *On Your Toes*, and to Broadway itself in the dance musical.

> We may have come unknowingly upon a successor to the old musical form, a musical show that is not a comedian's holiday, but a dancer's, or, let's just say, not a jesting but a dancing comedian's holiday. . . . The best talent, the highest vitality, most of the beauty and all of the gayest humor is not in the words but in the design and movement of the dance.[10]

How was it that a young Russian immigrant choreographer, within three years of his arrival and using the music of top American songwriters like Rodgers and Hart, could work such a transformation on Broadway dance? To answer this question, we need to backtrack.

THE DIAGHILEV DIASPORA

Balanchine was neither the first nor the only Russian ballet master to bring his talents to the United States. Nor was he the first ballet-trained choreographer to work on Broadway. Albertina Rasch, who had been classically trained in Vienna, whose dance troupe was a fixture on Broadway, and who had worked with Fred Astaire on his ballet with Tilly Losch in *The Band Wagon*, was very popular.[11] Fokine and Adolph Bolm had already relocated to the United States, and Bolm and another former Diaghilev dancer, Theodore Kosloff, had already choreographed for the movies. In 1922 Bolm, who had established himself in Chicago, would premiere his ballet *Krazy Kat* to jazz-inspired music by John Alden Carpenter. This new wave of Russian dancers would transform American dance.

In 1933, the year Balanchine came to America, a new troupe of his fellow ex–Diaghilev Ballets Russes choreographers and dancers took New York by storm. In New York, the company initially called themselves the Monte Carlo Ballet Russe. (It and related break-away companies frequently changed directors and went by many names. I will refer to any of these companies as the "Ballets Russe de Monte Carlo," or just the "Ballet Russe," also in the singular, when it is clear that I mean one of these companies subsequent to Diaghilev's Ballet Russes.)[12] Their first, highly publicized appearance in New York was a sensation. They went on to tour the United States and gave many Americans (including the young Gene Kelly) their first view of a large professional ballet company. The Ballets Russe de Monte Carlo sought to capitalize on the mystique of Diaghilev's Ballets Russes. They acquired a significant amount of the Diaghilev repertory and, during their first year in Europe, hired Balanchine to continue the Diaghilev tradition with his own new ballets. But Balanchine, dissatisfied with company's management and ethos, left. He was replaced by Léonide Massine, another former Diaghilev choreographer.

The Ballets Russe de Monte Carlo differed sharply in ethos from Balanchine's own School of American Ballet and American Ballet Company. The Ballets Russe dancers capitalized on their exoticism and their connection with a legendary Russian dance past. Cut off from these roots by the Communist Revolution, and with Russian dancers hard to find, the company required the American and British dancers who began to replace retiring dancers to take Russian names and to identify completely with their Diaghilev and Euro-Russian roots.[13] From the beginning, however, Balanchine saw his company as American and of the mid-twentieth century. For him, the Diaghilev era (1909–29), of which he himself had been an important part, was over. It was time to move on to the New World.

For Balanchine, as for many Europeans, the embodiment of the New World was in the jazz music and dance brought by African Americans to Europe. Long before he came to the United States, Balanchine had been intrigued and inspired by jazz dance and dancers.[14] Balanchine probably first saw African American performers in St. Petersburg. Dance teams such as Jackson and Johnson (recorded by Nijinska in her memoirs) toured the Russian Empire as early as 1896, and several of Balanchine's early projects in St. Petersburg indicate that he was well aware of ragtime.[15] As a teenager he earned money playing for silent movies, a job that demanded knowledge of the latest popular songs. In his senior year at ballet school, Balanchine was the pianist in the ragtime band at his school. After his escape from Russia in 1924, he saw such African American performers as Clarence "Dancing" Dotson on the program when Balanchine and his four-member "Russian State Ballet" first appeared in England, at the Empire Music Hall in London. It is easy to imagine young Balanchine in the wings, watching this "eccentric" dancer, who "tapped and scratched in swinging counterpoint"—and was famous for whole-body movements like the "quiver" (related to the shimmy)—avidly studying and perhaps even trading steps with him.[16]

Probably most of the jazz dancers whom Balanchine saw in Russia were men. But things changed drastically when, as the newly appointed choreographer and a dancer for the Diaghilev company, Balanchine, like the rest of Paris, saw and was enthralled by the African American troupe known as the Revue Nègre, whose first performances in October of 1925 set off what the French called the *tumulte noir*—a craze for jazz and jazz dance.[17] Their star, the long-legged and rhythmically brilliant Josephine Baker, adored by the general public and avant-garde artists alike, would become Balanchine's first American muse and an important model for his developing style. Balanchine "adored" the way Baker moved: more than fifty years later, when he was choreographing his last masterpiece, *Mozartiana*, he interrupted his work to remember and praise her "beautiful long legs" to his dancers. Balanchine became Baker's good friend; he would coach her in ballet, choreograph small numbers for her, and invite her to performances and rehearsals. They may have had an affair.[18]

Only eight months after the Revue Nègre opened, Balanchine's *Jack-in-the-Box* reflected Baker's influence, pursuing a theme that would preoccupy him throughout his life. A "black ballerina" and two "white ballerinas" dance with a jumping jack against a background of white, then black cardboard clouds moved by mimes. Ornella Volta concludes that the black ballerina "was directly inspired by Josephine Baker" (Fig. 3.1a),[19] and the only two images we have of the ballet seem to bear this out. In the photos—by Man Ray—Alexandra Danilova reproduces Baker's signature bent-kneed squat but balleticizes it by placing it on pointe (a device that Balanchine would employ again in his modernist ballets scored by Stravinsky) and, with Stanislas Idzikowski, begins a lift that may resonate with Baker's show-stopping entrance, her long legs in a semi-split position, on the back of Joe Alex. Elements from jazz dance also infuse such ballets as *La Pastorale, Le bal*, and *Apollo*, in which Terpsichore, the god's favorite Muse, swings her hips as she prances toward him holding a lyre (his symbol) and in which Terpsichore's long legs would be shown in splits both on the floor (another of Josephine's signature moves) and balanced on his shoulders—a classicized version of her entrance with Alex in the Revue Nègre as well as an extension of ideas that Balanchine had already been pursuing in Russia.[20]

Balanchine would put his observations of black male dancers to use in a role he created for himself. In his *Triumph of Neptune*, which premiered on December 3, 1926, he danced the role of a "Negro dancer" (Fig. 3.1b). Impressed with his vivid characterization, Cyril Beaumont described

a dance full of subtly contrasted rhythms, strutting walks, mincing steps surging backwards bendings of the body, borrowed from the cake-walk, the whole invested with a delicious humor derived from the mood of the dance, a paradoxical blend of pretended nervous apprehension and blustering confidence.[21]

It is not surprising, then, that even before he came to America Balanchine envisioned his company as starting with an equal number of African American and white students. As his sponsor, Lincoln Kirstein, excitedly wrote in a letter to Chick Webb: "4 white

FIGURE 3.1 (a) An André Derain design for Balanchine's *Jack-in-the-Box* (1926), aquarelle on paper. Wadsworth Atheneum Museum of Art, Hartford, Ella Gallup Sumner and Mary Catlin Sumner Collection. (b) Balanchine as Snowball in his ballet *The Triumph of Neptune* (1926). Bibliothèque de l'Arsenal. (c) Josephine Baker on pointe in a Casino de Paris revue, *Paris en joie* (1932). Balanchine may have coached her.

girls and 4 white boys, about sixteen years old and 8 of the same, *negroes*. . . . He wants to proceed with new ideas and young dancers instead of going on with the decadence of the Diaghilev troupe."[22] He would teach them and provide them with a repertory so that they would learn by performing. Balanchine's school would be used as a basis for the development of his own (American) generation's unique movement and the time and place in which they were dancing.[23]

Balanchine's experiences in Paris and London also introduced him to Astaire and Gershwin. The latter's fame had spread to Europe after the 1924 premiere of *Rhapsody in Blue*, and Balanchine was well aware of Gershwin's work. He was introduced to Astaire in 1926 when the Gershwins brought *Lady Be Good* to London. We can't be sure that Balanchine saw this, but we do know that he saw the Astaires in *Funny Face* in 1928 and, like most of the London audiences, fell in love with it; his understanding of Astaire as a great dancer stems from this time. Astaire's outlaw style nourished Balanchine. He recognized that, like his own work, it blended Old and New World forms to create new ones.

The incorporation of African American movements and music with classical music was nothing new in Europe. Massine and Satie had referenced ragtime in their 1917 ballet *Parade*. In 1923 Diaghilev's competitor Jean Börlin produced, for the Ballets Suédois, Milhaud's *La création du monde*, with sets by Fernand Léger, and Cole Porter's *Within the Quota*, with sets by Gerald Murphy. Balanchine continued the trend with his jazz-inspired movements in his ballets of 1926–28. And Gershwin's bringing together of elements of jazz and classical music in *Rhapsody in Blue* was extended to dance by none other than the Ballets Russes star Anton Dolin, who knew both Astaire and Balanchine. Dolin's ballet *Rhapsody in Blue* was created for the short-lived Dolin-Nemchinova Company; it premiered on April 16, 1928, in Paris.[24] Dolin was "the spirit of jazz," and Vera Nemchinova, also a Ballets Russes star, was the "spirit of the classics."

BALANCHINE AND DUKE

Balanchine was first introduced to the circle of the Gershwins and Astaire in Paris through Vladimir Dukelsky, later known as Vernon Duke—a Russian immigrant composer who would go on to work with Balanchine on Broadway and in Hollywood. Dukelsky, who straddled the worlds of classical and popular music, would become to Balanchine what Gershwin was to Astaire. A close look at their relationship illustrates how young immigrant artists born and trained in the musical traditions of the Old World mingled them with New World styles they met in the West.

Dukelsky and Balanchine first met in the summer of 1925 as Diaghilev's newest protégés. Only twenty-one years old, they were both part of the Jazz Age generation. Dukelsky had been hired as Diaghilev's new young composer soon after Balanchine joined the company. His score for Massine's ballet *Zéphire et Flore* was created during Balanchine's first summer with the company, and Balanchine's first wife, Tamara Geva, was in the cast. Dukelsky and Balanchine seemed destined to be friends: both had had their lives interrupted and shaped by the Great War and the 1917 Revolution, emigrating when it became clear that not only their professional but also their personal lives were in danger.[25]

Both had a thorough grounding in classical music.[26] But to the consternation of their elders and mentors, Diaghilev in particular, both adored jazz.[27] The difference was that Dukelsky was far ahead of Balanchine in his knowledge of American popular music, for by the time he met Balanchine he was already a friend of George Gershwin. Under Gershwin's tutelage he had begun to write in a jazz as well as a classical idiom and to experiment with bringing the two together.

In 1922, when Dukelsky was seventeen, his family immigrated to New York. There the young Russian émigré led a kind of double life, composing symphonic music and playing jazz in restaurants and cabarets to support his mother and brother. Even before Balanchine met Gershwin, Dukelsky knew him and had played his music. (He had fallen in love with "Swanee," to which he was introduced in Constantinople while his family awaited visas to America.) Dukelsky actually met the twenty-four-year-old George Gershwin through the singer Eva Gauthier, who had incorporated Gershwin into her largely classical repertoire but also, according to Dukelsky, sang some "pretentious and excessively dissonant songs of mine at a concert of the International Composers Guild."[28]

Gershwin and Dukelsky were fascinated by each other's talents and training. Gershwin was impressed with Dukelsky's conservatory training with Reinhold Glière in theory and composition, his wide-ranging knowledge of music literature, and in particular his "rich playing" and "lush harmonies"—the musical language of a kid raised in the Euro-Russian School and imbued with the colorist, folk song–influenced work of Rimsky-Korsakov, Borodin, Glazunov, and Tchaikovsky.[29]

But while impressed with his accomplishments, Gershwin was suspicious—and, one suspects, a little jealous—of Dukelsky's training in Russia and the younger man's confidence in his arsenal of academic musical devices. "Those European boys have small ideas, but they sure know how to dress them up," he told Dukelsky bluntly after hearing a piece by Arthur Honegger.[30] Dukelsky, for his part, fell in love with the freshness and vitality of Gershwin's music. Gershwin was

> a superbly equipped *composer* . . . not just a concocter of commercial jingles. His extraordinary left hand performed miracles in counter-rhythms, shrewd canonic devices and unexpected harmonic shifts. The facility for abrupt yet felicitous modulations, the economy and logic of the voice-leading, and the over-all sureness of touch were masterly in their inevitability.[31]

In his autobiography, *Passport to Paris*, Dukelsky chronicled what Gershwin taught him and how it changed his life and his attitude toward popular music. Once, after playing Gershwin his latest work (a "cerebral piano sonata"), George bluntly advised the impoverished young immigrant, "There's no money in that kind of stuff . . . no heart in it, either. Try to write some real popular tunes—and don't be scared about going lowbrow. They will open you up!" That phrase "They will open you up!" was a kind of epiphany for Dukelsky: "It stayed with me all my life," he wrote.[32] Jazz was not just a way to earn money; it was real musical nourishment.

Thus Dukelsky and Gershwin became friends and colleagues—the slightly older man mentoring the younger, but also taking Dukelsky's advice seriously. Under Gershwin's influence, Dukelsky started writing popular songs under the name Vernon Duke while continuing his work as the concert composer Vladimir Dukelsky. (It was Gershwin who suggested the new "American" name, which Dukelsky would later legally adopt.)[33]

Gershwin brought Duke into his circle of friends and patrons—the best and brightest of Broadway's young composers and lyricists and the New York socialites who admired them. "Dukie," as the Gershwin brothers called him, was a regular at the Gershwin family's apartment, where his fluent Russian endeared him to the brothers' St. Petersburg–born father and where George would famously entertain his guests with his latest songs, brilliantly improvised at the piano. Ever generous to his younger colleague, Gershwin would often invite Duke to play.

For his part, the young Duke became Gershwin's champion among his circle of expatriate Russian and European composers. In the period preceding *Rhapsody in Blue*, Duke recognized and respected Gershwin's potential as a "serious" composer in a way that many of Gershwin's colleagues did not. These colleagues, Duke wrote,

> could be divided into two separate groups. The first group consisted of the "lowbrows" of the Broadway stage and song publishers' retinues. The second group—almost entirely hostile—was composed of musicians and writers of modern music, who were patronizing at best and openly scornful as a rule. Both groups, with some dissenters, had one idea in common: they felt that George should stay on Broadway and regarded his Carnegie Hall escapades with suspicion or somewhat prejudiced curiosity.[34]

Duke was convinced they were wrong. He championed Gershwin to his concert-hall colleagues and continued to encourage his friend. Gershwin and Duke discussed the range of musical literature as well as techniques of orchestration, harmony, and counterpoint.

Indeed, Duke was present at the creation of *Rhapsody in Blue*, which Gershwin was preparing for the Paul Whiteman concert, "An Experiment in Modern Music"; this, as Richard Crawford points out, was meant "to put on public display the artistic properties of jazz music."[35] Duke remembered sitting in Gershwin's apartment and listening to him develop the famous opening theme. And, sitting proudly in a box provided by the Gershwins, Duke rejoiced with his mentor when Gershwin premiered this landmark work at Aeolian Hall on February 12, 1924.

It was to Duke that Gershwin entrusted the task of arranging the piano solo version of *Rhapsody*. He also asked Duke to create "piano copies" (publishable voice-and-piano versions) of his songs "Araby" and "Somebody Loves Me."[36] "I was quite proud," Duke later said, "of the 'fill-ins' I provided for *Somebody Loves Me* and was amused to find that they were used in the stock orchestration—obviously, the arranger thought them eminently 'Gershwinesque.'" Gershwin also entrusted him with the ghostwriting of "a black and white ballet—a simple bit of ragtime for a high-kicking precision routine for the Tiller girls who were to appear in the 1924 George White's *Scandals*."[37]

Gershwin was as supportive of Duke's symphonic ambitions as he was of Duke's popular music. His commissions were offered in part to help Duke earn the money to get to Paris to further his "serious" music career. Thus, it was with Gershwin's help that Duke was able to make the trip to Paris in 1924, whence he sent his mentor news of his progress. Once there Duke connected with the Russian expatriate community. An introduction to Diaghilev was arranged through Pavel Tchelitchev, a painter and friend of Balanchine's, and Valitchka (Walter) Nouvel, Diaghilev's business manager.[38] The result was Duke's first ballet, *Zéphire et Flore*.

Almost as soon as Duke was commissioned for the new ballet, he began trying to connect Gershwin with the Ballets Russes. As early as the summer of 1924 he had written to Gershwin, "I spoke about you to Diaghilev and played nearly all your tunes to his secretary, who finds them amazing. I also have an interesting proposition for you. Do come to visit me in Paris before I leave."[39] This may have been part of the reason for Gershwin's visit to Paris later that year. A letter from Ira to George places the composer in Paris only a week before the premiere there of *Zéphire et Flore* on June 15, 1925. And we know that Duke and other Diaghilev composers met with Gershwin around this time.

Zéphire et Flore premiered in Monte Carlo on April 28, 1925, and it established Dukelsky as a young composer to be reckoned with. Diaghilev proudly proclaimed Dukelsky his "third son"—after Stravinsky and Prokofiev.[40] Poulenc was exceptionally enthusiastic.[41] Prokofiev, who also liked the ballet, would go on to become Duke's mentor.

The problem was that while Prokofiev and Diaghilev encouraged Duke's classical compositions, they viewed his jazz career with suspicion. Prokofiev once refused to look at one of Duke's compositions because it was written on jazz manuscript paper. And when Diaghilev found out that Duke was moonlighting as a songwriter for one of Charles B. Cochran's London revues, he declared him a "whore"—this after trampling on the young man's top hat.[42]

Duke had no such problem with Balanchine, who, like Gershwin, was perfectly at ease with Duke's love of both jazz and classical music. Balanchine had also admired Duke's music for *Zéphire et Flore*. He and Duke began to work on a new ballet for Diaghilev called *The Three Seasons*.[43] When the Ballets Russes moved to London for the winter season in November of 1925, Balanchine and Duke lived in rooms adjacent to each other in Torrington Square, where their friendship deepened.[44] They hung out together in local restaurants, and it is from this time that Duke remembers Balanchine hauling out his old guitar to sing pop songs in his heavy Russian accent. A favorite was "Everybhody loves my bohby, but my bohby don't love nobhody but me"—a work written by the African American composer Spencer Williams, who wrote for Josephine Baker and also toured Europe with jazz bands between 1925 and 1928.

For Balanchine, Duke was an ideal bridge builder between the worlds of popular and classical music. Equally at home with the Ballets Russes and Broadway crowds, a native Russian-speaker and fluent in English, Duke would hardly have passed up the opportunity to introduce Balanchine to George Gershwin when he came to London at the very beginning of 1926 to prepare for the London premiere of *Lady Be Good*. Despite Diaghilev's disdain for jazz, he was well aware of the impact of Gershwin and of jazz forms on young fine-art composers and choreographers: in 1925 Gershwin's *Rhapsody* was broadcast on the BBC in a widely publicized concert, and the French duo pianists Jean Wiéner and Clément Doucet played two-piano versions of it and other Gershwin songs around town.[45] American popular music was the rage. Diaghilev finally responded to Duke's urgings and decided to add an American score to the Ballets Russes repertory. In 1928 Duke took the impresario and Prokofiev to the European premiere of Gershwin's Piano Concerto in F. The composer was there too, and the next day Prokofiev asked Duke to bring Gershwin to his apartment. But though George "played his head off" and Prokofiev "thought highly of his gifts," his verdict on Gershwin's concerto was that it was "formally amateurish" ("32 bar choruses ineptly bridged together") and "good jazz and bad Liszt." A commission never materialized.[46]

Jobless after Diaghilev's death in 1929, Balanchine gained direct experience with popular music and popular dance while employed in music halls and vaudevilles in France and London. Working in the immensely popular Cochran revues of 1929, 1930, and 1931 and in Sir Oswald Stoll's variety revues at the Empire and Alhambra Theatres, he staged numerous dance sequences for popular audiences. Cochran's revue incorporated a song by Rodgers and Hart, who must have first learned of Balanchine then.

ON BROADWAY: *PORGY AND BESS*, *ZIEGFELD FOLLIES OF 1936*, AND BALLET

When Balanchine immigrated to America in 1933, Duke, now back in New York, continued to build bridges between his friends.[47] Balanchine acquired Duke's agent, the notorious "Doc" Bender—a former dentist and real ballet enthusiast, and also a friend of Lorenz Hart as well as his agent. Duke was writing the score for *Ziegfeld Follies of 1936*, Ira Gershwin was writing the lyrics, and Duke and Josephine Baker, a star of the show, enthusiastically supported Balanchine for the job of choreographer.[48] Balanchine fit in easily, hanging out with Duke, Ira, George (who would stop by *Follies* rehearsals), and others working on the *Follies*.

Balanchine clearly loved what he heard. His warm friendship with the Gershwin family and his correspondence with Ira Gershwin would last until Balanchine's death.[49] As we have seen, he had already requested that Gershwin write the score for his first ballet on American themes, *Alma Mater*. Balanchine also acquired *George Gershwin's Song Book*, an expensive illustrated hardcover containing eighteen of Gershwin's virtuosic piano arrangements of his own songs.[50] He kept it throughout his life and would later use it as the basis of the 1970 ballet *Who Cares?* Perhaps inspired by the example of Duke's work with Ira, Balanchine would also try his hand at writing his own popular songs—both music and lyrics. Unlike Duke, he never succeeded in creating long-lasting contributions to the Great American Song Book, but songwriting was for him a lifelong avocation.[51] A song written with the composer Arthur Schwartz, a friend from those days and the composer of the Astaires' last Broadway show, *The Band Wagon*, was published just before his death. Rodgers and Hart, for whom Balanchine would choreograph four of their most important Broadway shows (*On Your Toes, Babes in Arms, The*

Boys from Syracuse, and *I Married an Angel*), were also an inspiration. Balanchine particularly admired Hart's lyrics, and the two were close enough that Balanchine, fearing for his alcoholic friend's health, would comb the streets in the early morning hours after one of Hart's notorious benders, picking him up from the gutter and taking him home to sober up.

Balanchine's love of the popular-song repertoire extended musicals both on the stage and on film. He arrived in New York at the very beginning of Astaire's movie career, and his knowledge of the songs Astaire introduced in his films was prodigious. In the 1970s two of his dancers, Bonita (Bonny) and Elyse Borne, invited him to dinner at their father's home. They were the daughters of Astaire's arranger and rehearsal pianist, Hal Borne, and Balanchine had finagled an invitation to their house for dinner during a company trip to Los Angeles. "My father got out all his sheet music," said Bonny Borne, "and the two of them spent the entire evening sitting at the piano singing through his entire repertory. Mr. B. was in heaven; he knew and could sing the lyrics to *everything*. It was as if the two of us didn't exist."[52]

Balanchine heard not only Gershwin's popular songs but also excerpts from his latest and most ambitious project, *Porgy and Bess*, which took as its subject African American life in Charleston, South Carolina. It drew on rural African American music for its inspiration and put it within the context of European opera. Duke was deeply involved in *Porgy* and very excited about it. (While *Follies* was in rehearsal at the Winter Garden Theatre, *Porgy* was running at the Alvin, just a short walk away.) Gershwin again used Duke as a sounding board and advice giver for the opera in "interminable nocturnal discussions."[53]

Not only did Gershwin hone his classical-music skills while writing *Porgy and Bess*, he also dug further into the black music on which his own music had always drawn. Now he went beyond the boundaries of urban jazz to research its deepest roots in rural African American culture. He spent June and July of 1934 researching the gospel, blues, and other musical traditions of African Americans in the South Carolina islands. Duke spent that summer living with the Gershwin family in a vacation home on Fire Island, where he learned of those musical adventures through George's letters home.[54]

Duke and other friends of George's from the *Follies* were bowled over by this masterwork. "The tunes we all listened to around George's piano—'Summertime,' 'It Ain't Necessarily So,' 'I Got Plenty of Nothin'—were now clothed in appropriate orchestral garb and shone with a new and dazzling brilliance," said Duke.[55] And indeed, as Duke has indicated elsewhere, Gershwin's gift for melody, interesting harmonies, and fascinating rhythms was now bolstered by his command of orchestration and vocal part writing, which had made a quantum leap.[56] *Porgy* was also marked by Gershwin's deepened knowledge of rural gospel and blues: the melismatic singing and polyrhythmic clapping, the call-and-response techniques, and the wailing and keening vocal lamentations punctuated by shouts—all these informed and strengthened this landmark work.[57]

The show impressed another *Follies* star and friend of Balanchine: Josephine Baker, who took time off her rigorous rehearsal schedule to attend *Porgy and Bess* with

Balanchine. Thrilled and touched, she lost no time announcing that she wanted to play Bess when it premiered in London.[58] We have no record of what Balanchine thought, but he certainly knew of Duke's and Baker's opinions, and judging from his response to Gershwin's other works, it is hard to imagine that he wouldn't have fallen in love with this new kind of opera. The 1940 all-black musical *Cabin in the Sky*, with music by Duke and staged and even financed in part by Balanchine, would reflect the influence of *Porgy and Bess*.

Three months after the October 1935 premiere of *Porgy and Bess*, on January 30, 1936, *Ziegfeld Follies of 1936* opened at the Winter Garden Theatre. Just as Duke and Ira Gershwin had followed *Porgy and Bess*'s progress, so George Gershwin had paid frequent visits to *Follies* rehearsals.[59]

George Gershwin now watched how the ballets of Duke and Balanchine used their own distinctive blending of Old and New World influences. The ballets from *Ziegfeld Follies of 1936* would, more than any other, forecast the kinds that would be introduced into film musicals. Duke's music reflected his Euro-Russian musical roots as well as the syncopation and tonalities of American jazz, yielding a new form of symphonic ballet score that, like *Porgy*, moved outside the boundaries of both popular and classical music traditions. At the same time, Balanchine combined the jazz, tap, and social-dance forms of the New World, the innovative modern movements of the Diaghilev choreographers, and the traditions of the Euro-Russian *danse d'école*. As in the Diaghilev ballets, the sets, costumes, and designs were carefully coordinated with the ballet.

Scenery, costumes, and some uncredited direction for *Ziegfeld Follies of 1936* were provided by a newcomer, Vincente Minnelli, who was quickly accepted into the Duke-Balanchine-Gershwin circle. Born the year before Balanchine and Duke, Minnelli would go on to become a renowned director of MGM musicals in the 1940s and 1950s, working with Astaire and Kelly. Having moved to New York from Chicago after studying at the Art Institute of Chicago and working as a window dresser, photographer, and director and designer of stage shows in Chicago, he was strongly influenced by the Diaghilev company and its employment of avant-garde artists to create sets and costumes using everything from the colors of the Fauves to the odd-angled, empty spaces of the Surrealists. In New York he had quickly moved up the ranks to become the designer and director of the highly praised 1935 musical revue by Arthur Schwartz and Howard Dietz, *At Home Abroad*. He got a studio apartment near the recently established Museum of Modern Art, and soon his apartment, which Gershwin's friend Kay Swift dubbed the Minnellium, became a locus for the Gershwin-Balanchine crowd, including Lincoln Kirstein and Edward Warburg, who were on the board of the Museum.

Minnelli worked uncredited with Balanchine and Duke on dance numbers in *Ziegfeld Follies of 1936*, and in the program the numbers they did were clearly distinguished from the more routine dance numbers.[60] The term "choreographer" was new to Broadway, and Balanchine was prominently credited as the "celebrated choreographer and former director for Diaghileff," to distinguish him from the ordinary "dance director," Robert Alton (who himself would go on to be an important choreographer for film musicals).[61] The pieces that Balanchine, Duke, and Minnelli did would become models for the ballets in film musicals directed by Minnelli and the team of Gene Kelly and Stanley Donen. In the ballets "Words without Music," "Night Flight," and "Five A.M.," Harriet Hoctor and Josephine Baker performed not with the ordinary *Follies* chorus "girls and boys" but with guest dancers from Balanchine's own American Ballet, who refused to sign contracts until they were assured that they would not be required in any of the show's more routine numbers.[62]

A preliminary look at evidence uncovered by my research for the Popular Balanchine project allows us to make some reasonable conjectures about how this first group of the Balanchine-Duke–Ira Gershwin ballets looked and sounded.[63] We lack any moving images and any notes by either the choreographer or the composer, but hitherto unpublished scores, a few surviving photographs, set designs, and even cartoons, as well as bits of description from both contemporary accounts and reviews, make it clear that the ballets probably departed from the Broadway norm.[64] We know the least about the two ballets written for the classically trained Harriet Hoctor, but evidence so far suggests that they were closer to the Diaghilev ballets in conception: modern-art settings and modernist movement mingled with ballet. Minnelli's Giorgio de Chirico–influenced set designs for "Words without Music: A Surrealist Ballet" could have fit into any Diaghilev ballet of the 1920s (Balanchine's own *Le bal*, for example). And the few photographs we have reveal that Balanchine's dance vocabulary was distinctly modern—tending more toward German Expressionist forms of movement. In the ballet's opening moments, three figures stand, their shadows played by other figures who lie on the ground in front of them and repeat their gestures in a prone position. In another photograph, the strange shadowy figures form an amorphous mass that supports Hoctor high in the air. It is hard to conjecture much about the Hoctor ballets and their scores. A preliminary analysis reveals that musically, "Words without Music" seems to be the most conventional of Duke's scores—basically a symphonic arrangement and extension of Duke's popular song "Words without Music."

"Aero Ballet (Night Flight)," also written for Hoctor, is closer to the modernist scores for the Diaghilev ballets. You can hear hints of the rich and colorful harmonies and orchestral palette of Duke's late nineteenth-century Russian teachers and models, but the primary influence seems to be the more transparent and innovative tapestry of varied orchestral textures and colors of his French colleagues—Debussy and, especially, late Ravel. The ballet is modern in its subject as well: it reflects the new aviation era and the excitement ignited by Charles Lindbergh's solo Atlantic crossing, Amelia Earhart's adventures, and the publication of Antoine de Saint-Exupéry's poetic evocation of flying at night, *Night Flight (Vol de nuit)*, from which the ballet seems to have taken its title.[65] As one critic described it, the "Aero" ballet was "a fantasy that has [Hoctor] hovering like a released and almost transparent soul over an aeroplane's grim shadow . . . a triumph of ballet technique and genuine imagination."[66] Unfortunately, we have yet to discover photographs of this ballet, so we can't say much about the choreography. A newspaper cartoon and the intrigued descriptions of critics tell us of the setting, and that Hoctor rotated her arms and spun around the stage like a propeller.[67] These ballets are the direct ancestors of the Minnelli and Kelly movie ballets.

However, it was in his "ballet" for Josephine Baker that Balanchine most notably aimed, with a mixture of Old and New World ways of moving, to "glorify the American girl" (in Florenz Ziegfeld's words) by creating a dance for this American muse, with whom he had first fallen in love in Paris. Choreographing for her in Paris, he had drawn both on her skills as a jazz dancer and on some of her newly acquired skills in ballet (Fig. 3.1c).[68] While she would never become a professional ballet dancer, she took her dance lessons seriously, just as she did her voice lessons. After a decade there, Baker's body had begun to absorb and transform both Old and New World movements. Now the toast of the city, fluent in French, and a star of operetta and movies as well as the music hall, she was very different from the young and relatively untried chorus girl who had left New York in 1925 to appear in the Revue Nègre.

Duke's score and Balanchine's choreography reflect this blend of the Old and New Worlds in the mature Baker. They depart from the strict orthodoxy of both Broadway show tunes and the symphonic repertoire, moving toward the development of a new form. Around the AABA form of a tender and nuanced musical-theater song, Duke shapes a score in which you can hear not only the syncopation and blues-inflected tonalities of Gershwin's *Rhapsody in Blue*, but also Duke's own Euro-Russian roots. Balanchine, for his part, creates a miniature *ballet d'action*—a narrative in dance that expands on Ira's poignant lyrics to tell the story of a tragic female, a modern descendant of the romantic-ballet tradition, who yearns for something she cannot have. Adoring men dance with her in a mysterious dreamlike setting. These shadowy, black-clad figures, as one viewer put it, carry Baker around "like a queen,"[69] supporting, lifting, and swaying with her glittering figure until rude reality interrupts. A photograph suggests that the romantic-ballet narrative conceits also incorporate a dance vocabulary that gives a new, streamlined diagonal line to the dancer's shape and a more varied, expansive, and choreographed port de bras, including, in one pose, a combination of the lyre-shaped arm of classical ballet and the angular placement of one hand on the hip. The men who frame Baker's form suggest, above all, Balanchine's idol Astaire: one in particular leans back to frame Baker with angled arms and cocked wrists.

Duke's score combines classical compositional techniques with popular-music forms.[70] The music of the opening section—clearly for mime and dance—sets the scene in a modern big city. It suggests the bustle of traffic and the manic gaiety of the party guests: we can hear the influence of the opening bars of *An American in Paris*. After a time the guests leave, and the mood changes. Baker is alone. She walks to the mantle, turns out the lights, and begins to sing (Fig. 3.2a). Ira Gershwin's bittersweet lyrics and Duke's yearning and poignant melody suggest a sophisticated woman who is relieved when her public mask can be taken off and she can enter "a world of her own."

Baker walks to the sofa and falls asleep. Now, in her dreams, Baker will truly enter that world of her own, which Duke indicates by leading into the dream sequence with the melodic material that accompanies that lyric. One by one, four male dream figures step from the shadows to dance with her.[71] The music is not so much developed as

FIGURE 3.2 *Ziegfeld Follies of 1936*: (a) Josephine Baker folds her arms across her body protectively as she sings "Five A.M." From the program, Billy Rose Theatre Division, New York Public Library for the Performing Arts. (b) Baker singing "Five A.M." surrounded by four men. From the program. (c) Newspaper cartoon of Baker and four men, uncredited. (d) Suzanne Farrell and Arthur Mitchell in Balanchine's 1968 restaging of the ballet *Slaughter on Tenth Avenue* for the New York City Ballet. Photo by Martha Swope, courtesy of New York Public Library digital collection.

fragmented—as a dream might be—with musical events appearing and disappearing suddenly. The dance builds in intensity as the dream devolves into a nightmare, and it ends when Baker opens the door of her apartment to reveal the exaggerated shadow of one of her admirers she sings about. He then disappears, and, calming herself, she returns to the song and final dance sequence.

This dream-ballet sequence, as Christian Matjias points out, uses fragments of musical material first heard in the song. Like the other Balanchine Broadway ballets and films to follow and like its most well-known descendant—Rodgers and Agnes DeMille's *Oklahoma!* dream ballet, "Out of My Dreams"—Duke focuses on the melodic materials used for a key moment in the text, "I Live in a World of My Own," dressing and varying this phrase in orchestral colors and textures and a harmonic language that reflects a variety of Euro-Russian and African American musical influences to create the dream world she now enters. The music of the dream ballet responds very closely to what we know about the action of the dance: the individual entrances of the dream figures can be discerned, and the arc of tempo and mood changes corresponds with our knowledge of Baker's emotional journey as suggested in the lyrics and the few stage directions in the script. Despite the dreamy atmosphere, the rhythmic pulse, though variable, is always discernible, and it is clear that some rhythmic motifs are meant to support specific dance movements.

The close ties between music with action in "Five A.M." hint at Balanchine and Duke's close working relationship, something Duke confirms in his autobiography. Balanchine showed Duke what he wanted musically "by sitting down at the piano and improvising the sort of music he needed," then "dancing out whole chunks of it, humming to himself, throwing himself on the floor and saying at intervals, 'Here I want about a minute of music for the guests . . . tra, la, la . . . tra la lee. Something like that; now . . .' as he ran from the room. 'That's where the dancer comes in, like this . . .'—a hop and a couple of turns—'about twelve bars. You see?' I saw."[72] Duke and Balanchine's ways of working together, with the choreographer guiding and indicating the outline of the dance and the dramatic action to take place, was, as noted earlier, a practice that extended back into Euro-Russian ballet tradition. The score is dance- and dancer-driven, written specifically for the choreography and the dramatic action, often with the actual dancer in mind. Adolphe Adam's score for the ballet *Giselle* (1841) and Tchaikovsky's scores for Petipa's and Ivanov's ballets follow detailed instructions as to the number of measures, tempo, and time signatures needed. Balanchine seems to be adhering to this model, but, as a musician himself, he prefers actually to demonstrate his ideas by improvising on the piano, giving Duke a vivid experience of the kind of music and choreography he needed—not just written directions of the meter and tempos, but, importantly, the sense of weight shift and flow of the dance, the quality of the movement, and its placement onstage. These face-to-face working sessions between two old friends not only allowed for a close interchange and spontaneous development of ideas, but made for a good time as well—much as with Gershwin and Astaire.[73] Astaire and later Kelly would interact similarly with composers, music directors, orchestrators, or arrangers to demonstrate how they wanted music to fit with the dance.

Baker and Balanchine also worked hard on the *Follies*. The rehearsals were rigorous and exhausting. "I rehearsed for weeks from two to six pm and again from 9 pm to midnight," she told a Harlem journalist. Halfway through rehearsals, most of the dances planned before her arrival were scrapped and replaced with new ones. But Baker was happy with the changes, even if she had to work harder to learn the new choreography, for she was desperate not to be stereotyped. Her director was of the same mind. As Baker excitedly explained to the same reporter:

One morning, in the middle of rehearsals, the director suddenly appeared in the auditorium. He was John Murray Anderson, the most famous director of American revues. He shook his head saying, "We must change everything. That won't do at all." I was in despair. Then he explained what he meant and I discovered that he was paying me a compliment. He meant that the numbers, which had been written for me, were too much like those that colored performers had done the last few years in New York revues. "You are different Josephine, do you understand that? You are from Paris. It's stupid to let you sing Harlem songs. You must give us something new."[74]

The *Follies* began its previews on December 30 at the Boston Opera House and went on to Philadelphia in mid-January. Fanny Brice, the other female star of the *Follies*, received rave reviews; with some exceptions, Baker's ranged from lukewarm to negative. Brooks Atkinson, the powerful critic of the *New York Times*, was dismissive: "Miss Baker has refined her art until there is practically nothing left of it." He pointedly compared Baker unfavorably not with Brice, but with the Nicholas Brothers, who followed Baker. After the "too refined" Josephine, the Nicholas Brothers, Atkinson wrote, "restore your faith in dusky revelry."[75]

Time was openly racist:

Josephine Baker is a St. Louis washerwoman's daughter who stepped out of a Negro burlesque show into a life of adulation and luxury in Paris during the booming 1920's. In sex appeal to jaded Europeans of the jazz loving type, a Negro wench always has a head start. The particular tawny hue of tall and stringy Josephine Baker's bare skin stirred French pulses. But to Manhattan theater goers last week she was just a slightly buck-toothed young Negro woman whose figure might be matched in any night club show, and whose dancing and singing might be topped practically anywhere out side of Paris.[76]

The repercussions of the magazine's review spread far beyond the world of the arts. Baker had been a source of pride to the African American community. To be sure, there was some jealousy and dissension, but in general Baker was welcomed back to Harlem as the hometown girl who had made good—a black woman who had become a wealthy and internationally famous celebrity. Her highly publicized visits to Harlem filled the streets with well-wishers. Members of the African American arts community as well as the black public in general saw Baker's appearance in the *Follies* on Broadway as a step forward in the fight to end segregation in the arts. The reception white American critics afforded her was dismaying, and the *Time* reviewer, in particular, made it abundantly clear that the deep, powerful currents of racism in American life were still determining white reactions to Baker and indeed all black performers. A furious editorial appeared in the *Chicago Defender*, a leading African American newspaper:

We are loath to believe that the editor and managing editors of *Time* lie in such a low and degraded mental channel. . . . Even *Time* must realize that the prestige of the white man in the last analysis must be maintained by the white man's own behavior, that his claims to "superiority" over the black man can be sustained only by the white man evidencing a higher culture than those whom he seeks to belittle.

While we have long since recognized that those claims have not in fact any moral foundation yet we have offered no evidence specifically to the contrary, knowing that from time to time the evidence would be offered by just such article[s] as the one now under discussion.

The vile word wench is not the language of cultured gentlemen nor does it necessarily classify those to whom it is applied. The very thought of applying such a word to a woman has its birth in a diseased mind. . . . We would like to believe that the editors of *Time* were unconscious of its use. But our better judgment makes us know that in this case they were fully conscious of what they were doing.[77]

Bewildered and hurt, Baker's response to her reviews was to threaten to pull out of *Ziegfeld Follies of 1936*, and her supporters had to persuade her not to return to Paris immediately. Could French and American audiences be *that* different?[78] Balanchine himself seems to have been happy with her performance. His own assessment of the situation was blunt and to the point: "They didn't like [Baker] because she was American. If she had been French, they would have gone wild; but an American Negro from Harlem—people said, 'Who the hell is she, who does she think she is?'"[79]

But there was another, unspoken, unacknowledged layer to the problem of Baker's reviews for the *Follies*, and it had nothing to do with her vocal equipment, her French accent, or the sophisticated setting provided for her in "Five A.M." It lay in Balanchine's choreography. A young African American official for the National Urban League, Donald Wyatt, took his wife to see the Philadelphia previews of *Ziegfeld Follies of 1936*. They went especially to see Baker.

We had heard about her, so we went. In a number called Five A.M. the Balanchine choreography was great, and Josephine was great. But the audience, mostly white, was unable to accept the public adoration of a black woman by four handsome young white men.

Most blacks didn't like it any better, but as a sociologist, I felt this is where we needed to be going, to the point where there would an interracial performance accepted by both sides for its artistic value.

At the end of the number, the boys lifted her into the air and ran off the stage with her, and there was total silence.[80] Nobody clapped. Then the tempo of the music picked up and the Nicholas Brothers made their entrance tap-dancing like mad, and everybody was relieved, and burst into a tremendous wave of applause.[81]

As Wyatt suggests, Balanchine's choreography had broken a powerful taboo. To American audiences in 1936, close physical contact between a white man or woman and a black woman or man onstage was immensely shocking. As Josephine herself told Fayard Nicholas, "These people here, they don't want black people to touch white people."[82] Balanchine was crossing into territory so forbidden that George Church, who danced with Baker, remembers an "avalanche" of threatening letters from disgruntled audience members: "How dare you?," "You Nigger-lover," "I'm gonna get you."[83]

For Baker in *Ziegfeld Follies of 1936*, Balanchine created a dance in which a black woman and white men interacted in the same physical and psychological space. They moved intimately and naturally in a dream world that belonged to them both. And he made it clear in the choreography's attitudes of tenderness that a black woman had as much right to dream of being cherished and loved as her white counterparts.[84]

The photograph reproduced as Fig. 3.2b illustrates this clearly. Baker leans back dreamily, eyes half closed, her body protectively framed by three white men, one of whom gazes at her in open adoration. His posture suggests that he is either about to fall or has risen from a kneeling position at her feet. In a cartoon drawing of the same moment, the artist (perhaps using the photo as a model) shows a similar pose (Fig. 3.2c).

It is this particular image, however, that provides the final clue to Balanchine's breaking of a taboo. Though the actual dancers were white, the artist presents them as racially stereotyped black figures derived from minstrelsy, and the caption reads, "Josephine Baker, the returned expatriate, goes a bit African." Robert Baral speaks of "black and white" lovers who "flit across her mind."[85] Some critics suggest that the dancer's faces were covered. *Variety*'s critic described the dancers as "four shadowy, black masked men."[86] Wyatt's description suggests, however, that the masks may have appeared *after* the preview performances—perhaps in response to audience complaints. In any case, even if the dancers wore masks, would it have been so hard to distinguish their race? They would have had to be gloved and their necks and ears blackened. In any case, the "guests" that attend Baker during the first part of the number were not specifically identified as black.

There is also a noticeable difference in the way the cartoon artist presents Josephine and the other dancers. The cartoon figures suggest an entirely different mood from that of the dance we know from descriptions, pictures, and Duke's music. The song is wistful and poignant, the music soft, lyrical, and yearning. The music for the dance itself plays on the contrast between this sweet legato theme and a more agitated, staccato, syncopated section—darker and more despairing in mood and tone. The dance section, which was probably written in close conjunction with Balanchine, is balletic in nature and symphonic in scope. It is impossible to imagine where the overt, brassy sexuality of the cartoon figures—in which a grinning Baker preens herself framed by exaggerated black stereotypes—might come from. So although Balanchine did not observe the taboo on interracial physical contact, the cartoon artist did, changing the dancers' poses and features in a deliberate or perhaps unconscious act of censorship.

Balanchine had violated another unspoken rule as well: he had presented a black woman in a dance that was not readable as black, exotic, or other. Rather, he placed Baker in the European romantic tradition that until then had been reserved for white women. The pictures, descriptions, and texture and tone of Duke's music all suggest that in this number Balanchine presented Baker as someone to be, as Wyatt put it, "adored by men." Baker's colleague Maude Russell sums it up: "At that time, nobody wanted to see a colored girl being twirled around with four white boys and dressed up like a queen."[87] Balanchine's attitude toward women is well-known: his muse of the moment was placed on a pedestal, and her distinctive personality and body became Balanchine's feminine ideal. She can be earthy and sensual, but she is also a woman to be adored, cherished, and inspired by—a woman to whom men owe fealty. Always she remains beyond the artist's reach, unknowable and unattainable. Balanchine thus may have worked with an African American woman—a jazz dancer—to develop a style that mingled Old and New Worlds. But like all of his American colleagues, both white and black, he was learning the hard way that if he wanted to develop his outlaw style in America, he would have to do it with white women. This problem would plague him throughout his career, and it would often come down to the same issues he encountered with Baker. In the ballet tradition, dancers partner each other in the most intimate ways. Blacks and whites intertwined aroused white Americans' most deep-seated fear: miscegenation. Balanchine constantly had to field complaints of parents who saw their children in adagio class being partnered by members of another race. This taboo on physical contact, then, joined with resistance to bringing a black woman into the nineteenth-century romantic tradition of adoration and idealization of the woman. Balanchine may have wanted to "glorify the American woman," but what if she happened to be black?[88]

Baker, rightfully furious, returned to Paris, where the prejudice was less virulent. Balanchine continued to seek out African American dancers. He greatly admired the Nicholas Brothers and used them whenever he could for prominent dancing roles on Broadway in *The Ziegfeld Follies* (1936) and *Babes in Arms* (1937). (He and Rodgers and Hart built the theme of race prejudice into *Babes in Arms*: a racist stage manager orders the kids, named, perhaps at Balanchine's suggestion, "Ivor" and "Igor," off the stage during the finale of the young company's big show, but they go on anyway, "Ivor dancing like mad, crying enormous tears as autos offstage honk their approval. The cheering and clapping make Ivor hoof and cry all the more as the curtain falls.")[89]

BACK TO *ON YOUR TOES* AND "SLAUGHTER ON TENTH AVENUE": DUKE, BALANCHINE, GERSHWIN, AND RODGERS AND HART

The climate created by the Diaghilev diaspora, *Porgy and Bess*, and Balanchine's and Duke's mingling of styles in *Ziegfeld Follies of 1936* created the atmosphere that produced Rodgers and Hart's *On Your Toes* and made it relevant to the concerns of New York audiences. The vitality of jazz as a key American art form had been stressed by musicians and writers both black and white, with the advent of the Harlem Renaissance. Questions of New World and Old World, jazz and classical music, high-brow and lowbrow had engaged music. Now these same questions were put into high relief in a musical comedy about the meeting of American jazz dance and Russian ballet.[90] *On Your Toes*, with Balanchine as choreographer, is a satirical look at the invasion of the Russian émigré ballet community and its impact on American performing arts and artists.

By 1936 expatriate Russians were everywhere in America, intimidating and alluring audiences in small towns and big cities with their art pedigrees and exotic glamour. The press played them up as exemplars of their craft, and young Americans, especially would-be ballerinas, signed up for lessons at their new dance studios. Among the most prominent was Balanchine's School of American Ballet, but many other Russian-run studios, big and small, were springing up across the country. Balanchine and Dukelsky were only two of the phalanx of Russian composers, musicians, choreographers, and dancers who began to take over U.S. stages and studios. Fokine and Massine created new works and remounted many of their Diaghilev ballets for the various Ballets Russes clone companies crisscrossing the country from the 1930s to the 1950s with such Russian stars as Alexandra Danilova, Irina Baronova, Tamara Toumonova, and Igor Yousevitch, as well as those with English and American roots who, like Alicia Markova (Alice Marks), Anton Dolin (Patrick Kaye), and Mark Platoff (Mark Platt), had felt it necessary to "Russianize" their names.

But the Russians were not the only ones satirized in *On Your Toes*. George Gershwin was also a target. More than anyone in America, Gershwin was identified with the attempt to bring jazz to the concert hall. The hero of *On Your Toes*, Phil Dolan Jr. ("Junior"), is a young American vaudevillian who leaves the stage to become a music teacher at "Knickerbocker University." His student "Sidney Cohn" writes a "jazz ballet," and Junior persuades a Russian ballet company to mount it. Junior himself is pulled into dancing in the climactic jazz ballet, "Slaughter on Tenth Avenue," opposite a Russian ballerina (Vera Barnova). (In the film version, Junior also becomes the composer himself.) Junior joins a Russian ballet company to write the score.

This jazz ballet climaxes his adventures with a company that is a thinly disguised portrait of the Ballets Russe de Monte Carlo.[91] "Vera Barnova," the temperamental ballerina, resonates with the name of the young Ballets Russe star Irina Baronova; "Serge Morosine" is the Ballets Russes dancer-choreographer Léonide Massine; and the leader of the company, "Alexandrovitch," is in part the vain and jealous Diaghilev, but even closer to Colonel Wassily de Basil, a ruthless wheeler-dealer of the first order who ran the Ballets Russe with Léon Blum and soon took it over entirely. (Balanchine left the company partly because he was fed up with de Basil.)

Throughout *On Your Toes*, Balanchine contrasts ballet with tap dancing to tell the story of the clash and eventual meeting of cultures. Balanchine's takeoff on Fokine's *Scheherazade*, "The Princess Zenobia Ballet," has Junior trapped onstage with the male corps de ballet. Panicked, he reverts to his vaudeville roots, hoofing alongside his horrified colleagues' *sautés*, with hilarious results. But "The Princess Zenobia Ballet" was another kind of statement as well. Here Balanchine presented an entirely new attitude toward Russian ballet in a way that no one outside his own culture could do. His takeoff was affectionate: he liked and admired Fokine, but he saw him as part of the past. Balanchine was not afraid to take the mickey out of the sacred Diaghilev repertory. In so doing, he announced his independence from even Diaghilev's modern ballet forms. He pointed a new way forward. *On Your Toes*, wickedly funny, crystallized in dance what would now become a central aesthetic concern of musical-theater and film-musical dance: the relationship between Old World dance (read ballet) and New World dance (read jazz dance) as well as music.

On Your Toes' climactic dance sequence, "Slaughter on Tenth Avenue," uses elements of both forms to create what Junior calls a truly "American . . . jazz ballet"—one that fuses the two techniques (and their musics) into that "something . . . new." As he had in "Five A.M.," Balanchine creates a *ballet d'action* to tell a story in a modernized form of mime as well as dance. Again, a romantic ballet plot is given a modern setting: a lonely hoofer yearns for a beautiful dance-hall girl, only to lose her when she altruistically stops a bullet meant for him. The star of *On Your Toes* was Tamara Geva, Balanchine's ex-wife (and still good friend). Geva, trained at the Imperial Ballet School, had incorporated jazz movement into a few of her previous Broadway appearances, some of it choreographed by Balanchine.[92] Balanchine thus had a fully trained ballet dancer at his command, one with an affinity for jazz movement—someone whom Balanchine knew intimately, had danced with many times, and could communicate with in his native language.

This dance established the American jazz ballet, a genre that would be developed on both Broadway and in the movies in the 1930s, '40s, and early '50s. In "Slaughter," Balanchine fused the skills of the African American tap dancer and the chorus-girl kick line with elements of ballet movement within the context of a short-form *ballet d'action*.[93] In this he was assisted by the African American jazz dancer Herbie Harper, who coached Balanchine and Ray Bolger in rhythm tap.[94] Balanchine, on the other hand, drew on the classical dancer's ability to turn out, which allowed for a wider range and expansiveness of leg and arm motion, and combined it with the jazz dancer's more fluid and active torso and hips, angular body shapes, off-balance positions, and preparationless flow of movement, which was not only tightly integrated with but interacted with syncopated rhythms. The blend is exemplified in one of the climactic musical and dance moments in "Slaughter," in which Balanchine transformed the routine chorus line into a powerful and affectionate tribute to the syncopated strutting of jazz dancers in Harlem and on Broadway. Like Rodgers's score, Balanchine's choreography depended for its impact on a combination of techniques drawn from the Old World and the New: the interdependent sharing of weight developed in the ballet pas de deux, furthered by Balanchine's innovative partnering techniques, and the flexible back and arrow-straight line created by the ballerina's leg, which stretched out from hip to toe, responding with the musical precision of the cakewalker and tap dancer to the music's syncopations. Arching back over her partner's supporting arm, Tamara Geva's drooping head and torso seemed to disappear into the shadows as she shot first one leg and then the other into the air and propelled them forward, over and over. In an effect both spectacular and surreal, her moving legs seemed disembodied (Fig. 3.2d).

"Slaughter on Tenth Avenue" is also a *ballet d'action* that uses modern mime in the manner of Fred Astaire. Instead of the European symbol system, Balanchine substitutes characteristically American gesture. (In the film of "Slaughter," he actually quotes Astaire in *Top Hat*, as the shadowy form of the hoofer crouches low over the pimp's body and freezes in position.) He uses American tap as an essential element of the drama, turning a trope from classical ballet hilariously on its head. Like the hero of the nineteenth-century ballet *Giselle*, the hero has to keep dancing until he is rescued—and it is an exhausting task!

It is thus one of the first ballets that functions as an essential element in the plot of a musical, ingeniously tying up its various threads in music and dance. Balanchine was not the very first to mingle jazz and classical dance for a jazz ballet. Such a blending had been in the air since at least 1928, when Dolin and Nemchinova toured England with his immensely popular ballet based on *Rhapsody in Blue*.[95] But we can be sure that everyone sat up and took notice of the way in which Balanchine was playing with these genres and, in doing so, producing what Edith Isaacs called "the change in emphasis in musical comedy from the jester to the dancer." She summed up the season:

> Although "choreography by George Balanchine" might indicate that something creative would be added to the conventional pattern of dance routines, that is not enough to make you realize, until the rapidly paced show is over and you begin to think about it, that what you have seen is an innovation. Nor is this only because *On your Toes* is a dancers' show, with as much satire and as much skill in the Princess Zenobia ballet and "Slaughter on Tenth Avenue" as there usually is in half a dozen skits but even more because the audience recognizes both the skill and the satire, although it is never expressed in words but only in a heightened movement, an exaggerated ballet position, a burlesqued composition, movement, a costume out of line, an overdone arabesque, and again, even more because the audience enjoys its own appreciation and applauds the performance with zest.
>
> When you have the artist and the audience, you have a theatre form, and there they are—dancers, choreographers, dancing chorus and responsive audiences. So perhaps instead of being at the end of our hope of comedy, we are making a fresh start in a new direction, one in which the progress of the comic dance is quite in line with what is taking place in every other part of the whole dance world.[96]

4

BALANCHINE IN HOLLYWOOD

Jazz Ballet for the Camera

AS RODGERS AND Hart joined Balanchine to salute and satirize Gershwin and Russian ballet on Broadway in *On Your Toes*, the Gershwin brothers answered *On Your Toes* at the movies—this time with their old friend and Balanchine's dance idol Fred Astaire. *Shall We Dance* (1937) was another tongue-in-cheek look at the clash and eventual reconciliation of Old World and New, of Russian ballet and jazz (now called swing). Astaire is Petrov, a Russian ballet star, who woos a reluctant tap dancer played by Ginger Rogers. She softens when he reveals his true American identity (Pete P. Peters, Philadelphia, Pa.) and his love of American jazz dance—along with his ambition to mix ballet and swing to create a new form. As in most of *On Your Toes*, the final extended dance sequence contrasts the two styles, with the ballerina Harriet Hoctor played off against Rogers's tap dancing. Astaire dances with them both to a Gershwin ballet score that contrasts a Ravel-influenced waltz and a lush symphonic arrangement of "They Can't Take That Away from Me" for Hoctor and Astaire with the upbeat, syncopated "Shall We Dance," to which Astaire exhilaratingly taps with a chorus of dancers masked to look like his beloved. The camera swings from one set to another, ending affirmatively on Astaire and Rogers singing the finale; tap and ballet dancers fill the stage as the curtain falls.

Shall We Dance may have whetted Gershwin's appetite for ballet. He was well aware of Balanchine and Russian ballet's growing hold on the public's imagination. (Even Busby Berkeley had gotten into the act. His 1938 *Golddiggers in Paris* featured an American nightclub owner who, to rescue his finances, disguises his Broadway showgirls as ballet dancers.) Gershwin had proven himself as a composer of opera; why not ballet? His experiences of the last few years had been clearly leading in this direction, with the example of Duke's ballet scores for the *Follies*, Rodgers's "Slaughter on Tenth Avenue," and of course, *Shall We Dance*.[1] After the premiere of *Porgy and Bess* in October of 1935, Gershwin had gone on a cruise to Mexico with Edward Warburg and Lincoln Kirstein, patrons and advocates of Balanchine's company American Ballet.[2] It is likely that they discussed a commission, for Kirstein and Warburg were still on a mission to mount American-themed ballets with American composers. Ballet was truly in the air, and Gershwin may have begun thinking about creating his own. Three years later, in 1938, a spate of such ballets from Gershwin's colleagues Aaron Copland, Virgil Thompson, and Jerome Moross would make their appearance: Thompson and Lew Christensen's *Filling Station*, Copland and Eugene Loring's *Billy the Kid*, and Ruth Page and Moross's *Frankie and Johnny*. Gershwin had by then planned to create his own ballet with its own original score for the movie *The Goldwyn Follies*, which was also slated to appear in 1938. But Gershwin's deteriorating health was to make this impossible.

For Gershwin, one of the attractions of *The Goldwyn Follies* was surely the chance to create ballets in collaboration with his friend Balanchine, Broadway's hotshot new choreographer.[3] The Gershwin brothers had planned to set aside a six-week period at the end of the actual songwriting for *The Goldwyn Follies* to prepare a new, full-scale ballet score that combined classical and jazz forms ("Swing Symphony") for Balanchine and his dancers.[4] Tragically, Gershwin developed symptoms of the brain tumor that would eventually kill him, and he was unable to write the new score. He offered the use of *An American in Paris* instead, and this projected ballet almost came to fruition: the music was edited and fitted to the scenario, the choreography and camera angles planned—but the ballet was scrapped. Balanchine and Gershwin's old friend Vernon Duke was called in to create the scores for two remaining ballets.

However, we can conjecture what Balanchine's "American in Paris" ballet for *The Goldwyn Follies* might have looked and sounded like, and how he worked to create a new ballet for a new medium. The scenario, written by Ira Gershwin, has been published, and its layout clearly reveals Balanchine's own ideas. The original program notes for Gershwin's 1928 tone poem *An American in Paris* had been written by Deems Taylor, and Gershwin himself had suggested a narrative. The aim was "to portray the impressions of an American visitor in Paris as he strolls about the city, listens to the various street noises, and absorbs the French atmosphere." Ira Gershwin's and Balanchine's detailed ballet scenario, titled "Exposition," retains the "American" protagonist but adds characters and changes the context, tracing the movement of the dancers through various locations with, in some places, an indication of the actual style of the choreography.[5]

Remarkably, a score also exists, edited by Balanchine with George Gershwin's blessing. Recalled Balanchine:

> I went to visit him and found him lying in bed in a dark room. He had a towel against his head and was obviously in great pain. He said to me, "it is difficult for me to work now, but I'll be all right." He knew I was trained in music, so he also

said, "Do what you must, I know it will be good"—he had more confidence in me than Goldwyn did then! "And when I'm all better we'll do our ballet just the way you want it." A week later he was dead.[6]

With Gershwin's blessing, then, Balanchine choreographed the ballet and edited the music of *An American in Paris*, creating a *ballet d'action* for film in which a romantic ballet theme (a yearning man chases an unattainable woman) is modernized. The now standard theme of the meeting of Old and New World music and dance forms—jazz and the classics—is explored. At an international exposition a schoolgirl, Vera Zorina, is pursued by the American tap dancer Paul Draper; they dance through the various colorful national pavilions, but in the end boy loses girl. (Gene Kelly's own "American in Paris" ballet, thirteen years later, is a variation on this Ira Gershwin-Balanchine theme.)

Balanchine, excited about planning a ballet made especially for cinema, actively choreographed the camera movement and editing to be integrated with music and dance. He worked with the great cinematographer Gregg Toland, from whom he learned about camera lenses, movement, framing, and editing. Sets were built, costumes were made, shooting schedules were set. The "American in Paris" ballet was completed, but it was cut from the movie. No film record has been found.

AN AMERICAN IN PARIS: THE SCORE

A recently discovered source can help us gain some idea of what Balanchine and the Gershwins envisioned. Balanchine's personally edited and annotated piano score for *An American in Paris* is archived among his personal papers in the Harvard Theatre Collection. The score is missing pages, but when it is examined against Ira Gershwin and Balanchine's detailed scenario for the ballet and within the context of Balanchine, Duke, and Gershwin's relationship, a great deal is revealed, although many questions remain.

Balanchine's score shows that, with Gershwin's permission, he reconceived Gershwin's tone poem for the ballet, freely rearranging and reordering the original musical structure by cutting and pasting chunks of material. Balanchine penciled in markings in Russian in the score (Figs. 4.1 and 4.2) to indicate locales, action, and sometimes characters that correspond to a section of the scenario. No specific steps are indicated. "Spain" (Fig. 4.1, №9, Испанія) presumably indicates the Spanish scene on the curtain, and on the next page of the score, the Russian for "runs away" (Fig. 4.2, №10, убѣгает) and later "pulls at the curtain" (теребит занавѣску) may indicate Draper's running to the curtain and opening it. He writes the feminine form of "Gypsy" (Fig. 4.3, №11, цыганка) right after this, at the start of a tranquil few measures, and this might mean that a Gypsy woman appears before the shift to flamenco (a dance with which Gypsies are associated). In the original Gershwin, agitated music follows immediately, but Balanchine pastes over the start this, perhaps indicating cutting, and so the pages I display don't tell us what music he uses for the flamenco. Further examination and analysis of Balanchine's markings are needed (Figs. 4.1–4.3).[7] His aim is

FIGURE 4.1 George Gershwin, piano score for *An American in Paris*, edited with markings by George Balanchine. After "Calmato," Balanchine has penciled in Испапія (*Ispániya*, "Spain"). All three score pages are courtesy of the Harvard Theatre Collection and the George Balanchine Trust. © The George Balanchine Trust. BALANCHINE is a Trademark of the George Balanchine Trust. Currently located in the Harvard Theater Collection, Houghton Library, Harvard University. Courtesy of the George Balanchine Trust.

clearly to make the music support the narrative flow of this *ballet d'action* as detailed in the scenario, as well as to support the various solo, pas de deux, and ensemble dances through which characters are revealed and the story is told.

As in the *Ziegfeld Follies* ballets, then, it is the choreography and the scenario that drive Balanchine's reorganized "American in Paris" ballet score. In the scenario, the male

FIGURE 4.2 Gershwin score with Balanchine's pencil markings, p. 11. At the top right, убѣгает (*ubegáyet*, "runs away"). Middle right, теребит занавѣску (*terebít zanavésku*, "pulls at the curtain"). Lower left, цыганка (*tsygánka* "Gypsy female").

protagonist (Paul Draper) searches for his schoolgirl ballerina in each of the national pavilions of the fair. One is the Spanish pavilion.

We follow Draper. He rushes to a guide and gesticulates: Have you seen her? Guide shakes head—no. There is a Spanish rural scene painted on the curtain nearby. He runs to this and opens the curtain. The rhythm of the music changes

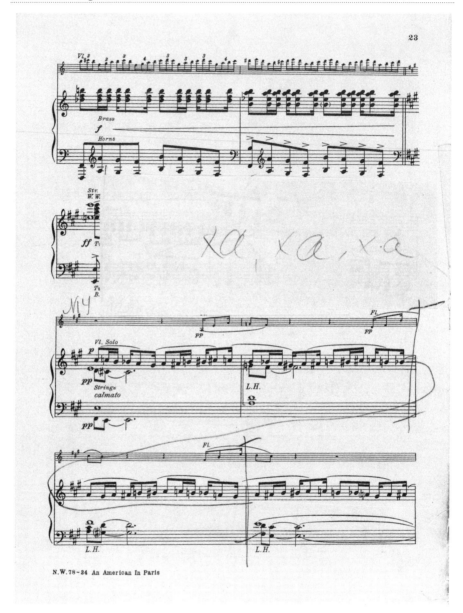

FIGURE 4.3 Gershwin score, p. 23, pasted over by Balanchine with xa, xa, xa (*kha, kha, kha,* "ha ha ha," i.e., laughter).

immediately to flamenco, and we are in the Spanish village. There is a wild dance in progress.[8]

The scenario also tells us that Balanchine wanted to add rhythmic layers to Gershwin's original structure. He gives a rhythmic motif to the schoolmistress, who supervises the group of schoolgirls of which Zorina is a part. "Every now and then, the schoolmistress uses a certain rhythm in clapping her hands to call her pupils to order." This is heard in the sequence that takes place in the American Café, which also adds many more rhythmic layers. This sequence also demonstrates that Balanchine and Ira Gershwin drew directly on George Gershwin's research in the South Carolina islands for *Porgy and Bess*. The scenario says:

> In the American Café, the orchestra is swinging and we see vague figures doing modern American rhythms. Draper comes out of his daze and the figures become clearer and off on the other side he sees Zorina. Draper's tapping excites the spectators. To help the basic rhythm, they start to clap hands in the style done in small Negro churches in Florida and the Carolinas where often there are two distinct rhythms going against each other. At a climax . . . there is a sudden dramatic stop in the music and clapping and Zorina finds herself doing a step to the beat we have previously seen done by the school mistress.[9]

On another page of the score, Balanchine pastes in the words "kha, kha, kha" (Fig. 4.3), indicating the "ha, ha, ha" of loud laughter. Whether this refers to a rhythm or to laughter that pauses the action I do not know.

AN AMERICAN IN PARIS AS A CINEMATIC BALLET

Balanchine was proud of the new ballet. It demonstrates Balanchine's own ideas about filming ballet, with camera angles, editing, and movement choreographed and integrated with the choreography of the dancers. When he arrived in Hollywood in 1937, he already knew something about movies from his stint as a silent-film accompanist in St. Petersburg, where he learned how to improvise and integrate music with the moving image. He and his classmates from ballet school went to see D. W. Griffith's *Intolerance* in 1919, and classmates remember Balanchine and Lida Ivanova acting out scenes from this epic.[10] Furthermore, Balanchine was associated with the young, postrevolutionary avant-garde group FEKS (Factory of the Eccentric Actor). The FEKS saw jazz, circus, music hall, cinema, and American movies as new and vital sources of artistic nourishment.[11] Balanchine held dance classes for his young colleagues; one of his pupils was Sergei Eisenstein, before he began his film career with *Strike* and *October*. We don't have proof that Balanchine saw either film, but there is a good chance that he was well aware of Eisenstein's innovations in film, especially since the filmmaker visited Paris to show his works while Balanchine was in the Ballets Russes.

Most important, Balanchine danced in the first sound film made in England, *Dark Red Roses* (1929), for which he choreographed a small dance sequence for himself and two other colleagues in the Diaghilev Ballets Russes. This was a mini–dance drama in the manner of the company's nationalist Russian ballets. A betrayed warrior (Balanchine) discovers his wife (Lydia Lopokova) with her lover (Anton Dolin) and takes his revenge by cutting off his rival's hands. (The situation echoes the betrayal moment in Fokine's *Scheherazade* that Balanchine would parody in *On Your Toes*.) The ballet reflected a parallel situation in the movie plot, in which a cuckolded Englishman realizes his wife's betrayal while watching the dance. Thus, even before he came to the United States, Balanchine was absorbing (consciously or unconsciously) ideas about integration of the movie narrative and dance.

Balanchine took movies as seriously as he did stage musicals, and both as seriously as ballet for the stage. In fact Balanchine felt, as he put it, that the "responsibility of working in motion pictures is *greater* than in the theatre because the artist is addressing, not a selected group of people, but large masses of people over the world." Balanchine felt, as did Gene Kelly, that film's unique qualities allowed for the democratization of the dance-going experience. You don't have to be able to afford the best seats to enjoy the show:

> In the film, ballet is visually equally complete no matter from what seat in the auditorium one looks at it. The camera does the work. In the theatre a person sitting high in the balcony sees only heads and thus has only an incomplete (and distorted) view of the ballet performance. The movies correct this error of the theatre and make it possible for *every* member of the audience to enjoy ballet fully.[12]

Balanchine understood well the conceptual difference between film and stage, and he was eager to exploit the unique possibilities of the new technology:

> The frame of the screen is a far more movable thing than the frame of the theatre: the ballet is not bound to a visual square of thirty or forty feet. The same applies to the space and movability of the settings. It is far easier to create a complete space fantasy on screen than on the stage. Natural elements like wind, light, and sound can be more freely applied to the screen than to the stage and thus become far more important additions to classic ballet than they are on the stage. Also the spectator sees a stage ballet always from the same angle and distance. *On the screen, however, the spectator moves with the camera and thus can see the ballet from a wide range of angles and distances*. He may even feel himself amidst the dancers. This imposes *completely new problems for the choreographer*: it makes his task far more intricate and difficult, gives him new riddles to solve and a wide range of possibilities for his invention.[13]

How did Balanchine solve these riddles? For one thing, he took complete control. In Figure 4.6n he is peering through the viewfinder to check out the frame composition. Like Fred Astaire, Busby Berkeley, and later Gene Kelly, Balanchine not only directed his film ballets but also choreographed them—choreographing the camera movement, editing, and lighting as well as his dancers while working with the best cinematographers in the business. In *The Goldwyn Follies*, it was the legendary Gregg Toland; the following year, 1939, Toland would win the Academy Award for cinematography for William

Wyler's *Wuthering Heights*. And just a couple of years later, in 1941, he would be responsible for the brilliant cinematic effects in Orson Welles's *Citizen Kane*.

Toland and Balanchine were the same age, both born in 1904, and they became good friends. Toland taught the young choreographer about lenses, lighting, camera angles, and movement. Together the two worked out a special technique of filming dancers from slightly below—by digging a trench and placing the camera in it—to compensate for screen distortion and to give the dancers that long, long look that Balanchine so admired. And Toland and Balanchine worked together to take advantage of the three-strip Technicolor process that was just then coming into its own. (*The Goldwyn Follies*, filmed a year before *Gone with the Wind* and *The Wizard of Oz*, won an award for color cinematography at the Venice Film Festival.)

Balanchine's approach to dance cinematography was very much his own. He admired the advances in dance filmmaking pioneered by Astaire, but he was also enthusiastic about Berkeley and his use of the moving camera. *Gold Diggers of 1933* was released during Balanchine's first year in America, and he studied Berkeley's and Astaire's films before making *The Goldwyn Follies*. Astaire's first film with Rogers, *Flying Down to Rio*, also appeared around this time, and it was followed by *Roberta*, *Top Hat*, and *Swing Time*—all of which Balanchine would have seen before working on *The Goldwyn Follies*.

Balanchine's work reflects a combination their two approaches. Like Astaire, he placed the full dancing body—usually during solos—at the center of the action. At the same time, in contrast to Astaire but like Berkeley, he used camera movement and a variety of camera angles and special cinematic effects to enhance the narrative told in song and dance, in both its formal and its dramatic aspects. The camera became an active participant in the dance. In this, his ballets in *The Goldwyn Follies* and *On Your Toes*—especially *On Your Toes*—are precedent setters for the film ballets created by Minnelli and Kelly and by Stanley Donen in the 1940s and '50s, including, most famously, Kelly's 1951 *An American in Paris*.

For their "American in Paris" ballet, Balanchine and Toland had worked out an elaborate plan. It was already on the shooting schedule, all sets and costumes made, camera angles plotted, and the choreography completed. Proud of their work, they excitedly showed it to Sam Goldwyn, who was maneuvered by the enthusiastic Balanchine from one odd-angled camera position to another, insisting that the studio head view each segment through the aperture of the constantly moving camera. Goldwyn was more irritated than impressed. "He thought [he'd settle into his chair]," said Vera Zorina, "and see us pretty girls dancing around . . . . Instead, he had to move his chair every three minutes."[14]

It all was too arty for Goldwyn. "The miners in Harrisburg won't understand it" was his alleged verdict. Zorina was appalled: "He didn't seem to understand that Balanchine was way ahead of his game in choreographing for the camera and not the theatre."[15] The "American in Paris" ballet was dropped from the shooting schedule. Balanchine was furious. He walked out for two weeks (taking Zorina with him), even though he was still under contract to provide more ballets.

It was Vernon Duke who saved the day. Ira Gershwin called him in to help finish the picture for which his brother had created his last songs and in which his buddy the "Tiflis pixie" (Duke's nickname for Balanchine) was making his film debut.[16] Duke stepped in to help tie up musical loose ends and write the remaining ballet scores. He now helped persuade Balanchine to stay. Back together again, the old *Ziegfeld Follies* team—Duke, Balanchine, and Ira Gershwin—went to work. Balanchine and Duke created two ballets ("Water Nymph" and "Romeo and Juliet"). "Romeo and Juliet" retains the blending of Old and New World forms that was also a subject of the "American in Paris" ballet. The jazz-loving Montagues and classical Capulets battle in music and dance on the streets of an updated Verona to Duke's classical and jazz variations on his and Ira's song "I'm Not Complaining." Juliet (Vera Zorina) and her relatives, members of Balanchine's company, dance on pointe; the Montagues, recruited from the ranks of Hollywood hoofers, "get down" and tap.[17] The dance battle isn't polite (Fig. 4.4a). One ballerina abandons all dignity to end-rush her opponent, knocking her rival unceremoniously onto her bottom. In the end (unlike in Shakespeare's original), the lovers survive, and the two families and the two styles are united (Fig. 4.4b). Not all of "Romeo and Juliet" is jazz influenced, however. Zorina especially loved adagio dancing. "It suited me temperamentally and physically," she said, "with my long legs, high extension, and flexible back."[18] Balanchine gifted his muse with a beautiful Technicolor close-up (Zorina recalls with pain the blinding klieg lights) and a slow pas de deux with William Dollar in which the modern lovers are transported briefly back to Shakespeare's Verona, and Balanchine, as he had in *On Your Toes*, makes much of his ballerina's long legs, one of which, in a remarkably sensual gesture that became a Balanchine signature, she wraps around Romeo to pull him to her.[19] Their tragic end, by poison and sword, is succinctly and touchingly evoked in two small gestures before they sink to the ground. Balanchine and Toland's use of a long, slow dissolve precisely timed to the music is a technique used again and again in movies. As the modern-day lovers stand gazing at each other, their images seem to morph into their Renaissance counterparts. The low-angle camera is used effectively, and the editing, carefully matched to the music,

(a)

(b)

FIGURE 4.4 Balanchine, *The Goldwyn Follies* (film, 1938): The Montagues (tap dancers) and Capulets (ballet dancers) (a) face off and later (b) reconcile.

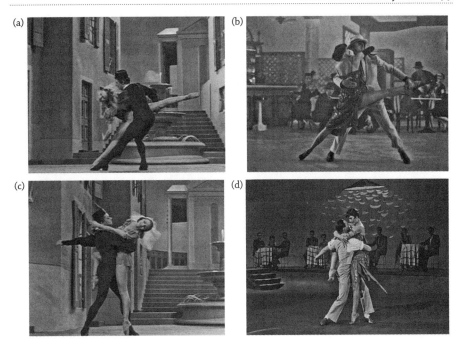

FIGURE 4.5 (a, c) Balanchine, *The Goldwyn Follies* (1938): Zorina and Dollar as Romeo and Juliet in the jazz-meets-classics sequence. (b) Astaire and Charisse, *The Band Wagon* (1953). (d) Kelly and Charisse, *Singin' in the Rain* (1952), Broadway ballet.

moves from a close-up to a long shot without interrupting the shape and momentum of the dance or the dramatic clarity of the story.

Balanchine's use of balletic movement would inform the dances of both Kelly and Astaire. Figure 4.5 compares images from Romeo and Juliet (Figs. 4.5a and c) with Astaire (Fig. 4.5b) and Kelly (Fig.4.5d) each dancing with Cyd Charisse. Charisse is representative of the ballet-trained dancers (like Leslie Caron and Vera-Ellen) who would gradually replace tap dancers in the film musicals in the 1940s and '50s as partners for Astaire and Kelly. Both Balanchine's stretched-out partnered arabesque for Zorina and Dollar (Fig. 4.5a) and Astaire and Charisse's equally stretched out jazz-dance variant (Fig. 4.5b), as well as Zorina's and Charisse's attitude devant position, in which the woman seems to "hook" her partner (Figs. 4.5c–d), call for the turn-out, leg extension and flexibility, foot control, and training that ballet technique provides.

ON YOUR TOES AND STAR SPANGLED RHYTHM

In *The Goldwyn Follies*, New World jazz and Old World classical forms bump up against each other. It's a kind of novelty. But in his next film—*On Your Toes* (1939), a film version of his Broadway show—Balanchine would blend elements of the two forms using more active camerawork as a choreographic element.

FIGURE 4.6 "Slaughter on Tenth Avenue" ballet in *On Your Toes* (film, 1939), the stage musical within the movie, described in the text, including (m) close-up of Zorina's upside-down head during the pas de deux, and (n) Balanchine peering through the camera to gauge the frame composition for this.

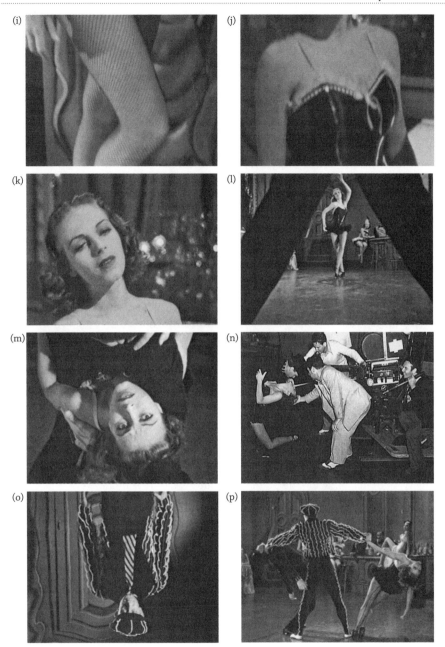

FIGURE 4.6 Continued

The Goldwyn Follies had been a disappointing experience for Balanchine. It is the film by which he is best remembered, but in the end, because of Goldwyn's rejection of the "American in Paris" ballet, he could not do all that he wanted with the film medium. What he accomplished in the film version of *On Your Toes* contains the seeds of a new way of filming dance that would blossom in the generation of dance choreographer moviemakers who followed him.

Balanchine's special approach to dance cinematography is illustrated by his "Slaughter on Tenth Avenue" ballet (Fig. 4.6), which concludes *On Your Toes* and serves as the denouement of the dramatic narrative. Balanchine completely reconceived the "Slaughter on Tenth Avenue" sequence for the camera, setting up shots that employed dramatic changes of lighting, exciting camera angles, the moving-crane camera, and variable film speeds to tell the story of doomed love between a dance-hall girl (Vera Zorina) and her lovestruck "customer" (Eddie Albert).

Here, unlike with *The Goldwyn Follies*, Balanchine was free to use all of the devices he had learned from Toland, Astaire, and Berkeley. The cinematographers of *On Your Toes* were, like Toland, among the best: James Wong Howe filmed the first part of the film, and Sol Polito was the cinematographer for the "Slaughter on Tenth Avenue" ballet. Polito had been the cinematographer for Berkeley's *Gold Diggers of 1933* and *Forty-second Street*, so he was experienced in filming extended dance sequences with the liberal use of the boom camera, moving from close to medium to long shots at varying heights and from different angles, dramatically timed to the split-second changes of lighting and music. The ways Balanchine and Polito combined camerawork, music, mime, and dance to convey dramatic information swiftly and succinctly can be seen by analyzing Albert's first encounter with Zorina as the dance-hall girl. Balanchine starts with a tight close-up of Zorina as she bends over the rim of the stage to caress Albert, her would-be lover, as he reaches up to her from the nightclub floor (Fig. 4.6a). As their faces and hands gently come together, a disembodied hand insinuates itself between them (Fig. 4.6b) and gradually forces Albert's head back (Fig. 4.6c) as the camera pulls back to reveal little by little the figure of her pimp inserting himself between them (Fig. 4.6d). Zorina, whose tender expression becomes increasingly remote, slowly and sadly straightens up, while the pimp holds out his hand for money (Fig. 4.6e), which we see him pocket (Fig. 4.6f). Now he slowly lowers her increasingly limp body to the floor while Albert, offering his hand to the girl, sinks to his knees (Fig. 4.6g). We see a close-up of his hand, in a chivalric gesture, cushioning her foot as it touches the floor (Fig. 4.6h), and the camera sidles up her leg (Fig. 4.6i) past her torso (Fig. 4.6j) to her head (Fig. 4.6k).

In the seduction dance that follows, Balanchine uses the moving camera to dramatize the couple's growing attraction, which climaxes when we see Zorina slink toward Albert, framed by his spread legs, through which the camera glides toward her (Fig. 4.6l). As Zorina succumbs to Albert's embrace, Balanchine arranges a close-up of Zorina upside down (Fig. 4.6m; this is the shot that Balanchine is shown setting up in Fig. 4.6n). Cradled by Albert, she bends back in his arms only to see the pimp approach—seen from her point of view, upside down—to interrupt their reverie (Fig. 4.6o). Now the gradual pushing-away gesture and the slow camera pull-back that began their encounter ends it as the pimp once again inserts himself between the two lovers. The camera gradually pulls back, and we see the pimp standing between them, pushing their bodies until they tilt away from him on either side like an opening fan (Fig. 4.6p).

Both Berkeley and Astaire are influences here. Berkeley's camera had dollied through the spread legs of a long line of generic chorus girls in a *Gold Diggers* movie filmed by Polito, but here the technique is used to tell an intimate and personal danced love story. Dramatic close-ups of Zorina as the camera zooms in and out are a visual theme of the ballet, but these close-ups never interrupt the shape and momentum of Zorina's actual dancing, in which Balanchine follows Astaire's model by keeping his distance, being sure to frame her so that she has enough room to shape the space within the frame, although the angle is kept low to lengthen the legs.

To be sure, some of the close-ups are there for purely practical purposes as well, for Balanchine was working with a number of big handicaps. While the camerawork and mime are impressive, the dancing isn't. Eddie Albert was not a trained dancer. For the dance sequence, originally done by Ray Bolger on Broadway, Balanchine employed Herbie Harper (uncredited), whose presence the cinematographer disguises by focusing on his legs and feet. To make this interesting, Balanchine choreographs the "corpse's" convulsive response to Junior's furious kicks and stomps. Zorina, too, looks awkward. Like many of her generation of ballet dancers, she could not maintain the speed, the musical precision, and, above all, the "flow" that Balanchine so admired in jazz dancers and would breed into his next generation of ballet dancers.

In this sequence, Balanchine uses variable film speeds to speed up or slow down the movement. A comic mime scene between two waiters is speeded up to hilarious effect, and the transition back to normal speed is synergized so beautifully with the music one doesn't notice the "bump."[20]

Rodgers' score for the film ballet "Slaughter on Tenth Avenue" is driven by dance and mime and coordinated with camerawork as well. Balanchine uses Rodgers's sensuous, stretched-out signature melodic theme as a leitmotif for the lovers throughout the ballet at especially intimate moments. It accompanies their very first encounter (Fig. 4.6a). It repeats as the camera sidles up Zorina's leg (Fig. 4.6i), and it accompanies Zorina as she moves sensuously toward Albert, framed by his legs (Fig. 4.6l). Finally, it accompanies Albert as he tenderly picks up his lover's dead body. Various musical devices are used to highlight body movements. Glissandos, for example, emphasize the arc of Zorina's arms, and also her entire body, as she somersaults backward. The melody of the children's nursery-rhyme song "Three Blind Mice," a slang term for police, accompanies them when they invade the speakeasy in which the action takes place.

Balanchine was fascinated by filmmaking, and he worked hard to provide Zorina with special settings and brilliant cinematic effects. A successful example is a segment of *Star Spangled Rhythm*, one of the many patriotic movies produced during World War II to boost morale both among the troops and on the home front. It was made in 1942, not too long after the Japanese attack on Pearl Harbor, and it relates to Kelly's and

Astaire's interest in special effects. A lonely soldier somewhere in the hot Pacific sings to an autographed pin-up of Vera Zorina. He falls asleep and dreams of his glamour girl dancing through a fantastic winter landscape. At the end of the sequence, Zorina seems to step from the picture frame onto his bedside table: he reaches for her just as she begins to dissolve into nothingness.

Here the romantic conceit of nineteenth-century ballet is updated and Americanized. The romantic prince who searches vainly for his beloved is replaced by an ordinary GI Joe, and the song "That Old Black Magic," by Harold Arlen and Johnny Mercer, describes his feelings in contemporary American vernacular: he's "in a spin, loving the spin I'm in" under her spell. This sequence was also cited for outstanding cinematography in a 1943 issue of *American Cinematographer*. The stunning backlighting and shimmering snow effects are the result of Balanchine's collaboration with another extremely inventive cinematographer, John Seitz (inventor of the matte shot), and he worked out the pioneering effect that ends the sequence with Edward Jennings.

Balanchine's exciting use of a swiftly moving camera on a crane gives the viewer the sense of gliding along with Zorina as she darts through the snowy landscape—a forecast of Kelly's street dances, in which the same effect is used. This sequence is so seamlessly edited that it seems to take place in one long unbroken shot, yet at least nine different camera set-ups were used. This means that Zorina faced the formidable task of maintaining the illusion of a unified flow of movement even though she was constantly interrupted while the bulky camera was shifted to capture her from different angles.

THE WATER NYMPH BALLET AND OTHER WORK WITH ZORINA

Most of Balanchine's contribution to film has gone unrecognized, however, for it is another *Goldwyn Follies* sequence, the Water Nymph ballet, for which Balanchine is most often remembered as a filmmaker. This may have something to do with Goldwyn, who scotched the "American in Paris" ballet but was extremely proud of the Water Nymph ballet. The studio publicity department let it be known that "great art" was being created on the Goldwyn lot, and Goldwyn himself proudly escorted a stream of reporters to view the filming. Goldwyn gave Balanchine star treatment—unusual for a mere "dance director," as choreographers were known at that time in the movies. Photographers were dispatched to capture his arrival in Hollywood. Balanchine's dancers were provided with luxuries unheard of by ordinary Hollywood hoofers: special practice spaces were built to Balanchine's specifications, and private rest areas, lined with cots for the dancers to stretch out on, were created on the soundstage. One of Balanchine's dancers, Ted Weamer, remembers their special drinks wagon, laden with Cokes on ice. Hollywood stars such as Marlene Dietrich and Gary Cooper made pilgrimages to view the Russian ballet master and his company of toe dancers. As long as he lived, Goldwyn would screen the Water Nymph ballet as a kind of "dessert" to impress dinner guests at his Hollywood home.

For Goldwyn, Balanchine's ballet was a sign of his and his studio's contribution to high culture. And indeed, the Water Nymph ballet comes closest to some of the ballets Balanchine created for Diaghilev (and later for the Ballet Russe de Monte Carlo). The Water Nymph ballet and Duke's score, with its echoes of Ravel and Debussy, could easily have fit into a Diaghilev program of the late 1920s or a Ballet Russe de Monte Carlo program of the early 1930s. The influences are largely European, and jazz is nowhere evident: the choreography for Vera Zorina and members of Balanchine's American Ballet company combine pointe work with lyrical adagio movement that shows the influence of modern dance.

Watched from the shadows by her would-be lover, Zorina, clad in a short, tight gold tunic, slowly rises, dripping, from a pool of water framed by a Greek colonnade (Fig. 4.7a). ("Will be verrry sexy!" Balanchine gleefully promised his ballerina.) Zorina is welcomed and dressed by handmaidens and goes on to waltz happily with an adoring young mortal, played by a tuxedoed William Dollar, surrounded by revelers reminiscent of the guests of Balanchine's European party ballets such as *Cotillon*. All too soon, though, a warning from the gods in the form of a windstorm disrupts their revels, and the nymph returns reluctantly to her watery home.

Again Balanchine uses a standard romantic ballet conceit. The water nymph, or undine, is one of those elusive romantic heroines that were so popular in the nineteenth century. She is a mythical creature, like the Sylph in *La sylphide* or the Swan Queen in *Swan Lake*—or, in literature, Hans Christian's Andersen's Little Mermaid. But this theme is updated in a semi-Surrealist set with echoes of de Chirico—the neoclassical sculptured horse that rears up in the background appeared also in Balanchine and de Chirico's ballet *Le bal* (1929) for Diaghilev's Ballets Russes. But whatever the setting, the nymph is an unattainable ideal: men pursue this beautiful and mysterious female, but she remains always just beyond their reach.

The Water Nymph ballet was hilariously parodied two years later in Walt Disney's own contribution to high culture, *Fantasia* (1940), and Balanchine seemed to enjoy the joke. The reference to Balanchine's Water Nymph ballet is now lost on audiences, but during its own time, many would have recognized it. Instead of the slender Zorina, a humongous hippo rises from a pool of water framed, as in the Balanchine ballet,

FIGURE 4.7 (a) Vera Zorina in Balanchine's Water Nymph ballet in *Ziegfeld Follies* (film, 1946). (b) The dancing hippo in Walt Disney's *Fantasia* (1940).

by a Greek colonnade (Fig. 4.7b). Hippo handmaidens clothe her in a delicate, transparent tutu (totally inadequate to conceal her acres of flesh). A windstorm disrupts their revels, with disastrous results.[21] Marge Champion, who was later to become, with her husband, Gower Champion, one of moviedom's most prominent dancers, and who was trained by her father, Ernest Belcher, a respected British ballet master who settled in Hollywood and opened a school, modeled the movements for the hippo in pointe shoes. She saw the parody as for the most part an affectionate one. Champion idolized Vera Zorina and viewed her as a role model. *Fantasia* has continued to influence generations of children all over the world on video and DVD, and its brilliant parody is often an American kid's first introduction to ballet.

Balanchine's contribution to dance in film is now largely forgotten except for its very weak echo in *Fantasia*. Years later, as he was writing his autobiography, Minnelli, who had been so happily nourished by his work with Balanchine in the Broadway *Ziegfeld Follies of 1936*, found the Water Nymph ballet disappointing. It is interesting to speculate, though, what would have happened had Gershwin not died and Goldwyn not shut down the "American in Paris" ballet, with its fascinating camera angles and juxtaposition of jazz and ballet, or if Gershwin had lived to create the "Swing Symphony" ballet with Balanchine and Toland. The echoes of Balanchine's "American in Paris" ballet exist in the Minnelli-Kelly *American in Paris*, and we know that the two men spent hours with Ira Gershwin sifting through his brother's unpublished and forgotten songs. They undoubtedly saw his and Balanchine's own scenario for *An American in Paris*. Kelly, of course, completely rechoreographed the ballet, and he and Minnelli not only plotted their own camera angles and movement, but also reedited the score to fit Kelly's choreography. But the echoes of Balanchine's ballet remain as Kelly's tap-dancing American, like Balanchine's Draper, chases his elusive ballerina ideal (Leslie Caron) through the Paris of his own imagination. Powerful echoes of "Slaughter on Tenth Avenue" (both the Broadway and film versions) remain, in subject, style, and innovative camerawork, in Kelly's own rechoreographed "Slaughter on Tenth Avenue" for *Words and Music* (1948) as well as his speakeasy pas de deux with Cyd Charisse in the Broadway ballet in *Singin' in the Rain*. The same holds as well for Astaire's dance with Charisse in the final sequence of "The Girl Hunt Ballet," choreographed by Michael Kidd in Minnelli and Astaire's *The Band Wagon*.

Balanchine's attempt at technical innovation bombed in *I Was an Adventuress* (1942), when, working with cinematographer Edward Cronjager, he created a twelve-minute *Swan Lake* which is in some ways brilliantly and inventively filmed—until a moment at the very end, when size relationships become a problem. Balanchine's "Lake of the Swans" sequence was featured in the publicity for *I Was an Adventuress*:

> Lasting 12 minutes, the longest ballet yet presented on the screen, the story is unfolded in a weird fog effect. A score of fog machines vaporized mineral oil, partially condensed it with dry ice and blew it across a huge sound stage. Balanchine figured out a slow motion technique by which the camera could record Zorina's famous leaps without blurring them. With cinematographer Edward Cronjager,

he made 200 tests before he evolved the right speed for clearly showing Zorina in the air and yet not slowing her up too much.

The studio used 40,000 square feet of quarter inch plate glass, costing 15,000 dollars, for the first all-glass set constructed in Hollywood. Art directors Richard Day and Joseph C. Wright created a forest, a lake, and a castle. The glass was first hung and then cut into the right shapes. At the finish of the film, the set was destroyed, inasmuch as the glass was too fragile, after being cut into lacy tree shapes, to be moved.

The studio gave the picture one of the longest shooting schedules in Hollywood this season, 97 days. Balanchine rehearsed the ballet scenes for one month. Filming of the dance required a week.[22]

After *Star Spangled Rhythm*, Balanchine increasingly devoted his attention to building the company that would become the New York City Ballet and to the School of American Ballet. His relationship with Zorina, his Broadway and movie muse, also came to an end. But Balanchine then adopted a new muse, Maria Tallchief. With Tallchief he would explore further the lessons he had learned from his experiences on Broadway and in the movies and exploit his intensive study of Astaire in order to alter and extend the classical ballet tradition of which he was a part in the making of modern ballets for the New York City Ballet, to which he would devote the remainder of his life.

Balanchine still maintained his ties with Hollywood, however, and always considered working again in movies. A project to make a movie of the life of Anna Pavlova, with Tamara Toumanova and Igor Youskevitch, got him excited but was never fully funded. He happily accepted Goldwyn's commission to choreograph the film *Hans Christian Andersen* (1952), but when the projected shooting schedule had to be shifted and came into conflict with the New York City Ballet's season at City Center, he withdrew from the project. (Roland Petit ended up choreographing the movie.) Balanchine nonetheless had an impact on the story. Francis Goldwyn, Sam Goldwyn's wife, who often advised her husband, recorded Balanchine's extensive comments to her, and the typescript exists in the Goldwyn papers.

Balanchine and Nicholas Nabokov also collaborated on a script for a projected movie of *Nutcracker*. It never materialized, but it was resurrected from his files after Balanchine saw *Star Wars*. Enthralled by this fantasy and its special effects, he tried to interest George Lucas in the project but was unsuccessful.[23]

ASTAIRE INFLUENCES BALANCHINE

I began this chapter by discussing how Balanchine and the diaspora of Russian ballet influenced both the Gershwins and Astaire in *Shall We Dance*. But Astaire also influenced Balanchine. Balanchine's groundbreaking work *The Four Temperaments* (1947), a radical alteration and expansion of the ballet tradition in which he was raised, "is steeped in George's contemplation of Astaire," insists Tallchief, the choreographer's wife and dance muse. "As a result, it marked a new beginning, a conscious departure from the Maryinski for him." Tallchief's performance in this ballet was famous. "Rehearsing and performing the ballet and discovering what George was doing firsthand was thrilling."[24] *The Four Temperaments* and other works of the 1940s and '50s, *Orpheus* and *Agon*, as well as *Allegro Brillante* and *Symphony in C*, would transform the look of the American ballerina and American ballet in general, and its influence would spread around the globe.

Tallchief's argument for Astaire's influence is backed up not just by the written word, but, perhaps more convincingly, by the videotapes she created for the Balanchine Foundation to document how the ballet master worked with her. In the tapes she coaches young dancers in the roles Balanchine created for her at this crucial time in his career. In each session Tallchief, in a long-standing ballet tradition, employs one of the dancer-choreographer's most common and powerful teaching tools: metaphor and visual demonstration. She shows the movement to them and at the same time gives them a verbal metaphor or simile—a word or phrase that suggests not just the precise body position but the subtle feel, look, and quality of the position. Tallchief's most consistent and vivid descriptor in every one of these coaching sessions and interviews is "like Fred Astaire"—even in ballets that appear, in costume and music, to be from very different worlds. From the overtly modernist ballets *Four Temperaments* (music by Hindemith) and *Orpheus* (Stravinsky) to Balanchine's nineteenth-century music ballets—the "tutu" (or sometimes short-skirt) ballets—*Allegro Brillante* (Tchaikovsky) and *Symphony in C* (Bizet), she again and again cites Astaire's ways of moving to describe the way Balanchine wanted his dancers to look and dance. In *Allegro Brillante*, for example, Tallchief uses Astaire to demonstrate Balanchine's new dynamic, streamlined look for the dancer's body (Fig. 4.8a; cf. Astaire and Charisse in Fig. 4.8b).

The streamlined, dynamic diagonal line was a hallmark of Astaire's work, and it undermines key rules and assumptions of classical ballet: the emphasis on symmetry, equilibrium, and balance. When a classical dancer goes off balance in a nineteenth-century ballet, she recovers it before she goes on. When she jumps, she seems to resist the pull of gravity by remaining upright in the air and landing in a balanced and stable pose. Balanchine, like Astaire, was not interested in stability and security; he was interested in dynamism, in the thrill of the vector created by a diagonal as opposed to the stability of the vertical standing position. "Not so much turnout," Tallchief counsels her dancers. "Streamlined . . . like Astaire." She warns them, too, not to interrupt the flow of the diagonal line created by the body from head to toe.[25] In the score, the step is actually labeled the "Fred Astaire step"—turned in and pushing away with the arms, with her partner behind her (see again Figs. 4.8a and b).[26]

Tallchief also asks the dancers to "flow" from one step to another, without breaking the continuity of the movement with an intermediate step that prepares for the next, as is common in classical ballet. "He loved the smooth flow of Astaire," says Rosemary Dunleavy, who worked with Balanchine and, with her photographic memory, is in

(a)  (b)

FIGURE 4.8 (a) Maria Tallchief teaching an "Astaire" pose to demonstrate Balanchine's new dynamic, streamlined look for the dancer's body. She is coaching Deanna Seay of Miami City Ballet in *Allegro Brillante*, choreography by George Balanchine © The George Balanchine Trust. Courtesy of the George Balanchine Foundation Interpreters Archive and the George Balanchine Trust, Miami Beach, Florida, January 1999. Photo Bryon Rushton. (b) Astaire and Charisse, *The Band Wagon* (1953).

charge of maintaining the repertory at the New York City Ballet.[27] The "seams don't show" when a dancer moves from one position to another.

Balanchine continued to refer to Astaire and his flow many years after Tallchief's era. Paul Boos, who danced in the New York City Ballet during Balanchine's last decade and now mounts Balanchine ballets worldwide for the Balanchine Trust, says that Balanchine regularly referred to Astaire in rehearsal, most often using him as a supreme model of a dancer who flowed seamlessly from one movement to another through space—a quality that Balanchine very much wanted in, and in some ways even insisted on, in his own ballets. Balanchine did not like the look of dancers who, constrained by ballet's traditional rules of preparation for every step and an abstract, geometrical ideal of shape, were unable to achieve flow.[28]

There are other references to Astaire penciled in throughout Balanchine dance scores. "Fred and Ginger" is one, and it indicates another of Astaire's influences on Balanchine's choreography. "He loved Astaire's partnering," says Dunleavy. For Balanchine, as for Astaire, couple dancing (ballet's pas de deux) was a key form. Balanchine turned away from the shadowing, supportive role of the male in the adagio section of the nineteenth-century pas de deux. Man and woman move constantly and interact continually. There is a real give and take as they circle each other, exchange places with arms and fingertips linked in ever varying patterns, and move in close, then pull away. And Balanchine, like Astaire, explores counterbalance, often going beyond his model as his dancers tilt precariously away from one another. Like the swing-out movement in the Lindy hop, which Astaire also loved, each partner does his or her part in holding them both up.

Many the qualities that Balanchine uses in his ballets are derived from the Africanist elements of jazz dance that he encountered before he left Europe.[29] His work with Josephine Baker and his observation of other black performers in Paris are part of the picture, just as Astaire himself was powerfully influenced by Africanist styles. In Astaire, however, Balanchine saw someone who, like himself, blended a variety of influences, including ballet, to create a style that wasn't tap dance, wasn't ballroom dance, and wasn't traditional ballet, but combined elements of them all to create a new style.

He saw Astaire, for example, as someone for whom the pas de deux was a key form. Balanchine loved Astaire's partnering. "He loved the way Astaire presented the woman," says Dunleavy—the interaction between the male and female dancer, as opposed to the shadowing and supportive role of the late nineteenth-century male dancer. Balanchine also loved the way Astaire used his hands and fingers in partnering, avoiding tight, heavy, bunched-up grips. In one of the loveliest moments in *Allegro Brillante*, Balanchine uses a partnering technique often employed by Astaire that can also be found in European social dance, in which its roots may lie: instead of holding hands, the woman rests her hand and upper arm gently on top of her partner's outstretched arm.

Balanchine also saw Astaire as someone who could use dance to create and develop a dramatic relationship between a man and a woman—not the detailing of a specific narrative, but a multilayered relationship between two people. Balanchine today is popularly known as the creator of plotless, "pure dance" ballets, and he is associated with similar movements in the mid-twentieth-century visual arts. But no matter how stripped down Balanchine's costumes and sets were, no matter how abstract his titles, Balanchine created a world of human relationships onstage. "There is no such thing as abstract ballet," Balanchine often said. "Put a man and a woman onstage, and you already have a story."[30] In Astaire's partner dances Balanchine saw a model that eloquently spoke to and inspired him as an example of modern American relationships.

Perhaps most of all, he loved Astaire's freedom, says Dunleavy. Astaire, as we have seen, was interested in the concept of line—the creation of beautiful shapes in space, but without sacrificing the flow of movement—especially at high speed. In ballet, the dancer tries to achieve an abstract geometric ideal not just when at rest, but in movement from one moment to the next. It is an unachievable goal, although its illusion can sometimes be sustained onstage for brief periods by consummate artists. Astaire was not committed to maintaining a perfect shape at all times onstage, and the shape he carved out in space was a more natural configuration of the human body—turned in with feet parallel, along with the aesthetic acknowledgment of the body's many joints (broken or cocked wrists) rather than an unbroken line. Like Astaire and his African American predecessors, Balanchine activated the pelvic area—movement initiated from the pelvis and leading with the hip.

Like African American dancers, Balanchine loved drags, slides, and chugs—but like Astaire, he developed and expanded the line created by these movements and used it with dancers on pointe. Rather than placing the foot carefully and precisely in one position or another, dancers on pointe as well as in flat shoes could drag or slide the foot from one position to the other—*Agon* is a good example, and so is *Rubies*, and of course *Who Cares?* But even in more romantic ballets, drags can be spotted.

One of the most striking things that Balanchine learned from Astaire was his way of shifting weight—that is, transferring the weight from one foot to another, as we all do when we move. Tallchief and Arthur Mitchell cite *Symphony in C*, in fact, as the work in which Balanchine showed them how to "move like Astaire." At first, *Symphony in C* looks like a standard classical ballet, about as far away from Balanchine's modernist ballets such as *The Four Temperaments* as you can get. A really close look at its inner workings, however, shows something else. Here's Tallchief:

> I also believe that Astaire was in the back of George's mind when he worked on *Theme and Variations* and *Palais de Cristal* [now known as *Symphony in C*]. I'd already seen that George used a step in both I'd seen in many of his ballets. It was a kind of jeté, which is a jump in which the weight of the body is thrown from one foot to the other. Astaire performed it in several of his films; he didn't do in it the classical style though, he didn't do what we call the temps lié, step, jeté combination. After all he was dancing in tap shoes. But his body moved just the way George wanted his dancer's bodies to move.[31]

Arthur Mitchell also points to *Symphony in C* to explain how Balanchine wanted his dancers to be able to shift their weight, to move off center, to tilt on a diagonal, and, as he says, to "dance on the edge" but still feel centered and in control, both in his radically modernist works such as *The Four Temperaments* and *Agon* and in more "classical" works such as *Symphony in C* and *Theme and Variations*.

> I would say that the ballet that taught me most how to move in *Agon* was in *Symphony in C* . . . . It's off the leg into the hip using jazz. I was off-center, but even when you are off-center you are still centered . . . . You take a triangle and you move it on its axis; it is still centered. A lot of people fall to the side and think it's off-centered, but it's a tilt. I understood the breaking down, that I could be off-centered. Understanding that, I could be off-center but still be centered. That was what was exciting for me . . . . I like living on the edge, but to able to dance on the edge—when you hit it there is a sense of joy.[32]

"If I were living in a different country," said Balanchine, "I would choreograph differently. I choreograph for American speed and kinetic energy." Ballet traces its beginning to lessons of grace and etiquette: the unhurried, serene, and modestly contained movements that were meant to signify nobility of character and status. But, as Balanchine counseled his dancers, "Don't be polite!"[33] The fearless, space-eating vitality of his dancers reflected the behavior he saw all around him in America, and in the dancers in the movies as well.

EPILOGUE: *CABIN IN THE SKY* ON BROADWAY

The all-black Broadway musical *Cabin in the Sky*, Balanchine and Duke's next project, premiered on October 25, 1940. It climaxed the young Russian friends' almost fifteen-year relationship, and was their most ambitious and personally meaningful undertaking, one on which they were producers as well as creators. Balanchine, who instigated the project, invested his life savings when he and Duke failed to get enough backers.[34]

Cabin in the Sky was conceived by its creators as a musical-theater piece, but in some ways it tried to do in dance what *Porgy and Bess* had done in opera: portray the lives of rural African Americans in a dance form that grew, in part, from a fusion of Franco-Russian and Africanist dance. Its all-black cast included such members of the original *Porgy and Bess* cast as Todd Duncan and Rex Ingram. As Gershwin had done for *Porgy and Bess*, Balanchine went beyond urban jazz resources to the roots of African American culture. In Paris, London, and New York Balanchine had seen and loved the North American urban versions of black dances: the Charleston, snake hips, rhythm tap, the Lindy hop. Now, like Gershwin, he went further—but not to the Carolina islands.

Instead, Balanchine sought out the young African American dancer-choreographer and anthropologist Katherine Dunham. Originally from Chicago, Dunham had done her research in Haiti on the Afro-Caribbean dances developed by slaves shipped to the Caribbean and their descendants. She had initially trained in ballet with a Russian teacher in Chicago, Lumilla Speranzeva. Her own choreography and the technique she eventually developed blended elements of her Russian ballet training with her discoveries in the field—adding isolations of the shoulders, torso, and hips and other elements from her Caribbean research as well as elements of Latin American, African American, and modern dance. Balanchine admired her work, and when she opened a school in New York, he sent his students to study with her.[35]

Although originally uncredited, Dunham is now recognized as the co-choreographer with Balanchine of the Broadway *Cabin in the Sky*. We know from Dunham herself that she and Balanchine worked together to blend their dance ideas. The choreography has been lost, but we can assume that Balanchine studied Dunham and her troupe's distinctive ways of moving and collaborated creatively with her to help organize, arrange, edit, and enhance an overall result that fit with the dramatic narrative of the show and worked with the music devised by Duke. Balanchine admired and encouraged her movement style—especially her free use of the "pelvic girdle"—and, with his pluralistic approach, he would have added his observation of Dunham's movement vocabulary, along with Baker's and Astaire's, to the crucible in which he was creating his own outlaw style. Dunham spoke of their choreography as a "merging," and herself used a metaphor similar to the melting pot: it was "a kind of making a cake batter, very smooth, you know, and not picking out little bits of it here and there."[36]

Although Dunham and Balanchine worked well together, they were forced, as with Josephine Baker, to deal with racist assumptions about what types of dance were "appropriate" for blacks. Dunham's style was far removed from tap dance. Halfway through the rehearsal period, the backers began to pressure Balanchine to include the upbeat tap-dance numbers that they believed the public expected of an all-black show. They secretly lined up another choreographer and threatened to fire Balanchine. Balanchine, along with Duke and set designer Boris Aaronson, stood firm, and in the end they won—but, as Dunham commented sadly, this was the kind of treatment that whites wanting to work with African Americans would have to struggle against over and over.[37]

Constance Valis Hill has written a convincing argument for *Cabin in the Sky*'s placement alongside such landmark "Americana" musicals as *Oklahoma!*[38] She argues that the African American subject has been a factor in its "non-recognition." For de Mille in *Oklahoma!* the sound and look of American music and dance came from Anglo-American folk songs and dances from Appalachia and the western plains; *Cabin in the Sky* demonstrates once again that for Balanchine and Duke, America's most vital and interesting artistic nourishment came from African Americans, who brought their distinctive and transformational aesthetic to America.

Cabin in the Sky would go on to be made as a movie in 1942, but it was not directed by Balanchine. Rather, it became the film-directorial debut of Vincente Minnelli—the man with whom Balanchine, Duke, and Ira Gershwin had created their first Broadway "ballets" from *Ziegfeld Follies of 1936* ("Words without Music," "Night Flight," and "Five A.M."). In 1940, the year *Cabin in the Sky* opened on Broadway, Minnelli had been brought to MGM by the producer Arthur Freed. Freed, like his friend Ira Gershwin, was himself a lyricist, and his songs with Nacio Herb Brown ("Broadway Melody," "Broadway Rhythm," and "Singin' in the Rain") were written for the earliest film musicals. A great admirer of the Gershwin brothers, Freed adored *Porgy and Bess* and had tried unsuccessfully to acquire it for MGM. *Cabin in the Sky* was his next choice, and he recognized Minnelli as a man who was aesthetically in tune with the composers he admired.

Minnelli would go on to become one of the most distinguished directors of Hollywood film musicals. Supported by Freed's production unit devoted to film musicals, he would promote the use of the dance musical and the film ballet form with Fred Astaire and Gene Kelly, drawing on his experiences with Duke, Ira Gershwin, and Balanchine in *Ziegfeld Follies of 1936*. As we shall see in the next chapter, Gene Kelly, as a dancer-choreographer just coming into prominence, would also respond enthusiastically to Balanchine's innovations on Broadway and to the Diaghilev diaspora. The influence of tap dance would increasingly be diminished by a new pluralist style developed by Kelly and his peers (Jerome Robbins, Charles Walters, Michael Kidd, and Jack Cole) in which elements of ballet technique and extended dance storytelling alongside new forms of jazz dance would become a requirement for younger dancers. Astaire's influence was still foundational, but his own style would be increasingly affected by the change: his partners in the late 1940s and '50s (Vera-Ellen, b. 1921; Cyd Charisse, b. 1922; Leslie Caron, b. 1931) would be ballet trained. Modern dance, too, with the codification of its vocabulary in the 1930s by Martha Graham and Doris Humphrey, would also enter the picture (especially with Jack Cole, Agnes de Mille, and Hanya Holm). Importantly, the story of the development of musical-theater dance has overlooked Katherine Dunham's incorporation of syncopated rhythmic elements into the body of the dancer and articulated by isolations of its parts in *Cabin in the Sky*, as well as George Balanchine's use of this style as a storytelling element within the context of a musical.

5

DANCING WITH THE CAMERA

Introducing Kelly and Donen

ONE OF THE young American dancer-chorographers most interested in the new wave of Russian ballet brought by George Balanchine and the Diaghilev diaspora to America was Gene Kelly, who settled in New York in the mid-1930s just as Balanchine, Duke, and Rodgers and Hart were beginning their ascent. Born in 1912, and therefore about half a generation younger than Astaire and Balanchine, Kelly was part of the "swing generation," named for the new variant of jazz that came with the advent of the big band and the Lindy hop era. By the time he was in his twenties, sound cinema was well established, and Astaire-Rogers movies were the rage. Tap flourished in Harlem and on Broadway. So did the interest in the relationship of New World and Old World musics and dance exemplified by Balanchine and the Gershwins in *On Your Toes* and by Astaire and Rogers in *Shall We Dance*. Balanchine had opened his new School of American Ballet, and by 1935 his American Ballet Company was ensconced as the resident dance company of the Metropolitan Opera. By 1940 a new company, Ballet Theatre (later American Ballet Theatre), was in operation. Modern dance, increasingly dominated by the post-Isadora and Denishawn generation of Martha Graham, Doris Humphrey, and Charles Weidman, was growing more and more prominent. Kelly's swing-generation peers in dance included Charles Walters (b. 1911), Jack Cole (b. 1911), Michael Kidd (b. 1915), and Jerome Robbins (b. 1918), all of whom, like Kelly, would go on to work in musical films and be influenced by this rich stylistic atmosphere. (Agnes de Mille too, although born earlier, in 1905, would rise to her greatest fame in musical theater in the 1940s with *Oklahoma!* She drew on ballet, modern dance, and American folk dance but was not particularly interested in jazz dance.)

Like Astaire, Kelly wanted to craft his own style to the music of Gershwin, Kern, and Porter, and like Astaire, he would choose to work in the no-limitations atmosphere of Broadway and musical films, where he would combine his knowledge of a variety of styles—and, following Astaire, of everyday movement—to set the music of American popular song, first in musical theater and then in film.[1]

Kelly's dance education was (like that of Astaire and others of his time and place) typically eclectic. While Astaire, an intuitive creator, hesitated to classify and analyze his work, Kelly clearly recognized that his style was pluralist, a "freewheeling mixture" of various styles of dance and sports based on "the beat of our jazz music and on the melodies of our native composers."[2]

Unlike Astaire and Balanchine, who came of age in the teens and twenties, Kelly and his generation were shaped by the Great Depression (he was sixteen at the time of the stock market crash) and then by World War II. These two cataclysmic events would strongly affect his attitudes toward life and dance as well as his subject matter. Also unlike Astaire, Kelly arrived at the idea of professional dancing relatively late. Coming from a proud, upwardly mobile Irish family, Kelly was headed to university, and for his family the purpose of dancing was not only to learn deportment but also to earn money for his education and keep themselves afloat during the Depression. He and his siblings were sent to dancing school by their mother, who wanted them to have, as Kelly put it, culture and the advantages of the upper middle classes.

Kelly's younger brother, Fred, had ambitions for the stage, but Kelly, who majored in economics at the University of Pittsburgh, was destined for law school. Early on, though, he learned from his dance classes that, like his brothers and sisters, he had talent and could pick up steps quickly—and that he truly loved movement of any kind. His training was eclectic, a "mélange of many things," including basic ballet and ballroom dancing. He also learned Irish step dancing, in which the body is held upright and the legs execute wonders of tricky footwork, and performed with Fred and the rest of the family. Gene was particularly impressed by the vitality of George M. Cohan, whom he saw in *Little Nellie Kelly* when he was seven years old. (He quotes the "Cohan walk" in the "American in Paris" ballet as a signature American move.)

Kelly also found that he had a talent for teaching kids to dance, putting on shows for neighborhood organizations. Eventually the Kelly family would take over a dance school, increasing its success by naming it after its talented and most famous son. Kelly's dances involving children would become a hallmark of his repertory. His mother helped manage the school, and teaching was a family affair. Kelly approached his dance studies with a perfectionism that would become legendary, and he had a photographic memory for dance. He picked up dance steps from the vaudeville and musical-theater performers who played Pittsburgh as a tryout city. He remembered later seeing the Ziegfeld and George White shows.

Like Astaire, Kelly learned by watching and learning from the African American dancers Frank Harrington and (like Balanchine) Clarence "Dancing" Dotson, and he later remembered being impressed by both Bill Robinson and John Bubbles. Dotson's originality impressed Kelly, who admitted to "pinching several of his steps" for his own use.[3] But although Kelly, like Astaire, admired and learned from African American tap dancers, his approach to tap, unlike Astaire's, would be powerfully shaped by his initial exposure to Irish dancing. Though he certainly could "swing" when he wanted to, he was not as focused as Astaire on the off-the-beat aspect of tap and the unexpected starts, stops, and explosions of "crazy" rhythm that lay at the heart of Astaire's dancing. Kelly favored balanced and symmetrical phrasing and more regularized patterns—one phrase to the left, another to the right, with clearly defined, repetitive cadence patterns—that sometimes ended with acrobatic steps. (Minnelli called them "flag-waving" steps.) His tap embroidery created a balanced filigree of sound that enhanced rather than played against an underlying pulse.[4]

But Kelly's approach to tap was even more powerfully influenced by the ballet boom of the 1930s—both by the innovations brought to Broadway in the Balanchine–Rodgers and Hart musicals and by the Diaghilev diaspora as represented by the Ballet Russe de Monte Carlo. In 1933 the company came to Pittsburgh, where, the first night, he saw works by Fokine, Balanchine, and Nijinsky. He was enthralled. Like most Americans, he had never seen a professional ballet company of truly high caliber, and he described it as a revelation, a "life-changing" experience, that would motivate to him to switch from his pre-law studies to pursuing a career in dance.[5] Captivated at the first performance, he cut all his classes and went to see them every night of their run. He became, by his own admission, "a balletomane," traveling to New York regularly to see them, and to see other performances of ballet whenever he could.

Crucially, these experiences introduced Kelly to the innovations of the three choreographers whose work entranced him that first night in Pittsburgh. Kelly marveled at their varied dance vocabularies. Following Fokine's theories, they took new kinds of subjects for dance and altered and expanded the vocabulary of academic ballet to fit with the stories they told or moods they conveyed—from Fokine's nonnarrative but historically evocative homage to French romantic ballet, *Les sylphides*, to Nijinsky's *Afternoon of a Faun*, which traced a brief, lustful encounter between a nymph and a satyr, its dance vocabulary modeled on the stylized postures of these mythological characters on ancient Greek pottery and concluding with a convulsive hip thrust mimicking ejaculation. Then there was Balanchine's witty dance story *La concurrence*, about the rivalry between two fashionable tailors in a small French town. With designs by the Fauvist André Derain (who had also designed Balanchine's *Jack in the Box*) and music by the French composer Georges Auric, the ballet introduced Kelly to the French modernism of the Diaghilev Ballets Russes' postwar era, an era that was still very much a part of the sensibility of the subsequent Ballet Russe de Monte Carlo. Full of dramatic incident, this ballet showed the young Kelly the many ways that a story could be told in music and movement alone, from modern full-body mime to dance—mingling dance character portraits of the tailors and their customers to trace the dramatic arc of their rivalry and their eventual reconciliation. A wide range of dance influences yields a fouetté competition between the tailors' two daughters and a solo—described by one of its dancers as "jazzy" and Chaplinesque—by one of the would-be customers (a hobo) who is initially rejected by the tailors but embraced with open arms when he strikes it rich.[6] (Kelly could also have gotten the flavor of jazz dance in Massine's famous solo in his ballet *Union Pacific*, the Ballet Russe de Monte Carlo's attempt at Americana, which entered the company's repertory the following year.)

Kelly was "just crazy" about this kind of ballet, both conceptually and technically. He cites ballet's "immeasurable" gift to him, which, like the sports he played as a teenager, endowed him not only with physical strength and agility but, more important, "a certain kind of line and form" that even the gymnastics he practiced couldn't. This line and form would become a hallmark of his style: Kelly combined the look of a gymnast with some elements of ballet, but Kelly was more like a character dancer (*demicaractère*) than a *danseur noble*. Kelly's proportions, with his compact, muscular frame, would have led in ballet to villager and mime-heavy roles as opposed to those of the nobleman or prince—a type that carried over to the roles he played on film. To be sure, like Astaire and Balanchine, he would streamline the balletic form he used, but his line and look were his own, less idiosyncratically angled and relaxed than Astaire's, his upper body more taut and presentational. Unlike Astaire, too, he liked standing and moving in plié, legs bent slightly at the knees as if always ready to spring—also a quality found in the stance of many sports.[7]

That first encounter with the Ballet Russe de Monte Carlo motivated Kelly to seek out ballet training at the highest level he could find. To this end, when school was over, he went to Chicago to study in the summer with Berenice Holmes at the Chicago National Association of Dance Masters. The American-born Holmes had been the pupil and then partner of the former Diaghilev star dancer Adolph Bolm, who had been trained in the Russian Imperial Ballet tradition and then appeared with Diaghilev's Ballets Russes, where he stunned Paris audiences in their opening 1909 season with his powerful and heroic dancing as the chief warrior in Fokine's *Polovtsian Dances*. Unlike Nijinsky, whose androgynous persona made him perfect for roles such as the Spirit of the Rose, the puppet Petrouchka, and his own half-man, half-animal Faun, Bolm exuded masculinity, and his virtuoso jumps and turns were legendary. He left Diaghilev in 1917 following the company's one and only trip to the United States in 1916–17, remaining in America, where he became an influential teacher in Chicago in the 1920s and San Francisco in the 1930s and '40s. Bolm was also a choreographer. His ballet for Stravinsky's *Apollo*, created in America, preceded Balanchine's— and Berenice Holmes was the first to dance Terpsichore. He also worked briefly in Hollywood.

Through Adeline Genée, Astaire had grown up influenced by the Bournonville tradition, which delighted in quick footwork (*petit allegro*). His training with Cecchetti's protégé Albertieri gave him some connection to the Russian tradition in the sense that the Italian Cecchetti had worked for a time in Russia and then with the Diaghilev company. But Cecchetti's training was more strongly tied to the romantic past. Kelly's teachers and models came from the dancers of the Diaghilev diaspora—like Bolm, who, although exposed to Cecchetti, had also participated in the reforms of Fokine and others. The Russians used higher extensions and more space-eating and higher jumps, and they were known for their powerful, athletic male dancers. Kelly admired Holmes's ability to dance "like a man," the strength of her double turns *en l'air*, and the way she could land in a "perfect fifth [position]." He speaks of his "great rapport" with her and the debt he owed her when she was willing to design a training program for him, with intensive lessons in the summer, after which he would go home to work on his own, like "a boxer in training."[8]

Kelly attributed his accelerating progress in ballet not just to Holmes, but also to the gymnastics in which he had excelled in high school and college. Gymnastics, Kelly explained, gave his body "the same kind of muscular training that you take years of ballet basics to acquire." Gymnastics, like ballet, also "cultivated a long line," and like Astaire, Kelly was aware of its power and visual effectiveness. From ballet Kelly also became acquainted with turnout. Unlike Astaire, he found it useful, although he never developed it to the extent that ballet dancers do. Again from ballet, Kelly would cultivate, to an even greater extent than Astaire, the use of extended legs. Also unlike Astaire, who depended on extensions of ballroom partnering technique, Kelly became intrigued with the concept of ballet partnering, its interdependent sharing of weight, as well as lifts, in which the male carries the female. Cyd Charisse describes the difference between Kelly and Astaire in terms of the use of lifts: her husband, she remembers, could always tell which one she had been rehearsing with by the bruises she would sustain from working out tricky lifts with Kelly.[9]

Like Balanchine, Holmes was open to all forms of dance, and Kelly remembers going with her to jazz clubs at night to watch the dance and music there. (Her mentor, Bolm, had also been open to jazz. His ballet pantomime *Krazy Kat*, named after the popular comic strip and set to early jazz-inspired music of John Alden Carpenter, premiered in 1922, although Kelly would have been too young to have seen it then.) In summer studies in Chicago (a city Kelly visited for at least five years running), he also took classes with the ex–Diaghilev dancer Alexander Kochetovsky, who was known for his prowess in *demi-caractère* and folk dance. Later, when he went to New York, Kelly studied, as Jerome Robbins did later, with Ella Dagonova, an American who had toured with Anna Pavlova. From all these mentors Kelly learned to scrutinize his body for the precise placement, alignment, and shape that classical dance demands.

Kelly also read "everything I could lay my hands on about ballet,"[10] including treatises by Carlo Blasis (1797–1878) and Noverre, and he learned about the reforms of Fokine, whose notion of the modern one-act *ballet d'action* would influence Kelly's film work. Betsy Blair, Kelly's first wife, remembered Kelly reading Arnold Haskell and Cyril Beaumont, critics and historians who helped to introduce the English-speaking world to the history and criticism of ballet and to promote the burgeoning of companies in England inspired by Diaghelev's Ballets Russes.[11] Fokine urged choreographers to abandon the strictly academic vocabulary of a preestablished repertoire of steps and develop whatever movement style expresses "the particular mood of and the period in which the dance is set." Kelly, who conceived of his dances as creating a character and forwarding a plot in what was then being promoted as an integrated musical theater (and eventually film), applied this precept of Fokine's to the dances he created.

Astaire too was an actor-dancer, but Astaire felt comfortable breaking out of his role to provide dances purely for their entertainment value and formal interest—dances only tenuously tied to the plot—and reveling in his ability to create intricate and offbeat rhythms. Kelly's dance movements were, with some exceptions, first and foremost character driven.

In the interest of creating character and atmosphere with his movement, Kelly, to be sure, used tap, but also used foot sounds to tell stories: the cowboy's galloping horse and the chugging locomotive with which he amuses French children in the "I Got Rhythm" sequence in *An American in Paris* are examples, and an even more famous one is the deliciously squishy, waterlogged sound of his taps in *Singin' in the Rain*.[12] They show that Kelly's major interest here was in creating character and atmosphere, rather than in a tap dancer's virtuoso display. Most of his movements in this dance are exquisite variations of everyday movement—usually play. His dance steps are straightforward and on the beat, unlike the rhythm tap of Bubbles and his cohorts, Astaire's idols.

Kelly quickly became aware of the developing ballet scene not only in America, but also in England and the rest of Europe, in response to the Diaghilev company and its spin-offs. He would follow this world, carefully cultivating friendships with its choreographers and dancers and seeing as much ballet as he could; Betsy Blair remembered him sitting through long, technical conversations with Balanchine in Los Angeles. Ninette de Valois recalled visits and chats at the Royal Ballet. Claude Bessy, director of the Paris Opéra Ballet, respected Kelly enormously as a ballet professional. (Kelly's ballet *Pas de dieux* was commissioned by the Paris Opéra Ballet in 1960; Bessy revived it in 2014.)[13] According to the assessment of the ballet dancer and choreographer Igor Youskevitch:

> If Gene had decided to abandon Hollywood and concentrate on stage work, there is no doubt in my mind he could have become a most distinguished and important choreographer. Some of the things he did in "Circus" are evidence of that. And where his own dancing is concerned, although he does not quite have the noble bearing for a Prince Siegfried in *Swan Lake*, if he had continued to work in the field of serious dance, he would surely have been one of the finest character performers in contemporary ballet.[14]

Kelly would later draw on dancers from these companies (including Bessy) for his all-dance movie *Invitation to the Dance* (1956). This was Kelly's heartfelt tribute to the art of ballet, to which he had been introduced on those "life-changing" nights in the company of Diaghilev choreographers. It conveyed his response to the reforms of Fokine and the varying styles of modern ballet. And it allowed him to choreograph for those ballet dancers whom he especially admired: Tamara Toumanova and Diana Adams, both protégées of Balanchine; Igor Youskevitch; and two young French ballerinas, Claude Bessy and the very young Claire Sombert.

Kelly also studied Spanish dancing. Astaire had watched and learned from Eduardo Cansino, Rita Hayworth's father; Kelly studied with her uncle Angel Cansino. He also watched and absorbed ballroom dancing, so popular in the 1930s and '40s. Growing up as he did during the great age of silent cinema, Kelly was influenced too by swashbuckling stars like Douglas Fairbanks Sr., who did his own stunts, scaling castle walls and jumping gracefully from heights and over barriers of every kind. Kelly fell in love with the way Fairbanks moved, recognizing his movement as balletic and citing his "classical air," his "long line," the "style and grace" in his brilliant swordplay, and the tie between fencing and the positions of ballet.

After Kelly graduated from college, he faced a big decision. Would he go on to law school, continue in the successful family dance-school business and choreograph shows for kids in Pittsburgh, or try his luck as a dancer-choreographer in New York? He turned in his first semester's tuition and dropped out of law school.

Kelly had become good enough to audition for and be offered a place in the Ballet Russe de Monte Carlo—but in the end he decided against joining the company.[15] His late start meant that he might never catch up to the great dancers he idolized. Thanks to his expanded viewing experience, he realized that, as much as he loved the Monte Carlo ballet, and for all the modernist innovations that he seen in the Diaghilev repertory, they too were part of the Old World. Kelly shared the view that Balanchine had articulated in his affectionate but wickedly witty parody of Fokine in the Princess Zenobia ballet in *On Your Toes*. Kelly understood that Balanchine too had built on and evolved from the Ballet Russe and was exploring a new look that that drew on the new ways of moving in the distinctive culture of America. Throughout his life, he would point to the New York City Ballet as the key revolutionary movement in American ballet. Outside of Balanchine, he complained, who "years ago had forgotten more than anybody knew, classic ballet was in the same mold."

Besides, Kelly's ambitions had now moved beyond just being a dancer. He saw himself, like Astaire, as a creator, a choreographer. "I knew that I had to find a way to dance my own kind of dance." He wanted to dance to the popular music of his time, and he wanted to do it where that music was valued, in musical theater and film. Accordingly, Kelly looked to make a career in New York and the musical theater. He had been traveling to New York to see dance of all kinds; now he decided to move there. He arrived as the Balanchine–Rodgers and Hart collaborations were at their height, and it is clear that he was aware of Balanchine's work in the Rodgers and Hart shows *On Your Toes* (1936), *Babes in Arms* (1937), *I Married an Angel* (1938), and *The Boys from Syracuse* (1938). Balanchine presented him with a model for how a choreographer could fuse multiple dance influences and vernacular movement, and for how extended dance-drama sequences or "ballets" could be incorporated into a musical and used to move the action forward.

"Slaughter on Tenth Avenue," in both the stage and film versions, of *On Your Toes* clearly made a powerful impression on Kelly. A decade later, in 1948, he would create his own version of "Slaughter" in the Rodgers and Hart biopic *Words and Music*. The sequence followed Balanchine's conception in subject and vague outline but, unsurprisingly, focused more intensely on the male dancer. Balanchine and Polito's camerawork and their use of the musical moving camera and editing to tell a story in dance must have been influences here and would reappear in Kelly's later film ballets (see chapter 9). Kelly's choreography was his own—now in the pluralist style developed by

Kelly and his colleagues of the swing generation.[16] However, our first glimpse of Kelly is surely a modernist take on Nijinsky's Faun: In his first "dance," he slowly wakes up, spread-eagled on a bed in his tiny New York flat, stretching, turning, and testing his limbs, as he prepares for the day. A variation of this would appear later in the opening of *An American in Paris*

All this, however, was a long way off. Kelly's first role was as a specialty dancer in Cole Porter's *Leave It to Me* in 1938, and he won a major role in the John Murray Anderson revue *One for the Money*. He also continued his work as a choreographer in the summer of 1939 at the Westport Country Playhouse, where he met Betty Comden and Adolph Green (who would later write the screenplays for *On the Town* and *Singin' in the Rain*). And Kelly had a hand in choreographing for the stage in New York—not only his own dances for *The Time of Your Life* and *Pal Joey*, but also for the musical *Best Foot Forward* (1941) and for shows at the nightclub Billy Rose's Diamond Horseshoe.

Kelly greatly admired modern dance and dancers and championed their significance as dance revolutionaries, "exploring the outer limits of dance." He saw its creators as colleagues and friends rather than mentors. He did not see them as major influences on his own style. "The big thing I got from modern dance was pure inspiration"; they "broadened my horizons," but "it wasn't my bag." Ever on the lookout for good male dancers to watch, he became friends with Charles Weidman, who actively promoted male dancing in a field dominated by female pioneers, and remembered him with great warmth. Kelly felt was he was "underrated as a dancer"; he admired Weidman's comic ability in his parody of silent films, called *Flickers*. He also admired the young Mexican American José Limón, a protégé of Doris Humphrey, who combined inspiration from modern dance (particularly Humphrey) with music and dance from his own Mexican heritage (e.g., *Danzas mexicanas*, 1937). Limon would also dance in two shows choreographed by Balanchine. Of the matriarchs of modern dance, Kelly himself was impressed by Doris Humphrey, but he idolized Martha Graham ("my goddess"), whom he saw at her annual concerts at Needle Trades High School. He preferred her "far out" works like *Ekstasis* to the more accessible *Appalachian Spring*. *Every Soul Is a Circus* aroused not only his praise but his passion. Kelly told a friend that Graham's dancing made him want to "make love to her . . . except I used the four-letter word." When Graham sought him out at a modern dance concert in New York to praise his dances and film choreography in *Living in a Big Way* (1947), he was startled and thrilled: "Here was my idol and my goddess who was happy to see popular stuff."

Kelly also loved and was inspired by folk dance and courted his wife-to-be Betsy Boger (a.k.a. Betsy Blair) by introducing her to it. Blair remembers the exhilarating evenings they would spend together going to various community dance halls around New York, where they would try out the dances of a different ethnicity every night. "Gene and I and his friend playwright Dick Dwenger loved to do this—one night Polish, one night Greek—Gene knew them all." They would dance the night away and feast on the spread of home-cooked delicacies that had been laid out.[17]

MAKING AMERICAN DANCE

Like many of his colleagues in all styles, Kelly was interested in creating what he called "American Dance"—a theme that was part of the aesthetic dialogue in many American art forms in the first half of the twentieth century, from Zangwill's young composer through Kelly's era. In many ways, the "Americana" sought out by ballet and modern dancers was part of a desire to define the artistic identity of a nation within a high-art context, whether ballet or modern dance. It was serious and sometimes fraught business. But Kelly's version of what was American did not stand outside the popular mainstream; it was an integral part of it. Kelly, like Astaire, saw himself as a popular entertainer as well as a serious creator, and to him this dual role presented no contradiction. His dance was, he said, "strictly aimed at enjoyment." It was there to "lift people" and to "make them happy"—to convey the joy of dance. Of course, not all of Kelly's dances were joyful, but the basic aim was always to entertain and entrance his audience.

However, Kelly was also interested in creating a character in dance, and the characters he created, with a few exceptions, were "American," but of a different sort from those by Astaire. Kelly's breakthrough appearance on Broadway was a role in William Saroyan's Pulitzer Prize–winning play *The Time of Your Life*, in which he played the character of Harry, described by Saroyan as "a natural born hoofer who wants to make people laugh, but can't."[18] In his next role, as the star of Rodgers' and Hart's *Pal Joey*, he played a related character, whose sleazy charm was both attractive and repulsive.

Kelly admired *Pal Joey*'s choreographer Robert Alton, whom he saw as an important mentor and with whom he would create a dream ballet sequence for the musical. Alton insisted, said Kelly, that dance should always tell a story, a lesson Kelly would also have learned from his readings on the *ballet d'action*. Alton would go on to work at MGM as a valued film choreographer, working with both Astaire and Kelly. Larry Billman credits Alton with being the first to break up standard precision chorus lines into smaller groups. Kelly also later remembered that Alton had each group respond to different aspects of the musical structure while at the same time maintaining the coherence of the whole. Balanchine did this in his choreography as well, and Alton had worked alongside Balanchine in the *Ziegfeld Follies of 1936*. Interestingly, Kelly felt that the focus of Balanchine's work on Broadway was always first and foremost on his central female dancer, his muse, building the choreography around her. To Kelly's satisfaction, however, Alton paid equal attention to the chorus.[19]

That led to Kelly's career in films. David O. Selznick saw him perform and brought him to Hollywood. Kelly's first films, however—and his most important subsequent ones—were made with the Freed unit at MGM, who bought his contract from Selznick. His first film, *For Me and My Gal*, was directed by Busby Berkeley, and it teamed him with Judy Garland. Garland was the one who introduced Kelly to film-acting techniques, and by watching Berkeley, Kelly began to understand the potential for the use of the moving camera in film dance.

When he first came to California in 1941, Kelly was seen mainly as a performer—an actor who could dance. Kelly's first look at his work on film in *For Me and My Gal* would pique his interest in the problems and potential of directing dance in cinema—which, he immediately grasped, was entirely different from stage dance and held vast and unique potential. He began to want increasing control over how he was presented onscreen. In *Cover Girl* (1944) he would choreograph and direct his own dance sequences, and this would eventually lead to his directing entire musicals.

As a performer who also wanted to direct, to control how he would be seen onscreen, Kelly faced special problems. He needed someone whose eye he could trust, who could make sure that his careful and precise plans were being carried out behind the camera while he was performing in front of it—and who could help teach and demonstrate his choreography when he was occupied. For *Cover Girl* he hired two assistants, Alex Romero and Stanley Donen, and with the latter he would form the closest of creative relationships.

THE YOUNG STANLEY DONEN

Stanley Donen, twelve years younger than Kelly, had also started out as a dancer.[20] Born in 1924 and raised in Columbia, South Carolina, he was inspired to become a dancer at the age of nine after seeing Fred Astaire in *Flying Down to Rio*: "I was never so moved by anything as seeing Fred Astaire dance."[21] Over the next few years he studied tap dancing both in South Carolina and in New York City, where his family spent part of every summer and where he saw many Broadway musicals. Donen's interest in dance was combined with an interest in film and photography. As a child he was given an eight-millimeter movie camera, and he remembers how he loved to take it "in the car and, as the car was moving, photograph the highways, trees, and signs passing by." He remembers, too, being fascinated "by the placement of the camera in such a way that I could make something appear to be gigantic in the frame when it might be minuscule in reality."[22] An avid moviegoer, he admired the musicals of Ernst Lubitsch and René Clair, as well as Astaire—and like Vincente Minnelli, he was especially impressed by Rouben Mamoulian's *Love Me Tonight*. (In later years Donen told Mamoulian that he would often rewatch *Love Me Tonight* before beginning any film-musical project.)[23]

After finishing high school, Donen came to New York at the age of at sixteen and got his first major job, performing in the chorus of *Pal Joey*—where he first met Kelly. Impressed by the older man's (Kelly was twenty-nine) choreographic creativity and charisma, he responded eagerly when Kelly took him on as a dance assistant in New York for the musical *Best Foot Forward* (1941). Kelly choreographed the show, and Donen not only assisted him but also performed in the chorus. In the fall of 1942, after a summer at the University of South Carolina, Donen got a job as assistant choreographer and stage manager for the George Abbott musical *Beat the Band*. In 1943, after Arthur Freed bought *Best Foot Forward*, Donen followed Kelly to Hollywood, eager to learn about making movies. Soon afterward Kelly persuaded Charles Walters to take Donen into the chorus of the film version of *Best Foot Forward*. But Donen's career as a performer was short: he was happier working behind the camera.[24]

Donen began film work with Kelly as one of his two assistants on *Cover Girl*.[25] In the beginning Kelly was clearly in control, and there is no doubt that he was the most significant influence on Donen's commitment to the integrated musical—and to staging songs and dances in choreographic terms. But there is some dispute about the way their creative partnership developed as their careers progressed. According to Saul Chaplin, who worked with them as a musical director on *Cover Girl* and *On the Town*, "In every case, Gene was the prime mover and Stanley an eager and talented pupil."[26] Donen paints a different picture. Here he speaks of the time of *Cover Girl*:

> You see, Gene and I were young and excited about working with each other and had fun doing it—we never got to bed before 3 or 4 o'clock in the morning and we'd get up again at 6 o'clock and go back to the studio . . . nothing is more fun than finding someone who stimulates you and who can be stimulated by you. The result, rather than just adding up two and two, it multiplies itself, and you find yourself doing much better things—you are both carried away on the crest of excitement. . . . A good collaboration, if you have it, means that you are not greedy about who did what, who did this or that, and you both enjoy being with each other—which is rare. While it is happening you really don't remember what anybody contributes, because you both like to stimulate each other; and from this stimulation an idea may come, even if one person got the idea the other is the catalyst. You can never be sure where to divide the credit.[27]

Donen's is a good description of any creative partnership. It seems reasonable to assume that Kelly—twelve years older than Donen and with an established reputation in Hollywood by 1944—was initially the dominant personality in their relationship. And it is apparent that as far as the actual choreography was concerned, it was always Kelly who was at the helm. Clearly, though, as Donen's confidence grew and he gained experience from outside assignments on his own, the two became increasingly interdependent and equal in their relationship. By the time of *On the Town* (1949) and *Singin' in the Rain* (1951), they were truly co-directors. Donen would also branch out on his own as a director of musicals, directing his first idol, Astaire, in *Royal Wedding* (1951) and *Funny Face* (1957), and also directing *Seven Brides for Seven Brothers* (1954) and other films. And Kelly would form close partnerships with Minnelli in *The Pirate*, *An American in Paris*, and *Brigadoon*.

Cover Girl was made at the same time as Minnelli's *Meet Me in St. Louis*. Kelly not only danced the lead but, with Donen's assistance, directed the dance sequences. These sequences show that Kelly and Donen already shared Minnelli's attitudes to the making of musical films in their use of song and dance as vital elements in the narrative structure and in their exploration of new and inventive ways to use the camera.

THE STREET DANCE: "MAKE WAY FOR TOMORROW"

The dance sequences in *Cover Girl* are the earliest good examples of the Kelly-Donen team's style.[28] *Cover Girl* (made at Columbia) was directed by Charles Vidor, and the film as a whole is a rather long-winded and unwieldy backstage musical. It is saved by its brilliant score and its fresh and inventive dance sequences. The songs, by Jerome Kern, were among the last by this great innovator of the American musical theater, who, as the composer of *Showboat* (1927), had been one of the pioneers of the integrated musical form and who was to die a year after *Cover Girl*'s 1945 release.[29] Kern's songs were orchestrated and arranged by Carmen Dragon and Saul Chaplin. (Chaplin would go on to work closely with Kelly and Donen in other films.)[30] The lyrics were written by Ira Gershwin, who, after George's death in 1937, had been forced to seek new collaborators. Ira, too, would become a valued colleague on later projects.[31] Already a close friend of Minnelli, Garland, Chaplin, and Freed, after *Cover Girl* Kelly was part of that circle as well. Later they would work together on *An American in Paris*.

The dancing for *Cover Girl* utilized the talents not only of Kelly, but of Rita Hayworth, a virtuoso dancer who was sadly underemployed as a sex goddess in most of her films, and whose uncle Angel Cansino had trained Kelly in Spanish dance. The dance sections with Kelly and Hayworth were directed jointly by him and Donen. These were of crucial importance for the Kelly-Donen style. In them we see the two young directors laying the foundation for their future work, establishing models for the dance forms, character types, and filming techniques that they would develop, extend, and refine in their later films, changing forever the face of the American film musical.[32]

It was in *Cover Girl* that Kelly and Donen developed what I call the "street dance." It would become a regularly repeated formula in their musicals, culminating in related dances in *On The Town, An American in Paris, Singin' in the Rain*, and *It's Always Fair Weather*. As my term implies, the street dance takes film dancing off the stage and out of the ballroom, into the everyday environment of the city street. The genre continued in other films—most notably *West Side Story*—and later in the form of street-dance videos, for later directors and choreographers have drawn from the Kelly-Donen models.

"Make Way for Tomorrow" is Kelly's first statement of this dance type. Unlike several of the other songs and dances in *Cover Girl*, "Make Way for Tomorrow" is tightly woven into the plot, much like any song in *Meet Me in St. Louis*. The passage from dialogue to song to dance is a dramatic fit, arising naturally out of the situation and feelings of the characters. Just as Esther in *Meet Me in St. Louis* expresses her deepest feelings in song, Kelly and his friends express them in dance.

Chaplin, who was the assistant musical director of *Cover Girl*, makes clear how important this dance was to Kelly, how carefully he planned for it, and how unusual the integration of song and dance with plot was for the other films he had worked on:

> He laid out everything he thought might affect the number: the set, the other
> characters, the method of shooting, the plot to where the number occurs, his and

Phil's [his co-star, Phil Silvers] attitude—everything. I recall thinking to myself, "This is impossible. I can't write anything that has to take all of those elements into consideration." . . . I never [before] had the luxury of being able to read the entire script, study the situation that included the song, formulate ideas concerning its content, then write it. The best I could do was read about five or six pages before the spot where the song occurred and the same number of pages after it. . . . I had become accustomed to reading from page 49 to 52. No way with Gene. . . . He was always concerned with the entire project.[33]

Chaplin also makes clear that—as in the Minnelli films—the orchestrator-arranger on *Cover Girl* played a role equal in importance to the composer's. To him fell the task of arranging the songs to fit the dance steps and the drama they conveyed. This could involve considerable alteration of the song's structure—as well as the writing of additional musical material not only for individual numbers, but for the musical fabric that underlies and unites the film's many sequences. When it came to the dance numbers, this involved working closely with Kelly as he developed his choreography and integrating the musical arrangement not only with the dance steps, but with Kelly's and Donen's camerawork and lighting.[34]

"Make Way for Tomorrow" introduces and explicates the high-spirited camaraderie of the three central characters, whose close and caring relationship will be one of the film's major themes. These characters are the first of the Kelly trios—sometimes duos—of dancing "buddies" or "pals" who will express themselves most naturally in dance and song, and whose friendship will be a central subject of most of his and Donen's films, from *Anchors Aweigh* through *Take Me Out to the Ball Game, On the Town, An American in Paris, Singin' in the Rain,* and *It's Always Fair Weather.*[35] The buddies are usually men, although in *Cover Girl* and *Singin' in the Rain* a woman is one member of the trio. Whether male or female, though, their behavior to no small extent reflected the relationship between these two young directors.

The "Make Way for Tomorrow" sequence begins in a small dockside oyster bar in Brooklyn, where Danny (Kelly) and his two friends, Rusty (Rita Hayworth) and "Genius" (Phil Silvers), come to relax after their performances at Danny's small nightclub. The friends, neophyte performers, discuss their dreams for the future with a friendly waiter. They order oysters every Friday, they explain, in the hope of finding a "lucky" pearl that will augur a rise in their fortunes. While bantering with the waiter, they pry open their oysters and, finding them empty, try to recover their spirits by singing. Twirling exuberantly on the revolving counter stools and accompanied by the restaurant pianist, they begin singing of brighter days to come.

A chorus of the song is sung in the restaurant (Fig. 5.1a); then, tracked by the camera, the trio march out onto the street, link arms, and continue their singing outdoors (Fig. 5.1b)—dancing with, on, and around the paraphernalia they find there in the dockyard (Fig. 5.1c). Genius uses garbage can lids as cymbals, Danny uses a bucket as a drum, and Rusty uses a breadstick commandeered from a restaurant customer as an imaginary flute (Fig. 5.1b). Danny and Rusty grab some oars and row vigorously, while Genius, astride bales of rigging, rhythmically bails out their imaginary boat (Fig. 5.1d). As they dance further down the street, a passing policeman watches them with suspicion. When he twirls his nightstick threateningly, the trio of friends stop dancing and tiptoe hurriedly down the street in rhythm, exploding again into dance

FIGURE 5.1 *Cover Girl* (1944), "Make Way for Tomorrow": An ordinary street and high-spirited friends—the beginning of a long tradition of Kelly and Donen street dances.

FIGURE 5.1 Continued

when they turn the corner out of his sight (Fig. 5.1e). Continually tracked by the camera—which moves alongside the curb just ahead of them so that we see them in full figure, framed by the facade of each building they pass (Fig. 5.1f)—they skip exuberantly down a city street.

Encounters with passers-by are choreographed into the dance. The trio dance up and down the steps of each building they pass, rhythmically startling two lovers who embrace at the top of one set of stairs (Fig. 5.1g). They whoop and holler around a mailbox commandeered as a drum (Fig. 5.1h), then tap-dance out a greeting to a milkman making a delivery. Returning their salute, the milkman enthusiastically responds in kind, jauntily swinging his bottles (Fig. 5.1i). Another dance encounter is with a drunk who follows the trio delightedly, his weaving steps a charming counterpoint to theirs. The dance climaxes as the dancers skip up and down their own front steps (Fig. 5.1j) and the drunk applauds (Fig. 5.1k). The dance is finally brought to a close by the reappearance of the firm but benevolent policeman (Fig. 5.1l), at the sight of whom the trio conclude their antics and tiptoe guiltily indoors.

Kern's "Make Way for Tomorrow" is a vigorous, upbeat march, characterized by an ever-rising melodic line. Its bright, confident tone musically reflects Ira Gershwin's lyrics, with their clever internal rhymes, which express the three friends' optimism and their determination to succeed, just as the dance reflects their youthful enthusiasm and their camaraderie: "To the blues just refuse to surrender."[36] Changes in tempo, orchestration, and arrangement characterize the dance and comment on it wittily. The uplifting march, reinforced by the dancer's taps, is presented first in a fife-and-drum-corps orchestration. As the emotional temperature builds, we hear orchestral references to Sousa (the piccolo embroidery of the theme) and—during the "rowing" section—the swelling of waves.[37]

Far from being rigorously foursquare like Sousa, though, this march, like the dance, "swings": early on, Rusty and Danny, using oars for props, pluck imaginary bass fiddles (a standard jazz underpinning), and when the dancers explode into the long street for the most exuberant and expansive section of the dance, we hear a swinging big-band arrangement that adds to the mounting excitement. As the dancers meet each passerby, changes in tempo and arrangement refer musically to the dance as it changes to accommodate a new character or prop: a characteristic tom-tom beat,[38] the juxtaposition of low resonant drums and high-pitched wind instruments, and a harmonic stress on fourths is a movie-music cliché used to suggest Native Americans. The milkman's dance is similarly clichéd: in its reliance on fiddle with banjo underpinning and its change in tempo and accent, it transforms "Make Way for Tomorrow" into a "Turkey in the Straw" type of country-dance reel. As in a reel, the dancers face each other, and their percussive steps beat out a characteristic rhythmic pattern from this well-known fiddle tune. In a wonderful musical moment, the offscreen sound of the milkman's truck horn rhythmically punctuates the close of this musical section. The song is again transformed, as a passage of rapidly alternating ascending and descending scalar passages musically mimics the drunk's staggering steps. And all the while the syncopated tapping shoes of the dancing trio interact like percussion instruments with the music, adding to its interest and vitality.

Thus is the street dance defined: a street in an urban setting, the incorporation of ordinary street objects into the dance (found-object props), and choreography based on variants of walking, skipping, and running steps or children's street games, all accompanied by a swiftly moving camera that parallels and enhances the dancers' movements with its own. The policeman who motivates the end of the number will also be seen again in other street dances—most notably "Singin' in the Rain." He helps to emphasize the idea of the dancers as *enfants terribles* who, in response to the music and their own high spirits, temporarily become children in an adult world, flouting convention by transforming the street into a music-and-dance playground. Part of the street dance, too, are passersby, who may either, like the milkman, enter into the dance or, like the drunk, form a delighted audience that applauds enthusiastically at the end of the number. These elements will make up a street-dance iconography that will appear again and again, in whole or in part, in all later Kelly-Donen (and some Minnelli) musicals. (See chapter 8 for the subsequent development of the street dance.)

The street dance has its predecessors in the musicals of the 1930s. One of the most important is Maurice Chevalier's musical walk down the street in the opening of Mamoulian's *Love Me Tonight*, in which, as in "Make Way for Tomorrow," the passersby are incorporated into the number. Indeed, any of the Lubitsch, Clair, or Mamoulian sequences that present characters who sing as they ride or walk through the streets can be considered, in a broad sense, to be prototypes of this form. In *Broadway Melody of*

1938, Eleanor Powell and George Murphy also tramp through the streets of New York singing in the rain.

The street dance's primary prototypes, though, can be found in the films of Fred Astaire, who made walking into dance an established convention, and who began many of his dances with a simple but brilliant variation on this everyday movement. (George Gershwin, in fact, wrote music specifically inspired by Astaire's casual but elegant stroll in the Astaire film *Shall We Dance*.)[39] In *Damsel in Distress* (1937), with songs by George and Ira Gershwin, Astaire performs amid the traffic of a busy London street ("I Can't Be Bothered Now," Fig. 5.2) and walk-dances twice down a garden path ("Things Are Looking Up," Fig. 5.3). Donen himself traces the source of the street dance to Astaire (as well as to Lubitsch). Speaking of the street dance in *Cover Girl*, he says:

> It is hard for me to believe that was the beginning of that kind of thing because I know all those Fred Astaire numbers so well and it wasn't an original conception to have them doing a dance on the street. Lubitsch and Astaire had both done it. Not in exactly the same way, it's true, but I think the difference is that it [*Cover Girl*] had more vitality.[40]

Astaire, too, like Kelly in "Make Way for Tomorrow," had incorporated everyday objects into his 1930s dances—props that were transformed by his rhythmic manipulation of them into magical extensions of his hands and feet. In musicalizing everyday objects and making them, in effect, dance with him, he established a tradition that we see repeated in "Make Way for Tomorrow." The most famous of these objects—so well-known that they became emblems for the dancer—were his walking stick and his top hat, but there are many more: the soda siphon that he uses rhythmically to punctuate the opening phrases of the song "No Strings" in *Top Hat* (1935) and the Art Deco sculpture that becomes his dancing partner in the same song, among others. Just as Kelly and his buddies vault over fireplugs, skim curbs, and dance up and down brownstone stairs, so too does Astaire jeté over sofas, engage chairs in dance, and (in *Damsel in Distress*) hop rhythmically onto a moving London bus.

(a)    (b)

FIGURE 5.2 Astaire, in *A Damsel in Distress* (1937), "I Can't be Bothered Now," uses his umbrella as (a) a rhythm stick and (b) a support in a leap.

FIGURE 5.3 Astaire, in *A Damsel in Distress*, "Things Are Looking Up." Note the varied camera angles as Astaire (a) walk-dances down a garden path to woo Joan Fontaine, playing an English aristocrat, using (b) turnstiles and (c) a garden bench as props, and (d) dancing up a grassy slope.

But though Astaire initiates street dancing in *Damsel in Distress*, Kelly must be given credit for definitively stating and developing this form—a form that, more than any other, would become identified with him and would ultimately affect Astaire as well.

DANCE FOR THE COMMON MAN: THE URBAN AMERICAN BOY NEXT DOOR

Despite these parallels between the dances of Astaire and Kelly, in crucial ways Kelly's street differs from Astaire's in *Damsel in Distress*, reflecting concerns that became salient during the Great Depression and Roosevelt's New Deal response to it and continued through the war years. Kelly himself, as a concerned political liberal involved in the debates of the day over the plight of the common man in America, was involved. (The famous 1942 speech of the committed New Deal liberal Vice President Henry Wallace, in which he characterized the twentieth century as "The Century of the Common Man," was given soon after the United States entered World War II; Copland's *Fanfare for the Common Man* was composed the same year in a musical echo of it.) Instead of a studio-recreated central London or a carefully landscaped English garden and wood, in "Make Way for Tomorrow" Kelly and his friends move through an ordinary street in a Brooklyn dockyard. And the objects that Kelly, Hayworth, and Silvers incorporate in their dance are similarly items that can be found on any city street, a far cry from the fashionable Art Deco furniture in the elegant hotels, nightclubs, country clubs, and manicured gardens where Astaire romped.

The choreography that Kelly devises for "Make Way for Tomorrow," like Astaire's, is grounded in everyday movement but transformed for his own body type and dance persona. He uses a repertoire of movements derived from the games that Kelly himself played as a child in Pittsburgh, movements with which many urban working-class Americans could identify—teetering on the curb, vaulting over fire hydrants, skipping along the sidewalk.

The street and choreography of "Make Way for Tomorrow" fit in with the working-class American character that Kelly portrays in *Cover Girl* and will continue to develop throughout his career. His stocky, compact, clearly muscled body, completely unlike Astaire's slender, elegant, greyhoundlike shape, fits with this character and with the street choreography he devises for himself—choreography he infuses with a distinctively aggressive energy that differs radically from Astaire's casual nonchalance. It is the punch you can feel in the Mickey Rooney character in the Berkeley backyard musicals—and in the urban street-tough character that James Cagney (also a dancer) developed in his films. Like Cagney's, Kelly's body is that of an athlete or a laborer, not Astaire's American entertainer or bon vivant at home in the elegant male attire of café society. "Put me in a tuxedo," Kelly once remarked, "and I look like a truck driver going to Mass on Sunday."[41] For Kelly, there was also a real class distinction between his style and Astaire's: "Mine was a plebeian style and Astaire's was an aristocratic one."[42] In line with this, Kelly saw a strong link between his choreography and sports. He himself had excelled not only in gymnastics, but in hockey. Later in his career, in his Emmy-winning television program *Dancing, A Man's Game*, he would link dance movement to all sports, comparing the techniques of boxers, baseball players, tennis champions, competitive skaters, and others to techniques used in dance. I've already mentioned the influence of gymnastics for Kelly and its link with ballet's long line. But other sports were very important, especially street sports. As Kelly explains, sports that require specially prepared spaces and expensive equipment such as tennis rackets and golf clubs (with which Astaire dances in *Carefree*) are for rich people who can afford them. Soccer, he explains, is on the other hand a "poor man's sport." All you need is a ball or even a crumpled-up newspaper to kick around. In soccer and related street sports, the stance is low and close to the ground and you "bump into each other a lot"[43]—a stance we see in Kelly's dance vocabulary.

Perhaps the most striking difference between Astaire's and Kelly's street dances can be seen in the way the dances are filmed and performed. Compare Astaire's London street dance "I Can't Be Bothered Now" in *Damsel in Distress* and Kelly's "Make Way for Tomorrow" in *Cover Girl*. When Astaire steps off the curb to dance amidst the traffic (Figs. 5.2a and b), he turns the street into a little stage. Its boundaries on either side of him are clearly defined by a mostly static camera that frames him from the front. The rear boundary is defined by a backdrop of continually moving traffic. Within the space framed by the camera, Astaire performs a dance that could, with little alteration, be performed effectively on an actual stage.

However, in another section of *Damsel in Distress*, Astaire dances not on the street but through an expansive, landscaped English wood and garden (Fig. 5.3). Following him through this long, extended area, the mobile camera, now no longer confined to a limited space nor committed to a frontal orientation, follows him freely, photographing him and his partner at various points in the dance from a variety of angles and positions.[44]

Kelly's street, like Astaire's garden, in *Damsel in Distress*, is a long, expansive space, and he uses every inch of it in his equally expansive choreographic program. So the dance had to be recorded by a mobile camera that could photograph the performers from a multitude of angles.[45] The camera gave a specifically cinematic orientation to a dance that was no longer frontally oriented, but planned to be filmed from many different angles, the separately positioned shots then edited together. This parallels to some extent Minnelli's conception of film dance, as presented, at about the same time, in the party sequences in *Meet Me in St. Louis*, and in his work later with Astaire in *Ziegfeld Follies* and *Yolanda*. Still, an important difference between the older director and his younger colleague should be noted: in order to capture the dance from multiple angles, Minnelli relies more heavily on the moving boom camera—active in height as well as depth. In "Make Way for Tomorrow"—and, as we shall see next, in "Alter Ego"—the camera is less expansive in gesture and less active in height than Minnelli's. In "Make Way for Tomorrow," it is primarily editing that transports us through space to view, now from the front, now from the side, the dancers as they cavort singing through the streets.

"SOMETHING THAT HAS MEANING FOR THE CAMERA": THE "ALTER EGO" DANCE

In *Cover Girl*'s second street dance, Kelly and Donen dealt even more powerfully with the problem of making dance cinematic. As with "Make Way for Tomorrow," the "Alter Ego" sequence could only have been done in film. Its use of special visual effects presages a series of experiments with film dance that this directorial team undertook in their subsequent films. Kelly and Donen searched for a way to portray psychological conflict on the screen, where theatrical devices of the stage would have failed—to find "something that has meaning for the camera." Like "Make Way for Tomorrow," the "Alter Ego" street dance is carefully integrated with the dramatic action. It paints a complex psychological portrait of Danny and his conflicted feelings at this crucial moment in the plot.

Rusty has failed to meet Danny and Genius at the oyster bar for their post-performance ritual. Her friends realize that she is out with Noel Wheaton, a wealthy upper-class impresario who wants to sponsor her stage career—thus breaking up the trio. Danny leaves the restaurant and walks angrily down a deserted, run-down, storefront-lined street. It is deliberately stark and stripped down, a bitter contrast to the cozy, populated residential area through which he had skipped so high-spiritedly with Rusty and Genius in "Make Way for Tomorrow." Its somber late-night colors—and the tint of the film, deliberately darkened to contrast with the more high-keyed palette of the rest of *Cover Girl*—reflect Danny's mood as he tries to reconcile his love for Rusty with the jealousy and anger he feels toward her benefactor.[46] As he walks along, the audience hears (in a whispered voice-over) the words of the debate taking place in his mind as he tries to work out his conflict. He passes a deserted storefront and pauses to confront his mirrored image. It stares back at him, becoming, in effect, a visual metaphor for the opposing side of the argument. After a moment he moves on to avoid looking at his reflection, but when he passes another window he is again forced to confront himself. He crosses the street to avoid his image and meets yet another reflection head-on in another window (Fig. 5.4a). This time, however, the reflection takes on a life of its own and speaks directly to him: "Don't be such a hard-headed Irishman for once. If you really loved Rusty, you'd let her go. . . . You have nothing to give her. Wheaton has everything."

Danny again turns away abruptly, but the image now leaps from window to window, trailing him as he moves faster down the street, shouting, "Hey Danny, you can't run away from yourself. You'd better make up your mind about this, and I'm going to see that you do it now." Finally, jumping out of the window onto the street, Danny's "alter ego" (a transparent image of himself) confronts him directly, and the two perform a vigorous *pas de deux*—a battle in dance—that becomes a visual metaphor for Danny's conflicted thoughts (Figs. 5.4b–d).

The music for this sequence draws on two songs that have been associated with different aspects of Danny and Rusty's relationship. The first, "Long Ago and Far Away"—one of Kern's most masterful—is their love song, and we first hear it in the film in a lush, leisurely arrangement to accompany a slow, romantic song and "walking" dance—reminiscent in mood of Astaire and Rogers's more passionate ballroom duets, such as the "Never Gonna Dance" sequence in *Swing Time*, also to a Kern score. The second, the exuberant "Make Way for Tomorrow," has been used, as we have seen, to express their friendship and optimism about the future. Both are now arranged and orchestrated to match the "Alter Ego" dance's despairing and sometimes violent mood. But these two references appear embedded in newly composed music that is largely dance driven: that is, Kelly's step patterns, so specifically expressive of the battle with his alter ego and thus his psychological conflict, determine not only the arrangement and orchestration, but the melodic phrases themselves—which are not Kern's but probably Saul Chaplin's. In short, staccato phrases they parallel now the pattern of the dancer's feet, now the arc of his arms, now the quick shifts of weight and abrupt starts and stops of this tension-filled dance drama.[47] The alter-ego image begins the battle by compelling Danny to stop walking and begin dancing (Fig. 5.4c)—forcing him to imitate, in sequence, each of the alter ego's own dance gestures. Gradually, however, Danny begins to hold his own. Tracked by the camera, the images chase each other down the street, dancing on street props: lampposts, stairs, a fire escape (Fig. 5.4e). At one point, in a wonderful gesture, the images even leapfrog over each other. Finally they pinwheel down the street together (Fig. 5.4f), and Danny, having chased the alter ego back into his window, defiantly hurls a garbage can at it,

FIGURE 5.4 *Cover Girl* (1944), "Alter Ego": the alter ego (a) confronts Kelly, then (b–d) leaves the window and compels him to stop running and dance. Kelly (e) chases the alter ego up a fire escape, (f) makes forceful turning jumps toward the camera with the alter ego, and (g) once the alter ego has returned to a window, hurls a garbage can at him.

shattering the glass (Fig. 5.4g). His personal devil thus subdued, he turns and walks off in silence.

The "Alter Ego" dance demonstrates Kelly's attempt to portray a character in depth by choreographing not only a dance metaphor for his complex personal conflicts, but a specifically *cinematic* dance metaphor. How could he convey inner conflict without counting on the empathic relationship between audience and actor? As Kelly has explained, what works on the stage doesn't always work on the screen. In front of a live theater audience, he could show his character's conflict "with a few contortions and a fall to the floor." On the screen, "that falls flat—the personality is missing and you have to replace it with something that has meaning for the camera."[48]

The most striking cinematic gesture in the "Alter Ego" dance is, of course, the transparent alter-ego image itself—an innovative visual idea that made a strong impression on contemporary critics and audiences. (Donen claims this idea as his.) The roots of the "Alter Ego" sequence, as well as the ideas for other experimental Kelly-Donen cinematic dance sequences, can again be found in the work of Astaire, whom Donen acknowledges as a major influence. In Astaire's "Bojangles" sequence in *Swing Time* (1936), the dancer had used a double-image device related to the alter-ego effect when he danced in front of three enlarged images of himself. These images, however, unlike the transparent alter-ego image, were shadowy shapes that paralleled the dancer's movements—until the end of the number, when they took on a life of their own and walked offscreen. Astaire had employed other such cinematic dance devices as well, among them the slow-motion dream dance in *Carefree* and the "Funhouse" sequence in *Damsel in Distress*, in which the dancers' images were distorted by trick mirrors. As Donen acknowledges,

> everybody minimizes what extraordinary cinematic ideas Fred Astaire had in those pictures. . . . They had a gigantic impression on me. When he did Bojangles, it was an incredible piece of film with shadows of Astaire behind dancing with himself in front of him. I was about nine or ten years old then, and I must have seen it forty times. And it was that which made these huge impressions on me to do cinematic dancing ideas. . . . Then, later, Kelly and I did the double exposure thing in *Cover Girl* and the mouse thing in *Anchors Aweigh*, but the spark to me for all that was Fred Astaire, without question.[49]

Less immediately obvious than their use of this alter-ego image—but just as important for subsequent film dance—was Kelly and Donen's coordination, in the "Alter Ego" dance, of camera and choreography. Like Minnelli's use of the camera at the same time, Kelly's moving camera serves a dual purpose in this sequence: it not only records the dance gesture but enhances it, and enhances the drama that the dance plays out. A good illustration of this is at the beginning of the dance, when the alter ego literally pulls Danny into the dance (Fig. 5.4c), making him imitate the alter ego's steps. Danny tries to resist, and the two skirmish in dance. When Danny succumbs, the two finally dance simultaneously (Fig. 5.4d). At the moment they begin to dance together, the camera—which has up to now been static, photographing them frontally—begins to track back, moving in time to a turbulent and disturbingly dissonant arrangement of "Long Ago and Far Away" while Danny and his reflection, dancing now in tandem, move with it down the street and directly toward their audience, as if also compelled by it and the music. Thus, through its motion the camera that glides in front of them doubles the impact of their dancing. Putting the audience under the spell of the alter ego, it compels us to dance as well.[50]

CAMERA ANGLES AND FRAMING

Camera angles too are integrated with the "Alter Ego" choreography, as is the way in which the dancer's body is positioned within the frame. These techniques establish a model for subsequent Kelly-Donen dances. The camera views Kelly from either side, from the back, and at oblique angles, turning and cutting to aim from various directions. In each case the viewer is given what Kelly felt was the optimal view for the choreographed gesture: "I always move the camera for the numbers, and I can't remember one where I didn't. The reason is that in constructing a dance, I know there's a certain angle that you can look at that is the most advantageous angle. You can't always be turning and facing one way."[51] Importantly, most shots—whether from the front or the side—include the dancer's full figure, surrounded by enough space not only to include the complete dance gesture, but also to allow the dancer to shape the space within which he is working in height, to each side, and in depth.

Framing crucially affects the impact of any dance. The audience must be able to perceive not only the full line of the body, but also its relationship to the space surrounding it. Choreographers understand this instinctively, but not many directors did; Minnelli, Kelly, and Donen were among the few exceptions. In this, too, they followed in the footsteps of Astaire, who, as a dance-film pioneer, always insisted that his directors take fully into account the relation between the shape of the screen and the shape of the dancer—a relation far different from that of the dancer to the proscenium stage, where the dancer is a less dominant element in space.

The aspect ratio for these films—the ratio of the width to the height of the frame—was the "Academy ratio," 1.33:1. This held for the bulk of Kelly's films, and for Astaire's, and for most of the Freed unit films. This standard screen size was in many respects ideal for the dancer—it coordinated well with human proportions and indeed emphasized them. Kelly's frames allowed him to dominate the space and at the same time gave him room to move in the space around him and to shape it. In his last three films, Kelly would be forced to adapt to the new and unwieldy aspect ratio of Cinemascope, ranging from 2.35:1 to 2.55:1, in which the dancer becomes lost in the huge space that surrounds him.[52]

As it had for Minnelli, the way the variously angled shots were edited together posed new problems for Kelly and Donen, adding yet another level of complexity to their task. Astaire faced this problem less frequently: his camera moves to document the dance without interruption—gliding parallel to the dancers and thus allowing them to complete the dance in one long take so that theirs is the major movement onscreen. Astaire's directors and the dancer himself, like a dancer on a stage, had only to contend with the internal shape, flow, and momentum of the dance itself.[53] Kelly and Donen faced a different problem. Instead of filming the dance in a single long take, they had to film it in a series of short ones to allow for a variety of camera set-ups. This meant that the dancer had the formidable task of remembering and sustaining the flow and dynamism of the dance as a whole while being constantly interrupted.

In addition, the editing together of shots in the "Alter Ego" sequence added a new and specifically cinematic pulse to the dance. To achieve it, Kelly, like Minnelli, insisted on meticulously linking his editing to the accompanying music. Cuts from one shot to another occur directly on musical beats and also at times parallel changes not only in tempo, orchestration, and song section, but also in dance gesture. Kelly's description of how he worked with the editor Adrienne Fazan on the dances for his film *An American in Paris*, made with Minnelli, makes this process clear (and also provides an insight into how he edited the "Alter Ego" sequence). At the cutting stage of the film, he says, he "had a steady day to day work relationship" with her: "When you get a good cutter like Adrienne, you say 'Now in the middle of that turn on the third beat of the bar, as I'm turning, cut to this other angle' and it won't look like a cut."[54] Kelly's words reveals his concern with making the cuts as unobtrusive, as integrated with the flow of the dance, as possible.[55]

Determined to create specifically cinematic dance, Kelly and Donen came to recognize other problems specific to film dance as opposed to stage dance. One is the two-dimensional nature of the medium; another is the absence of the empathic audience-performer relationship of a live performance. Kelly's words show an explicit recognition of these problems. What's mainly lacking on the screen as opposed to a three-dimensional stage space is "the kinetic force. On the stage you can do certain things, but I found out very early when I came to Hollywood that a dance I could do on stage that would hold up for seven minutes would boil down to about two minutes on the screen." His diagnosis: this "is mainly due to the lack of physical or kinetic force"— but also, "the personality of the dancer is missing in pictures. You're with the audience in the theater. You look at them and you can embrace them and they can embrace you so to speak, or you can hate each other, but you get no direct response from the screen. It is so remote from the empathy of the live theater."[56] As dancers often do, he described this using metaphors: "I would compare dancing basically to sculpture and the motion picture to painting. So the difficulties we have in transferring a dance onto film are simply those of putting a three-dimensional art form into a two-dimensional panel." He sought to convey on the screen "the kinesthetic, the musical expression of the real dance form."[57]

The use of the particularly long, deep space of the street as a forum for Kelly's dancing may be in part a response to these concerns. The use of the street in the finale of the "Alter Ego" dance seems almost to be a textbook solution. With his movement enhanced by the camera that glides in front of him, Kelly launches a frontal attack on the audience—pinwheeling up the full length of the street directly toward the viewer in a fast-moving series of turning jumps (Fig. 5.4f), as if to mark out for the viewers the distance covered and to will them to feel his physical presence.[58]

Kelly's drive to compensate for the loss of the impact on the audience of a live body in real space may also account for some aspects of the particularly athletic and forceful dance style Kelly developed for his films: his extraordinarily vigorous tap attack, his repeated acrobatic stunts, and his stress on open and expansive gestures of the arms and legs. It may also account in part for Kelly's major weakness as a performer, especially in his early films: his tendency to overplay. This hadn't been a problem for him onstage, he insisted: "On Broadway I was a damned good actor. I could hit that fourth balcony without any trouble at all. But I needed to see three thousand pairs of eyes to do it." The screen was different—though, as his words show, he later saw the way he coped with all this as problematical. "I had a tendency to overact"—and for this, he didn't entirely let himself off the hook. "Of course, my initial defense was to say 'but why the hell didn't the director tell me'—like a kid blaming his mother for not telling him that if he walked down the street without looking where he was going, he'd fall into the sewer. And, in some of my straight roles, I often fell into the sewer." The problem, indeed, as he saw it, was more general: "I was trying to give a performance all the time, and in pictures that's about the worst thing you can do."[59]

Kelly's greatest roles incorporate that characteristic of overplaying and make good use of it—as can be seen in his "ham actor" roles in Singin' in the Rain and The Pirate. But that tendency to project just a little too much, the almost aggressive friendliness and enthusiasm that emanate from the characters he portrays, is also an important part of that particularly American, ordinary, boy-next-door type that Kelly developed in dance and song, a type very different from the urban sophisticate, well traveled and familiar with the manners and mores of upper- and upper-middle-class life in England and on the Continent.[60] Danny McGuire, with his small, unpretentious nightclub in Brooklyn, inhabits a world far removed from Astaire's Manhattan, and as we have seen, the "Alter Ego" dance results from the conflict of these two worlds and the classes they represent.

Kelly's ordinary American musical hero would be more fully developed and presented in the street dances he created throughout his career. And the dance language—both in the use of the camera and in the dance vocabulary he uses—that he would develop for his street dances would have a wide-ranging impact on American musical film, culminating with Jerome Robbins's street dances in West Side Story and later with Michael Jackson's use of the street in his revolutionary music videos. In Kelly's next films, though, dancing in the street would take on another aspect of his character. Both Anchors Aweigh and On the Town reflect the concerns of a nation at war, so Kelly would be put in uniform, and Americans would respond to a new musical hero: the dancing military man.

Film-Dance Genres

6

SONG AND DANCE AS COURTSHIP

THE PLOT OF almost any American genre film made between 1927 and 1957 includes a courtship: boy meets girl, boy courts girl, boy marries girl. In westerns and gangster films, courtship becomes a subplot, with the conflict between men of opposing groups (cowboys and Indians, gangsters and police) taking central stage. In comedies and romantic dramas, however, the courtship is almost always the plot's central element. And this is most vividly true in the case of the American film musical. The love story is American, set to music, with songs and dances that portray and celebrate many or all the stages of the romance. The relationship often follows a predictable pattern: the meeting (hero and heroine encounter each other for the first time), the chase and rebuff (the man chases the woman—though sometimes the roles are reversed—and, annoyed or embarrassed, she refuses the pursuer's ardent advances even though secretly attracted), the seduction (he persists in his advances and wins her affections). The couple may revel in the euphoria of love, but usually there is some kind of plot complication (circumstances conspire to break up their relationship). Ultimately, though, we arrive at reconciliation and finally marriage, or the unmistakable promise of one.

Some musicals concern the courtship and little else: the plot's central concern is "getting the girl" (Mamoulian's *Love Me Tonight*; Sandrich and Astaire's *The Gay Divorcee*; and Minnelli and Kelly's *The Pirate, Swing Time*, and *Seven Brides for Seven Brothers*). In the "backstage" musicals (the *Gold Diggers* and *Broadway Melody* series, *Singin' in the Rain*, and *The Band Wagon*) the courtship is intertwined with "putting on a show": the stages of courtship parallel the making of a star and the success of the show. In musicals with other subjects (the family, for example, in *Meet Me in St. Louis*, or the war buddies in *It's Always Fair Weather*), something else vies for center stage, though courtship remains one of the film's most important elements.

At the heart of the presentation of courtship in the dance musicals I discuss is a musical number that I will call the "seduction song and dance." It was Astaire who set the model for this movie form, first on Broadway and then in the film musical. The dance usually takes place when the hero, whose every effort to win the heroine has been ignored or rebuffed, finally woos and wins her through dance. The seduction dance is often a linchpin of the plot, a crucial turning point in the action. At the beginning of the dance the hero and heroine are either virtual strangers or mere acquaintances; by its end they are both in love. The dance is the formal means through which the transfer of emotions occurs—taking the place of the "first kiss" in romantic dramas and enlarging and expanding with choreographed gesture that prosaic first physical contact into an encounter of mythical proportions. The couple's encounter is opened up, and we are presented with a series of moving pictures that—especially in Astaire's dances—suggest multiple levels of meaning and feeling.

As with almost any narrative work, what holds our attention isn't the bald and simple narrative, but the devices that draw us into the story and lead us to care about it. In a musical, the devices are music and dance, which together convey the varying emotional shades and nuances of what's happening between the man and the woman. More than any other film dancer of his era, Fred Astaire understood and exploited dance's power to achieve this effect, and it was he who set the model for this dance genre, first on Broadway and then in the early film musicals of the 1930s. His brilliant and subtle variations on the seduction dance would span the entire Golden Age of musicals, from his dances on Broadway through Hollywood's 1957 *Silk Stockings*. Kelly in turn modified the seduction dance in the 1940s and '50s to suit his own individual style and the interests of a new decade, influencing Astaire in turn. Along the way other dancers presented their own variations of the form—Donald O'Connor and Vera-Ellen, Marge and Gower Champion, Bob Fosse and Debbie Reynolds. But the seduction dance, as we shall see, also stems from a long tradition in stage dance. Astaire simply rejuvenated and expanded it in his outlaw style for the modern era and its new medium of film.

The archetypal seduction dances in the Astaire and Rogers films were brilliantly described first by Arlene Croce and then by John Mueller, who detailed every one of Astaire's film dances. An early example of the form, "Night and Day," occurs in Astaire's second film with Ginger Rogers, *The Gay Divorcee* (1934).[1] By the time Astaire developed his seduction dances for film in his early 1930s, he had had more experience creating, practicing, and dancing increasingly intricate and varied couple dances with his sister Adele than many dancers get in a lifetime. Since the two more often danced as brother and sister, however, the erotically charged romantic form seen in "Night and Day" was a departure in style for him. In his only Broadway show without his sister, *The Gay Divorcee*, Astaire assumes the new role of a romantic musical hero and pursues a lifelong mate. This quest paralleled Astaire's real-life courtship of Phyllis Potter, who would become his wife, and for whom he had had to overcome obstacles more serious than those in any Broadway musical.

Phyllis was, in fact, a real divorcee who had a four-year-old son from her first marriage, and whether the script for *The Gay Divorcee* was in any way influenced by her situation is a matter for conjecture. The lyrics of "Night and Day" certainly describe Astaire's feelings as recounted in his autobiography and in his letters. He was obsessed by her. And she took her time to come around. In the 1930s divorce was rare and a far greater social stigma than it is now. Having been burned once, she was wary. As a professional entertainer, Astaire was, in the eyes of her Boston Brahmin circle, below her in social status, and she always tried to maintain a certain distance between herself and his entertainment community even after they were married. And Astaire's mother was always a problem. "I honestly think that mother would be happy if I just did nothing but work and come home early every night," he wrote his sister. "Damn it—it's all so difficult and unfair Delly—and I don't want to lose this girl. . . . All the girls that I've liked in the past have gone off and married—one can't expect them to wait forever—not that I want any of those in the past cause I never asked any girl to marry me until this one and I mean it." Mother," he wrote, will "have a fit I suppose if I get married to anybody within the next ten years. I don't know what she expects me to do—keep a couple of tarts or play with myself."[2]

As his romantic interest on the stage, Astaire's partner, Clare Luce, was a more sensual and sexually mature dance presence than Astaire's tomboyish sister. So, in addition to the real-life parallel, the danced courtship took on a kind of intensity, power, and seriousness—along with an open sensuality new to the choreographer. Astaire himself describes it as "an entirely new dancing approach" for him.[3] The stage version of "Night and Day," which can be seen in a film clip made by Fred Stone, whose daughter Dorothy took over the role after Claire Luce, looks very close to what ends up in the movie, where the dance takes place about a third of the way through. As for the movie version, Arlene Croce observes that "for the first time in films, dance becomes the subject of a serious emotion between a man and a woman." Having met and fallen in love with Rogers in the film's first moments, Astaire is determined to woo and win her. Rogers, however, responds to his verbal advances with continued rebuffs. Finally, finding the heroine alone in a deserted dance pavilion, Astaire makes one last attempt to ingratiate himself, and he sings to her. The song (Cole Porter's "Night and Day") softens Rogers's resistance, but it alone is not enough: after it's over she turns and walks away. Undiscouraged, Astaire now tries dance. As the music of the song continues, he urges Rogers onto the dance floor, where the pursuit-rebuff tactics characteristic of this courtship are played out as the dance's opening gestures: she walks away, he follows and stops her; she walks in the other direction, he stops her again (Fig. 6.1a). Finally Rogers allows herself to be drawn into dance (Fig. 6.1b). But the battle is not over. During the dance Rogers again tries to escape the seductive pull of her wooer (Fig. 6.1c). She actually strikes Astaire in a stylized gesture, and he falls back, stumbling the length of the floor (Fig. 6.1d). Undeterred even by this, he continues his pursuit in dance, and Rogers's gradual acquiescence becomes clear in the phrasing of the steps as the balance of power shifts. By the dance's central section the couple move in total accord (Fig. 6.1e). The end of the dance demonstrates Astaire's victory and her capitulation: he guides her to a couch at the side of the dance floor, and she sinks down on the cushions, seemingly too weak to walk (Fig. 6.1f). As she gazes up at him, mesmerized, Astaire signifies the success of his seduction by brushing his hands together above her as if to say "mission accomplished" (Fig. 6.1g). He offers her a cigarette (a standard Hollywood euphemism for postcoital relaxation and bliss). Song and

FIGURE 6.1 Astaire and Rogers, pursuit-rebuff and final acceptance, *The Gay Divorcee* (1934), "Night and Day": Rogers's vacillation between accepting and rebuffing Astaire's advances is built into the dance.

dance have accomplished what words could not. She is now in love with him (Fig. 6.1h). These elements—a song sung by the man to soften the woman's resistance, followed by a dance that plays out the tentative approach-avoidance tactics of early courtship and concludes with the woman's capitulation, and relaxation at the end—will be repeated, in whole or part, in various guises in Astaire's films throughout the 1930s, '40s, and '50s.

THE ROOTS OF ASTAIRE'S COURTSHIP DANCES IN DANCE HISTORY

Astaire and Rogers's seduction dance in "Night and Day," however new to film, grows out of a dance tradition that extends at least as far back as the Middle Ages. The dance floor has always been a major site for Western courtship; for centuries it was one of the only public spaces where young men and women could openly mingle in a space and time devoted solely to social intercourse between the sexes. As the Renaissance dancing master Cesare Negri explains, "The male and female naturally seek one another—and nothing does more to stimulate a man to acts of courtesy, honor, and generosity than love . . . *if you desire to marry you must realize that a mistress is won by good temper and grace while dancing.*"[4]

The "good temper and grace" meant to be displayed in courtship dance reflect, in part, the ideals of courtly love: the woman as idealized figure, aloof and seemingly unattainable; the man as ardent pursuer and champion, who must earn her affection by proving himself worthy of her. But, as Negri also explains, there was a very down-to-earth and practical purpose to couple dancing: "Dancing is practiced to reveal if lovers are sound and in good health. And they are permitted to kiss their mistresses in order that they may touch and savour one another, thus to determine whether they are shapely or emit an unpleasant odor as of a bad meat."[5] During dances, then, normal societal rules of behavior were temporarily suspended, and couples could interact, as Astaire and Rogers do, both emotionally and physically—touching, talking, and flirting with eyes, mouth, and hands, and maybe even brief but thrilling full-body contact.

In this way, Negri goes on to say, dancing *"becomes an essential in a well-ordered society."*[6] In the Renaissance Italian and French courts, where court ballet was slowly becoming a professional theatrical form, the love relationship was one of the primary subjects and sites for dance. One of the first officially recorded and published ballets, Balthasar de Beaujoyeulx's *Ballet comique de la reine*, was created to celebrate a noble wedding at the French court in 1582.[7] And of course, courtship continued in the social dances. A mandatory part of any nobleman or -woman's education was to learn the intricate footwork, complex patterns, and postures of such dances as Negri's *La caccia d'amore* (The Hunt of Love), which incorporate approach-avoidance maneuvers distantly related to the Astaire-Rogers courtship dances.[8] An extremely accomplished dancer, Louis XIV played leading roles in court ballets, and his mistresses performed in the ballets he produced and appeared in. It was his reign that saw the establishment of the Académie Royale de la Danse in 1666.[9] Elizabeth I also loved dance: her favorite, "La Volta," allowed men and women to come into contact for an exhilarating moment as the male, holding his partner tightly and using his thigh for leverage, lifted and whirled the female through the air, her skirts flying. (Gwyneth Paltrow and Joseph Fiennes fall in love while dancing a rather subdued recreation of "La Volta" in *Shakespeare in Love*.) Astaire used a modern and more expansive descendant, most notably in the finales of the courtship dances "Pick Yourself Up" in *Swing Time* and "The Yam" in *Carefree*.

Dance retained its importance at the French courts until the revolution in 1789. Marie Antoinette was described as an especially graceful dancer. Like Louis XIV, she appeared in ballets staged at the court of her mother, Maria Theresa, in Vienna, where she was raised, and at Versailles, where she spent her married life. (Her countryman Mozart, who played for her as a child, wrote many social and court dances and was an enthusiastic social dancer as well.) Lack of documentation means that we are unable to recreate precisely how courtship was danced onstage before the nineteenth century, but it seems that in the early nineteenth century it was still a primary subject. As in film musicals, whatever else the ballet was about, the marriage plot was a primary theme around which choreography was organized and the female body displayed.[10] In these ballets male and female dancers carry out a courtship in dance: they either meet and fall in love in stylized movement, or one dancer dances for the other in an attempt to attract a mate.[11]

Take, for example, the first-act pas de deux of *Giselle* (1841), one of the few survivors from the romantic ballet repertoire of the first part of the nineteenth century, with which Astaire was familiar. (*Giselle* was still in the repertoire when Astaire and his mother saw it with the great Russian ballerina Olga Spessitsiva in the title role in 1927 at the Paris Opéra.)[12] Albrecht, a nobleman, disguises himself as a peasant in order to court Giselle, a village maiden. Like Ginger Rogers, Giselle at first shyly rebuffs her suitor's ardent advances, but we can sense her attraction to this amorous stranger as she hesitantly moves toward and then away from him in a series of choreographed approach-avoidance maneuvers that climax when she abandons all caution and accepts his invitation to dance. They circle the stage in exhilarating jetés, a balletic parallel to Astaire and Roger's climactic dance embrace. (Fig. 6.2 compares stages of pursuit-rebuff in *Giselle* with corresponding stages in Astaire's dances.)

Later in the nineteenth century, courtship dances in professional ballet become more erotic. In the act 2 pas de deux from *Swan Lake* (1877), Prince Siegfried pursues the trembling swan princess Odette, whose ambivalent behavior parallels Giselle's and Rogers's (though Rogers, an emancipated 1930s woman, shows anger, not fear). But when Odette finally capitulates, her feelings are expressed in one of the most sensual pas de deux of this or any other era as she melts trustingly into her suitor's arms, opening and stretching her pliant body in response to her lover's tender manipulations.

Seduction dances can vary in tone and style from the serious and swooning to playful flirtation, but the game is the same. The cheeky, tomboyish heroines of the comedy ballets *Coppélia* and *Napoli* take pleasure in cheerfully taunting their suitors before succumbing. Film-musical courtship dances do not always have to be as serious

FIGURE 6.2 Comparison of the choreographed pursuit-rebuff tactics played out by Astaire and Rogers in "Night and Day" in *The Gay Divorcee* (1934, right) parallel the pursuit-rebuff tactics that precede the first-act pas de deux of Albrecht (Johan Kobborg) and the peasant maid Giselle (Alina Cojocaru) in a Royal Ballet performance of the French romantic ballet *Giselle* (1841, left).

in tone as "Night and Day." A dance that follows the same pattern but in an entirely different mood and style is the Astaire-Rogers-Berlin film *Top Hat* (1935). "Isn't It a Lovely Day," the Irving Berlin song with which Astaire woos a reluctant Rogers in this film, is cheerful and breezy, and the tap dance with which the couple follow it is equally ebullient, full of witty challenges and exchanges between the two partners. It is all very different from the grand passion of "Night and Day." Like the latter, however, it is

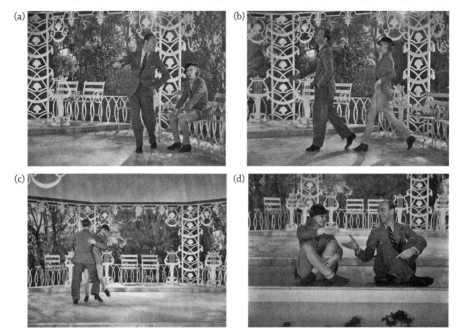

FIGURE 6.3 Cheerful seduction: *Top Hat* (1935), "Isn't It a Lovely Day." Astaire (a) offers Rogers his arm to bring her into dance, and (b) she follows, walking; (c) they start to dance together and then (d) shake hands to seal the relationship.

used by the hero as a seduction device after all other tactics have failed. Again, the song softens the reluctant heroine, and the dance that follows melts her completely. And again, the shape of the dance parallels the heroine's gradual acquiescence to the hero's advances. This time, however, in line with the mood of the song, instead of pleading dramatically with her, Astaire jollies Rogers into dance by walking rhythmically in front of her, as if daring her into movement (Fig. 6.3a). When, unable to resist, she joins him (Fig. 6.3b), they at first dance separately: she eyes him warily as he throws out one after another of a series of challenge steps that she follows and tops. Her total capitulation comes when they begin to whirl around the floor together, arms entwined (Fig. 6.3c). At the dance's end they shake hands, but the dance has conveyed a deeper feeling (Fig. 6.3d). Later in the film she jubilantly tells her friend Bedini—and the audience— the dance's meaning for the plot: "I've seen him, I've talked to him, I've *danced* with him!" Her tone and emphasis make it clear that "dance" is a synonym for love.

THE MODERN WOMAN IN ASTAIRE'S COURTSHIP DANCES

It is in lighthearted courtship songs and dances like "Isn't It a Lovely Day" that we can most clearly see the New World body language and behavior that Astaire brings to his couple dances. The danced courtship played out here is a relationship of equals;

it involves friendship as well as love, and Astaire's partner, much like his sister, is a modern American woman who can give as good as she gets. One of the most graphic and startling examples of this new kind of relationship can be seen in one of the courtship dances in one of his earliest films, *Roberta*.

This is not to say that the romantic concept is abandoned completely. Women in dance musicals are every bit as prized as the heroines of romantic ballet, but they belong to a new world and a new century, and their movement and manner reflects the century of women's suffrage. She is the woman who bobs her hair, shortens her skirt, and unapologetically enters the job market. Onstage she was embodied in Fred's spunky, sharp-witted, outspoken sister, Adele, who more often played his friend than his lover. In screwball comedies, she's Katherine Hepburn, Myrna Loy, Rosalind Russell, and Jean Arthur. In the Astaire-Rogers films, she is Ginger Rogers, and she reveals it in song and dance. In *Roberta*, it is she who sings the courtship song, and she who sets the terms in the song "I'll Be Hard to Handle."[13]

We don't have to worry about Astaire's reaction to the warning. Long before she finishes, his reaction shots show his admiration for her style and her talent, and something else too: he's turned on, and the conversation and body language that serve as a prelude to the courtship dance make that clear. Rogers plays a spunky, ambitious small-town girl from Indiana who leaves Depression America to make her fortune abroad by impersonating a Polish noblewoman living in postwar Paris. Turns out that Astaire is also a midwestern boy out of a job, the leader of a jazz band—and he's on to her. Turns out, in fact, they've grown up together, and we are in the process of watching the rekindling of their early romance.

The dance that follows the song (Fig. 6.4) expresses in Astaire's outlaw style the new body behavior and interaction of modern American men and women. For one thing, it starts on the floor, where Rogers plops down next to Astaire, who, leaning back on his elbows, sprawls with his legs extended in front of him (Fig. 6.4a). It's a pose that definitively leaves polite Old World behavior behind. Like Astaire, Rogers is wearing trousers—a relatively new item for women, one that Katherine Hepburn was just beginning to promote in a parallel career. Unconfined by a skirt, Rogers's legs are free to splay or bend as she likes. (At one point, her back to the camera, Rogers awkwardly hauls one leg up in front of her to stretch it [Fig. 6.4b] and then sits down, arms akimbo, legs stretched out in front of her [Fig. 6.4c].) In the kind of high-spirited, competitive horseplay that you can still see wherever American teenagers hang out, they nudge, lean, and bump up against one another with shoulders, elbows, hands, hips, eyes, and smiles. She takes a swipe at him in response to a mock insult, and he catches her wrist in the air before her blow can land—holding it and turning it suddenly into the first step of a dance in which friendship begins to grow into something else (Fig. 6.4d). It's the same idea as in the beginning of *The Gay Divorcee*, but this danced-out game of seduction is a fun one, begun so causally and walked into so naturally that we almost don't see it coming. Playful dance and mime battles (Figs. 6.4e and f) in which both give as good as they get culminate in a joyous dance frolic (Fig. 6.4g), followed by their happily exhausted collapse into a couple of chairs at the dance's end (Fig. 6.4h).

FIGURE 6.4 The modern American woman: Astaire with Rogers in trousers in *Roberta* (1935). Note the casual, informal body language, the lighthearted games of pursuit-and-rebuff, and the happy collapse at the end.

Astaire makes an art form of slouching. He rarely stands balanced equally on two feet, instead leaning on one supporting leg, the other crossed negligently in front of him. His walk is loose-limbed and relaxed. All this, along with his horseplay with Rogers, is far removed from the polite, upright posture and measured steps of the more formal Europeans by whom they are surrounded in this movie.

GOOD SONG, GOOD DANCE

Dance, however, is only one part of the tool set employed by the musical seducer. In the musical, film song and dance are inseparable parts of a whole. Astaire, along with Kelly and other film-musical performers, saw themselves as song-and-dance men and women: the music and lyrics they sang and danced to were the key to the very heart of the film musical's power to enchant and inspire not only us, the audience, but also the choreographers who created and performed the dances. As Hermes Pan, Astaire's close friend and assistant choreographer, remarked, "Bad song, bad dance." George and Ira Gershwin, Cole Porter, Irving Berlin, and Jerome Kern inspired Astaire's dances; and in turn, his singing and dancing inspired them to produce some of their greatest music.

Take Porter's song "Night and Day." It shares with most popular songs the overall structure of verse followed by a chorus. The verse is the introduction section, setting the situation and mood for the chorus, which is repeated several times. The throbbing, repetitive lyric with the pulsing one-note ostinato, "Like the beat, beat, beat of the tom tom . . . , / Like the tick, tick tock of the stately clock," evokes the obsessional rumination, the kind of body-and-mind takeover, that the lover experiences. He can't get the heroine out of his mind: "So a voice within me keeps repeating 'you, you, you.'" The chorus, "Night and day, you are the one," which is what most of us remember from the song, is a succinct and poetic declaration of love and an implied appeal to the beloved to return it.

Porter's verse and chorus here serve as the "thesis" (as Gene Kelly once described it) of the courtship dance that was created to follow it. In musical terms, this means that the song is the theme, and the musical dance-drama becomes a series of variations meant to demonstrate the emotional trajectory of the evolving relationship. Like the score of a *ballet d'action*, music underlines, enhances, and interacts with every moment of the dance. For example, as Astaire urges Rogers onto the dance floor, the musical introduction (the verse) is repeated sotto voce, its relentless ostinato building up tension as Astaire pursues the recalcitrant Rogers, blocking her path in each direction as she strides, almost in panic, across the dance floor to escape him. The explosive pounding of the bass drum dramatizes the moment when Astaire in desperation forces a confrontation, grabs her hand, whirls her around to face him just as the chorus ("Night and day, you are the one") begins, and dances pleadingly in front of her in a final, desperate effort to draw her into dance. The powerful climax, when the dancers whirl around the floor, clasped tightly together, is enhanced by the most musically and lyrically dramatic section of the chorus, and there is a dramatic change of key for the most passionate of Porter's lyrics: "Night and day deep in the hide of me, / there's an oh such a hungry, yearning, burning inside of me." And a specially composed musical tag, like a long orchestral sigh, is inserted to parallel Roger's supported melt into a seated position at the very end.

These are some pretty obvious musical enhancements, but the score for this dance is studded with varied and subtle compositional devices: changes in tempo, dynamics, rhythm, and instrumentation, and insertion of countermelodies and accents to push the dance-drama forward, enhance it, and comment on it. These devices fit a long-standing dance tradition in which ballet composers such as Adolphe Adam, Cesare Pugni, Riccardo Drigo, Léo Delibes, and Tchaikovsky worked in tandem with their choreographers to create music tailored measure by measure to the choreographic story or drama, and also to the particular performers featured in the central parts, promoting their strengths and hiding their weaknesses.[14] (Mozart once remarked, "I write an aria to fit a singer like a good suit of clothes.") The same was true in early opera, of which ballet was an important part.

The music for these song-and-dance variations, in line with a long tradition in musical theater, was created not by the song's composer, but by the music director with his staff of orchestrators and arrangers. The composer of music for ballet and opera was, for the most part, the sole creator of the music published under his name, notating precisely its melody, harmony, orchestration, tempo, and dynamics. In contrast, the composers of the dance-film musicals I discuss were responsible (usually) only for the song's melodic line and its harmonies. The task of arranging the song for orchestra, voice, and dance was given to the person listed in the screen credits as the music director and, under him, the orchestrator. These people, in conjunction with Astaire, Pan, and other choreographers, worked out the variations or exposition of the song thesis or theme and the dance that followed it. (Hal Borne performed this task in the Astaire-Rogers musicals.) The musical director, the orchestrator, and their colleagues not only assigned various combinations of instruments to play the song's melody and its harmonic accompaniment, but were allowed to determine the kinds of harmonies used. They were also given license to invent countermelodies or motifs and incorporate them into their arrangement, to determine the song's tempo and dynamics, and, in most cases, to alter or expand the song's structure to interact with and enhance the dance. In so doing they performed a role almost equal in importance to that of the composer—one that was crucial to the effectiveness of the choreographer-dancer and of the dance itself.[15]

GENE KELLY AND THE COURTSHIP SONG AND DANCE

Astaire set the general template for film choreographers to follow in his songs and dances, but later choreographers would alter and expand that template in their own ways. Like Astaire, Gene Kelly places his courtship songs and dances at crucial points in the plot and uses them to demonstrate the protagonists' growing affection for one another. And like Astaire, he worked in tandem with orchestrators and arrangers to create a dance that would be effective. But though Kelly's dances relate in plot placement and general idea to those of his predecessor, they differ radically in other ways. Kelly transforms Astaire's general model into one that not only fits more closely with his own dance style (and the new, "ordinary American" character type he presents in his films), but reflects his new interest as a film director by using the camera and editing as another element of the choreography. Here the orchestration works with the moving camera as well as the dancer.

"You Were Meant for Me," the courtship song and dance in *Singin' in the Rain*, follows the general pattern established by romantic ballet and by Astaire. But Kelly adds a new element: participatory camera movement. Astaire had taken brilliant advantage of the cinematic medium, transcending the limitations of the audience-proscenium relationship by giving every member of his audience the best seat in the house. For the most part, his dances were filmed from the front. Much of the time the camera remained at a prescribed distance from the dancers moving parallel to them, as if, as Croce put it, the viewer were "watching every moment from an ideally placed seat in a theater."[16] The choreography itself was for the most part planned to be viewed frontally. In Kelly's courtship dances, in contrast, the camera functions equally with the choreography and music to convey the drama of seduction played out in this dance form, and the choreography was planned to be seen from a variety of angles. The couple's growing attachment is now illuminated not only by body gesture, but by camera gesture as well. In "You Were Meant for Me," camera movement dramatizes the pivotal moment of the courtship dance-drama, that moment of surrender when the heroine, after the usual period of hesitancy (Fig. 6.5a), wholeheartedly accepts the hero's invitation to dance (Fig. 6.5b). At that crucial point the camera, which has until then been following the dancers' movements on their own level, suddenly takes flight (Fig. 6.5c). Hanging high in the air, riding an orchestral crescendo, it frames the couple from above and then, exhilaratingly, swoops down, around, and toward them as they circle the floor ecstatically (Figs. 6.5c and d), providing a visual metaphor for the lovers' emotional high. Once on the ground (Fig. 6.5e), the camera continues to move as the couple dance together, finally gliding into a waist shot as he lifts and turns her lovingly (Fig. 6.5f). Kelly's expressive camera also dramatizes visually the moment at the dance's end that tells us that the couple has arrived, through dance, at love (Figs. 6.5g and h). The couple stand transfixed, gazing at each other, while the camera glides slowly back on a musical diminuendo until the two become the furthest point in the scene—the still point of emotion at the apex of a triangle of deep, empty space.

Kelly's orchestrators, like Astaire's, worked closely with the choreographer, and "You Were Meant for Me" is a good illustration of the orchestrator's ability not only to help transform a mediocre song into a memorable one, but to set the stage for a seduction in dance. Like "Night and Day," "You Were Meant for Me" climaxes the hero's obsessive search for his beloved (Debbie Reynolds), which ends on an empty soundstage. Here Kelly charmingly reveals the conventions of the courtship dance genre itself. He places his beloved on an electrician's ladder for a "balcony," uses a wind machine to

FIGURE 6.5 A truncated pursuit-and-rebuff follows the song "You Were Meant for Me," from *Singin' in the Rain* (1952). (a) Debbie Reynolds turns away from Gene Kelly after he declares his love for her in song. The camera movement dramatizes the moment when the hesitant heroine wholeheartedly accepts the hero's invitation to dance. (b) The camera, which has until then been following the dancers' movements on their own level, suddenly (c) takes flight.

gently blow her hair, turns on a battery of multicolored arc lights, and activates a mist machine to create a romantic atmosphere. The only convention left unexposed is the most crucial: the music. Kelly's demonstrations are enhanced by the loveliest of orchestral colors—the only effect not pointed out by Don himself. Each flick of a light or fan switch is accompanied by a layer of sound that, like the imagery Don creates, gradually accumulates to create both a musical atmosphere to parallel the visual one and a musical "cushion" on which Don can sing and the two can dance.

Similarly, in *An American in Paris*, the song and dance "Our Love Is Here to Stay" with which Kelly woos and wins Leslie Caron also traces the trajectory from approach-avoidance to capitulation as the lovers dance along the night-lit banks of the Seine accompanied by Conrad Salinger's masterful arrangement of one of Gershwin's most poignant songs. Here Kelly and Minnelli use the space in a new way. The long, narrow quai on which Kelly dances is a studio recreation, designed by Preston Ames, of the Quai de la Tournelle in back of Notre Dame Cathedral. The lighting design was created by the cinematographer Ray June, who was called in to relight the set when the lighting of the initial cinematographer failed to come up to Minnelli's and Kelly's standards. The scene and its dance sequence have inspired a number of filmmakers. Salinger enhances the beginning of this intimate "walking" pas de deux with an equally intimate chamber group featuring violin, oboe, clarinet, and French horn, which swells briefly into a rhapsodic section for strings at the dance's climax and fades away as the dance concludes—this time as the dancers, not the camera, move away from us into the distance, their tightly clasped arms signaling their emotional transformation.

Kelly develops another type of courtship dance too, one that has its roots in the history of dance. Instead of dancing with his object of adoration, he tries to convince her to love him by demonstrating in dance the skills that display why she might want to. It is part of the old Western iconography of courtly or chivalric love: Lancelot demonstrates his prowess before Guinevere, and she falls for him. In medieval manuscript illuminations, noblewomen watch admiringly as knights battle in tournaments to prove their love (Fig. 6.6). In the Renaissance, specialty steps such as the competitive "tassle kick" demonstrated men's agility and strength before admiring ladies. The intricate, jumping steps of the galliard also served this function. (Women could perform the galliard too, but their movements were limited by their long skirts.) And in the nineteenth-century *ballet d'action* solo, male and female variations perform roughly the same function: the male dazzles the female by dancing in front of her, or she dances for him—from Odile's thirty-two fouettés in *Swan Lake* to the virtuoso male show-off dances of the cape-swirling toreador Espada in Petipa's ballet *Don Quixote* (1869) to the Saracen knight Abderakhman, who woos the titular character in *Raymonda* (1898).

Astaire, on the whole, preferred the emotional and physical interaction of the pas de deux, but occasionally he draws from the tradition of the male display dance as well. Indeed, he precedes Kelly in its use in film. In *Carefree* (1937) he tries to charm Rogers, who watches (Fig. 6.7a) as he shows off his virtuosity, power, and precision not only as a dancer but as a golfer: his clubs become rhythm instruments and dancing partners. An intricate Highland fling between crossed golf clubs (Fig. 6.7b)

FIGURE 6.6 Illustration of chivalry from the Manesse Codex, 14th century: ladies watch from above as knights battle.

is followed by driving a series of balls in great, graceful arcs far out onto the green (Fig. 6.7c). Unlike Kelly's dances, this one doesn't do its job of eliciting her adoration: Ginger, irritated, walks away during the dance. When Astaire looks up triumphantly (Fig. 6.7d), she's gone.

Astaire grew up dancing with his sister; Kelly danced with his brother Fred. The interaction was side by side, but it could also be competitive. Kelly, as a serious gymnast, was also used to displaying his powerful arms, his jumping, balancing, and swinging ability, and his beautiful line before cheering audiences. The courtship dance from *Anchors Aweigh* (1945) enacts the fantasy of an American sailor played by Kelly, who imagines himself the other side of the knight figure: the bandit-hero, a Robin Hood or Zorro type. To impress his lady as she watches from her balcony (Figs. 6.8a and b), the bandit, swathed in a cape, performs a stunt-studded, tango- and flamenco-flavored dance ("La Cumparsita") that emphasizes, in its repeated posturing, not only his strength and agility but also his masculine figure (Figs. 6.8c–f). Balletic forms are used as well (Fig. 6.8g). He scales the wall of her castle (Fig. 6.8h) and swings, à la Douglas Fairbanks, to her side (Figs. 6.8i and j), where, overwhelmed by his choreographed display of manly daring, she collapses into his arms (Fig. 6.8k). The final shot brings us back to reality, and the success of the fantasy seduction is signified by the sailor and his girl in a parallel embrace (Fig. 6.8l).

A less pretentious and very funny version of this type of balcony courtship dance will follow in *The Pirate* (1947), a musical set somewhere in the Caribbean islands in the nineteenth century. Its expanded form also makes it into a film ballet, and

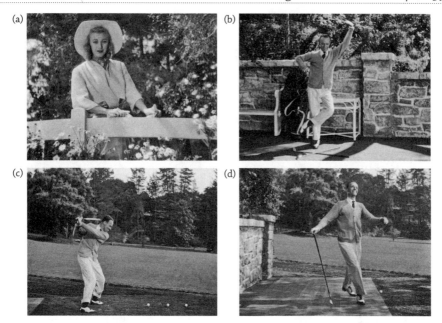

FIGURE 6.7 *Carefree* (1938), golf dance: Rogers watches from above as Astaire tries to dazzle her with his golf mastery.

I'll discuss it more at length in the chapter on that genre (see Fig. 9.3). But it also serves as a seduction dance in which Kelly shows directly the impact of Russian ballet as passed down from Adolph Bolm through his ballet teacher and also from Balanchine's affectionately satirical takes on Fokine. Kelly is Serafin, a strolling player who seduces his reluctant heroine (Judy Garland) as he shows off in dance while she watches, shivering with delight. The joke is that in real life Serafin is dancing in an ordinary town square and his aggressive leaps and shouts, his swordplay and barrel turns, are actually directed at a tired donkey that has collapsed and is stranded in the town square, as well as at members of the local militia. But Garland's imagination turns him into a warrior-pirate whose dance vocabulary, enhanced by Minnelli's moving camera, parodies not only the Fokine choreography for the *Polovtsian Dances* that made Bolm famous but also the melodramatic feats of derring-do of Kelly's idol, Douglas Fairbanks Sr.

In 1957 Astaire would use Kelly's variation (the "woman on the balcony" and the Spanish dance) on his own theme in a film that he made with Kelly's collaborator Stanley Donen. In *Funny Face* (1957), thirteen years after Kelly's seduction dance in *Anchors Aweigh*, Astaire wins the affections of Audrey Hepburn by performing a flamboyant flamenco-style dance using his raincoat as a toreador's red cape and an umbrella as a sword in the courtyard of a Paris hotel as she watches delightedly from her balcony (Figs. 6.9a–c).[17] Now controlled by Donen, Kelly's collaborator, with input from Astaire, the camera moves to enhance the drama—filming from a variety of angles and actively moving. To be sure, the greater proportion of the dance is more

FIGURE 6.8 *Anchors Aweigh* (1945), fantasy sequence to "La Cumparsita." (a–b) Kathryn Grayson watches from her balcony as Kelly tries to win her over. (c–d) Kelly "being Spanish," with elements of flamenco and other forms. (e–g) Kelly being balletic. (h–j) Athletics à la Douglas Fairbanks, climbing, leaping, swinging, and finally sliding down the pole into her arms on the balcony. (k) The final shot brings us back to reality, and the success of the fantasy seduction is signified by (l) the sailor and his girl in a parallel embrace.

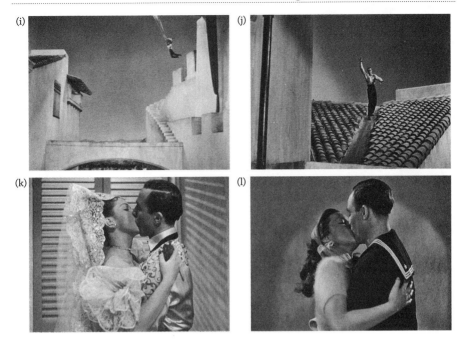

(i) (j) (k) (l)

FIGURE 6.8 Continued

frontal than many of Kelly's of that period; but it is clear that Astaire is responding to a new style of camerawork and working with it in his own way.

Ideas that we have seen in both Astaire's and Kelly's dances are united in yet another film directed by Stanley Donen and choreographed by Michael Kidd, three years before *Funny Face*. *Seven Brides for Seven Brothers* (1954) contains one of the most monumental of film courtship dances—you could call it a kind of apotheosis of the form. In this dance, the ritual of courtship in dance is multiplied by six, as six backwoodsmen brothers simultaneously woo their girls during the course of a barn-raising dance. As in the Kelly "balcony" dances, the brothers in *Seven Brides* attempt to impress their girls with their virtuosity. This time, however, they must do so in direct competition with a group of rivals—the townsmen. The competition between the two groups is played out as a dance challenge in the dance's central section. The girls also participate in this monumental courtship dance, dancing back and forth between the rival groups and designating the winners choreographically by vaulting into their arms at the conclusion of the dance.

Just as the moving camera enhances the drama of seduction in *Singin' in the Rain*, so too does the filming technique in *Seven Brides for Seven Brothers* work to enhance the drama of courtship, with its central theme of competition and challenge. Here, however, it is done not so much by camera movement as by editing. Images of the brothers and their rivals, each man in turn demonstrating his skills, are rhythmically contrasted from different angles while they move at an ever-quickening pace as the challenge dance builds to a peak of excitement.

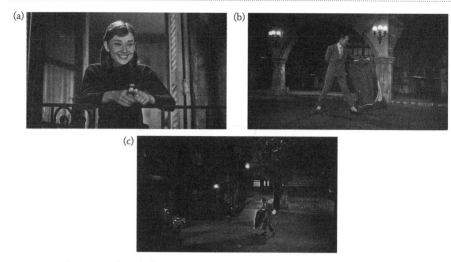

FIGURE 6.9 *Funny Face* (1957), "Let's Kiss and Make Up." Astaire and Donen's own witty variation on chivalric and Spanish imagery as Astaire tries to win over Audrey Hepburn, who watches from her hotel balcony.

One of the last of the courtship dances in the Golden Age of film musicals virtually replays the first, conforming to an amazing degree to the blueprint given us by Astaire in *The Gay Divorcee*. As danced twenty-three years later by the same performer and to music by the same composer, this dance takes place in the Cole Porter musical *Silk Stockings* (1957), a remake of Ernst Lubitsch's 1930 comedy *Ninotchka*, directed by Rouben Mamoulian (Fig. 6.10). In *Silk Stockings*, Astaire, as Steve Canfield, an American film producer, attempts to woo and win a visitor from another culture—a Soviet commissar named Ninotchka (Cyd Charisse). Just before this last courtship dance begins, when Astaire turns down the lights and turns on the music to set the scene for his seduction in dance, Ninotchka, recognizing the beginning of a clearly defined American ritual, unknowingly does a favor for future film and dance historians by identifying and labeling the form in her next lines of dialogue:

NINOTCHKA: Is this what is known as "the courtship"?
STEVE: Yeah, the "build up," the "pitch."
NINOTCHKA: Then I shall take out my little black book and make notes.

As in "Night and Day" from *The Gay Divorcee*, Astaire first tries song ("All of You"), then dance, to win over his reluctant partner, and, as in that first courtship dance, the pursuit-rebuff tactics characteristic of the initial stage of the lovers' relationship become the opening gestures of the dance itself. In this last of Astaire's courtship dances, however, the metaphorical meaning of the act of dancing—its implications for the couple's relationship—is made more explicit than in any of the previous examples of the form. In the dance's first section, Astaire dances pleadingly in front of Ninotchka, who,

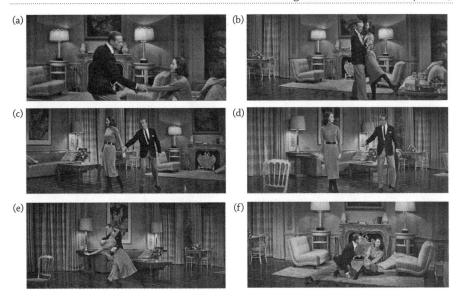

FIGURE 6.10 *Silk Stockings* (1957): From pursuit-and-rebuff to love.

true to form, obstinately remains seated on a couch in front of him. Taking a chance, he pulls her forcibly up from the couch (Fig. 6.10a). Most of her body resists, but a wayward leg lifts involuntarily, as if to go into arabesque (Fig. 6.10b); she looks at it disapprovingly while he smiles knowingly. They both know what this gesture means. Disturbed, she walks away from him, but of course he follows and stops her (Fig. 6.10c). After a few stylized walking steps, she finds herself, again involuntarily, in fifth position (Fig. 6.10d). Troubled, she looks down at her disobedient feet while Astaire wags his finger at her knowingly. Feeling herself unable to resist the dance, Ninotchka, like Rogers more than thirty years before, now turns, grabs her coat, and walks determinedly toward the door as if to escape. Astaire, true to form, follows and blocks her path. Then, like the heroines of so many musicals before, she surrenders completely to dance (Fig. 6.10e) and thus to love, as mesmerized, she and Astaire, mission accomplished, sink to the floor (Fig. 6.10f).

The great courtship dances of the two decades between *The Gay Divorcee* and *Silk Stockings* have become part of the collective unconscious of generations of filmmakers and audiences. Astaire and Rogers's dances are referred to in countless films. So are Kelly's. Billy Crystal (*Forget Paris*) and Woody Allen (*Everyone Says I Love You*) directly quote Kelly's courtship dance with Caron along the banks of the Seine in *An American in Paris*, using it as a symbol of romantic love, lost and found.

The long afterlife of Astaire's and Kelly's courtship dances, their firm roots in the history of dance, and their hold on the public imagination are clues to their relevance to all of our lives. Film musicals are often portrayed (mostly by American critics) as frivolous, irrelevant forms. Breaking into song or dance is downright silly. Our Puritan heritage makes dance (that is, display of the body) and song suspect, and, as a young country and unlike Europe and Asia, we do not have traditional theatrical forms (opera and ballet, or song-and-dance epics like the *Ramayana*) that convey ideas and emotions in song and dance. Musicals are also viewed as feminine and/or gay and therefore of lower status. (Westerns and mysteries are just as stylized and illogical as musicals, and just as fantastic, but no problem there.) Musicals' subject matter, however—mate selection, bonding—are among the most important things we as humans do, and language, while important, is not always the key to the matter. Geoffrey Miller, Robbins Burling,[18] and others have pointed to how, in the evolution of our species, gesture and body display parallels language and courtship. Courtship is practically universal among humans and other animals, and courtship dances are central to mating in certain species. Body language—moving toward or away, gestures of tenderness and rejection and of frustration and anger, as well as visual and aural signals of health (body symmetry, complexion, vigorous movement, shape, class)—all are communicated by sound and image.

Film musicals put the ordinary American (male and female) center stage and poeticize their body language during the period of courtship. The greatest of their songs and dances come closer to presenting their feelings in the multivalenced language of movement and music than could any dialogue. During their heyday, film musicals were presented to an audience who were doing this same kind of bonding with their senses themselves: the arm around the back of the chair, the sudden touch of knee or thigh, the thrilling reach across the body for the popcorn in the other person's lap.

Romantic love is also a topic held suspect. Some cultural historians argue that it is nothing more than a socially constructed phenomenon valorized in the medieval romance—a pretty myth that masks a hard, cold socioeconomic contract between two families in order to ally their powers and maintain (or increase) their status within the larger community. There is validity to that, and I am not a scientist or specialist in this area. But recent research in brain chemistry and human behavior has shown that aspects of romantic love are not only real but may be universal, and that the powerful drives it involves serve our primary evolutionary purpose. The psychologist Dorothy Tennov has invented the term "limerence" to describe the series of psychological and physiological behaviors associated with what we call romantic love. She clearly distinguishes it from other kinds of love—maternal, fraternal, and long-term marital.[19] Since then, others have built on this research to investigate exactly what goes on in the human brain and body during this state. But these investigations are by no means the first. Stendhal tried to analyze romantic love "scientifically" in his book *Love* (1822). Tennov follows his lead with more modern scientific and investigative tools, conducting extensive interviews across a large sample of couples who describe themselves as "in love." Neuroscientists are continuing her work with brain imaging and chemical analysis.[20] Limerence, which can last from six months to three years, has a number of characteristics: idealization of the love object, intrusive thinking and fantasizing about the beloved, obsessional behavior in an attempt to "catch" the beloved, and, when that love is reciprocated, euphoria. The drive for those in limerence is to unite in all ways with the beloved. If the love is not reciprocated, limerence will eventually die down, but while it survives (as all of us who have been rejected by a beloved have experienced) it can be as hellishly painful as the joy of limerence can be blissful.

As time goes on and brain research continues, there will be more, and more definitive, findings in these investigations. But scientific study confirms that the song-and-dance genres that have developed in the film musical correspond to characteristic stages in the period of limerence leading to union, and that they accurately and poetically describe something very real that most humans experience. This is only common sense; but common sense about love can arouse suspicion in the sophisticated. We now have scientific evidence that these feelings reflect a change in brain chemistry, chemical changes that are as powerful as those of any drug, and that withdrawal is just as difficult as withdrawal from drugs. Cole Porter's "Night and Day" and Astaire's dance to it poeticize this state, as do other songs and dances in film musicals. Berlin's "Cheek to Cheek" and Astaire's passionate dance on the song's theme of the euphoria evoked by dancing with his beloved ("Heaven, I'm in heaven") is another.

Courtship songs and dances are, to my mind, key to the success of a musical film— and it is the quality of the score (and its arrangement) and the power of the songs and dances that lie at the heart of the film musical's enchantment. During the first decade of sound cinema, it was Astaire and his composers who set the highest standard for consistent brilliance of score, song, and dance, and it was Astaire who set the model for many of the song-and-dance numbers. His inventions would become characteristic musical and dance devices not only for the Golden Age of film musicals, but beyond it.

The shadows that had immured France exploded. The tall soldiers, dressed in khaki and *chewing their gum*, were living proof that you could cross the seas again. They *ambled* past, and often they *stumbled*. Singing and whistling, they *stumbled* along the sidewalks and subway platforms: *stumbling*, they danced at night in the bistros and laughed their loud laughs, showing teeth white as children's. Jean Genet . . . declared loudly on the terrace of the Rhumerie that these costumed civilians had no style. Stiff in their black and green carapaces, the occupiers had been something else!

—Simone de Beauvoir, *The Prime of Life* (1962; emphases added)

7

FREEDOM INCARNATE

The Dancing Sailor as an Icon of American Values in World War II

SIMONE DE BEAUVOIR is describing the American soldiers who liberated Paris following the invasion of Normandy on June 6, 1944. (Fig. 7.1a shows American soldiers in France during this period.) Watching these "laughing," "gum chewing" young Americans as they "ambled" and "stumbled" through the streets and bistros of Paris, she is struck by their distinctive way of moving and behaving. She and her friend the writer Jean Genet contrast it with the more formal carriage and manner of the German occupiers. This fresh way of moving, she writes in the memorable phrase "freedom incarnate," literally embodies the liberty these soldiers will bring to her and her compatriots: "For me, these *carefree* young Americans were *freedom incarnate*: our own and also the freedom that was about to spread—we had no doubts on this score— throughout the world."[1]

This chapter takes up a genre that flourished briefly with World War II and then ceased as prevailing attitudes toward the military changed, especially with the Vietnam War. Military-leave film and stage romances became increasingly popular subjects during the war and the postwar years.[2] America's entrance into World War II changed American society and made a powerful impact on dance in musicals on Broadway, in ballet, and in films.

Only two months before the Normandy invasion, in April of 1944, these same military men had been the subject of a new ballet by the young American choreographer Jerome Robbins (see Fig. 7.1b), born in 1918 and thus only six years younger than Gene Kelly. Robbins's dance education, like that of Astaire and Kelly, was eclectic. He studied modern dance as well as ballet, Spanish as well as jazz dance, and a variety of other forms and styles. Like Astaire and Kelly, he was interested in everyday American movement. He loved Astaire and also Balanchine. He had appeared in 1938 in the

FIGURE 7.1 (a) Citizen-soldiers: American GI buddies who participated in the liberation of France in 1944 take a break by the side of the road. From Boivin, *La manche liberée* (1994). (b) Sailor buddies on leave in New York in 1944 look for fun in Jerome Robbins's ballet *Fancy Free* (1944). Members of the original cast: Jerome Robbins, John Kriza, Harold Lang, Janet Reed, and Muriel Bentley. (c) Three sailors wandering through Times Square in 1945. Photo by Herbert Gehr, courtesy of TimePix. (d) The three sailor buddies of *On the Town* (film, 1949) tour New York.

musical *Great Lady*, choreographed by Balanchine, and in 1940 in the Balanchine-Duke musical *Keep Off the Grass*.[3]

Fancy Free was both set and premiered in New York City, a major port of embarkation for the soldiers and sailors who would take part in the invasion and where many of them would enjoy their last shore leave before being sent to war in Europe. American involvement in World War II was at its height, though the United States had been at war since December of 1941, when the Japanese attacked Pearl Harbor. American boys were being sent in record numbers to the South Pacific and Europe from both the East and West Coasts. Robbins was not in the military, but at twenty-six he was only a little older than most of these young fighters, and he must have identified strongly with them. He watched and mingled with them as they enjoyed their precious days of freedom hanging out in the streets, canteens, and bars of New York. And, like de Beauvoir, he tried to capture their distinctive way of moving in the ballet, which he called *Fancy Free*, from the phrase "footloose and fancy free."

And indeed the opening of *Fancy Free* incorporates all the movements that de Beauvoir would later notice: these "carefree" young men "stumble," pushing and shoving each other into off-balance positions. And they "amble" in a kind of relaxed, aimless walk that suggests their openness to experience. They shove and scuffle and lean on one another. Like Astaire, Balanchine on Broadway, and Kelly, Robbins transforms ballet mime into American vernacular gesture. One sailor outlines the curves of an hourglass figure to suggest that they go chase girls; another wags his fingers in a "trucking" gesture from popular dance to suggest that they go dancing; another makes fun of this attempt by holding his nose. They enter a bar, order beers, and play rock-paper-scissors to decide who pays. We still see all this male adolescent horseplay in hamburger joints and pizzerias and on school playgrounds and street corners across America. Robbins of course theatricalizes it, editing it, subtly organizing it, and fitting it to music. The dance is full of physical stunts no ordinary adolescent can do—Robbins's dancers are highly trained artists, after all—but its vernacular base is unmistakable. He concludes this opening section by choreographing one of the most typical characteristics of the American military man of the time—gum chewing. One sailor offers his friends a stick of gum; each one peels away the wrapper, crumples it, and uses it to play a game they've obviously played many times before as, one after another, they flick the shiny wads across the stage to see who can launch them the farthest. It is a game that sums up their close but competitive relationship, and Leonard Bernstein, the musical's composer, builds this little game into the score, musically enhancing the trajectory of each pellet as it arcs across the stage.

Fancy Free was Robbins's first ballet for American Ballet Theatre. He was tired of the Russian-based ballets in his company's repertory: "I had just spent I don't know how many years dancing with Ballet Theatre at the point where it was completely Ballet Russified. . . . And for one whole year I did not get out of boots, Russian bloomers, and a peasant wig, and I thought, 'why can't we do ballet about our own subjects, meaning *our* life here in America?' "[4]

As we have seen, however, Robbins was not the first to put American dance subjects on the ballet, modern dance, or Broadway stage, and he was well aware of his precedents. A decade before *Fancy Free*, in 1936, as both he and Kelly were aware, Balanchine had fused jazz and ballet in the Broadway and Hollywood versions of *On Your Toes*. And like Kelly, he knew about Graham's *American Document*, and about *Frankie and Johnny* and *Filling Station*.[5] He would presumably have seen Katherine Dunham's and Balanchine's work in the Broadway production of *Cabin in the Sky*. During Robbins's teens there was also Massine's 1934 ballet *Union Pacific* for the Ballets Russe de Monte Carlo. Robbins knew about Agnes de Mille's choreography in *Rodeo* (1942), set, like *Billy the Kid*, to a score by Copland. She created ballets with American subjects, but they drew largely on a legendary American past. *Fancy Free*, in contrast—and like Kelly's and Astaire's work—could not have been more up to the minute. Said Robbins:

During the war years . . . the kinds of people I described in the ballet were all around us. At that time we were dancing at the old Metropolitan Opera House, which was situated at 40th Street and Broadway. Times Square was right there, and that was all bubbling out over us. We saw it everywhere we looked—the kind of incident, the kind of people, the kind of kids that were dancing then. . . . There are some steps in the ballet that I actually saw sailors do in a bar.[6]

Reviewing the first night of *Fancy Free*, Edwin Denby was struck by how successfully Robbins captured "how people live in this country . . . its dances are witty, exuberant, and at every moment they feel *natural*. . . . There isn't any of that coy showing of 'folk material' that dancers are doing so much nowadays." And Denby recognized "all sorts of references to our normal dance-hall steps, as they are done from Roseland to the Savoy; trucking, the boogie, knee drops, even a round-the-back done in slow motion."[7] There are also references to tap dance, which many American youngsters were taught at dancing school and for school performances.[8]

Even the choice of the number of dancers came from close observation: Harold Lang, who was in the original cast, tells how "when we were in New York, between rehearsals and performances at the old Met, often Jerry, Muriel [Bentley] and I would be wandering around Times Square and Jerry would point out, 'Did you ever see one or two sailors? No, you always see *three*. . . . There are always *three* together'" (Figs. 7.1b–d).[9]

In *Fancy Free* Robbins makes use of an absolutely up-to-the-minute subject: sailors on shore leave. But while he may have been the first to put American sailors on the ballet stage, he was by no means the first to present them to American audiences. Dancing military men had already been used as musical subjects in American movies: Astaire, one of Robbins's idols, was a dancing sailor in *Follow the Fleet* (1936), into whose dances Astaire had of course incorporated vernacular movement. But in the 1940s the sailor, like the street dance, would become most prominently identified with Gene Kelly, who would make something of a specialty of the dancing military man. Kelly first presents his dancing sailor in the film *Anchors Aweigh*, which was choreographed and filmed the year *Fancy Free* premiered. Like Robbins, Kelly was interested in incorporating everyday movement into his work. Robbins would have seen *The Time of Your Life* and *Pal Joey*. And like Robbins, Kelly frequented the streets, bars, and dance halls of New York and Los Angeles to see how ordinary Americans moved and then incorporated those movements into his choreography.

Again like Robbins, Kelly introduces in *Anchors Aweigh* not only the dancing sailor, but dancing sailors—plural—with their buddies. Kelly and his pal, played by Frank Sinatra, are stationed on the West Coast in the port city of San Diego, and they spend their precious leave time exploring Hollywood. Joe and Clarence, the film's singing, dancing sailors, stand with Robbins's sailors at the head of a line of military men who will become new American musical heroes for the war and postwar years, in the same way that Astaire's top-hatted gentleman was a cultural emblem of the 1930s. It is as a musical man in uniform, often a sailor, that Kelly will create some of his most memorable screen heroes, from *As Thousands Cheer* (1942), *Anchors Aweigh* (1945), and *On the Town* (1949, a film version of the stage musical that would grow from *Fancy Free*) to *Invitation to the Dance* (1954) and *It's Always Fair Weather* (1955).

Kelly, like Robbins, preferred sailors to soldiers for his dancing characters. There is one very practical dance-related reason for this, and it relates to Kelly's interest in line. Kelly himself tells us that the ordinary seaman's uniform, with its close-fitting jacket and hip-hugging trousers in either blue or white, was an ideal outfit for a dancer: its uniform color and unbroken line function like a dancer's unitard to reveal and emphasize the line and flow of the body, while its bell-bottomed trousers, jaunty cap, shoulder flaps, and rakish tie inject an element of fantasy—of costume—into everyday life.[10] The uniform thus provides a way in which a character could stand out without being unnatural, could be both "ordinary" and fantastic at the same time.

The dancing sailor also has a long history, of which Kelly and probably Robbins were well aware. In America it extends as far back as the eighteenth century. Beginning in 1785 and until the end of the century, John Durang toured widely with his specialty dance, the sailor's hornpipe. (Interestingly, the sailor is the only type of American serviceman associated with a specific dance.)[11] Across the Atlantic there were also, of course, the singing and dancing sailors in Gilbert and Sullivan's operetta *H.M.S. Pinafore* (1878). In 1925 Serge Diaghilev commissioned Léonide Massine and Georges Auric to create *Les matelots* for the Ballets Russes, a ballet that, like *Anchors Aweigh* and *Fancy Free*, took for its heroes three sailor buddies, one of them an American.[12]

The sailor costume (and the institution it signified) also gave the character license for otherwise unacceptable public behavior, especially during the war and immediate postwar years. The sailor on leave was treated indulgently by a public that saw him as a guardian hero of the nation. Because he had been prepared to sacrifice his life to maintain order, he had the right to bend the rules just a little. His carefree attitude and his desire to pack as much boisterous fun into the short time allotted him while he was on shore leave made him the ideal musical hero; song and dance seemed appropriate vehicles for the expression of what the public perceived as the sailor's natural qualities.

Part of the excitement and poignancy of *Anchors Aweigh*, *Fancy Free*, and *On the Town* comes from the idea of shore leave—that hiatus between tours of duty that gave a special urgency to the romance of the dancing men and women.[13] Says Betty Comden of *On the Town*:

There was a tremendous emotional base for the story line. The fact that there was a war on was working for us all the time; the fact that these boys had just twenty-four hours beginning with their coming off the ship and ending with their saying goodbye and getting on a ship going who knows where. . . . In wartime it had a tremendously poignant feeling.[14]

Fancy Free and *Anchors Aweigh* put those emotions into dance. Muriel Bentley, who played the first girl in *Fancy Free*, remembers:

The whole attitude of so many young people at that time was very disoriented. And we, the dancers, were living right in the middle of it. On tour, when we could get a train, the Ballet Theatre cars would be hooked up to the troop cars. All those soldiers and sailors and ballet troupes, in strange places and different towns. We were uprooted and although we had a very carefree attitude, we were also very tentative about relationships. There was a certain brashness and carefree feeling mixed with sensitivity, almost a timid quality. We were all so terribly young, not necessarily young in years, but kind of innocent, and rather lonely. Our attitude was one of wanting to be close to one another but knowing that it couldn't last. So that there was this constant reaching out, but knowing that it was only temporary. You can see that in the choreography.[15]

Yet *Fancy Free* and *Anchors Aweigh* were concerned not only with relationships between men and women, but also with that special bond of loyalty that developed between servicemen working together, fighting for the same cause, and sharing the same dangers. During these years the buddy bond, a combination of kidding and caring, like the theme of shore leave, became an important subject for dance in musicals, on the stage, and in film.

Robbins establishes that bond in the opening moments of *Fancy Free*. As he says in his libretto, "One should feel immediately that the three are good friends, used to bumming around together, used to each other's guff . . . that they are in the habit of spending their time as a trio, and that, under all their rough and tumble exterior, there is a real affection for each other, a kind of, my buddy, feeling."[16]

That "my buddy" feeling also pervades *Anchors Aweigh*. At the beginning of the film we learn that the main characters, Joe and Clarence, have earned their leave because of their heroism in battle. Joe (Kelly) is, in fact, responsible for saving the life of Clarence (Frank Sinatra), and he continues to be responsible for his buddy throughout the film. Suppressing his growing attachment to Susan (Kathryn Grayson) because of his buddy's infatuation with her, Joe spends most of the film helping his buddy win the girl whom he himself loves. Similarly, Clarence conceals his own interest in another female friend because he thinks Joe wants him to like Susan. Only when the two men understand that neither will be hurt can they act on their real feelings.

The buddy bond also provides the motivation for a genre of song and dance, the "buddy song," which first appears in *Anchors Aweigh* and carries through others of the genre. In "I Begged Her,"[17] the first song and dance in the film, Joe and Clarence unite, in locker-room fashion, to boast to their pals of their prowess with women, which they claim to have demonstrated on their first night of leave. Each praises the other extravagantly in a song that, restricted by the Hays Production Code, uses the word "kiss" as a euphemism for sex. The song is given its comic undertone by the fact that the audience knows that both Clarence and Joe are lying outrageously. They have, in fact, failed

FIGURE 7.2 (a) Sailor Kelly cheers up a little Mexican girl (Sharon Macmanus) in *Anchors Aweigh* (1945). (b) An American GI cradles a child victim of the war in the South Pacific; *Newsweek*, February 19, 1945. Photograph courtesy of *Newsweek*. (c) Ex-GI Kelly amuses French children in *An American in Paris* with "I Got Rhythm." (d) Sailor Kelly, in *Anchors Aweigh* (1945), liberates the kingdom of Jerry the Mouse by teaching him to dance.

miserably in their pursuit of female companionship. In its down-home language, and especially in the irony of the situation in which it is sung, "I Begged Her" reveals a great deal about these two American archetypes. Both are from those "average" families celebrated in the Frank Capra and MGM family movies. The character played by Sinatra in *Anchors Aweigh* and later *On the Town* is the softer of the two—an American innocent, awkward and inexperienced, who, lacking the Kelly character's more assertive stance toward life, needs to be mothered—at the beginning of the film by his pal and, by the end, by a strong comic female who takes the initiative in the relationship. Physically, Sinatra also fit this role: his skinny physique is the subject of a running gag throughout this film and others of the series. Kelly's character, Joe, is the leader of the pair, good-hearted and aggressively friendly, his vulnerability and naiveté often masked by a defensive, cocky veneer.

Robbins draws similar contrasts between hard and soft character types in *Fancy Free*: the sailor originally danced by John Kriza is the shy, sweet, vulnerable character, and he is played off against his more confident, harder-edged friends. However, whether shy or sharp, the sailors must present a united and cocky front to the outside world, a facade that masks any fear. This behavior conforms to the standard social norms for American men, intensified here by their uniforms. As Robbins explains: "Well, everyone that went into the armed forces felt he had to behave the way the public expected him to behave. A sailor in New York had to be cocky. He wanted to appear not to be afraid of the city, especially if he came from out of town. Once you put on the uniform, that's the way you behaved."[18]

This new emphasis on male friendship is a distinguishing feature of *Fancy Free*, *Anchors Aweigh*, and their film-musical successors. Most previous ballets had focused on heterosexual romantic relationships, and most other film musicals of the 1930s placed the romantic male-female relationship at the heart of the film. In every one of his films, Astaire's male sidekick was a comic foil, inept and one-dimensional, who contrasted with and thus pointed up Astaire's own virtues. In *Anchors Aweigh*, although Clarence's awkwardness is used to create comic situations, he is Joe's equal. And Joe too is made the butt of jokes. In any case, it is clear that in this film, as in dancing-sailor films to follow, the friendship between Joe and Clarence vies for pride of place with romantic love. And like the courtship, it becomes an important subject and motivating force for song and dance in the Kelly-Donen films and in *Fancy Free*.

Close male friendship had always been a feature of westerns and war movies, and it intensified during the war years.[19] In Robbins's *Fancy Free*, a homoerotic subtext should be considered. John D'Emilio, in his chronicle of homosexuality in America, has pointed out that World War II marked an important step forward in the self-recognition and formation of a group identity for gays and lesbians, when young men and women from all over America were brought together in the armed forces to live in close conditions in same-sex groups.[20] As an active (although closeted to the general public) gay man, Robbins was part of a homosexual cohort active and influential in the arts, including some of the original creators of *Fancy Free*: the composer, Bernstein, and the dancers John Kriza and Harold Lang. The sailors whom Robbins so closely studied on the streets of New York were erotic objects for him as well as research material for his new ballet. Another factor was the gay artist Paul Cadmus's painting of sailors on shore leave, *The Fleet's In*, which was suggested to Robbins as the subject for a ballet by his friend Mary Hunter. Robbins was intrigued with idea of sailors on shore leave but rejected the model of Cadmus' s painting as too raunchy.[21] It must be remembered that homosexuality was illegal in the United States through almost all of the twentieth century (in some states until 2003), and any homosexual caught in the act could be prosecuted as a felon. Although *Fancy Free* may indeed have homoerotic undertones, it is clear that the musical was intended to be seen, on the surface, as a portrayal of American heterosexual males on the lookout for a good time with members of the opposite sex and competing, often aggressively, for women's favors.

In any case, it is in *Fancy Free* and *Anchors Aweigh* that Robbins in New York and Kelly in Hollywood use the dancing sailor to present a very particular American character, a type that differs in behavior from its European counterpart. He is a man whose casual manner and relaxed, spontaneous behavior mark him as the boy next door, a citizen-soldier rather than a member of a specially groomed and trained military class.[22] Nowhere is this more clearly presented than in the Olvera Street dance in *Anchors Aweigh*, in which Kelly presents the dancing sailor as the "made to be a good dad" children's friend (Fig. 7.2a; cf. Figs. 7.2b and c).

The Olvera Street dance takes place on a studio recreation of the street of the same name in the Mexican quarter of Los Angeles. Joe has come to a restaurant in the quarter that is a frequent meeting place of the buddies. Peering through the restaurant window, he sees the woman with whom he has fallen in love seated with his pal. Out of loyalty to his friend, he decides to leave the two alone. Turning sadly from the window, he notices that he is being watched by a solemn-faced little Latina girl. Partly to cheer himself, and partly to please her, Joe dances with her.

The dance begins when the sailor bows politely and offers the child his arm. The little girl accepts it solemnly, and the incongruous couple two-step gravely to the "Mexican Hat Dance." In the dance's center section Joe attempts to cheer the child by performing for her, incorporating objects found in the street. He "plays" some hanging ceramic pots with candlesticks he finds among the pottery stand's wares. He improvises a jump rope from some string. To climax the dance, he swings the little girl in a breathless polka around the fountain at the center of the set. The camera, which until this point has remained relatively quiet, responds to the increase in tempo, dynamics, and dance activity by grandly swinging back and up.

A children's dance like the Olvera Street dance was an ideal vehicle both for Kelly's personal dance style and movie persona and for the dancing military man. It allowed him to incorporate legitimately the street games and elements of play on which many of his dance ideas were based into a form that confirmed the hometown-boy good-father-to-be character that he portrayed in most of his films. After *Anchors Aweigh*, Kelly's dances with children as a military man or someone just out of the army would be incorporated into several of his films, including *Living in a Big Way* (1947), *An American in Paris* (1951), and *Invitation to the Dance* (1956).

But Joe's character, as portrayed in dance in this segment—his boyishness, his sweet concern for the little girl—also crystallized in dance an image that by 1944 had become part of the national consciousness. The American military man, as portrayed in national journals and in the movies, was seen as a kind of boy hero—symbolic, in a sense, of the supposedly free-spirited and classless society from which he emerged.[23] Joe, who comforts the brown-skinned girl (she is listed in the film's credits as a "beggar girl"), is the dance reflection of thousands of GI Joes. In newspaper and magazine images, especially after the invasion of Europe, the American military man was presented as a sort of children's savior, distributing chocolate bars, bubble gum, and canned goods to European or Asian children.[24] The good-humored boyishness of the American soldier, himself just out of childhood, is an important part of this image. His willingness to involve himself in the child's world, to play, further confirms his benevolence; he is an unsophisticated and gregarious citizen-soldier, temporarily in uniform; his enemy is the professional German or Japanese soldier, portrayed in the media as a part of an inhuman military machine, itself the reflection of a rigid, vicious government.[25]

One of Kelly's most famous citizen-soldier dances appears in *An American in Paris*. As an ex-GI, he enchants a group of French children by using Gershwin's "I Got Rhythm" as the basis for an exuberant and interactive song and dance game on the streets of a postwar Paris still recovering from the German occupation (Fig. 7.2c). Another dance sequence that presents the sailor as a children's hero makes a very direct connection between his behavior and the idea of freedom or liberation. In the "Worry Song" sequence in *Anchors Aweigh*, Kelly invents a song-and-dance allegory on the theme of liberty, combining live and animated figures, to amuse a group of schoolchildren. We see him first striding in slow motion through a cartoon landscape, playing a pennywhistle, while we hear Joe's voice narrating the tale. At one point in the narrative, the sailor suddenly stumbles and falls through a hole in the ground. The camera follows him through the dark, narrow tunnel of earth from which he emerges into an animated cartoon landscape populated by sad-faced animals who silence his whistle, explaining to him that the king of their country has banned all music. Incensed, Joe promises to investigate the situation. In the palace's throne room he confronts the cartoon country's monarch, Jerry the Mouse, who explains that the law was created because he himself does not know how to sing or dance. Joe proceeds to teach the mouse by example, and the two dance exuberantly together ("Worry Song," Fig. 7.2d). The opening section of this sequence particularly exploits the casual, carefree manner of the sailor as he runs, jumps, and rolls in the grass on his way to the magical kingdom. Kelly's dance with the mouse becomes more of a routine, but it too uses ordinary walking, quotations from popular dances, and gestures of play as part of the choreography.

In this sequence, song and dance are presented as metaphors for freedom, and Joe embodies that freedom. By teaching Jerry to sing and dance—to move the way he does—he liberates him and the other members of the cartoon kingdom. When *Anchors Aweigh* was being written, choreographed, and made in 1944, Americans were well aware that an invasion of Europe was being planned, although they had no idea when or where it would take place. They knew too that, successful or not, it would mark the beginning of the end of the war. Although successful, the invasion of Normandy, on June 6, 1944, was a horrific event in which many were killed and wounded.[26] Joe uses popular movement to tell a tale in dance about how democracy will triumph with ease. Like the cheeky citizen-soldiers in *Fancy Free*, Joe is de Beauvoir's "freedom incarnate" in dance, and as his real-life counterparts did the year *Anchors Aweigh* was made, he "liberates" a country. By the time *Anchors Aweigh* was released in 1945, it could be read as a metaphorical musical celebration of the Allied liberation of Europe.

Joe and his descendants in *On the Town* crystallized this image not only for Americans, but also for those English and European audiences to whom these films were distributed and widely shown. (*Fancy Free* was taken to England in 1946 by the American Ballet Theatre.) More Broadway shows and films that feature this type followed, the most famous being the Broadway show *On the Town*, which reunited the Bernstein and Robbins team and brought in Betty Comden and Adolph Green to write the script. Helping to distribute this image even more widely, Kelly and Donen in 1949 adapted *On the Town* with some (though not all) of the Bernstein score, replacing the original Broadway stars with the *Anchors Aweigh* team of Kelly and Sinatra and, as the third buddy, Jules Munshin. How established the convention became in the minds not only of Americans but internationally can be seen, for example, in Tom Stoppard's 1976 comedy *New-Found Land*, a play within the play *Dirty Linen*, which evokes a utopian New York as envisioned by an Englishman using the dancing sailor on shore leave as an important part of his imagery, while he quotes the opening lines from the first song in *On the Town*: "New York, New York! It's a wonderful town!"[27]

Anchors Aweigh and *Fancy Free* mark the beginning of a high point in the American public's confidence in the military. But de Beauvoir's vision of a free and open Europe, as represented by those freely moving young Americans, did not come to pass. With the Cold War and the descent of the Iron Curtain, Americans begin to lose confidence in the military, and the dancing sailor lost his validity as a cultural icon. Kelly and Donen's last film as a directorial team, the ironically titled *It's Always Fair Weather* (1955), reflects this change. In it the three buddies of *On the Town* are reunited after ten years. This time, however, they are dancing GIs. Their wartime solidarity is established in the opening montage as they slog and battle through the hardships of the European ground war. Back home at war's end, they celebrate in the streets of New York City, reeling from bar to bar in a street dance that mingles joyful exuberance with drunken anxiety and anger (Fig. 7.3a). At its end they are sent on their way by an affectionate but realistic bartender who warns: "Hey, hey, boys, the war's over, people don't love drunk civilians the way they love drunk solders." Ten years later they reunite, and as they have aged they have become disillusioned and embittered. Their confidence has been shaken, and time and social change have eroded their once close and caring relationship.

In the song and dance "Once I Had a Friend" from *It's Always Fair Weather*, the three buddies use vernacular gesture to mourn the loss of their friendship and self-confidence. This time, however, the exuberance and energy are gone, and the dance, a quiet time step, uses a series of variations on the stamping, brushing "aw shucks" gestures with which each character conveys his grief, anger, and frustration. Somber workday clothes replace their uniforms. Strikingly, too, they dance in separate spaces, although united via Cinemascope by a three-way split screen (Fig. 7.3b).

Like the courtship songs and dances that come at the heart of other musicals, this song and dance mark a turning point in the plot: the characters, having reexamined

FIGURE 7.3 *It's Always Fair Weather* (1955), ex–war buddies disillusioned. (a) Drunk dance. (b) Mourning the loss of their friendship in song and dance, in separate spaces.

their feelings, will eventually be reconciled. But although *It's Always Fair Weather* ends on a positive note, its overall message is still, in comparison with earlier Kelly-Donen musicals, a sad one. The once inviolate bond of friendship has been broken, and the confident and cheerful sailors of the earlier films have become frightened and vulnerable in middle age. In its exploration in song and dance of male vulnerability, "Once I Had a Friend" has almost no predecessors in musicals.[28] The tune's offhand nonchalance—the sadness is underlying, expressed indirectly—allows these emotionally repressed American men to despair musically without ever stepping out of character.[29]

After *It's Always Fair Weather*, never again in the twentieth century would the dancing military man have potency as a musical image of confidence and freedom. During the Vietnam years the military became a symbol of oppression. The 1979 film musical made from Broadway's *Hair*, directed by Milos Forman, begins its first number with the burning of a draft card. Now it is those who actively resist conscription, the hippies, who are dancing and singing symbols of liberation. The dances, choreographed by Twyla Tharp—who was herself influenced by both Kelly and Robbins—are based, like theirs, on everyday movement and popular dance forms. Like their dancing-sailor predecessors, the hippies use dance and song as a symbol of freedom, but this time they are contrasted to the stiff, regimented, and faceless American military. In the opening sequence they startle an uptight young cowboy who has come to New York to join the army with their carefree demeanor and start him on the road to rebellion. Thirty years after *Anchors Aweigh* and *Fancy Free*, it is those outside the military who move as if they are "freedom incarnate."[30]

8

'S WONDERFUL

Euphoric Street Dances

JUST AS THE intricate and varying emotional texture of the courtship couple dance belongs to Astaire and will be forever identified with him, dances about the bliss of falling in love belong to Kelly. His best-loved dances come from this genre—and in accordance with his style and interests, they take advantage of the expansiveness of the street. "Singin' in the Rain" is the prime example, and another is "'S Wonderful," George and Ira Gershwin's compendium of slang tributes to love. In *An American in Paris*, Kelly and Georges Guétary ride a wave of euphoria, their inhibitions falling away and proper behavior cast aside as they stroll singing and dancing through the streets of Paris.

The euphoria dance is about what you feel when your big crush is around, or better yet, when you find out that the attraction is mutual. It parallels a song tradition that began long before the period under discussion. It can motivate even the most physically inhibited of us to move: as Leo Sayer sings, "You make me feel like dancing." And like the pursuit and capture of courtship, this feeling is a great subject for a choreographer.

Euphoria songs and dances were a standard part of the Broadway musical. "'S Wonderful," for example, started life in the Gershwin show of the same name, written for Fred and Adele Astaire in 1927. Thirty years later, in 1957, Fred Astaire and Audrey Hepburn sing it in *Funny Face*, now rewritten for the movies. (Kelly's version in *An American in Paris* came in 1951.) Or take Rodgers and Hammerstein's "I'm in Love with a Wonderful Guy," sung by Nelly Forbush, the naive army nurse from Arkansas (played by Mary Martin on stage in 1949 and Mitzi Gaynor in the 1967 film) as she frolics in the sand of a South Pacific beach after spending an enchanted evening with the French planter Émile de Becque. Hammerstein's lyrics for "Wonderful Guy" acknowledge the commonality of these ecstatic feelings. Nelly knows she is not unique; as she admits, she's "a cliché coming true." But her feelings are genuine, and she revels in this "conventional dither" as she exults over and over to her friends, "I'm in love."[1]

Ordinary people may indeed express the high that comes with love in clichés. But as my brief discussion of limerence in chapter 6 indicates, the feeling is genuine, remarkable, and even astounding when it happens for the first time. After the right hormones kick in at puberty, we experience a key change in brain chemistry, one that serves us in, so evolutionary biology tells us, the most important things we do as humans—reproducing and nurturing. The euphoria dance is about an actual physiological phenomenon now being explored by psychologists, anthropologists, and neuroscientists: the hormonal cocktail that gives a kick better than that from either champagne or cocaine. Or, as Ira Gershwin says in a *Funny Face* song, "I must find why my mind is behaving like a dancer."

Actually, lyricists of this genre can be impressively analytical about the phenomenon. Ira Gershwin expresses one lover's understanding of these new and seemingly uncontrollable feelings in the song mentioned earlier: "How Long Has This Been Going On?" from *Funny Face*. The singer addresses another feeling that comes along with the euphoria. It's not *just* bliss; there is also something else, a heightened emotional state that makes you see and feel everything differently. While it certainly has to do with sexual attraction, it is much more than that. The lover has entered into unknown territory, and bewilderment, awe, and wonderment are part of its topography. In *Funny Face* this feeling sends the earnest, repressed intellectual played by Audrey Hepburn swooping ecstatically around her tiny basement bookstore in response to a kiss from Fred Astaire. Inhibition swept away, she dances with an extravagantly trimmed hat, the trailing ribbons of glowing green, yellow, and orange chiffon punctuating the darkness of her drab workaday clothes and shop. Johnny Mercer's wonderful lyrics of "That Old Black Magic" for the Balanchine dance sequence in *Star Spangled Rhythm* draw on one of the most common metaphors to explain this feeling: witchcraft. So does Hart's "Bewitched, Bothered and Bewildered," describing the feelings aroused by Gene Kelly in *Pal Joey*, or E. Y. "Yip" Harburg's "That Old Devil Moon" from *Finian's Rainbow*, which debuted on Broadway in 1947 and became Astaire's final musical film in 1968.

Most of Kelly's euphoria songs and dances, though, express unadulterated bliss and the disinhibition that comes with finding a new emotional world. The expansive public space of the street was an ideal site in which to demonstrate this feeling in movement. And Kelly, working with Minnelli, adds to the repertoire of camera moves he established with Donen in *Cover Girl* with a more frequent and broader use of the boom camera (one attached to a crane and mounted on wheels) to express it. Balanchine had used the gliding boom camera to capture a GI's euphoric dream of his pin-up, Vera Zorina, running through a snowy landscape. Now Minnelli, working with Kelly, would manipulate the boom camera in ever more inventive ways to bring an exciting new dimension to street dances.[2]

A good example is the street dance "'S Wonderful" in *An American in Paris*, directed by Minnelli and choreographed by Kelly. By the time of *An American in Paris*, Minnelli's skill with the boom, like that of Berkeley a decade and a half earlier, had become something of a legend among filmmakers and technicians. Only a handful of directors and camera operators had mastered the technique of using it effectively. Directors too often used boom shots gratuitously, employing them for their breathtaking effect yet making no attempt to relate this to the dramatic action. Walter Strohm, the head of MGM's production department, noted this when he paid tribute to Minnelli:

> Minnelli loved to be on the boom and was very astute in using it, although it's a time consuming and costly thing because you could take a whole day just to rehearse and shoot one boom shot. Sometimes he did a whole day's work in one shot, which is rather interesting. Some days he would be on the boom all day rehearsing, riding it, and, when the end of the day came they would make the shot and that would be the whole scene. Well, there are very few directors you could allow to do that because they are not capable of visualizing and timing boom shots. They become very awkward and mechanical, and you become conscious of the boom and not the action. Booms are deadly to most directors. In fact, we had a rule—people hated it, but we had to have it because everybody wasn't Minnelli and everybody didn't know how to use the boom—so directors couldn't use the boom without my okay. . . . But, with Minnelli, some of his great boom shots were classic. I just used to love to watch his boom shots. The one he did on "'S Wonderful" with Gene is just a classic.[3]

In "'S Wonderful," Minnelli and Kelly present inventively not only the euphoric response of two characters to love, but the love triangle at the heart of *An American in Paris*—in a street song and dance that holds multiple layers of meaning and feeling. Kelly and Georges Guétary are in love with same woman. We know it, and so does their friend Adam—but they themselves are clueless. In the song "'S Wonderful," they confide their feelings to Adam, who, afraid of letting the cat out of the bag, nervously fumbles with his cigarettes and drinks his coffee with shaking hands as he desperately tries to change the subject ("Did I ever tell you about the time I gave a command performance for Hitler?"; Fig. 8.1a).

The emotional temperature rises as each proclaims his love ever more forcefully in speech until, as if unable to contain their feelings, they stand up and stroll, arm in arm, into song. The camera, on a level with them, parallels their movement, gliding precisely in tempo and pausing briefly while Kelly dances and Guétary sings to an audience of pedestrians (Figs. 8.1b–d). In "'S Wonderful," each singer tries to outdo the other in finding the word that expresses the emotional high he feels for the girl he loves, moving chromatically up the scale with every new description—and with Ira Gershwin adding increasingly silly and slap-happy call-and-response lyrics to the original laundry list, Guétary singing his love in French and Kelly rhyming him in English.

Kelly's choreography and Minnelli's boom camerawork parallel the emotion, the music, and the lyrics. The singers move in opposite directions down the street, shouting to be heard over the people and traffic as Minnelli's camera glides back and up to capture them. The pullback of the camera, precisely coordinated with the music, becomes a visual metaphor for the crescendo to the climax of sound and emotion that

FIGURE 8.1 *An American in Paris* (1951), "'S Wonderful." Beginning in a café where their friend Oscar Levant looks on and moving into a Paris street, Gene Kelly and Georges Guétary sing and dance their love, not realizing they are both in love with the same woman (Leslie Caron).

concludes the song. The camera's highest point coincides with the song's final note, then hangs in the air as the people in the street—carefully positioned to form, in color and compositional arrangement, a dynamic diagonal across the screen, at either end of which the two singers stand—applaud their impromptu performance (Figs. 8.1e–g).

Following Kelly's experiences with Minnelli in *An American in Paris*, Kelly and Donen's moving boom camera achieves a new level of fluidity and expansiveness, demonstrated in the most famous movie dance of them all. "Singin' in the Rain" incorporates almost every one of Kelly's conventions: it is a street dance that, like "'S Wonderful," expresses the hero's euphoric response to falling in love, making use of a dance vocabulary of Kelly's typical vernacular. "Singin' in the Rain" is also a kind of children's dance. Kelly performs a set of variations on the theme of playing in the rain as, drenched and euphoric, he abandons all sense of decorum, closes his umbrella, and dances in the pouring rain, using his umbrella as a prop rather than protection as he balances on the curb, gets thoroughly and happily soaked under a downspout, and, for a finale, stomps and splashes ecstatically in the street's deepest puddle (Figs. 8.2a–h)—until the appearance of a policeman who, like his counterpart in *Cover Girl*, puts an end to his musical games.

The song starts quietly. At first, the camera simply glides in tempo in front of Kelly as he strolls toward it. It becomes more active, however, after the dancer abandons himself to the rain, shuts his umbrella, shoulders it (a gesture enhanced by a glissando right up to the first note of the song), and begins to sing (Fig. 8.2a). When Kelly suddenly jumps up on a lamppost in his excitement, the camera exhilaratingly pulls back and up (Fig. 8.2b), then swoops in to capture, in close-up, his euphoric smile as he dismounts and leans drunkenly against the post. Passing a lighted shop window, he bows to a cardboard cutout (Fig. 8.2c), then partners his umbrella (Fig. 8.2d). After he gets thoroughly soaked under a downspout (Fig. 8.2e), this camera gesture is repeated a few steps further down the street when he opens his arms in an invitation to the heavens to soak him, and the camera responds by swooping low over his upturned face. At the emotional and musical climax of the dance, the camera sweeps exhilaratingly back, up, and around as Kelly catapults off the sidewalk and, using his open umbrella as a sail (Fig. 8.2f), traces a circle on the street while the melody is transferred to the brass in an emphatic restatement. We have seen the final camera movement at the end of "'S Wonderful" in *An American in Paris*, but here it parallels—every bit as effectively—a diminuendo: the camera pulls back and up slowly to give us a full view of the final poetic moment, the black-slickered policeman watching Kelly skip off down the street (Fig. 8.2h).[4] Kelly pauses briefly to hand his closed umbrella to a passer-by who is hunched over to protect himself from the downpour. He opens the umbrella, then hurriedly moves on as Kelly, drenched and happy, skips off.

As we have seen, Kelly saw a strong link between his choreography and sports—especially urban street sports like soccer. The most basic poor kid's sport is a street competition. Who can vault the highest over the fire hydrant? Who can balance most confidently on the curb? Who can jump off the curb and swing with impunity into the forbidden territory of that street our mothers won't let us cross? Who can get

FIGURE 8.2 A euphoric Gene Kelly sings, dances, and splashes in the rain in *Singin' in the Rain* (1952).

away with all these stunts without attracting the attention of the cop on the beat? In "Singin' in the Rain" and in other street dances, Kelly turns this urban child's play into art.

"Singin' in the Rain" is also one of the highest examples of the art of the arranger-orchestrator: the use of orchestral color and texture, harmonic structure, tempo, and rhythm in suggesting atmosphere and interacting with song, dance, and camerawork to convey the emotional and dramatic trajectory of the sequence. Indeed, "Singin' in the Rain" is a fine example of the ability of orchestrators to spin straw into gold. Compare the first appearance of "Singin'" in *Broadway Melody of 1929*, a brittle, up-tempo, ricky-tick arrangement sung by a chorus of tinny-voiced chorus girls. The vamp that leads into to it and continues under the song is meant to suggest the reassuring patter of the raindrops, but it sounds more like hail. Later Roger Edens and his colleagues in the Freed unit at MGM transformed the song in two different musicals with two brilliant arrangements that are completely different from each other. His big-band arrangement for the singer Judy Garland in *Little Nelly Kelly* swings the song and gives her wonderful musical and rhythmic games to play as she entertains a crowd at the policeman's ball. Eden's arrangement for Kelly is—in an established tradition that, as we have seen, extends back to Astaire and Balanchine film dances and before that to ballet scores in the nineteenth century—driven by both the dance and the drama, written in conjunction with the choreographer himself and made to enhance and interact with almost every one of his gestures. But the synergy of sound and moving image to create a larger unified whole is so brilliant that we never notice the musical and dramatic devices built into it. The score starts with the soft suggestion of the most imitated of clock chimes that bleeds into the vamp (whose first phrase is a swung version of Westminster's third-quarter chime) as Kelly kisses his beloved goodnight, then waves away his chauffeur as the vamp, on strings, moves up a key when Kelly takes it up in vocables ("doo di doo do") to accompany his rhythmic walk. The lead into the song and dance is subtle and natural seeming.

Kelly's dance is a deceptively simple-looking and exquisitely executed series of tap variations on Arthur Freed and Herb Nacio Brown's "Singin' in the Rain" combined with walking, running, skipping, and jumping steps. The sound of his shoes, softened and slightly muffled by the water in which he splashes, embroiders and interacts with variations of the song's melody, countermelodies, colors, and textures provided by the orchestrators. Debussy and Ravel are an influence here: the shimmering textures and harmonies of their various water musics (*La mer, Une barque sur l'océan*) inform the orchestrations—for example, when Kelly scoops up water from the gutter onto the sidewalk in a breathtaking skim along the curb (Fig. 8.2g). The brass-choir sound of a big band powerfully reinforces Kelly's space-eating swing out into the street, and the danced variations on the song include various manipulations of the umbrella from simple to complex: Kelly initiates an orchestral glissando to a key change as he drags the umbrella along a series of fenceposts, and a variety of orchestral punctuation points and countermelodies, each tailored to the quality of each "umbrella variation," emphasize and interact with Kelly's gestures. The orchestrator even slips in one of the oldest musical tropes in musical history, the association of horns with state authority: it accompanies our (and the dancer's) first view of the policeman who will put stop to Kelly's antics (Fig. 8.2h).

After *Singin' in the Rain*, Kelly became increasingly daring in covering ever more varied and expansive spaces. He had planned for the dances in *Brigadoon*, for example, to be filmed on location in the highlands of Scotland. *On the Town* had been a real breakthrough—and increasingly, other films were not being shot on the studio back lots, but picking up and moving abroad. "It would have been so exciting," Kelly remembered, "to have the meeting of the clans for the wedding in the actual hills of Scotland." But the studio system was gradually breaking up, and the country's variable weather and a shortage of studio funds prevented this ambitious scheme. So Kelly had to be content with a studio Scotland. The Freed unit's art department tried its best to create the heathered mountain landscape, with plenty of rocks to clamber over, streams to ford, and stone fences to teeter on—in short, as many ups and downs as possible to satisfy Kelly's wish to dance over a varied and natural landscape.

In *Brigadoon* as in *Singin' in the Rain*, Kelly starts with a song and a walk, and as his inhibitions fall away he becomes ever more playful and daring, hopping and skipping through the landscape, testing his balance on a rocky wall that snakes up a hill. In *Singin' in the Rain* Kelly sang ardently to a shop-window mannequin; this time he confides his happiness to a cow, and farther down the road he tips his hat to a pig. Just as his waterlogged taps counterpoint the music in "Singin' in the Rain," Kelly, drawing on a long tradition, creates a "sand dance," embroidering his song with the softly gritty sound of his footsteps, then illustrating the lyrics choreographically—a swinging shift of weight—for "all the music of life seems to be like a bell that is ringing for me." Finally, all restraint abandoned, he tumbles down a hill, concluding the sequence by pitching his hat and coat into the valley below, almost shouting the last lines.

"'S Wonderful" concludes with the camera gradually pulling back and up to match the crescendo of music and emotion. "Singin' in the Rain," using the same camera technique, ends in a diminuendo while the camera, in a now-typical Kelly finale, pulls back and up as his character walks away from us at an even speed and gradually fades into the distance. "Almost Like Being in Love" repeats the technique of "'S Wonderful," this time moving gradually back and up to allow the audience to capture the full scope of the magisterial mountains that receive his voice. One wonders how much more effective it would have been if it had been done in a real landscape and not a painted one. For that, audiences would have to wait for Julie Andrews's paean to the Austrian Alps, "alive with the sound of music." Saul Chaplin, the musical director of *The Sound of Music*, was Kelly's close friend and colleague and had worked with him on *Cover Girl*, *Singin' in the Rain*, and *An American in Paris*; he was the only person Leonard Bernstein would trust with the arrangement of his music in *On the Town*, with its opening scenes in the Brooklyn dockyard. He and the director, Robert Wise, knew very well what a moving camera coordinated with crescendo could do in the mountains.

It's Always Fair Weather climaxes Kelly's series of euphoria street dances. Comden and Green's lyrics to André Previn's song represent a new twist in euphoria song

FIGURE 8.3 A euphoric Kelly on roller skates in the streets of New York in *It's Always Fair Weather* (1955), "I Like Myself."

texts: instead of just saying "I'm happy," the character attempts to analyze his feelings from a psychological point of view. Buoyed by the knowledge of Cyd Charisse's love, Kelly, as the small-time fight manager and gambler Ted, has stood up to the mob and refused to "fix" a game. For the first time, he feels good about himself, and it is her confidence in him that has done it: "If someone wonderful as she is can think I'm wonderful, I must be quite a guy." "I Like Myself" is closely related to similar dances in *Singin' in the Rain* and *Brigadoon*, but it has an even greater expansiveness in both the choreography and the space covered by the dance. Like "Singin' in the Rain," it is a street dance as well as a euphoria dance. Kelly varies the old formula, however, by using roller skates—yet another prop from the street that was particularly associated with children. According to his daughter Kerry Kelly, the skates came from a hardware store in Beverly Hills; Kelly had bought them specifically to teach his little girl to skate. By chance, Comden and Green, the scriptwriters, watched one of the lessons and, moved by Kelly's skill and grace, encouraged him to use it on screen.

Astaire and Rogers had already done an extended roller-skate dance—in *Shall We Dance* (1937), to Gershwin's "Let's Call the Whole Thing Off"—but they were not the first: Chaplin, one of Kelly's idols, had performed on them in *The Rink* (1916). But whereas Astaire and Rogers performed within the relatively limited and intimate space of a small skating area in a park (constructed on an indoor set), whose boundaries were clearly marked, rather like a stage, Kelly moves to a street set, using his skates to cover as wide a territory as possible, testing his skill and proving his daring by gliding nonstop around corners and across traffic-filled streets, whizzing past delighted pedestrians in arabesque, leapfrogging over fireplugs, gliding on and off the edge of the curb in a breathtaking variation on a similar step in "Singin' in the Rain" (Figs. 8.3a–h). Almost all of the dance and camera gestures of "Singin' in the Rain" are in fact repeated, expanded, and done at double speed. The finale does not conclude with a camera crescendo, however, and that is a mistake. The camera moves in straight onto Kelly's smiling face as he looks up to the camera and relies on an old choreographic weakness: repeating a virtuoso step one time too many.

ASTAIRE'S EUPHORIA DANCES

Though developed most famously by Kelly, the street dance, as we have seen, really begins not even with Astaire in *Damsel in Distress* (1937), but with Mamoulian's and Clair's singing and dancing Parisians in *Love Me Tonight* and *Le million*. Astaire's walk, of course, was enough to make a musical number: whether through London in "A Foggy Day" in *Damsel in Distress* (1938), on his shipboard stroll with Rogers and dogs in *Shall We Dance* (1937), or on Fifth Avenue at the beginning and end of *Easter Parade* (1948). In one of Astaire's final films, *Silk Stockings* (1957), the director, Mamoulian, follows Astaire's walking feet from his hotel to the soundstage where he works as a producer. All we see is a close-up of his brown suede shoes and pink socks: we don't need to see him full figure to know who he is. That same year a member of the younger generation, Stanley Donen, pays his own tribute to the tradition started by Mamoulian and Astaire and points toward the future of the street dance. Donen, now working solo directing *Funny Face*, uses the split-screen techniques he and Kelly had first employed two years earlier in *It's Always Fair Weather* to unite Astaire in time and space with Audrey Hepburn and Kay Thompson as they each explore their own favorite parts of the city in "Bonjour Paris."

In the early 1950s Astaire, perhaps in response to Kelly and the genre's increasing popularity, sometimes turns to street dances. "Anything you can do . . . " seems to be the message of two of his street dances in *The Belle of New York* (1952), directed by Charles Walters. Astaire goes Kelly one better: this time he dances in the air *above* the street—literally walking on air. Contemplating the kiss he has received from Vera-Ellen, Astaire sings, "When I kiss you I feel that we're six feet off the ground," and then proceeds to prove it as he levitates above Greenwich Village and explores the top of the Washington Square arch, at first tentatively and then with increasing confidence as he daringly tests his balance on the lintel and cornices and bounces in the air between three flagpoles, finally stretching out comfortably on one to sleep and dream.

Astaire ups the ante in "Oops," dancing on (and off) a horse-drawn trolley that glides through the city streets. Like Astaire's dance on the ceiling, it feels more gimmicky than his dances of the 1930s, but he is nevertheless a wonder to behold as he swings around poles, leaps from car to car, and jumps on and off the moving trolley, like Kelly skimming along between rainy sidewalk and gutter in "Singin' in the Rain," which was being made at the same time and at the same studio.

But Astaire clearly feels more comfortable when he doesn't have to be concerned with the expansive space and multiple camera angles that dancing in the street demands. "Dancing in the Dark," in a studio-recreated Central Park in *The Band Wagon*, directed by Minnelli, returns him to his true center. It is a courtship and seduction dance: the dancers move from distinct and separate emotional worlds to blissful unification. The dance space is more confined than Kelly's, and although Astaire and Cyd Charisse dance over benches and up stairs in their simultaneously lyrical and sensual pas de deux, it is the dance itself that is the major interest here. With the same partner Astaire very late in his career created one of his most brilliant dances, in which you can feel his new interest in covering the larger and longer spaces preferred by Kelly: in *Silk Stockings* he and Charisse move side by side over the length of two soundstages in a series of danced variations on Cole Porter's "Fated to be Mated" and "Paris Loves Lovers," arranged and orchestrated to accompany, in turn, Spanish (flamenco) and jazz rhythms.

CHANGING TIMES, CHANGING STREETS

In most of these street dances, the city is benign, and the use of street props is playful. Kelly's street dances are full of joie de vivre. He stops short of disrupting the passers-by and vandalizing the objects on the street. The street dances that follow, in line with growing class unrest and the developing drug culture, increasingly portray American streets as places of danger rather than delight. In *On the Town* (1949), New York and its citizens are bright and cheerful. We don't see vagrants or drug dealers, and the policemen, though stern, are benevolent. However, in two instances Kelly departs from this benign model. In the "Alter Ego" dance in *Cover Girl* and in the drunk dances in *It's Always Fair Weather*, the streets seem more threatening, and the dances are used to express dark aspects of human nature: anger, jealousy, and despair. In the "Alter Ego" dance Kelly works over his complex and conflicted feelings of jealousy by dancing down a deserted, rundown street with a transparent image of himself. The dance ends when Kelly angrily shatters the plate-glass window of an empty storefront to destroy his reflected alter ego. In *It's Always Fair Weather* (1955) three soldiers, panicked at facing their new lives at the end of World War II, reel drunkenly down Third Avenue, commandeer a taxi, shake up its driver, and dance noisily with garbage-can lids in a forbidding street shadowed by the tracks of the El.

Six years later, in 1961, the film version of *West Side Story* opened. In it Jerome Robbins adapts and expands Kelly's cinematic street-dance traditions by using a brilliantly choreographed mobile camera on a crane and rhythmic cutting to enhance the dance's excitement. But now the street dancers, fueled by gang warfare and racial tension, demonstrate their domination of the city streets they skim across and the fire hydrants they leap over. The passersby look upon them with fear rather than delight as they disrupt traffic and steal street-vendors' wares. The littered, rundown streets, with their broken windows and graffiti-defaced walls, reveal a society at war with itself, and the distinctive energy that Kelly used to portray enthusiasm and joy in "Make Way for Tomorrow" and "Singin' in the Rain" is now transformed into anger and alienation. The policemen who break up *West Side Story*'s dance fight are anything but benevolent: they threaten the boys and use them as pawns in a race war, offering to help the white gang, the Jets, clean up their Puerto Rican rivals, the Sharks.

By 1960 the terms "juvenile delinquency" and "street-gang warfare" had become buzz phrases in the American media. New York came increasingly to be seen as a frightening and dangerous place. The rise of popular interest in urban teenage gangs was dramatic. A search of *New York Times* articles from 1870 to the present under the keywords "juvenile delinquency" and "street gangs," or indeed any combination of another word and "gangs," reveals relatively few articles on the subject between 1929 and 1945. After that articles about street gangs increase steadily, peaking in the late 1950s and early '60s. A search of the *Reader's Guide to Periodical Literature*, which covers a wide range of popular magazines, reveals a similar trend.

But though the content of the street dance had changed, the filmic roots of *West Side Story*'s opening sequence (directed and edited by Robbins) are embedded in the Kelly-Donen street-dance tradition.[5] To this source Robbins adds the influence of Astaire and Balanchine, both of whom he idolized. He had seen at first hand the innovations that Balanchine, inspired by Astaire, had brought to his work in both ballet and in musicals on Broadway. In 1949, while Robbins was still working on Broadway, Balanchine invited him to become associate artistic director and a resident choreographer of New York City Ballet, where Robbins's understanding of the nourishment provided by jazz dance as developed by his African American colleagues and Fred Astaire on Broadway and in the movies, and his interest in working with dancers trained in Balanchine technique and style, could be developed as nowhere else. It is the combination of Astaire and Balanchine, along with the choreography of the camera and dancer developed by Kelly and Donen, that provides the foundation of *West Side Story*'s street dancing.

EUPHORIA AND DANCING ON THE CEILING

Not all street dances are euphoric, just as not all euphoria dances take place in the street. One of Astaire's most famous dances on the theme of euphoria takes place indoors. In *Royal Wedding*, directed by Stanley Donen, he uses the ceiling of a London hotel room as a new kind of dance space. The first steps he takes up the wall and onto the ceiling are tentative, but they become more and more daring, and by the end of the song he bounds over the chandelier, then spreads out next to it kicking his heels. It was Astaire, as we have seen, who first began to explore public and domestic interiors, large and small, as sites for dance—not just their floors, but on and with furniture of all kinds: chairs, tables, desks, couches, pianos, fireplaces, even the machines in the bowels of an ocean liner, as well as canes, umbrellas, hats, and, in another part of *Royal*

Wedding, even a hat rack. One would have thought that by the 1950s he had exhausted the possibilities. But in "You're All the World to Me," he and Donen combine them all in a room mounted on a device that could revolve in tempo with Astaire inside it.

Like "'S Wonderful," the euphoria song "You're All the World to Me" is a list, this time comparing the beloved to the lover's favorite places: "Paris in April and May," "New York on a silv'ry day."[6] Of course, as Lerner and Gershwin well knew, they were following a standard poetic device dating all the way back to before Shakespeare's sonnets. (Shakespeare has the edge, though. He enumerates life's beautiful things, then points out that even they have their flaws; his beloved is better: "Shall I compare thee to a summer's day?")

When *Royal Wedding*, Donen's first solo film, was made in 1950–51, Kelly was occupied with Minnelli on *An American in Paris*. "I've Got a Crush on You," a number cut from the film, celebrated the joys of falling in love and had Kelly rocketing around his tiny garret. So did "Tra-la-la-la," another indoor euphoria song and dance. As is typical, the dancer progressively sheds his inhibitions as he dances, but this time Oscar Levant, who plays Kelly's cynical sidekick, provides an ironic commentary on his ecstatic dancing. Levant, the composer, is intent on the creation of a "serious" work for piano, but Kelly forcefully interrupts, turning one of its motifs into a popular song form. (It's a version of the old swinging-the-classics theme.) Gradually Kelly's character draws his friend into the fun as he swings around the room and tap dances on the piano lid. At the finish, the two men sit together at the piano, banging out the final chorus and singing at the top of their lungs.

INFLUENCE OF THE STREET DANCE

The street dance, unlike the courtship dance, is not so much a culmination of a dance form with roots deep in the past of theatrical and social dance as it is the beginning of a new form. Created to take specific advantage of film as a medium, it launched an ever-expanding genre and also changed our concept of where dance could and should take place. It is linked directly with the development of what is now commonly called "site dance," which took off among postmodernists like Anna Halprin in California and the Judson Theatre Group in New York. Its most powerful impact has been felt on television and video and now in digital imagery, which will be touched on in the last chapter.

I have so far looked at three song-and-dance-film genres: the courtship dance, the military-buddy dance, and the euphoria dance with its street-dance variant. The military-man-in-uniform motif was short-lived. The euphoria and courtship dances I have described are relatively short, and they explore a single theme and sustain a single mood. But the interest in longer, more varied dance sequences in which a story is told and several moods are presented grew with the introduction of the kinds of extended dance dramas or ballets that were staged by Balanchine and Minnelli for Broadway musicals, and the increasing prominence of the dancers of the Russian ballet diaspora would be reflected in movies as well. The film ballet, as it was often called, is today most closely associated with Kelly, working with Donen and Minnelli (*On the Town, An American in Paris, Singin' in the Rain*). But the extended ballet or dance-drama sequence, though it was jump-started on Broadway by Balanchine and Minnelli in *Ziegfeld Follies of 1936*, in the Rodgers and Hart shows, and in the film version of *On Your Toes* by Balanchine, is first modeled in the movies of the 1940s and '50s by the dancer with whom the film ballet is least associated: Fred Astaire. In the 1940s with MGM's *Ziegfeld Follies* and *Yolanda and the Thief*, Astaire, working with Minnelli, would start an era in films in which, as on Broadway, "you couldn't put on a show . . . without a hallucinatory ballet."[7]

9

DREAMING IN DANCE

Astaire, Minnelli, Kelly, and Donen

BALANCHINE'S COLLABORATIONS WITH Minnelli, Gershwin, Duke, and Rodgers and Hart on Broadway and then in movies heralded a new era in which a "ballet"—often a dream ballet—became a standard feature of musicals. Gene Kelly's *An American in Paris* film ballet has become the most prominent example of this trend, but as we have seen, it came toward the end of a tradition that began in 1938 with the Balanchine film ballets for *On Your Toes* and the unrealized "An American in Paris" for *The Goldwyn Follies*. It was Balanchine's collaborator Vincente Minnelli who would initially carry on and develop the film ballet in the 1940s—and he would do it not with Gene Kelly, who became most closely associated with the form later, but with Fred Astaire. Astaire disliked the form, but, in the face of its popularity, had to adapt to it.[1]

The term "ballet," in its most popular and widely accepted meaning today, is any dance that uses the classical academic tradition called the *danse d'école*. Originally the term meant any theatrical dance arrangement. For Minnelli, Astaire, and Kelly, the "ballet" in film ballet meant the *ballet d'action* as developed by Noverre and made modern by Fokine with Diaghilev, a dance that tells a story or develops a character. The film ballet's vocabulary was made up of the new outlaw style of Astaire and later Kelly. For Minnelli and Kelly, a film ballet (or "ciné ballet," as Kelly sometimes referred to it) was also one in which the choreography of the camera participated equally in the storytelling: sound and moving image (with both the dancer and the camera moving) were synergized to convey a story or reveal a character's state of mind. I have chosen to use the generic term "film ballet" because that is the one used both by its creators and by critics, and because it fits with the original definition of ballet. However, "cinematic dance drama" or "film-dance drama" is a more precise label for the works discussed in this chapter.

The theme of the story told in these dance dramas has again to do with the vicissitudes of courtship: the search for an ideal mate and the euphoria and despair of courtship, now expanded in time and space and varied in setting. The lover and beloved investigate new aspects of their emotional lives by entering a dream world in which they are free to reveal their deepest and most contradictory feelings.

These ballets set a new style in production numbers at MGM, turning away from the lavish, often heavy-handed revue-format spectacles of the Busby Berkeley and *Broadway Melody* films of the 1930s. Instead, Minnelli offers some of the fantastic effects expected in the film-musical genre within a more intimate and dramatically coherent framework. The impact of Minnelli's quieter spectacles comes not from the piling up of ever more lavish sets, costumes, and visual effects, but from the coordination of dance, decor, music, and camerawork to play out the stylized drama of seduction at their core. Thus while Berkeley, the major promoter of the moving camera during sound cinema's first decade, influenced Minnelli in a general way, he cannot be seen as a primary influence on the young director. As Minnelli has stated bluntly: "Berkeley's large scale spectacles never moved me."[2]

ZIEGFELD FOLLIES: MINNELLI, ASTAIRE, AND THE MOVING CAMERA

The first Minnelli-Astaire dance dramas for film appear in the MGM film *Ziegfeld Follies*, released in 1946. "This Heart of Mine" and "Limehouse Blues" are the next landmark moments in integrating dance and camerawork to convey a drama in dance. *Ziegfeld Follies* was supposed to have been one of Astaire's last films before his retirement, but it turned out to be one of the first in a series of films he made for MGM, some of the best of which were made with Minnelli (*Ziegfeld Follies, Yolanda and the Thief, The Band Wagon*).[3] Astaire had retained full control over the camerawork in his films of the 1930s, preferring that the camera move in parallel with the dancer's movement, but not that it actively participate in the choreography as a formal or expressive device. In *Ziegfeld Follies*, however, he loosened the reins for the first time and trusted Minnelli to employ the mobile boom or crane camera in such a way that it *participates* in the dance.

In the *Ziegfeld Follies* dance drama, Minnelli had to employ the mobile camera both for dramatic purposes and for formal effects: with the assistance of the cinematographer George Folsey, who had so brilliantly filmed the "Skip to My Lou" and Christmas dance sequences in *Meet Me in St. Louis*, he tells the story by maneuvering his camera quickly and smoothly in height as well as depth, from long to medium to close shots, from high above the dancers to stage level, capturing telling facial expressions and gestures in close-ups, then gliding back to both reveal and enhance the sweep and scope of the dance as a whole. The pace of the camera blends rhythmically with the choreography and music, seemingly even being cued to the musical beat. So does the editing, which also shapes the sequence, though to a lesser extent. Impressively (and unlike much Berkeley camerawork of the 1930s), Minnelli and Folsey move the camera without obscuring either the line of the dancers, the shape of Astaire's overall choreographic design, or the essentially human scale on which the dance is planned.

The camera movement is integrated so closely with the music and dance gesture that even in the sequence's center section, when the restless camera is given its grandest and most sweeping gestures, it does not overwhelm or dominate the dancers or the dance. Rather, the camera movement seems to grow inevitably and logically out of the demands of both music and choreography. A close analysis of the center section of "This Heart of Mine," danced by Astaire and Lucille Bremer, demonstrates this clearly.

In the tradition of Astaire's courtship dances of the 1930s, "This Heart of Mine" can be roughly divided into four sections that trace, in general outline, a dance seduction. Here, however, the seduction is played out within the context of a film-dance drama involving mime as well as dance sequences. It is built around a song of the same name by the composer Harry Warren and the lyricist Arthur Freed, orchestrated and arranged by Conrad Salinger.[4]

As we have seen in these earliest films of his, Astaire's dances were pivotal moments in the drama, tracing the emotional roller coaster of courtship from the initial approach-avoidance tactics to the final ecstatic bonding. In "This Heart of Mine," Astaire continues this tradition but also expands it: an entire story is mimed and danced. Astaire plays the role of a jewel thief who, at an elegant party, falls in love with a woman (played by Lucille Bremer) whose diamonds he hopes to steal. He lures her into an extended ballroom dance; she falls in love with him and at the same time comes to realize his intentions. At the end of the dance she removes her necklace and hands it to him openly. Shamed, he returns the jewels, and the couple embrace.

"This Heart of Mine" relates to that old romantic ballet theme: a man chases a female ideal who seems forever beyond his reach. In *Giselle* (1841), as in "This Heart of Mine," a man with duplicitous intentions yearns for an idealized woman and is reformed by her. *Giselle's* hero loses his love to death, while in the film dance she becomes his. Whatever the century, however, it is the chase that gives the choreographer an ideal subject for dance.

The first and last sections of "This Heart of Mine" are presented entirely in modern full-body mime. Major and minor characters alike are introduced within the ballroom setting by a combination of movement, music, and camerawork. It would be hard to overstate the brilliance of the camera movement in this section. Minnelli and Astaire go beyond even Balanchine in the way they seamlessly move from one character to another. Astaire finally makes the first move to really ingratiate himself with his intended victim by singing to her, following the same overarching pattern he presents in his courtship dances: for a good portion of the song, the woman sits on a bench placed on the edge of a semicircular expanse of open floor, while her would-be seducer leans over her; she listens quietly and gravely, seemingly receptive but not actively responsive to his musical advances.

During the song's second verse (played simply and straightforwardly by orchestra alone) he draws her into dance—a dance based, as will be the entire sequence, on the theme of turning and circling. Although their hands touch as she allows herself to be turned continuously under his arm and he, in turn, circles her, their bodies rarely make contact. During this first section the camera remains fairly quiet, framing the couple for the most part from the front to let us absorb the song and the choreographer's initial dance statement. The second section introduces a variation for dancers, camera, and orchestra. The orchestrator arranges melodic material in ever more interesting guises. The song is repeated in a fuller and more expansive orchestration, and a prominent countermelody is introduced by the strings as the woman, as if to rebuff the man or at least to distance herself from his advances, turns away from him (and the camera) and moves to a higher level of the set—a sort of embankment that borders the floor on which they have been dancing. Undeterred, Astaire and the camera (which seems to sail through space) follow her. In an audacious visual gesture, the woman, standing motionless, glides along on a slowly moving track, while the man, in pursuit, dances after and then around her, the mobile camera paralleling his movements. (Such is Astaire's integrity as a choreographer that the trickiness of this effect does not compete for attention with the dance. Like all of Astaire's props, the moving-track floor is firmly integrated into the overall choreographic and dramatic design. As Rudolf Nureyev has said of Astaire, "He *justifies* his props.")[5]

The third section, in which the dancers return to the "ground" level of the set and the woman signals her willingness to respond to the thief's advances, introduces another layer of musical and visual activity. As Astaire and Bremer pose quietly at its center, his body framing hers, the floor begins revolving slowly counterclockwise while the camera, moving clockwise, glides slowly up and back. At the same time dreamlike immobile couples enter the frame, posed on the rim of the moving floor as a chorus of voices is added to the musical accompaniment. The couples lean against stylized, bare-branched trees that form a decorative, surrealistic bracelet around the couple. When the camera pauses at its highest point, the couples become active, circling the trees against which each leans.

The fourth and final section sets all forces in motion again. The dance seduction completed, the camera and dancers are given their grandest and most expansive gestures. The corps of dancers (and trees) glide magically to the second level of the set, where they form a continually moving backdrop for Astaire and Bremer, who are now alone on the still-revolving circular space. The choreographed pursuit-rebuff tactics played out in the initial stages of the dance now abandoned, the couple circle this space faster and faster, their new relationship graphically illustrated by the configuration of their bodies: as they waltz, she leans back trustingly in his arms and extends her own like wings. The camera rests quietly at the far end of the set as the constantly turning couple dance on a collision course with it. Finally, just before they meet it—and in the grandest visual gesture of all—they seem to set the camera in motion. The camera now sweeps up on a diagonal to the set's second level, riding on the nine repeated notes of the song's third line, the pedal-point effect created by their repetition seeming to support the camera. The final shot of the sequence gives us a view of the entire set head-on, with its several layers of movement. Then, the dance seduction completed, the couple turn and stroll away from us toward the stylized shell of the ballroom—circular, of course—at the back of the set. This shell adds a last layer of movement as it slowly glides open to receive them.

CHOREOGRAPHING COLOR AND LIGHT: "LIMEHOUSE BLUES"

The "Limehouse Blues" segment of *Ziegfeld Follies* takes the new film-dance drama form even further. It introduces the fantastic, dreamlike settings and dramatic lighting and color effects that, coordinated with music, would become a major characteristic of the dance dramas of Minnelli's subsequent films (Fig. 9.1). As its title implies, the setting for the sequence is London's Limehouse district at the beginning of the twentieth century—as visualized, however, by the director in a highly personal and stylized way.

To help him create his vision of Limehouse, Minnelli drew on two important collaborators: Irene Sharaff, who created the costumes and decor, and Charles Rosher, the cinematographer, who lit the multiple sets. Sharaff, who had originally designed the costumes for the stage and film versions of *On Your Toes* as well as Minnelli's first color film, *Meet Me in St. Louis*, here demonstrates that she was as much a colorist as Minnelli and as imaginative and willing to try brilliant and unorthodox color combinations and textures to stretch the Technicolor palette. She would become one of Minnelli's (and later Kelly's) favorite collaborators—on *Yolanda and the Thief*, *The Pirate*, and, most famously, *An American in Paris*.

Making use of his eclectic clipping file and book collection as well as at least one other previous film, Minnelli also drew from a wide variety of visual sources to form his final vision. The jazz classic "Limehouse Blues," by Philip Braham, originally performed by Gertrude Lawrence in *Charlot's Revue* (1924), may have been inspired in part by D. W. Griffith's *Broken Blossoms* (1919). Taking his cue from that film, Minnelli evokes the melancholy mood and dreamlike atmosphere of Griffith's remarkable wharf scenes by creating around his character a fog-suffused ambience that rivals that created by his predecessors and can be seen in part as a visual homage to Griffith (Figs. 9.1a and b).[6] Astaire too may have been influenced by *Broken Blossoms*: his portrayal of the dance drama's Chinese protagonist— his walk, stance, and facial expressions—closely parallel Richard Barthelmess's sensitive portrayal of a similar character in the Griffith film, although there is no other evidence that he studied or even saw *Broken Blossoms* before this sequence was shot. In any case, Astaire had long loved the song, and it was he who suggested the sequence.[7]

Though Griffith might have been a major influence, the "Limehouse Blues" sequence may also reflect the influence of one of Minnelli's favorite artists, James McNeill Whistler. Joseph Pennell and Elizabeth Pennell's biography of Whistler was the first study of an artist that the young Minnelli ever read,[8] and its impact on him was immediate and powerful: "Here was an artist with whom I could identify."[9] Minnelli especially related to Whistler's "penchant for titling his paintings with musical terms," and he took special delight in Whistler's "affinity for yellow," noting that the artist "painted the walls of his house in its most sunny shading."[10] It may be, then, that the fog effects created in the first section of the "Limehouse Blues" sequence are related to those Whistler paintings with musical titles (e.g., the various *Nocturnes*) in which London night and fog effects are captured on canvas. And certainly the beautiful, warm yellow space of the central section of "Limehouse Blues" derives ultimately from

FIGURE 9.1 *Ziegfeld Follies* (film, 1946), "Limehouse Blues." Choreographed color and light in the dance drama as Astaire pursues his ideal woman. Minnelli's camera follows Astaire and Bremer from Limehouse into a hallucinatory, boundaryless dream world of chinoiserie.

Minnelli's interest in Whistler's use of yellow (Fig. 9.1f). Though this is the first distinctive appearance of "Minnelli yellow," it is not the last—a warm, sunny yellow will recur throughout his films.[11] Another visual source for the scenes set in Limehouse is what Minnelli calls an "old English mezzotint."[12] The idea was not only to suggest the somber ambience of the Limehouse slums, but also to provide a dramatic contrast between this and the second section of the ballet, in which the Chinese man hallucinates an encounter with his beloved. For this section Minnelli drew on another visual source—eighteenth-century French chinoiserie (Figs. 9.1f and g).[13]

As it does in all of Minnelli's films, lighting combines with atmospheric elements— in this case, fog and mist—to create the director's portrait of Limehouse. The light fog that envelops the set is nuanced and varied by colored lights and shadow. These impart to the colors of the objects over which they play a subtlety, variety, and richness that contrasts vividly with the harsh and uninterestingly uniform colors presented in the Technicolor works of many of Minnelli's contemporaries, whose use of flat, overall lighting resulted in these films' slick, embalmed, and airless look. As he had in *Meet Me in St. Louis* the year before, Minnelli and his cinematographer, George Folsey, produced colored lighting and atmospheric effects that, in the Limehouse sequence, reveal for one of the first times the real potential of the still fairly new Technicolor process. Their work demonstrates conclusively that, under the right conditions, Technicolor could offer just as much subtlety and variety of tonal effects as the remarkably nuanced black-and-white films being produced at MGM in the later 1930s and 1940s.[14] It shows too that dramatic light and color effects could be effectively coordinated with music arranged for the purpose.

In line with Minnelli's predilection for introducing characters enmeshed in their environment, the camera finds Astaire, the ballet's central character, only after gliding down the street on which much of the action will take place—a street appropriated for the "Limehouse Blues" sequence from the set for the MGM film version of *The Picture of Dorian Gray* (1944). In its journey along the road, shrouded in pale brownish-yellow mist, at the end of which the dancer stands, it gives us a look not only at the stylized, weathered architecture of the Limehouse district, but also at its equally weathered inhabitants: an old woman who trundles a baby carriage in which a phonograph incongruously sits, a group of drunks who clown and dance in front of a basement café. Through the café windows we see, surrounded by soft, smoke-suffused light, a young singer—perhaps related to the Sybil Vane character in *Dorian Gray*. She begins singing "Limehouse Blues." It is only then that the camera "discovers" Astaire, the "Chinese man," standing to the side of the window, watching the drinkers' antics.

In the sequence that follows, Astaire plays out, in mime and dance, a fantasy romance distantly related to that of *Broken Blossoms*.[15] Like the Barthelmess character in Griffith's film, the Chinese man admires from a distance a woman with whom he is able to consummate a relationship only in dreams. We meet the woman when she pauses near Astaire to watch some costermongers ("pearlies") perform, their multiple rows of white buttons flashing through the mist (Fig. 9.1a). After a few minutes, when she moves down the street, Astaire and the camera trail her, pausing only when she stops in front of a store window to admire a prominently displayed fan (Fig. 9.1b). When she passes on, Astaire, followed by the camera, enters the shop and inquires, in mime, the price of the fan. Clearly unable to afford it, he nonetheless fingers it admiringly as, through the shop window, we see a group of thugs suddenly smash the window glass and snatch some objects from the display case. Police in the street respond with gunfire and Astaire is accidentally shot.

Amidst a hail of broken glass, he tumbles to the ground, dropping the golden-yellow fan. The camera drops to the floor with him, gliding in to a close-up of his hand as he reaches out toward the bloodstained fan lying just beyond his reach (Fig. 9.1c). This image slowly dissolves, and we enter the wounded man's delirious dream. The camera frames the fan from above as it floats in deep shadow among a cluster of seemingly weightless gold and blue lily pad–like objects, which, as the shadows gradually lighten, are revealed to be hats worn by figures that press around Astaire (Fig. 9.1d), who now stands erect and is dressed in deep red. The drifting boom camera continues to frame the dancer from above as he reaches again and again for the fan, which floats just beyond his reach. Most of the set at this point is in deep shadow; the hats and hands appear for the most part disembodied. Gradually, however, the lighting reveals that the fan is being held by Astaire's fantasy beloved (Fig. 9.1e).

The sudden appearance of several elaborately masked and fantastically costumed figures who emerge from the shadows to confront the dancer heralds a change in music, lighting, camera activity, and dramatic action. Astaire pushes through them and is at last able to grasp the hand of the woman whom he has followed. As if to express his joy and excitement, the set is suddenly illuminated, the music swells in volume, and the camera arcs back and up to reveal, now bathed in brilliant light, a deep, expansive yellow-orange "space" (it has no boundaries to indicate the joining of floor and wall) on which are arranged at intervals a series of silver-gray constructions around which groups of figures, costumed also in gray, are arranged (Fig. 9.1f). In configuration, these freestanding constructions, or sculptural forms, suggest those stylized architectural groupings (bridges and pagodas) and figures found in French chinoiserie. We're in another world, one created by the delirious man's hallucinatory image of the fan, where Astaire and Bremer, newly clothed in fantastic red garb, dance together at last (Fig. 9.1g).

The overall coloring of first section of the Limehouse drama, while subtle and variegated, has so far been deliberately subdued, as has been the musical accompaniment. Now, as the set is flooded with brilliant contrasting colors and light, the orchestration changes dramatically from soft, low winds and strings to a fuller orchestral palette, bringing in brass, chimes, and percussion. The dual effects emphasize visually and musically the contrast between the Chinese man's fantasy world and his drab real-life existence. This precise coordination of light and color and of the volume, texture, and timbre of sound to emphasize a dramatic moment in the dance will become a hallmark of Minnelli's and later of Kelly and Donen's dance dramas, and it was extremely difficult to achieve before the digital era. As Minnelli proudly explains, "We accomplished this by first lighting the set. The black shields—what the industry knows as 'gobos'—were placed in front of the lights. At a synchronized count, the shields were removed to unveil the lighted set" (compare Figs. 9.1e and f).[16] This effect will be seen again, not only in Minnelli and in Kelly and Donen's film ballets, but in Michael Powell and Emeric Pressburger's *The Red Shoes* (1948).

At the dance's conclusion, gold and blue fans blot out the dancers and cover the screen space. In a slow dissolve, the variegated pattern of blue and gold resolves gradually to an image of Astaire's hand, and we are returned to the Limehouse setting. The camera pulls back to reveal that the wounded man now lies stretched out on a bench in the middleground of the screen, framed by the shattered glass storefront window immediately behind him. After first passing by this window, his fantasy beloved, now escorted by a wealthy admirer, enters the shop. Unaware of the wounded man, whose eyes follow her every move, she picks up the fan she had earlier admired, then drops it in horror when she realizes that it is spattered with blood. She quickly leaves the shop, and the camera, following the direction of the wounded man's eyes and as if doing his bidding, glides suddenly up and out of the shattered window after her. On its way down the street, the camera again passes the basement café in which the singer who opened the sequence now completes her song as fog gradually covers the screen.[17]

YOLANDA AND THE THIEF: MINNELLI, SURREALISM, FREUD, AND THE DREAM BALLET

The ballet in *Yolanda and the Thief* builds on the *Follies* ballet techniques, once again with Astaire and Bremer. It expands the theme first explored in "This Heart of Mine" into a full-length movie: a con man falls in love with his victim, a young heiress, but this time the setting is the mythical Latin American country of "Patria," whose richest citizen, Yolanda Acquaviva (again Bremer), is targeted by the American Johnny Riggs, and the film ballet at its core is integrated into the dramatic fabric this story.

By the time of *Yolanda*, the trend set in motion by Minnelli and Balanchine in their *Ziegfeld Follies* ballets and Balanchine in the "Slaughter on Tenth Avenue" sequence for *On Your Toes*, "Peter's Dream" in *Babes in Arms*, and the "Aviator" ballet in *I Married an Angel* was in full swing on Broadway. Agnes de Mille's ballet sequence ("Out of My Dreams") in *Oklahoma!* (1943) arrived rather late on the scene, but like Minnelli's *American in Paris* in film, it became the most prominent example of the era.[18]

The ballet was often presented within the context of a dream (either day or night) imagined and expressed by a dance within a fantasy setting. However, dream and "vision" sequences were a standard feature of the music hall and of the nineteenth-century *ballet d'action*. (The opium dream in *La bayadère* is a good example.) Before that there were dream sequences in court opera ballets as well. (The ballet in Lully's *Atys* [1676] has both good dreams and bad dreams.) In the integrated musical, as in the *ballet d'action*, the device of the dream allowed the introduction of colorful, fantastic, and surreal elements, varied and elaborate dances, and, in the case of film, interesting and fantastical cinematic effects without violating the relatively rational nature of the plot and logical behavior of the protagonists.[19] The dream ballets in *Yolanda and the Thief* and *Oklahoma!* both fit into this model, as did the dream section of "Limehouse Blues."

The dream-drama form in *Yolanda* in 1945 also reflects a peak of popular interest in Freudian theory and his technique of psychoanalysis, which used dream interpretation as a key analytical tool for understanding human behavior. Although Freud's *Interpretation of Dreams* was first published in Europe in 1900, it wasn't until the late 1920s that his theory was popularized in America and Freudian terminology began to enter the vocabulary of American writers, musicians, and artists, many of whom— Gershwin, for example—went into analysis themselves. Minnelli, like many of his colleagues in film and musical theater, used the concept of dream interpretation as a dramatic device to show the inner conflicts of his characters. He and Balanchine used it in the dream sequence of "Five A.M.," their ballet for Josephine Baker in the Broadway *Ziegfeld Follies of 1936* ballet. Fred Astaire jumped on the bandwagon in 1938 playing a psychiatrist who falls in love with his patient, Ginger Rogers. In his short "Colorblind" dream dance sequence in *Carefree* (1938), Rogers reveals her unconscious attraction to Astaire (Fig. 9.2a).[20] In the dream ballet in *Yolanda and the Thief*, Johnny Riggs reveals his ambivalent feelings about Yolanda when his growing attraction to the young heiress conflicts with his desire to steal her money, and Gerry Mulligan explicates his complex personal and professional relationship with Lise in his reverie in *An American in Paris*.

Minnelli's interest in the dream state was also linked to his discovery of the Surrealist artists who themselves shared Freud's fascination with dreams and dream imagery— and who showed him a new way of organizing theatrical space.[21] In 1932, during his second year in New York, paintings by the Surrealist precursor Giorgio de Chirico, as well as Salvador Dalí, Max Ernst, André Masson, and Joan Miró, were displayed at the Julien Levy Gallery in the first major Surrealist group exhibition in New York.[22] In 1934 Dalí made his first trip to the United States in connection with an exhibition of his works at the Julien Levy Gallery in November and December of that year.

Minnelli's response to Surrealist imagery (and to the works of de Chirico in particular) and his attempt to translate it into theatrical terms for dance appear in the Balanchine-Duke-Minnelli ballet "Words without Music" in *Ziegfeld Follies of 1936*. This "surrealist ballet" was the first on Broadway, Minnelli tells us; Balanchine choreographed and Minnelli directed the number. Besides Minnelli's own description, his preliminary design sketch for the ballet is available.[23] The sketch shows a sweep of almost empty stage bounded on the left by an arcade that, in configuration and placement, suggests similar forms in works of de Chirico, and bounded on the right by another de Chirico-like motif—a disembodied classical head. Punctuating the stage space at wide intervals are three figures that, like many of de Chirico's figures, cast elongated shadows.[24]

Surrealist imagery also appears in the brief section entitled "Beauty" in the *Ziegfeld Follies* film. But it is in the *Yolanda and the Thief* dream ballet that we find his most ambitious use of Surrealist imagery to further plot and convey character relationships

FIGURE 9.2 (a) *Carefree* (1938), dream dance, to "I Used to be Colorblind." (b–d) *Yolanda and the Thief* (1945), dance-drama dream sequence.

and to create a vast and seemingly limitless "dreamscape" on which his characters will dance. The film medium gives Minnelli an edge over his Broadway counterparts, who were restricted to a small stage, single sight lines, and a small pit orchestra. Minnelli and the choreographers, Astaire and Eugene Loring, were liberated by the film medium—the moving crane camera, vast soundstages, and varied lighting and color equipment of the MGM studios. These tools for experimentation and development of the film ballet form allowed them to control and shape the images we see more tightly than any stage director could.

Foremost among these tools for Minnelli is, of course, the sweeping, gliding boom camera (and the expertise of his cinematographer from *Ziegfeld Follies*, Charles Rosher). Continually moving through the same space through which the dancers move, the camera becomes an active participant in the dance. The dramatic use of lighting coordinated with sound to set off and contrast certain sequences—the abrupt transition from brilliant light to sudden darkness—is another oft-used device. The décor participates as well. Just as the moving trees in the "This Heart of Mine" sequence of the *Ziegfeld Follies* film are part of the dance, so too do elements of landscape play an important role in the *Yolanda* sequence. This is most clearly seen in the final section, when the Surrealistic rock formations close in to trap Riggs. It is important to note, though, that *all* of the dance takes place framed by, in opposition to, and firmly placed *within* the décor. This even includes floor shapes. In the *Yolanda* ballet, the floor is not completely flat; rather, it has gentle hills and valleys that enter forcefully into the filming of the dance. At one point, for example, the dancers stroll up one side of a small incline, the camera starts at the other, and the two meet on the top of the "hill." Another of Minnelli's characteristic formal devices is the use of actors as elements of the decor. Arranged in groups as *tableaux vivants* or as solitary figures who are decoratively placed much like other elements of scenery, these frozen figures dot the surrealistic rock formations during the horse-race sequence in *Yolanda* and punctuate the landscape during the final pas de deux (Fig. 9.2d). Some, like the cigar-smoking "guardian angel" figure, serve a symbolic as well as a decorative function. Costumed by Irene Sharaff, they stand at the beginning of a long line of such images that culminates in the elaborate *tableaux vivants* of the "American in Paris" ballet. In a looser way, they also relate to the semi-immobile figures that dot the Bois de Boulogne in the establishing sequence of *Gigi* and dramatically freeze to form a framework for Gigi's entrance in the climatic Maxim's sequence of that film.

This new space, or dreamscape, in which the *Yolanda* sequence takes place has first appeared in the finale, "Beauty," of the *Ziegfeld Follies* film and now appears in an expanded form. The vast, seemingly limitless space created on the screen seems to have no beginning and no end. Boundaries between floor and walls are blurred or obscured. Punctuating the space are fantastic rock shapes from which protrude stylized bare tree branches. The space itself opens up unlimited possibilities for the movement of the sweeping boom camera, which completely undermines the proscenium-stage orientation of the theater and gives the dancers more space in which to move—and room for exciting new choreographic possibilities (Figs. 9.2b–d).

The expanse of seemingly limitless space created on film in the central section of *Yolanda*'s ballet is clearly the influence of both Dalí and de Chirico.[25] The use of rock formations and their placement suggest the influence of Dalí and, perhaps, Yves Tanguy.[26] The frozen figures that Minnelli places at intervals throughout the vast screen space may also be derived in part from the director's viewing of certain Surrealist paintings: these still and sober figures, strangely withdrawn from one another and their surroundings, suggest similarly isolated figures in works of René Magritte and Paul Delvaux.[27] To these possible visual sources, however, may also be added another—unrelated to Surrealist imagery, but closely linked to *Yolanda*'s Latin American setting: Minnelli says that the undulating outline of the rock formations were meant to suggest South American baroque architecture.[28]

THE PIRATE: MINNELLI AND KELLY

Although Kelly had worked briefly with Minnelli on a segment of the *Ziegfeld Follies* film, it was *The Pirate* that gave him his first chance to work extensively with a director he very much admired. The relationship between Minnelli and Kelly was to be important for both men. Minnelli describes it as "the most intense professional association that I'd ever had with an actor. One idea would meld into another, and little difference who started the train of thought."[29] Both were on the lookout for new and distinctive ways to coordinate moving image with sound. Both were visually and musically oriented, and both were perfectionists who were willing, even eager, to work painstakingly, frame by frame, to synergize the moving image of the dancer with music, color, lighting effects, and the moving camera. "We complemented each other so well," said Kelly; "Vince has an artist's viewpoint, an arty eye, and I have a dancer's eye."[30] Just as Kelly, like any dancer-choreographer, would scrutinize and coordinate every inch of the human body in motion and its relationship to the space around it within the limits of the frame, Minnelli would coordinate that moving body with light and shadow, color and texture, like a painter creating a visual world within the boundaries of a canvas.

Their contrasting temperaments—Minnelli's introverted and reticent, Kelly's extroverted and gregarious—seemed to complement one another. "Working with Gene was wonderful . . . wonderful," Minnelli later said, with his characteristically quiet fervor. "He understood what I wanted to say without my having to say it. He was as crazy about work as I was. We'd work at the studio all day, then go home and spend the evenings together working."[31]

As this remark indicates, Kelly—his appetite whetted by his work with Donen on the dance sequences in *Cover Girl, Anchors Aweigh*, and *Living in a Big Way*—came in *The Pirate* to take an increasing interest in the direction of the film as a whole. Although in the end it is clearly Minnelli's hand at the helm, Kelly and Minnelli were more to each other than just actor and director. Minnelli had Kelly participate in the planning and filming of *The Pirate*'s dance sequences, but he drew Kelly into other areas as well. His experience on *The Pirate* would thus provide for Kelly an insight into the mind and working habits of a master director. It would give him invaluable experience for the time when he and the young Stanley Donen would be entirely in charge of their own film.

Director and dancer alike conceived of *The Pirate* as an affectionate but tongue-in-cheek tribute to both silent and sound swashbuckler movies—presented in the form of, as Minnelli put it, "a fantasy, . . . flamboyant, swirling, and larger than life."[32] The role of Serafin, the strolling player who disguises himself as Macoco the Pirate to impress the girl whom, during the course of the film, he courts and wins, was patterned after two great screen romantic heroes. "Vincente and I thought we had one of the great ideas of all time for *The Pirate* because we thought that we could do a very big inside joke." The joke was to have him do Serafin in his own persona as an actor "in the style of John Barrymore, so that the public would recognize this," and the "pirate," Serafin as Macoco, "after Douglas Fairbanks Sr. and try to make it as swashbuckling as we could."[33] A ham actor and braggart whose boyish and vulnerable nature—like that of Joe in *Anchors Aweigh*—lies just beneath the surface, Serafin was a role that took unique advantage of both Kelly's strengths and weaknesses as a performer. It allowed him both to legitimately overplay and to legitimately incorporate the stunt-filled, athletic dance gestures of which he was so fond into his dance characterizations—characterizations that translated Fairbanks's hair-raising feats of physical daring into dance terms.

The most immediately noticeable of Minnelli's contributions to Kelly's style is the arresting visual framework that he provides for the dancer's movements. Following in the tradition of the beautifully lit and filmed dance-drama sequences for Astaire—especially the "Limehouse Blues" sequence in *Ziegfeld Follies*—Minnelli in *The Pirate* surrounds Kelly with the richest and most subtly varied visual atmosphere in which he had yet danced. In terms of its color, lighting effect, and imagery alone, *The Pirate* is one of the most beautiful movies of the era. Working with the cinematographer Harry Stradling, whose luminous lighting he had first admired in Jacques Feyder's *La kermesse héroique*,[34] and with Irene Sharaff, his old friend from his previous three musicals, Minnelli discovers and coaxes from Technicolor film a palette of colors that, in addition to deep, luminous blacks and snowy whites, includes a remarkably wide range of colors drawn from the pirate's treasure chest and the sea upon which he sails.[35] One thinks, for example, of Manuela's soft coral dress and jewelry, over which torch-light flickers in the hanging sequence; the violet lining of Serafin's cape, which he cunningly manipulates like bat's wings to form a dramatic framework for his actions; and the visually thrilling jumble of jewels (rubies, pearls, coral, turquoise, opals, emeralds, and sapphires) in the pirate's treasure chest, over which Minnelli's camera lingers lovingly again in the hanging sequence.

Widely varied ranges of lighting and atmospheric effects are also presented to us in this movie. Minnelli gives *The Pirate* a dramatic visual structure by rhythmically alternating day and night sequences: Port Sebastian and the village of Calvados are presented to us alternately bathed in brilliant sunshine and enveloped in deep, velvety, blue-black shadows. And at the center of the film, Minnelli and Stradling, in the by now well-established dream ballet sequence, present what amounts to a cinematic light show—a virtuoso display of continually shifting colored lights that surround Serafin as he dances.

Just as Minnelli's color and lighting effects add a new dimension to Kelly's performance, so too does his camerawork—in particular his use of the mobile boom camera—add another layer of interest to the dancer's street and courtship dances. In Kelly's previous film, *Cover Girl*, Kelly and Donen's use of the moving camera was, in comparison to Minnelli's, restricted, especially in height. Though a gliding boom camera was occasionally used, as in the middle and final sections of the Olvera Street sequence of *Anchors Aweigh*, another early film, it was not used continuously or with the ease, fluidity, and expansiveness with which Minnelli had employed it in *Cabin the Sky, Ziegfeld Follies*, or *Yolanda*. Before *The Pirate*, Kelly and Donen, to impart a sense of cinematic movement to their dance sequences, had depended more on the editing together of separately angled shots filmed by a camera that stayed and moved on the ground than on the boom camera. The collaboration between Minnelli and Kelly led to a new repertoire of moving boom shots and camera angles to capture Kelly's dance sequences.

Finally, in *The Pirate*, Minnelli offered Kelly, for the first time, a coherent, tightly structured musical and dramatic framework within which to integrate dance forms that he had developed in his previous musicals. In *Cover Girl, Anchors Aweigh*, and *Living in a*

Big Way, Kelly and Donen's imaginative and cinematically innovative dance sequences had functioned as islands in the midst of sprawling, loosely organized narratives in which music, dance, plot, and camerawork were sometimes only tenuously related. In *The Pirate*, Kelly's street and courtship dances were planned by the director and the dancer to fit seamlessly into a whole that—like *Meet Me in St. Louis*—came close to Minnelli's ideal of a movie in which all elements were fully integrated.

How did Minnelli's camerawork, decor, and lighting enhance the impact of Kelly's dances? *The Pirate*'s film-dance drama blends ideas from both men's previous films—the dream sequence in *Yolanda and the Thief* and Kelly's "balcony dance" in *Anchors Aweigh*. Like the former, it is set within the context of a dream which provides an insight into the thoughts and hidden desires of the dreamer; like the latter, it serves as the hero's seduction and courtship dance.

Kelly, as Serafin, a strolling player, seduces the reluctant heroine (Judy Garland) by pretending to be the notorious pirate Macoco. In this guise, while she watches, mesmerized (Fig. 9.3a), he performs a daring dance beneath her balcony. As he dances, the frame dissolves, and we see the heroine's vision of him as he dances out her idea of masculine prowess in a sequence that burlesques her adolescent vision of Macoco (Figs. 9.3b–d). He wields his sword with ever-increasing speed as if to cut down his enemies; he scales masts seemingly hundreds of feet high (Fig. 9.3c) and plunges his muscular arms into piles of jewels.

Kelly's choreography links to his training in ballet with Berenice Holmes and the Diaghilev Ballets Russes. Kelly's savage leaps and multiple turns draw directly on Fokine's *Polovtsian Dances*.[36] This was the ballet in which Holmes's teacher, Adolph Bolm, transformed the image of the male dancer in Paris, as he and his muscular warriors stunned French audiences accustomed to seeing women *en travestie* take male roles—just as Kelly would try to do in America. The virtuoso male dances in *Le corsaire* (whose title translates as "The Pirate"), the 1856 romantic ballet based on Lord Byron's eponymous poem, are also the choreographic ancestors of the dances in this film.

Lighting, decor, camerawork, and music enhance the dancer's choreographed demonstration of masculinity and help also to parody it. The expansive, borderless "dreamscape" is bathed in a red glow. Shadowy forms suggest razed buildings (Figs. 9.3b and e), and there is a tall mast for the pirate to swing up (Figs. 9.3c and d).

The lighting in particular is virtuosic, going well beyond the impressive effects in the *Yolanda* dance dream sequence. Coordinated with the movements of the pirate and his men, these explosions make this ballet an almost abstract sequence of moving colored light and shadow, illuminating the screen now blindingly with brilliant orange light, now with deeper reds and smoky whites. These great explosions of smoke and flame, varied in size and shape, are choreographed into the dance. Their sound is written as well into Conrad Salinger's witty arrangement of Cole Porter's song "Mac the Black"—itself an affectionate tribute to adventure-movie music as well as to the Rimsky-Korsakov and Borodin scores for the Fokine ballets *Scheherazade* and *Polovtsian Dances*, respectively.

FIGURE 9.3 (a) Judy Garland, as Manuela in *The Pirate* (1948), watches Gene Kelly as Serafin the actor as he performs stunts below her balcony. (b–g) In her imagination, Serafin is transformed into the pirate; (h) Serafin in "reality".

Minnelli's use of the camera is expressionistic, emphasizing the force and daring of the pirate's presence. His boom camera transports us freely through a space that—as in the *Yolanda* dream sequence—seems almost limitless. We view the action from multiple angles: from below, then high above the pirate as he swings up the mast of a shadowy phantom ship, the daring of his ride emphasized by the exaggeratedly low angle from which we view him. This camera angle is new to Technicolor film and made possible by a camera device developed by the MGM camera department in conjunction with Kelly to meet Kelly's and Minnelli's needs for this particular sequence. This was an adjustable mirrored lip that extended, only a few inches from the floor, from the bottom of the large Technicolor camera. The mirror could be adjusted to reflect the subject at the angle desired by the director, and the camera then shot down into the mirror.[37] The integration of all the elements—camerawork, choreography, lighting, decor, and music—in this sequence shows how intimate was the collaboration between its director and its central performer. It displays their like-minded approach both to film dance in general and to the film-dance drama in particular.

This unity of vision of director and choreographer distinguishes *The Pirate*'s dream sequence from its predecessor in *Yolanda and the Thief* in an important respect. In *Yolanda*, Astaire, moving away from much of his work in the 1930s, had "allowed" Minnelli's moving camera to participate in his dance. Still, *Yolanda*'s central pas de deux is a discrete unit, separable from the movement of the camera that frames it and tied to the floor on which it is performed. Although in broad outline *Yolanda*'s dance plays out a drama of seduction, that drama is a general one—framed by a proscenium arch, the dance could, with slight modifications, be incorporated into any one of a number of Astaire films. But Kelly's dance in *The Pirate* is inseparable from the camerawork he and Minnelli planned, and removing it from the context of the film and stringing it together without the camerawork would make it an essentially meaningless and formally unrelated series of movements.

ON THE TOWN, "A DAY IN NEW YORK": KELLY AND DONEN'S FIRST DANCE DRAMA

Minnelli's impact on Kelly would be next seen in his "Day in New York" ballet in *On the Town* (1949), a movie version of the Broadway musical that grew out of Robbins's *Fancy Free*, with choreography now by Kelly. Like its predecessors on Broadway and as in *Yolanda and the Thief*, the ballet takes the form of a dream or reverie in which the hero pursues a female ideal just beyond his reach and in which the hero's yearning and confusion, the emotional low point of the film, is dramatized.

As in *The Pirate* and in the Minnelli-Astaire film-dance dramas, lighting is coordinated with music to mark out sections and change mood: the set is suddenly plunged into darkness for the elegiac meeting of the two lovers at the barre around which the dancers twist and turn, paralleled by their shadows, which are cast against a deep red backdrop; the set lights go up again as the three couples dance (Figs. 9.4a–c), and then dim as Gabey is left alone.

Unlike with Minnelli, however, the moving boom camera, though active in height, does not play a large role in the "Day in New York" ballet, Kelly and Donen's first extended ballet sequence in a movie, and this may have been due to Donen's influence. The camera remains cautiously on one level, only gliding up and back to conclude the

FIGURE 9.4 *On the Town* (1949), "A Day in New York." Note the variety of movement as Gabey and his friends meet their dream girls and he relives his day.

sequence. Movement, however, is provided by rhythmic editing and fast camera pans as the lens moves back and forth to capture the three sailors as they skitter across the dance floor in Kelly's energetic choreography. The performance space, too, is shallower and more clearly defined than the seemingly infinite performance areas of the dance dramas in *The Pirate* or *Yolanda*, or even the "Miss Turnstiles" sequence at the beginning of the film. It is almost theatrical in effect: a frontally oriented, sparsely dressed two-level "stage," the back boundaries of which (a stylized New York skyline) are obscured when the set is darkened.

In terms of dance itself, the film ballet in *On The Town* demonstrates Kelly's ambition, as with Astaire and Balanchine before him, to blend in his own way both Old and New World forms. To play the pirate, Kelly had looked for inspiration both to Fokine and to Douglas Fairbanks's movie derring-do. In the film ballet of *On the Town*, Kelly, playing an American sailor, blends the everyday movement of his street dances from *Cover Girl*—walking, running, skipping—with elements of play, sports, and the friendly physical horseplay of American buddies. Like Robbins, who also combines these influences, he draws on the skills of the classically trained dancer for attention to the overall line of the body and its relationship to the shape of other dancers, as well as for the ability to stretch, extend, and rotate the leg. Like Astaire and jazz dancers, he wanted a seamless flow from one movement to another. To this mix, Kelly, again like Robbins and like de Mille and Michael Kidd, adds gravity-emphasizing modern dance with its use of the floor—knee slides, for example.

In order to do all this, Kelly now substitutes for four of the cast (Sinatra, Munshin, Garrett, and Miller) professional dancers who, like Kelly, have been trained in ballet as well as other forms. Jeanne Coyne, Carol Haney, Alex Romero, and Lee Scott, like Kelly and Vera-Ellen, were products of a typically American eclectic education, trained in ballet but also in jazz dance. (Coyne and Haney were Kelly's regular dance assistants, and Romero had assisted him in *Cover Girl*.)

In his choreography, like Astaire, Kelly combines stylized vernacular movements—running, walking, skipping, and jumping steps—with influences from a variety of dance sources, ranging from ballet to social dance (ballroom and folk) to sports, jazz, and modern dance. But the influence of Balanchine and the Diaghilev diaspora adds another layer of influence on his choreography, and this is among the characteristics that distinguish him as a choreographer from Astaire and link him with Robbins and others choreographers of his generation, likewise influenced by Balanchine as well as Astaire. Whereas Astaire might elaborate on ballroom or social dance or use rhythm tap, Kelly's turned-out stance, his emphasis on a long, stretched-out line, and his repertoire of turns and lifts have their origin in his classical training as well as gymnastics.

Kelly's style, as presented in *On the Town*, is a distant relative of the new and distinctively American dance style that Robbins, influenced by Balanchine and Astaire, presented in *Fancy Free* and the stage version of *On the Town*. Michael Kidd later used this style in the choreography for *Seven Brides for Seven Brothers* (1954). It demands the skills and resources of the classically trained dancer for speed, strength, flexibility, and ability to turn out for a wider rotation of the leg, and it calls on the devices of floor work developed by modern dance. But the style has a particularly American flavor in its freer and more relaxed port de bras, its rhythmically intricate coordination with the popular music to which it is danced, and, most of all, the distinctive energy and vitality that animates the dancers. Kelly's style, then, assimilates and amalgamates many influences. But like Astaire and like his cohorts, Kelly blends and transforms aspects of these disparate sources to create his own pluralist dance style.

THE RED SHOES AND THE BRITISH BALLET INVASION

Besides Minnelli's, Astaire's, and Kelly's responses to the American dream ballet, influence from outside the country would nudge the film ballet. This too had its roots in the Diaghilev diaspora. By 1949 the art of ballet had really taken off, and not just on Broadway. Balanchine was largely devoting his energies to his company, the New York City Ballet, which, after years of on-again, off-again activity, had finally found a home at New York's City Center. The various Ballet Russe touring companies still had immense appeal for audiences. Furthermore, a new American ballet company had been established in 1940 and was going strong. This was the Ballet Theatre (later American Ballet Theatre), from which would come a new generation of American choreographers and dancers. They were the products of the typically American eclectic dance training, but, unlike Astaire and more like Kelly, had a considerable amount of ballet training, some of them from the expatriate Ballets Russe dancers who had set up studios. Balanchine created some works for them, and they also performed ballets by Fokine and other Diaghilev choreographers. From Ballet Theatre would emerge two important choreographers for film dance, Jerome Robbins and Michael Kidd. Both would have a powerful impact on film dance.

In 1949 another ballet company that had emerged from the diaspora of Diaghilev dancers would invade New York and, like the Ballet Russe, would be taken to American hearts, crisscrossing the country almost every year in the 1950s and '60s. This was the Sadler's Wells (later Royal Ballet), founded in the early 1930s by Ninette de Valois, an Anglo-Irish dancer who in the mid-1920s had worked with Diaghilev, just as had Balanchine. England, like America, did not have a continually active ballet company and school such as had existed in France, Italy, and Russia for centuries. Diaghilev and his Ballets Russes had changed all that, and the diaspora of his dancers had had as profound an impact on England as on America.

One of their principal dancers was Moira Shearer, who had starred the year before in an English film, *The Red Shoes*, directed by Michael Powell and Emeric Pressburger. Staffed by Léonide Massine and a corps of British dancers, the film was a thinly disguised portrait of the Diaghilev company in which Anton Walbrook plays a powerful and manipulative impresario whose aim in life is to hire and develop a great dancer. The ballet of *The Red Shoes*—a fifteen-minute piece choreographed by Robert Helpmann, another Sadler's Wells principal—lies at the heart of the picture, and it soon gained cachet with art-house audiences, eventually becoming a cult favorite. *The Red Shoes* was a very Anglo-European take on ballet. Diaghilev was part of their history in a way that he would never be in America. Helpmann's film ballet at its center incorporated some references to jazz, German expressionism, and surrealism, but on the whole, the ballet was clearly rooted in the Euro-Russian and now English ballet tradition. After the premiere of *On the Town*, Arthur Freed acknowledged a kind of rivalry in his note to Kelly and Donen: "Powell and Pressburger can't shine your shoes: red or otherwise."[38]

The ballet of *The Red Shoes* pointed out, by contrast, how very far removed the American film ballet had moved from its original associations with any classical or European associations. The pluralist style developed by Astaire, Kelly, and Kelly's swing-generation cohort was now ingrained as the new vocabulary of storytelling dance in America. And its music and feeling were above all American. Rather than its content, it was the *length* of the ballet that convinced MGM to allow Kelly and Minnelli to create their most ambitious project. Saul Chaplin, the music co-director of *An American in Paris*, recalls: "There was a discussion as to whether to do a seventeen minute ballet, and I remember what finally sewed it up. There was a picture called *The Red Shoes* that came out that had a seventeen minute ballet and it was doing very well. That settled it. As long as they could do it, we certainly could do it, only do it better."[39]

Like the Gershwin score, the "American in Paris" ballet has the vigor, vitality, and undisguised enthusiasm of the New World. Like Gershwin himself, Kelly is the American who looks at the Old World anew and savors it, but with his own distinctive attitude and ways of hearing and moving. As with Gershwin, however, this ballet and others like it would be victims of the stereotypical highbrow/lowbrow divide. In the 1920s lowbrow jazz had been sniffed at, and its black performers were seen as unworthy of being taken seriously. The film ballet form was pretentious; the "ballet" form belonged to the trained European. Kelly, Minnelli and Donen were giving themselves airs. Like Josephine Baker, they should stick to American "revelry"—comedy dancing and the like. But in fact, they had remade the "ballet" in an entirely new medium and in a new dance language that synthesized sound and moving image in a new way.

KELLY'S AMERICAN IN MINNELLI'S PARIS

The ascendancy of the choreographer jump-started on Broadway by Balanchine with Minnelli and Duke in *Ziegfeld Follies of 1936* and by Balanchine with Rogers and Hart in *On Your Toes* is most clearly shown in *An American in Paris*, whose opening credits showcase "choreography" by Gene Kelly.

Listed in the opening credit sequence as the "American in Paris Ballet," the seventeen-minute dance drama that climaxes the series of dance dramas in both Minnelli's and Kelly's films. It is the longest and most elaborate in the series. Like the rest of *An American in Paris*, the ballet blends ideas from both director and star: Minnelli creates an elaborate and colorful framework for a dance drama that, in choreographic style, is distinctively Kelly's (Fig. 9.5). However, the ballet also extends back to Balanchine and Toland's discarded "American in Paris" ballet with its libretto, "Exposition," created by Ira Gershwin in consultation with Balanchine. To prepare for *An American in Paris*, Kelly, Minnelli and producer Arthur Freed had gone through the Gershwin catalogue of songs with Ira Gershwin, who was closely involved in the project, and they undoubtedly discussed the libretto. While Kelly went on to create his own libretto, two basic themes remain: An American man purses a female ideal through a variety of exotic locations. The man dances tap (New World) and the woman is on pointe (Old World). Can they make it?

Dramatically, this dance drama has multiple meanings. Like its predecessors in *Yolanda*, it is a dream sequence that serves as a dance character portrait of Kelly's character, Gerry Mulligan. It reveals his emotional state by recapitulating his relationship with his beloved, Lise. During the sequence Gerry meets Lise, courts her, and loses her. The ballet is also a visual and musical homage to Paris as inspiration for Gerry and his fellow artists. Like New York in *On the Town* and St. Louis in *Meet Me in St. Louis*, the city itself is a major character.

The woman (Caron) whom the dancer chases through the city, like Zorina in Balanchine's "American in Paris," like Vera-Ellen in *On the Town*, and like Lucille Bremer in *Yolanda and the Thief*, again has origins in romantic nineteenth-century ballet as well as Balanchine's film ballet for *An American in Paris*. She is his ideal, his muse—as is symbolized visually in the ballet's opening moments. Gerry, dressed in black, is seen standing within the space of his black-and-white sketch. On the ground in front of him

FIGURE 9.5 Ballet, *An American in Paris* (1951). (a) The predominantly black-and-white Beaux Arts Ball "rests the eyes" before the color-filled dream ballet. (b–c) Kelly's black-and-white sketch is suddenly flooded with color. (d) The Dufy-inspired Place de la Concorde. (e) "Utrillo" set: Kelly and his American military friends. (f) "Rousseau" set: Caron, on pointe, adopts the Cohan strut with Kelly and his buddies. (g–h) Varied color and light effects suffuse the dance. (i) By the steps of the Opéra, inspired by the colors and brushstrokes of van Gogh's *Sunflowers*. (j–k) Toulouse-Lautrec's sketch of the dancer Chocolat dissolves into Kelly's embodiment. (l) Caron as Jeanette Avril and Kelly as Chocolat dance amidst characters from Toulouse-Lautrec's paintings arranged as a *tableau vivant*.

(i) (j) (k) (l)

FIGURE 9.5 Continued

is a rose that has been associated with Lise earlier in the film—the red rose is the only spot of color in the frame (Fig. 9.5b). Gerry leans over and picks it up, and suddenly his sketch is flooded with color. Minnelli had already used this device in *Yolanda and the Thief* with Astaire: a red carnation becomes a symbol of the Yolanda he encounters in the dream ballet to follow. But this use of a flower as a symbol extends back to nineteenth-century ballet, particularly the ballet that Astaire went to with his mother in Paris and that Kelly certainly saw in his many viewings of ballet companies: the lily with which the spirit of Giselle signifies her presence.

Another of Minnelli's favorite devices is also used here: the all-black-and-white decor of the previous sequence (the Beaux Arts Ball) provides a dramatic contrast to the brilliant, multicolored mise-en-scène of the ballet that follows (Fig. 9.5a). "I thought it would give the eye a rest, so that when the black and white turned into color it would be so much more dramatic," explains Minnelli.[40] Similarly, the contrast of sepia tones in the opening of the "Limehouse Blues" sequence contrasts with its brilliantly colored dream finale, and the purple haze of the opening in the hanging sequence of *The Pirate* is replaced by multicolor at the conclusion of the sequence. Cecil Beaton would adopt the sudden shift to colors from black and white in the "Ascot Gavotte" sequence of *My Fair Lady*, both onstage and in the film.

Dramatically, the Beaux Arts Ball functions to bring the film's protagonists and the threads of the story together in one place, and the plot's denouement takes place within the festive framework provided by the party. Musically, the ball serves an ingenious double function: phrases from songs used as leitmotifs for the film's characters comment on the dramatic action and at the same time serve as a sort of musical finale in which the songs we have heard throughout the film are reprised.

This burst into color was an especially difficult effect to achieve. Preston Ames explains how it was done:

Vincente wanted to do the resolution of black and white to color in the studio. . . . How did we do it? Everybody had a different idea until the head of the Camera Department, John Arnold, was brought in and . . . introduced us to a photographic mirror or black-glass mirror. This gave you an opportunity to either see through the mirror or to photograph a reflection. So what we did at first was to see this sketch reflected into our mirror in black and white. Now, the color was in an identical sketch on the other side of the glass and that, at the moment, was not lit. As you took light off your black and white sketch and lit up the color one on the other side of the mirror, it became a perfect match dissolve, until all you saw was the color sketch. So we solved the transition by taking light from one image and putting it on another image.[41]

Musically, the dance drama is also a summing up of the movie. The themes from the *American in Paris* symphonic poem that have been heard in fragments throughout the film as leitmotifs for various characters and situations are now presented as parts of a coherent whole. The music for the ballet is based on Gershwin's original work and on first hearing seems indistinguishable from it, but in fact, as with the Balanchine "American in Paris," it is artfully edited to interact with the dance drama's choreography and camera movement (compare Figs. 9.5b and c). Kelly and Minnelli's "American in Paris" ballet, like the rest of the movie, is also a tribute to George Gershwin himself, whose memory motivated the entire project and whose loss, even after more than a decade, was still felt by his colleagues. To them, he was a giant in the field of music to which they were still devoting their lives and which would by the end of the decade, as their generation aged, fade in popularity along with the musical film. John Green, the music director for *An American in Paris*, who worked with Kelly on editing the score for his choreography, sums it up: "I don't know how to articulate it better. George is in my blood, that's all."[42] Arthur Freed writes, "In *American in Paris*, I wanted to hear the real Gershwin sound."[43] Freed conceived of the entire film as a sort of homage to Gershwin's music, not as a biography. A lyricist as well as a producer, he was a close friend of Ira Gershwin, and he bought the entire Gershwin catalog to choose from for the film, as well as the title and music for *An American in Paris*. The key musicians who worked on the film, John Green and Oscar Levant, had worked in some capacity with George and Ira Gershwin at one time in their careers. Saul Chaplin was close to Ira Gershwin and knew George's music extremely well, as did Conrad Salinger. Freed knew from the beginning that they wanted to do *An American in Paris*, and as he explained, he chose Gene Kelly for the central role over Fred Astaire because Kelly was more interested and accomplished in "ballet."[44] Kelly was too young to have met Gershwin but adored his music.

Visually, the ballet repeats, in a more elaborate format, ideas from Minnelli's previous film-dance drama sequences: the expansive, dreamlike space, the freewheeling mobile boom camera (more active than ever before), and the delineation and dramatization of each section by contrasting-colored lighting. The color and lighting effects are more subtle, varied, and impressive than in any of the previous Minnelli ballets, and they make this film a landmark in color cinema. The director called in a new cameraman, John Alton, especially to light this section, replacing Alfred Gilks, whose bright, flat lighting in the first part of the film displeased the director. Alton would make his name as a brilliant and innovative cinematographer and is today credited for creating the look of film noir. For this film, he worked with colored filters to create the complex light and color effects demanded by the director, who in this sequence clearly wanted the most dramatic and varied of colors to recreate the dream world of a painter.[45]

The ballet's sequences that take place on the set modeled on the Place de la Concorde are a good example of these virtuoso colored-lighting effects, and also of how carefully coordinated they are with the music and the camera movement. As the camera swoops and sails around them, the dancers move through clouds of mist that change continually in color and light quality in response to their movements (Figs. 9.5g and h). At the peak of a musical phrase, for example, Lise is raised aloft by Gerry. In response to the movement of her upraised arms and body, the light changes from soft blue to blinding white. Soon after, an arc described by her leg throws a blanket of rose over the set.

Transitions from one set (or section) of the dance drama to another are made by light changes coordinated with camera movement and music—some quite ingenious and without precedent in film. At the end of the section just described, for example, a shaft of light picks out Gerry and Lise in silhouette; as the music softens and slows to conclude this section the camera, starting in a medium-close shot, glides back and up at a forty-five-degree angle as they slowly lift their arms. At the peak of their gesture, when the camera is at its highest point—and paralleling a musical exclamation point—a brilliant yellow light suddenly illumines the set, and, as if by magic, we see the dancers dressed in completely different costumes within an entirely new setting, the Place de l'Opéra (Fig. 9.5i).

The sets and costumes of this dance drama are the embodiment of Minnelli's theories about the expressionistic, personality-revealing function of decor. They also give him a chance to pay his own visual homage to some of the artists he loves. Freed too loved French painting, and Irene Sharaff suggests that *An American in Paris* reflected this. "One must give tremendous credit to Arthur Freed, who is a very peculiar man with a great love for painting. . . . Arthur fell in love with the Impressionist painters, and *An American in Paris* was a story about Paris. I think he felt this was some way of showing his love for nineteenth century and early twentieth century painters."[46] Each set, representing a different section of Paris, is meant to suggest in style and imagery the work of an artist whom Gerry admires: the Place de la Concorde (Dufy, Fig. 9.5d); a flower market (Renoir and Manet); a street in Montmartre (Utrillo, Fig. 9.5e); a carnival, zoo, and park (Rousseau, Fig. 9.5f); the Place de l'Opéra (van Gogh, Fig. 9.5i); a cabaret interior (Toulouse-Lautrec, Figs. 9.5k and l); and overall, in its variety of beautiful color effects, as Irene Sharaff has suggested, Monet.[47] Works of each artist are not precisely recreated: As Minnelli says, "We didn't want to copy, just evoke."[48] As in previous Minnelli dance dramas, actors arranged in *tableaux vivants* (Fig. 9.5l) are a crucial part of this, lit and costumed to suggest representative images from the oeuvre of each painter.[49] Special attention was paid by all involved—especially Irene Sharaff, the costumer, who was an important participant in this project—to capturing precisely the distinctive palette of each artist represented. As a result, the range and subtlety of colors presented is entirely new to cinema. Under Minnelli's supervision, Sharaff and other members of the art department attempted—and, at times, succeeded—in creating a range of hues as varied and distinctive as that of any of the painters they evoke.[50]

Choreographically, Kelly's character dancing is carefully integrated with decor and camera movement. As in *The Pirate*'s ballet, his choreographed movement functions to create more of a series of dramatic cinematic images than a dance performance per se. Again as in *The Pirate*'s dance drama, there are few pure dance sequences; rather, a great deal of running and posturing takes place within the ornate decor. In the only extended dance sequence, one of Kelly's favorite images reappears: three dancers dressed as GIs (their uniforms enlivened by clearly visible brushstrokes painted directly on them by Sharaff) join Gerry in a dance that, in feeling, recalls sequences from *On the Town* and *Anchors Aweigh*, and that ultimately relates back to *Fancy Free* (Fig. 9.5e). As Kelly explained, these musical military buddies are used to suggest the particularly American qualities of the American in Paris. Their vernacular dance style (tap) and the Cohan strut (an idiosyncratic, stiff-legged walk associated with George M. Cohan) that they employ are contrasted with the pointe work of Lise and her friends to symbolize the difference between the two different worlds (Old and New) from which the lovers come (Fig. 9.5f).[51] As Kelly said: "I saw only two very clear ways to make an American really look American amongst all those French Impressionistic paintings." One was to have American servicemen figure somehow in the dance drama; the second, to include in the dance drama "tap dancing as opposed to classic ballet."[52] As Kelly explains, "This is an American looking at Paris, so we had the canes and straw hats and we walked like Cohan and we did a tap dance." For the zoo scene with surroundings in the style of Henri Rousseau, "as Frenchy looking as you can get," he chose to have his men "do everything the way George M. Cohan would do it, like an American would do it," and so make them "immediately identifiable as American." The little girls in the scene were "Frenchy as could be," in contrast to the men, who were to be emphatically American. "Now, you could go into the jungles of Africa and you'd know immediately that those fellows were Americans. That's what I wanted."[53] When Lise and her corps adopt the strut in the dance's final section, it is a dance symbol of their union with the Americans.

Some of Kelly's other dance ideas come directly from the works of artists to which the dance drama pays tribute. The stylized profile pose (one arm upraised) of the cabaret dancer called Chocolat in Toulouse-Lautrec's drawing of this performer is used as the initial gesture of a dance tribute to this artist (Figs. 9.5j and k); Lise, costumed as the dancer Jane Avril as portrayed by Toulouse-Lautrec in his poster for the Jardin de Paris (1893), dances Kelly's recreation of a can-can for an audience composed of figures drawn from the painter's oeuvre and arranged in *tableaux vivants*, including Oscar Wilde, Aristide Bruant, Yvette Guilbert, May Milton, and Louise Weber-La Goulue. These figures are arranged in an odd-angled composition that can be seen as derived, in general configuration, from Toulouse-Lautrec's *Au Moulin Rouge*. In the major shot of the sequence, an actress made up to resemble the face of a similar female figure in this work is illuminated dramatically from below by a green light and cut off laterally by the edge of the frame, paralleling the lighting effects and composition of this painting (Fig. 9.5l).[54]

"GOTTA DANCE," KELLY'S BALLET FOR *SINGIN' IN THE RAIN*

Following *An American in Paris*, the film ballet would become a standard element not only in MGM musicals but in those produced by other studios, resulting in self-consciously "artistic" ballets in the film musicals of the 1950s. Kelly would go on to make an all-dance film, *Invitation to the Dance*. For Minnelli and the team of Kelly and Donen, however, the "American in Paris" ballet marked the beginning of the end of the tradition that they themselves had brought to fruition. After this film, Minnelli would incorporate only one more film ballet into one of his musicals (*The Band Wagon*), and the Kelly-Donen team's last such effort would appear in the next film in the Freed unit series, *Singin' in the Rain*. In the dance drama with which it ends, "Broadway Rhythm," Kelly and Donen build on Kelly's experience in the "American in Paris" segment and employ the moving camera more expansively than ever before, putting a final stamp on the tradition of the film ballet.

The ballet is again essentially a *ballet d'action* which combines an *hommage* to Jazz Age Broadway backstage musicals with a modernized romantic ballet theme of the search for an unattainable woman, seen in the Balanchine Broadway and film ballets. Like *Singin' in the Rain* as a whole, the film ballet at its center affectionately and humorously comments on the forms and devices of earlier film-musical ballets, and in so doing sums up a tradition that *Singin' in the Rain* climaxes. As in the early backstage musicals and the *Broadway Melody* series of movies, Kelly is an aspiring young performer who comes to New York to dance on Broadway, inspired by its fascinating rhythm: "Broadway Rhythm, it's got me, everybody dance." His theme phrase, "Gotta Dance," repeated over and over, echoes the songs that paid homage to the new jazz rhythms and their irresistible, crazy rhythms.

Appropriately, "Broadway Rhythm" was one of those songs, and it and the other Arthur Freed–Nacio Herb Brown song, "Broadway Melody," around which the MGM orchestrators built the score were signature tunes for the series of MGM backstage musicals produced at the very beginning of the sound era and through the 1930s to rival the Berkeley *Gold Diggers* series at Warner Bros.[55]

As in these films and their companions made by other studios, the key, recurrent visual image—one that both starts and concludes *Singin' in the Rain*'s dance drama (like the "Dufy" Place de la Concorde in *An American in Paris*) is Times Square, with its rhythmically flashing neon signs suspended surrealistically in the air above an expansive space upon which Kelly sings and struts (Fig. 9.6a). In *Singin' in the Rain*, however, the black-and-white of the 1930s films explodes into brilliant colors that punctuate a deep blue atmospheric, seemingly limitless space surrounding a triangular, stylized Times Square in yellow.

In line with this opening set, the later ones through which Kelly moves are equally stylized, the colors bright and vibrant—deep reds, greens, blues, and yellows. Some seem, like the *American in Paris* sets, to be paintings come to life: distinct brush marks activate the surfaces of floors and props (Fig. 9.6b). And again as in *An American in Paris*, *tableaux vivants* (possibly a Minnelli influence) are used extensively and wittily. In the opening section, for example, a series of urban citizens, frozen in position, glides past Kelly on a moving sidewalk (Fig. 9.6c).

Minnelli's influence, as well as that of early modern dance, may be most clearly seen, however, in the rather heavy-handed central Surrealist set that visually relates to the dance-drama sequences in *Yolanda and the Thief* and the "Beauty" sequence of the *Ziegfeld Follies* film, and before that to Minnelli's Surrealist setting for Balanchine's "Words without Music" ballet for the Broadway *Ziegfeld Follies of 1936*. In this Surrealist interlude, Kelly, dressed in black, and Charisse, in a filmy white Isadora Duncan–esque white silk scarf, dance on a vast blue-gray horizonless space marked off by perspective lines in pink and punctuated at intervals by small silver balls placed on the ground (Fig. 9.6d). The dance that takes place on this set is the only uncomfortable moment in an otherwise fast-paced and witty American dance drama. It seems stylistically incongruent with the rest of the sequence.

In contrast is a witty section that, in dance, visual imagery, and camerawork, is a descendant of Balanchine's and Polito's film "Slaughter on Tenth Avenue"—this time using Kelly's own pluralist dance language and a female dancer completely comfortable with devices and rhythms of both ballet and jazz dance. Set in a speakeasy, it begins with one of Kelly's most dynamic short solos, accompanied by a hot, high-speed, big-band arrangement of "Broadway Rhythm." Its pulsating, syncopated opening propels Kelly forward and at the same time highlights his body gestures with instrumental riffs and ornamentations. With the breathtaking speed of a hockey player gliding over the ice, Kelly, his center of gravity low, digs into the ground for abrupt, on-a-dime stops, combining turned-in drags with whispered tap riffs and then suddenly levitating into dynamic, streamlined, slanted jumps (Fig. 9.6e). Kelly alternates into-the-ground and angular pirouettes with skimming just-above-floor turning jumps as he circles the floor in his own modernist version of one of the standard virtuoso enchainments of male variations of classical pas de deux.

FIGURE 9.6 *Singin' in the Rain* (1952), Broadway ballet. (a) The expansive Times Square set: Kelly's "gotta dance" as (b) he importunes agents on a colorful stylized set. (c) New Yorkers glide by him as *tableaux vivants* on a moving sidewalk. (d) He dances with his ideal woman in a Surrealist landscape. (e) Solo dance in a New York City cabaret. (f–h) Kelly and Donen's camera glides from Charisse's toe to thigh to head; compare with Balanchine's slide up the leg of Vera Zorina in "Slaughter on Tenth Avenue" (see Figs. 4.6n and o).

He ends it all with a dynamic knee slide and almost collides with Cyd Charisse's pointed foot, in a visual reference to Balanchine's camera trawl up the leg of Vera Zorina in *On Your Toes*—this time moving horizontally from the tip of Charisse's foot to her face (Fig. 9.6f–h). Kelly's pas de deux with Charisse makes use of her long extended legs, one of which at one point wraps around Kelly in a Balanchinian pose (cf. Fig. 4.5d).

Another section includes a variation on a common Astaire and Kelly dance theme: different dance styles and musical arrangement styles to the same melodic line. This time, as in *On the Town*, such variation is used as a visual and musical joke depicting the dancer's rise from obscurity to fame as he moves from performing in burlesque to vaudeville and, finally, to the *Ziegfeld Follies*. In a series of rhythmically edited images, we see the aspiring dancer travel with the same song from one setting to another. With each setting, the tempo and arrangement of the song and dance are modified to indicate the progressively more refined atmosphere of the establishment in which he performs. We first hear two lines from "Broadway Rhythm" played fast and loud as, dressed as a clown, he mugs his way down a line of chorus girls in a rowdy burlesque house. A more subdued but still cheerful arrangement accompanies him as, dressed in a red, white, and blue suit, he cakewalks down a line of similarly dressed chorines. Finally, a lushly orchestrated and stately arrangement accompanies him as he strolls, like Fred Astaire, singing the same song, down a line of opulently dressed *Follies* girls.

SATIRIZING THE FILM MUSICAL: *THE BAND WAGON*

The Band Wagon is, in part, another summing-up film, one that looks affectionately and with a satirical eye at the evolution of film dance—and at the meeting of ballet and jazz first explored in Balanchine's *On Your Toes* and Astaire's *Shall We Dance*. *The Band Wagon* explores Astaire's later career in relation to the new directions in which Kelly and Minnelli are taking the musical, along with Astaire's and Kelly's differing attitudes toward film dance.[56] It takes up Astaire's position within the world of stage and film musicals in 1953, focusing on Astaire's relation to a new style of dance influenced by the ballet boom of the 1930s and jump-started on Broadway with the success of *On Your Toes* and the other Balanchine–Rodgers and Hart shows—to the point where it was now almost a cliché to stick in a film ballet and to substitute dancers trained in ballet, such as Charisse and later Leslie Caron, for their tap-dancing counterparts. The satire is affectionate and tongue-in-cheek. As in their examination of early Hollywood with Kelly and Donen in *Singin' in the Rain*, Comden and Green, now working with Minnelli, spare no one, including themselves, in their witty and irreverent and at the same time loving look at the clash between two generations—and between two different concepts of the musical.

The Astaire character, Tony Hunter, modeled on the dancer himself, is a star of movie musicals whose career, after many successful years, has begun to founder.

In the film's opening scene, the top hat and cane that he used in his first movie, *Swingin' Down to Panama* (a reference to Astaire's early film, *Flying Down to Rio*), are being auctioned off, but there are no bidders. Hunter travels to New York in an attempt to salvage his career and, urged on by his scriptwriter friends Lily and Lester Marton and the prominent producer Jeffrey Cordova,[57] tries to update his image by participating in a show that, in the manner of the latest stage and film musicals, eschews a light-entertainment format in favor of one with, as he says, "significance and stature"—a modern musical version of Goethe's *Faust*. Like Kelly and Minnelli, Buchanan's Cordova is a multitalented director who seeks to expand the scope of the musical not only by incorporating into it themes and imagery from the "fine arts," but by raiding the world of classical dance to do so.[58] As Kelly and Minnelli had just done with Leslie Caron in *An American in Paris*, Cordova provides Astaire with a partner from a French ballet company rather than a tap dancer. To Astaire's increasing dismay, her lover (the show's choreographer—read Kelly) gives Astaire Kelly-style choreography to do—dances that require classical training (Fig. 9.7a). In a rehearsal sequence, Astaire virtually replicates a section of *An American in Paris* in which Kelly searches yearningly through a crowd of dancers looking for Caron (Fig. 9.7b), and much is made of Astaire's inability to lift his partner (Fig. 9.7a). Minnelli joins in the fun and further parodies himself in the agonizingly pretentious, climactic "Damnation Scene" ballet, in which explosions of smoke and flame reduce the dancers to fits of coughing and laughing. (The "exploding" decor and the jagged spotlight within which the dancers move makes it clear that *The Pirate*'s ballet is one of this satire's targets [Fig. 9.7c].)

In another sequence, the show's director (here again Minnelli satirizes himself) tries valiantly to coordinate an elaborate assemblage of moving scenery, lighting, and music. However, the heavily decorated revolving set refuses to function properly—its multiple floors move up and down seemingly at random. Dancers in elaborate costumes (some of them borrowed from the "American in Paris" ballet) struggle to keep their balance as the scenery on which they are poised, in Minnelli's distinctive *tableaux vivants*, glides out of control and the set is suddenly plunged into semi-darkness by the confused lighting operators. At the height of this confusion, and paralleling a climax reached by the orchestra that accompanies this section, the director, tangled in the set's wiring, is inadvertently hoisted aloft, from which point, hanging above his frantic company, he continues to shout directions (Fig. 9.7d).

Despite the satire, *The Band Wagon* concludes with a film ballet demonstrating that Astaire has won his snobby ballerina over to the world of jazz and popular entertainment. Indeed, the "Girl Hunt Ballet" is a parody of Mickey Spillane's detective fiction with the accompaniment of a swinging big-band score—not an investigation of inner emotions. The new style of jazz dance, however, now replacing tap dance, has been completely transformed by its absorption of Old World as well as New World styles. The new form is now called "jazz dance," but it demands ballet training as well as the ability to embody jazz rhythms with precision, while maintaining the ease, flow, and improvisatory quality of rhythm tap dancers.

FIGURE 9.7 *The Band Wagon* (1953). Old meets new: Astaire tries to work with a new generation of ballet-trained dancers, exemplified by (a) Charisse and (b) James Mitchell. (c) Minnelli parodies big dream ballets: in the "Damnation Scene" ballet, Astaire and Charissse try to make their way across the stage, blinded by explosions of colored light; clouds of smoke reduce the actors to fits of coughing and laughter. (d) The parody extends even to Minnelli's own dream ballets: confusion reigns as the director (Jack Buchanan) loses control of the elaborately moving scenery and gets tangled amidst the heavy sets. (e–f) Mickey Spillane dance drama, finale. Elements of ballet, jazz, and acrobatics in the new pluralist style. Astaire encounters Charisse in both sacred and profane guises.

The choreographer of the "Girl Hunt Ballet," Michael Kidd, who worked with Astaire on the ballet, was trained at Balanchine's School of American Ballet. Cyd Charisse was taught by another great Russian dancer-choreographer, Bronislava Nijinska, part of the Diaghilev diaspora who had settled in California. Kidd makes use of Charisse's long legs, which, with her ballet training, she can move, rotate, and stretch with the flexibility of arms. Astaire supports her in the stretched-out arabesques (Fig. 4.5b) that we first saw in Balanchine's pas de deux for Romeo and Juliet in the film *Goldwyn Follies*

(Fig. 4.5a). At the same time, Charisse, unlike Zorina, is completely at home with jazz rhythms. However, the syncopated rhythms once articulated by the feet in tap dance are absorbed into the body of the dancers (Fig. 9.7f). We don't "hear" their feet; rather, jazz rhythms are articulated by the entire body, especially through the isolations of shoulders, hips, and torso—techniques taught by Katherine Dunham and employed as well by Jack Cole in his own pluralist style, a blend of the latest jazz incarnation, bebop, with ballet, burlesque, modern dance, and *bharata natyam*. Cole's modern dance mentors Ruth St. Denis and Ted Shawn drew from the rich vocabulary of world dance. Cole goes a step further and seriously studies this classical Indian dance form.[59]

Echoes of earlier stage and film ballets—especially *On Your Toes*—are still there. This time Astaire chases an elusive woman (Cyd Charisse in two guises) through the streets of New York, but the final pas de deux takes place, like Balanchine's "Slaughter" and Kelly's "Broadway Ballet" in *Singin' in the Rain*, in a speakeasy, where Charisse is shot. This would be the last Minnelli-Astaire effort—and Astaire gives his director license to move the camera when he sees fit but trusts him to capture his full body during extended dance sequences (Figs. 9.7e and f). Minnelli, like Balanchine and Kelly, does occasionally interject close-ups for dramatic purposes, but without interrupting the flow of the dance. One close-up is remarkably similar to a device first used by Balanchine and Polito for the same purpose in "Slaughter" (Fig. 9.8a), when Charisse, leaning back over her partner's arm, spies danger upside down as another figure approaches (Fig. 9.8b).

The Band Wagon and *Singin' in the Rain* climax the tradition of the dance musical, but they also come in the last decade in which it would be truly viable. These films begin to mark as well the very beginning of the end of the careers of the great songwriters and the popularity of their form as an accompaniment for dance, and along with it, the careers of Astaire and Kelly. By the mid-1950s, rock and roll was starting to displace the song forms begun and developed in the Jazz Age—and it was the music that the next generation wanted to dance to.

The Band Wagon (1953) was the last of Minnelli's collaborations with Astaire. *Brigadoon* (1954) was his last with Kelly, and Kelly's last film with Donen was *It's*

FIGURE 9.8 (a) Zorina's upside-down head in Balanchine's "Slaughter on Tenth Avenue" in the film *On Your Toes*. (b) Charisse's upside-down head *The Band Wagon*.

Always Fair Weather. Though these two last films are filled with dance sequences, a film ballet is not among them. Nevertheless, Fred Astaire would appear in one more film ballet, *Daddy Longlegs* (1955), with Leslie Caron, Kelly's partner in *An American in Paris*. The dream ballet, choreographed by Caron's mentor Roland Petit, draws on all of the devices of the Balanchine-Kelly-Minnelli ballets, but this time the standard roles are reversed: the woman chases the man. Caron searches for Astaire through a series of multicolored sets, representing the various countries through which her ever-elusive ideal travels.

Making Film Dance

Plotting the movement of the camera is a form of
choreography.

—VINCENTE MINNELLI, in Minnelli and Hector
Arce, *I Remember It Well* (1974)

10

MAKING FILM DANCE

The Through-Composed, Through-Choreographed Musical

BEGINNING IN THE 1940s Vincente Minnelli, followed closely by Gene Kelly and
Stanley Donen, begin to conceive of entire movies as akin to dance, and of the role
of the director as akin to that of the choreographer: someone who works in tandem
with a composer to create an art form in which all movement, including the camera
and editing, is choreographed to a score. So far we've been talking about individual
song-and-dance sequences in musicals. When song and dance stop, as in many of the
Busby Berkeley films of the 1930s, dialogue takes over (and music may or may not be
heard in the background). Even in the Astaire-Rogers musicals of that decade, songs
and dances materialize like oases in the middle of a dialogue desert. Dynamized by
Astaire's singing and dancing, the audience must nonetheless return to earth and
await the next dance sequence, because while the musical scenes bear any amount
of repetition, the dialogue scenes tend to wear after multiple viewings. In any case,
in these films the characters either dance or they don't—and there is a clear distinction between musical numbers and the rest of the film. But in the second full decade
of sound film, the proportion of music to all action increases until, by the end of the
decade, practically the whole film is through-composed, and the distinction between
song, dance, and action is increasingly blurred. In dialogue scenes the music is no
longer musical wallpaper but, like a nineteenth-century ballet score, is studded with
leitmotifs and other compositional devices that are synergized with movement to
comment on the plot or drive it forward. Unlike a ballet score, however, dialogue and
sounds of all kinds are more and more intricately and rhythmically interwoven with
music and dance so that the whole is both formally and dramatically unified, becoming
more than the sum of its parts. The synergy of the elements turns them into something new and closer to dance than to any other art form.[1] The techniques developed

by these director-choreographers would profoundly influence filmmaking until they became so commonplace as to no longer be distinctive. In this chapter I will explore sequences that are not actually danced but, because of the way sound and movement are synergized, give the feeling of dance: the musical establishing sequence, the musical montage, and the musical finale.

THE MUSICAL ESTABLISHING SEQUENCE

> In a film or on a stage, you have to establish a style within the first five or eight minutes. You have to establish it on the level that you are asking the audience to accept it. It is on that level that the audience will feel and laugh. The audience, after that, will know what kind of an evening it should expect.
>
> —ALAN JAY LERNER, quoted in Donald Knox, *The Magic Factory* (1973), 41

Lerner's remark helps to explain what is going on in the opening moments of two model through-choreographed, through-composed musicals from the 1940s: Minnelli's *Meet Me in St. Louis* (1944) and Kelly and Donen's *On the Town* (1949). *Meet Me in St. Louis* was Kelly's favorite musical. So excited by the film was the young dancer and would-be director that he telephoned Minnelli and his wife, Judy Garland, after the premiere to enthuse about it. "We really couldn't get him off the phone," Minnelli said with a smile.[2] Kelly confirms this: "Most people think that the most important musicals are *An American in Paris* and *Singin' in the Rain*. To my mind they are *Meet Me in St. Louis* and *On the Town*."[3]

In the musical establishing sequence, the director makes clear his intention to tell the story in a specifically cinematic and musical language. The sequence introduces almost every major character, defines their relationships to one another, sets them within their environment, and gets the plot going, primarily by means of moving pictures linked to music. The dialogue is minimal and plays a secondary role. It is the succession of musically accompanied motion pictures through which the film's most important information is conveyed. From the very beginning, music will be as necessary and integral a part of the characters' surroundings and ways of expression as the spoken word.

Just as the characters are introduced musically, so too are they presented cinematically: their environment is dynamized and shaped by the moving camera and rhythm of editing. The director choreographs the camera: he frames people and objects rhythmically, now one way, now another, continually selecting and emphasizing. The sequence directs and focuses our attention on people, objects, and relationships as the director wills. Here is a camera totally freed from a frontal, theatrical, proscenium-stage orientation, a camera in almost continuous motion. Liberated from the pull of gravity, it glides through the opening locations—a Victorian house in turn-of-the-century St. Louis in *Meet Me in St. Louis*, the Brooklyn Navy Yard in *On the Town*. We view the characters from below and then from above; we track in front of them and then suddenly peer over their shoulders; we see them framed by banisters, window frames, and doorways. This camera movement and the images that it continually frames are carefully coordinated with the music. In tempo, dynamics, and orchestration, music is so closely allied with the visual images that at every point it enhances or comments on them. And even if no characters actually break into dance, the effect is the same as if they do.

What looks at first effortless in the sequence is actually an intricate, frame-by-frame coordination of a variety of sounds and a multilayered moving image, a coordination that fuses the skills of the director, choreographer, cinematographer, composer, orchestrator, and actors at the highest level. *On the Town* begins with a panoramic, poetic view of the city at dawn, fronted by the ocean, just as the sun emerges from the mist-shrouded skyline. The upbeat music of the credit sequence subsides into a quietly repeated musical phrase suggestive of water, and we hear, buried in the orchestra, an anticipatory phrase of the opening song, "New York, New York," played twice—the repeat moving a key higher—as the image dissolves slowly into another view of a now sunlit skyline, and the time, "5:57 AM," glides slowly in white letters across the screen (Fig. 10.1a). This image then dissolves into a view from high above the Brooklyn Navy Yard (Fig. 10.1b), and the "New York" leitmotif again modulates up a step, increasing the tension. Now, paralleling a descending musical phrase in the song, almost like a sigh, the camera glides slowly down from its omniscient position to focus from above on a pier against which a U.S. Navy ship is docked. Down the pier walks a tiny figure. This image slowly dissolves and the camera moves to the level of the figure to track it more closely: a blue-shirted, heavyset dockworker. Swinging his lunch bucket, the sun glinting off his yellow helmet, he walks the length of the pier (Fig. 10.1c) and then, as the camera glides up and back, lumbers onto a crane. As he walks, he begins to sing. His song, in its long, stretched-out phrasing, moving from high to low, is like a musical yawn: "I feel like I'm not out of bed yet." (Stretches.) "Ah-h-h-h."

Soon a piercing whistle suddenly interrupts his sung reverie, and the quiet, slow-moving sequence of images is disrupted by an abrupt cut to a close-up of the whistle ejecting steam (Fig. 10.1d). This visual and musical downbeat seems to galvanize the screen into activity as the camera returns to the pier. We are now given a head-on shot of a stream of white-uniformed sailors who rush, seemingly propelled by the whistle and the musical crescendo under them, off the ship and directly toward the camera. The dockworker stands in the right foreground of the frame watching them with amusement, and the time, "6:00 AM," speeds across the screen (Fig. 10.1e). The film's heroes, Gabey, Ozzie, and Chip (Kelly, Munshin, and Sinatra), separate out from the crowd and pause briefly next to the dockworker (Fig. 10.1f). Stunned by the view of the city in front of them, they are silent; then, recovering, they climax the mounting musical and visual tension by bursting into a song that pays tribute to the glorious view with a phrase that, now in full voice, gives words to the orchestral leitmotif of the initial opening sequence: "New York, New York . . . / It's a wonderful town!"[4] The camera remains in position as the dockworker, laughing at the sailors' enthusiasm, asks a question for the audience's benefit—"Hey fellas, what's the rush?"—and is answered almost immediately in song: "We only got 24 hours!" When the dockworker asks what they can do in just one day, the sailors again sing to him about the wonders of New York. The dockworker's question is also answered visually, by the sequence of images that follows. In a succession of shots cut together rhythmically, the trio is seen "traveling" with the song throughout the city. The excitement of this visual and musical tour mounts continually; the images—linked mostly by cuts and quick dissolves,

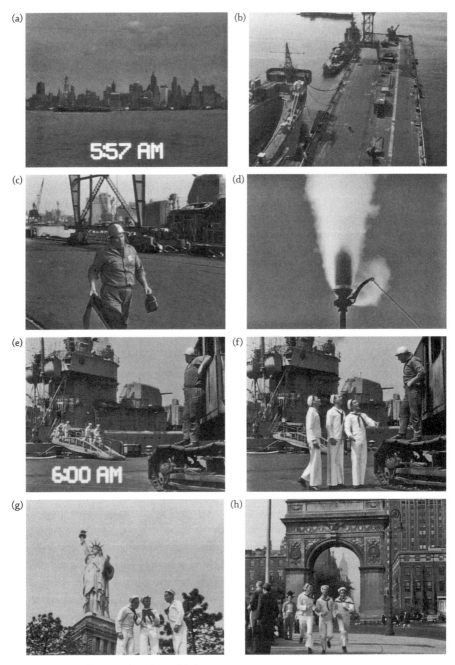

FIGURE 10.1 *On the Town* (1949), establishing sequence.

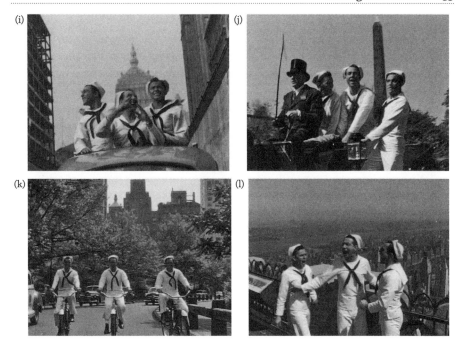

FIGURE 10.1 Continued

in contrast to the slow dissolves of the film's opening moments—succeed each other at an ever-quickening pace, paralleled by an increase in activity within the frame as the sailors move ever faster, walking and running, then riding on every form of transport (ferryboat, taxicab, horses, bus) as they visit the city's most famous sights, from Chinatown to the Statue of Liberty, from Washington Square to Fifth Avenue. In front of Grant's tomb, Sinatra fingers his ever-present guidebook, singing of the many famous places they have to cover in "just one day." The camera, constantly varying its position, frames them from various angles as they move, and the editing adds its own rhythm to the tune's propulsive pace (Figs. 10.1g–k).

The sequence finally comes to a visual and musical climax on top of a skyscraper, where, in the most dazzling series of images, the moving camera (attached by the intrepid young directors to a monorail constructed on top of the building) captures them surrounded by a panorama of skyscrapers and blue sky (Fig. 10.1l). Here the sailors seem to conduct the entire city in song, demonstrating its words by gestures—actually pointing out that "the Bronx is up and the Battery's down."[5]

The final verse of "New York, New York" returns the sailors to the ground as the camera pans swiftly and exhilaratingly down the front of the building to discover the trio (in a wonderful visual surprise) standing at its base. An elegantly coiffed young woman dressed in a stylish crimson outfit strolls rhythmically across the frame in front of them and Gabey, Ozzie, and Chip, now at the conclusion of the establishing sequence, respond to her appearance in song, introducing the theme of courtship. The song "New York, New York" has now traveled with its characters full circle around the city, illuminating the territory in which the important moments of the musical drama will be enacted. Thus it not only serves as a vehicle for introducing us to the film's central characters, but, linked to the traveling camera, it sets them in the film's environment. All this has been accomplished within the first two minutes of the film—using four lines of spoken dialogue.

The conventions of the through-choreographed, through-composed musical have now been established. We, the audience, will expect the characters to sing and dance as naturally as they talk. We can expect much of their speech and action to be synergized, in form, mood, and use of leitmotifs, with the orchestral music that, like the air they breathe, permeates the film's atmosphere. The New York City of the film, a setting that at first glance looks entirely real, is actually a city transformed and musicalized. In *this* city, music is an essential and natural element—the primary vehicle, in fact, for the expression of its citizens' most profound emotions. "The film's *soul* is musical," Stanley Donen has said of his musicals. "Berkeley's films weren't musical in their soul because there was always a rationalization for their singing and dancing."[6]

As I mentioned in the introduction, the musical soul of *On the Town* is presented cinematically: the music is wedded indissolubly to the moving picture. In this picture there are three kinds of movement. First, we have the movement of the characters within the frame. To this is added the movement of the camera—movement that activates the space within which the characters move. Finally, there's the movement provided by editing, which, in the transition from one shot to another by means of cuts or dissolves, imparts its own visual rhythm to the film. The effect of this combination of many-layered movement and music is, as I've noted, unique to sound cinema. Each medium enhances the impact of the others so that the pulse of the song is underlined and enhanced not only by the three sailors' rhythmic movements, but also by the movement of the camera, which shapes the space within which they move, and by the visual rhythm of the dissolves and cuts that interact with key changes as well as dynamics, orchestral color and texture, and words both spoken and sung. The basic conception is close to what a choreographer does, and its overall effect is similar to, although not the same as, that of dance. Much like an Astaire or a Balanchine who rhythmically coordinates the full resources of the body to reflect or interact with the warp and woof of the music as well as its emotional and dramatic mood, the director organizes all his visual resources to interact rhythmically with all kinds of sound.

Meet Me in St. Louis and *On the Town* each became a model for the through-choreographed musicals that followed. The model is not a rigid one, but its basic concept is almost always the same: characters and their settings in Minnelli and Kelly-Donen musicals are introduced and characterized primarily in terms that are musical and cinematic. We meet the characters singing, dancing, or (more rarely) speaking to a meaningful musical accompaniment, their environment shaped and dynamized by a moving camera and rhythmic editing that works in conjunction with the music to introduce and characterize them in a more succinct and yet richer and more poetic way than could any unaccompanied dialogue.

Often the songs in a Minnelli or Kelly-Donen establishing sequence—songs that characters sing or that accompany their actions—will travel with them, much as does the song "Meet Me in St. Louis" in Minnelli's film of that title and Bernstein's paean to New York in *On the Town*. By means of camera movement and editing, the songs are made to travel through space and time. A musical-visual form that takes unique advantage of the film medium, the traveling song serves as a unifying device.[7] Music links characters in disparate locations—sometimes in disparate time zones. Just as the song in *Meet Me in St. Louis* travels from character to character as they walk rhythmically around their family's midwestern Victorian home, where much of the action will take place, "New York, New York" introduces and travels with the three sailors from the ship through the city in their quest for love.

A synergy of music and moving image transforms the world of *Meet Me in St. Louis*, *On the Town*, and other musicals: what at first looks natural is really as artfully and intricately stylized as any musical or dance form, from ballet to opera. Thus the Smith family in *Meet in St. Louis* and the sailors Gabey, Ozzie, and Chip in *On the Town*, as well as the cities within which they move, become archetypes.

Not only audiences but also the younger filmmakers who loved these musicals were unaware of the very specialized skills and techniques necessary to create something so effortless-looking. What they didn't understand was that added to the hundreds, even thousands of hours required to hone the skills of singing, dancing, moving the camera, and editing was the development of techniques to coordinate them on film and the skilled technicians needed for such work. Jean-Luc Godard, who, like most of the French *nouvelle vague*, adored *On the Town*, eagerly asked Kelly to work with him to create film musicals. "I would have," said Kelly, but Jean "didn't seem to realize that you can't get in front of a camera and improvise a dance and hope to get the same results as we got in *On the Town* or *Singin' in the Rain*."[8] This misunderstanding is what weakened Kelly's ambitious all-dance film *Invitation to the Dance*. Filming away from the MGM studios, Kelly couldn't draw on the expertise, for example, of technicians who were used to moving the camera to musical counts, and his dancers didn't understand that rhythmic precision and placement (landing from a jump precisely on a mark) within the film frame was of critical importance.

MAMOULIAN AND *LOVE ME TONIGHT*

As Minnelli and his colleagues knew, techniques such as the musical establishing sequence and the traveling song, as well as the entire concept of the through-composed, through-choreographed musical, didn't begin with him but were created in the earliest years of sound cinema: specifically, in Rouben Mamoulian's *Love Me Tonight* (1932), with music by Richard Rodgers in one of his most wonderful scores, and lyrics by Lorenz Hart. Minnelli called it "a perfect example of how to make a musical," citing the complete integration of sight, singing, sound, and vision, and studied it as carefully as Balanchine studied the Astaire-Rogers films.[9] Stanley Donen agrees.[10] Mamoulian's

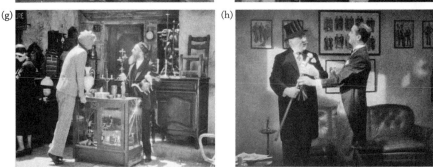

FIGURE 10.2 *Love Me Tonight* (1932), establishing sequence. (a) View of Paris. (b–d) The neighborhood of Maurice the tailor (Chevalier) and some of its inhabitants. (e) At his window Chevalier starts the "Song of Paree," then (f–g) walks to his shop, greeting his neighbors in song. (h) Inside, he sings "Isn't It Romantic?" to his about-to-be-married customer, who takes up the tune. The song then travels to a taxi driver, whose musician passenger (i) takes it up, to (j) soldiers who overhear it, and (k) to a gypsy violinist who plays it and (l) is overheard by Princess Jeanette (MacDonald). Their romance will be the movie's subject.

FIGURE 10.2 Continued

role as a director and innovator, not only in film but in stage musicals (*Porgy and Bess, Oklahoma!*), has been until recently too often overlooked.[11]

In *Love Me Tonight*, Paris, like New York in *On the Town*, wakes up musically, and rhythmically paced images show its citizens at work: the crescendo of sounds and rhythms they create climaxes with a song in which its hero, a tailor (Maurice Chevalier), like the sailors in the *On the Town*, pays affectionate tribute to his city ("The Song of Paris") and then ingeniously uses a traveling song, "Isn't It Romantic?," to connect the tailor in Paris with his beloved-to-be, Princess Jeanette, who languishes in her countryside castle waiting to be rescued from her boring, loveless life (Fig. 10.2; see the caption for the progression of the story). In this sequence Mamoulian—like Minnelli in *Meet Me in St. Louis* and Kelly and Donen in *On the Town*—relies not only on the traveling song to link the movie's main characters, but also, and primarily, on the musically accompanied moving camera to introduce them and their environment. And all this Mamoulian developed almost two decades before *On the Town*.

The various musical-visual devices introduced in this film will be used again and again by the most creative makers of film musicals. But Mamoulian can't be given all the credit for the devices that would become key elements in the through-choreographed musical. Joining him as pioneers in melding music and movement in various ingenious ways was René Clair, with his *Le million* of the same year, and Ernst Lubitsch, who made the great film musicals *The Smiling Lieutenant, The Love Parade*, and *One Hour with You*.

Meet Me in St. Louis and *On the Town* both follow a variation of the formula established by Mamoulian in *Love Me Tonight*. In *Yolanda and the Thief*, "A Day for Love" travels through space and time to introduce Yolanda and her surroundings and take her from the convent to start a new life; and in *It's Always Fair Weather*, "March" introduces the GI protagonists and travels with them through the war, demonstrating their bonding adventures visually and musically. In *Singin' in the Rain* we meet the characters even before the credit sequence begins as they whirl around in their bright yellow slickers and stride toward us singing the title song; soon afterward the traveling song "Fit as a Fiddle" presents the two central characters. In Donen's *Seven Brides for Seven Brothers*, "Bless Your Beautiful Hide" accompanies Adam Pontipee from his remote mountain cabin in the Oregon Territory to town, explaining his mission to find a bride. By the conclusion of the song he has indeed met her, and marriage follows in short order. In the complex opening of *An American in Paris*, Minnelli uses the moving camera to introduce the city, and as his camera climbs up the walls of the Left Bank *pension* in which the main characters reside, a succession of quotes from Gershwin works comments on the characters. Jerry, the artist around whom the story revolves, has the opening theme of *An American in Paris*. "How Long Has This Been Going On" comments ironically on the aging perpetual-student composer, Adam, on yet another scholarship. Gershwin's song "Nice Work If You Can Get It" introduces the cabaret star and bon vivant Henri Borel. The formula established by Mamoulian, Clair, and Lubitsch persisted in some of the most successful musicals of the second half of the twentieth century and into the twenty-first: from the opening of *West Side Story* to *The Sound of Music*, from *Cabaret* to *Hairspray*.

DANCE WITHOUT DANCING: CONRAD SALINGER AND THE ROLE OF
THE ORCHESTRATOR-ARRANGER

The impact and effectiveness of all of these techniques result not only from the manner in which they are staged, filmed, and edited, but from the songs themselves, as arranged and orchestrated to coordinate precisely, musically and dramatically, with the specific set of images we are given on the screen. We have already talked about the importance of the orchestrator to the courtship dance, the street dance, and the film ballet. As discussed in previous chapters, these musical effects were the responsibility not only of the song's composer and lyricist, but also of the members of the music staff, who orchestrated and arranged the song to be integrated, moment by moment, with the dramatic action it accompanied.

In the through-composed, through-choreographed musical, as in the film ballet, the musical director and orchestrator combine to perform a role even more crucial than that of the composer.[12] The importance of both the musical director and the orchestrator becomes even clearer when we realize that, in addition to setting the songs of others for song-and-dance sequences, the musical directors and orchestrators (despite often not being given screen credit) were often called upon to write original music to accompany and comment on action in the film, music that does not involve singing and dancing. They were thus responsible for creating the musical atmosphere that, in accordance with the aim of the integrated musical, continually surrounds and interacts with the characters as they move through the film. This was not just background music that functioned to create mood and atmosphere, but rather music that, incorporating significant leitmotifs, was carefully integrated with the characters' actions, lighting effects, and camera movement to express and propel the narrative forward.

In creating the musical fabric that runs almost continuously throughout the musicals I have been discussing, the musical director and the orchestrator performed a crucial role. Just as the director structures the film visually and dramatically, so the musical director and orchestrator, working with the director, put the musical meat on the skeleton. As Hermes Pan put it, "bad song, bad dance": a dance can only be as good as its music. This aphorism can be extended to the music for the whole film.

Aside from the composer of the songs to be arranged, it is not completely clear who was responsible for all the arrangements heard in a movie. Like medieval cathedral sculpture, film music was often the result of a group effort. John Green, a member of the music department at MGM, describes the process:

> There was no proud flesh, you know. We would look and see that it was four o'clock in the afternoon on a given day and say "Holy Jesus, this records day after tomorrow. I'll tell you what, Connie [Conrad Salinger], we've got Solly's [Saul Chaplin] two line sketch here. I'll expand it out to six lines, and you put it on the score paper.[13]

There was, however, one individual in the MGM music department whose style was clearly a dominant influence: Conrad Salinger.[14] He is currently unknown to film scholars and did not have the highest position in the music department. Very little is actually known about him. Yet his sound and style, probably more than any other, created the extraordinary sound of the finest musicals, from *Meet Me in St. Louis* to *Gigi*. André Previn, who began his career with the music department at MGM and who greatly admired Salinger, pays him tribute when he says that he himself always tries to imitate Salinger's "sound" when arranging American songs of the 1920s, '30s, and '40s.[15] The other orchestrators, too, Previn insists, tried to "sound like Connie." Alexander Courage, Salinger's fellow orchestrator on *The Band Wagon*, told me, "There was really only one 'sound' on those MGM musicals—that was Connie."[16] Green says that "aesthetically . . . Connie was unique."[17] Saul Chaplin, also an MGM musical director, sums it up:

> It's my considered judgment that Hollywood's major contribution to the musical film is Connie Salinger. He's the most imitated, and was simply the best for the kind of thing he did. Now, you didn't give him a big jazz thing to do, but for his orchestrations of ballads, his ideas of what went into them, and the eventual sound, he has been more imitated than, I think, even Debussy

and Ravel, by the guys out here who wrote those early scores. Connie was incredible.[18]

Salinger's sound, his style of orchestration, can thus be seen as a significant connecting link between the Minnelli and Kelly-Donen musicals. However different they may at times appear visually, musically they are closely related. Salinger's style reflects both his six years of training in French art music and his knowledge of the popular music of his native America. Conflicting sources place him as a student of Maurice Ravel, Nadia Boulanger, or André Gedalge in the early 1920s in Paris. (Chaplin is certain that he worked with Boulanger.)[19] Suskin simply says that he studied at the Paris Conservatoire but also lists him as a student of Gershwin's teacher Joseph Schillinger. And we know that he was one of the orchestrators for *Ziegfeld Follies of 1936*, on which Balanchine, Duke, Ira Gershwin, and Minnelli worked. His orchestrations of Kern's songs appear in Astaire's *You Were Never Lovelier*. But whether or not he studied with any of these people, his works reveal him to be part of that group of young American musical-theater musicians who, in the 1920s, were strongly influenced by impressionist composers—specifically, Claude Debussy and Maurice Ravel.

In his introduction to Alec Wilder's study of American song forms during the first half of this century, James T. Maher discusses this phenomenon:

It was during the 1920's that the young dance band arrangers were seized by the remarkable inventions in harmony and sonority of Debussy, Ravel, Delius . . . and composers of like creative resources. Some of them still recall with enthusiasm, and even a sense of urgency, their first encounters with French music of the early part of the century. "The older musicians thought the new French stuff was frivolous," one of them remembered not long ago, "they thought only German music was *serious*."[20]

To the list of French composers that exerted such a strong influence on these young American musicians, including Salinger, one may also add another: Igor Stravinsky. Like his American colleagues, Stravinsky was strongly influenced by Debussy—and also by American jazz. The impact of his early ballets for Diaghilev's Ballets Russes—*Petrouchka*, *Firebird*, and *The Rite of Spring*—can be clearly heard in several of Salinger's arrangements; a particularly good example is the festival sequence of *Yolanda and the Thief*, in which the effects of the music for *Petrouchka*'s crowd scenes can be clearly heard.

Salinger's music blends the innovative harmonies and rich and varied orchestral color and texture to be found in the works of Debussy, Ravel, and Stravinsky with the irregular, syncopated rhythms, the polyphonic structures, and the uniquely driving pace and vitality of American jazz. The resulting style, which, like Gershwin's, blended both classical and popular traditions, was uniquely suited to the tasks that Salinger and his associates were called upon to perform. His mastery of a remarkably wide range of

orchestral color and texture allowed him to create musical moods and atmospheres re-
flective of, and evocative of, a wide variety of visual and dramatic effects on the screen.
Salinger was particularly admired for the transparency of his orchestration—his ability
to create a rich tapestry of musical sound in which interesting and subtle orchestral
colors were both distinctly heard and yet blended together beautifully. His innovative use of winds in interesting combinations also won him admiration.[21] At the same
time, Salinger's grasp of and enthusiasm for American popular music meant that his
settings of songs by George Gershwin, Cole Porter, Hugh Martin, Nacio Herb Brown,
and Arthur Schwartz retained and even enhanced the pieces' distinctively American
freshness, wit, and energy. This distinguished them from the composers for dramatic
films at MGM, who were more likely to have come from the Austro-German tradition.
Salinger and his colleagues, to be sure, were guilty on occasion of overorchestrating.
The MGM orchestra, always rich and full, occasionally sounds too plush and glossy.
But on the whole, Salinger and his colleagues' arrangements are eminently suited
to the impressive catalog of American songs presented to us in the Minnelli and
Kelly-Donen films.

One of the orchestrator-arranger's specialties, as illustrated in the musical
establishing sequence, was to be able to create an entire score for a movie—not just
music for individual songs and dances or even for an extended dance drama—that was
shaped around the melodic material provided by the songs themselves, using them as
leitmotifs for certain characters and situations and combining them in various ways to
create mood and atmosphere for the action musically. We have already talked about the
black-and-white Beaux Arts Ball prelude to the "American in Paris" ballet, for example,
peppered with a variety of Gershwin's musical quotations that relate specifically to the
actions or mental state of the characters. But there are many other examples, ranging
from significant small moments to extended sequences.

As seen in his invention of the musical establishing sequence, one of the
hallmarks of Mamoulian's *Love Me Tonight* and the Lubitsch and Clair musicals was
to replace dialogue scenes, whenever possible, with a musically moving image to
convey a plot progression or complication. Let's examine a scene in *Meet Me in St.
Louis* as an illustration to give a sense of how Minnelli uses the technique of dance
without dancing.

THE GASLIGHT SEQUENCE IN *MEET ME ST. LOUIS*

The gaslight sequence illustrates clearly the use of coordinated choreographed camera
movement, lighting effects, body gesture, and music to replace dialogue and resolve
a plot situation. In the original screenplay for *Meet Me in St. Louis*, the gaslight sequence consisted of several pages of dialogue. Minnelli eliminated this and had the
protagonists play out the scene mostly in mime, punctuated only at intervals by hesitant phrases of dialogue. The actors' movements were then wedded to music that
incorporates fragments of a song (by Hugh Martin and Ralph Blane) sung earlier by

the heroine to describe her crush on "The Boy Next Door" as one of its themes, music that parallels almost every nuance of their changing relationship as, framed by the floating camera, they move through the deserted house extinguishing the gas lamps. Writes Minnelli:

> After the going away party for Esther's brother the relationship between the girl and the boy-next-door is established. It was very conventional, the dialogue realistic but banal. I supplied camera movement to eliminate these five pages of dialogue. Esther asks John Truett to turn out the lights for her . . . the action followed the two from room to room. It flowed smoothly but took considerable preparation. Lighting had to change as each of the dozen gas burners was extinguished . . . we took one full day for rehearsal—we probably could have shot those five pages in that time—but we got the scene first thing the next morning. It couldn't have been done without George Folsey's fluid and mobile work. He proved that my thoughts on the choreography of the camera weren't half-baked.[22]

Minnelli's use of the term "choreography" to characterize camerawork in the gaslight sequence is entirely appropriate, and the word applies equally well to Esther's and John's gestures, which, like the movements of the camera that frames them, seem almost musically timed. Their walk through the house is not so much a walk as a slow mime dance made up of their movements and the movement of the slowly gliding boom camera that sails along with them—now swooping down to examine them more closely, now pulling back so that we see their upturned faces framed by the chandeliers (whose softly tinkling glass ornaments are incorporated into the musical accompaniment). When, at the end of their journey, Esther begins to sing "Over the Bannister," it feels like a fitting and natural climax to the poetry of their gestures and the Folsey-Minnelli camerawork.

Lighting also participates in this musical journey. The gradual dimming of the gas lamps becomes a visual metaphor for Esther and John's growing intimacy, and like the actors' movements, it is integrated carefully with music: the dimming of the last two lights, leaving the two young lovers standing in a pool of moonlight that filters in through the stained-glass window, is, for example, coordinated with the last phrases of "The Boy Next Door," which swell up and then fade like the gas flames as Esther extinguishes the last two lights.

"Over the Bannister" sets the seal on the seduction. From the path of mere acquaintance and one-sided longing, the couple have now turned onto the road to love. As in the Astaire courtship dances, this emotional transformation takes place through song, but this time the choreographed camera takes the place of dance. The plot has turned. The moved and flustered John can offer Esther only an awkward handshake, when she—and we—want more; but no kiss is needed. The synergy of music and moving image has done the work: as in the courtship dances, it has expanded and poeticized their growing relationship.

The creativity of the orchestrator-arrangers working in the Minnelli and Kelly-Donen films and their ability to work with the director to synergize sound and moving image is used brilliantly in another device developed by Minnelli and by Kelly and Donen, though it was ultimately inspired by Mamoulian. From *An American in Paris* on, what I will call the musical montage will be an increasingly important formal and dramatic device for Minnelli and Kelly-Donen. It is prominently featured in Minnelli's next two films, *The Band Wagon* and *Gigi*, and in Kelly and Donen's *Singin' in the Rain* and *It's Always Fair Weather*. It is neither a song nor a dance, but rather a succession of moving images, depicting disparate events over time and space, accompanied by music, sometimes involving dialogue, and linked by dissolves. It will go on to powerfully influence both musical and dramatic films in general. Like a regular montage, the musical montage is made up of a succession of often unrelated moving images edited together to create a condensed, cinematic way of depicting a series of events over time.

In a musical montage such as the painting sequence of *An American in Paris*, however, the duration of the images tends to be longer and more extended than the quick, almost flash images of conventional montage, which may appear on screen for less than a second.[23] Each shot is packed with meaningful dramatic action and—another distinction—carefully coordinated not with background music, which, in a conventional montage in sound cinema, simply creates a generalized mood of gaiety or excitement or tragedy, but with an orchestral arrangement of a song or series of songs from the score, music that not only pushes the plot forward but comments on the images dramatically and interacts with them formally. The musical montage is in fact another number, like a song or dance—and again, the overall effect is close to the feeling of dance. It helps to propel the plot forward and develop the characters.

Although, strictly speaking, one could call the painting sequence in *An American in Paris* a montage, it is useful to distinguish between the musical montage and a regular montage. The painting sequence and the sequences that follow in Minnelli and Kelly-Donen musicals are longer in duration, and each of the sections that make up the whole is longer as well; they differ from the quick images of conventional montage. Accompanied by dramatically meaningful music, they are presented as distinct and coherent musical sequences that serve roughly the same purpose as a song or dance sequence within the overall structure of the film.

The painting sequence explicates visually and musically the development of the young artist Gerry's (Kelly) relationship with Lise (Leslie Caron) and his patron, Milo (Nina Foch), revealing during its course the growth of his love for Lise and, simultaneously, his increasing discomfort with the emotional situation in which his patron has placed him. We see him prepare for an exhibition that Milo has arranged for him.

The score for the painting sequence interweaves arrangements of fragments drawn from two Gershwin songs and a musical quotation from Gershwin's symphonic poem

FIGURE 10.3 *An American in Paris* (1951), painting sequence: Minnelli's musical montage shows the artist approaching his major exhibition while juggling the two women in his life. It conveys its story by means of a series of moving images edited together and linked by dissolves and cuts. Acting, camera movement, and editing contribute dramatically and formally to advancing the plot. The overall effect is close to that of dance.

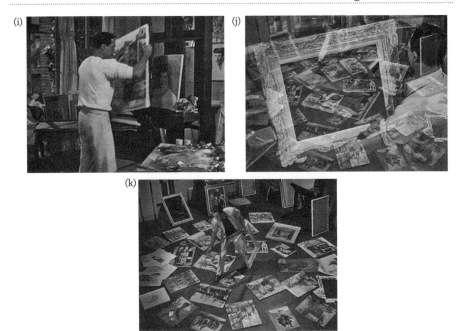

FIGURE 10.3 Continued

An American in Paris. Both songs serve as leitmotifs associated with two crucial stages in Gerry's developing emotional relationships, and they also follow his progress over time as he prepares for the exposition. The first is the euphoria song and dance "Tra-la-la," and the second is the courtship song "Our Love Is Here to Stay." Cheerful, up-tempo "Tra-la-la" travels with a rhythmic succession of images that show the painter working happily around the city as he prepares for the exhibition: we see him working in the Café Huguette, painting one of the children from the earlier "I Got Rhythm" sequence (Fig. 10.3a, dissolving), and painting at the Place de l'Opéra (Fig. 10.3b) and at the *quai* opposite the Cathedral of Notre Dame.

Salinger's orchestrations, which provide a musical commentary on the action, are precisely geared to the constant fluctuation of mood and dramatic import of the images, as well as their composition and color. At one point, for example, Minnelli's camera glides to a close-up of the painter's palette on which we see several shades of yellow; the painter adds a dab of white pigment and begins to mix rhythmically as the image slowly dissolves and the bright, high-key colors are transformed into softer shades of pale pink and mauve (Figs. 10.3c and d). Paralleling the color change and in tempo with the dissolve, the music also changes as "Tra-la-la" moves seamlessly into a softer, more lyrical arrangement of "Our Love Is Here to Stay" (Fig. 10.3e). The change in both music and color forecasts the appearance of Caron. The camera pulls back, and we see Gerry painting Lise as she poses near Notre Dame (Fig. 10.3f). The camera pauses briefly to capture this image, and then we see Caron drop the rose she holds as a prop. The artist leaves his easel to pick it up for her (Fig. 10.3g), and the camera glides toward them as they embrace. The song swells and then softens as this image dissolves into another (Fig. 10.3h). We now see the painting of Lise propped up on an easel in Gerry's studio. A new theme from the blues section *An American in Paris* accompanies Milo as she enters the studio and Gerry guiltily covers the portrait with another work (Fig. 10.3i). "Tra-la-la" accompanies the concluding image of the series. Kelly has finished his work and is now ready for his exhibition. In a visual finale, we see him in his studio, the camera taking a position directly above him. As he picks his way through the paintings, which form a kaleidoscopic pattern of brilliant colors around him on the floor, he chooses which ones to include in his exhibition and which ones to discard (Figs. 10.3j and k).

Ingenious, often comic and ironic combinations of image and sound are devices used often by Mamoulian, Lubitsch, and Clair and carried forward by Minnelli, Kelly, and Donen to drive the plot forward. In *Love Me Tonight*, an excruciatingly slow, funereal arrangement of the peppy turn-of-the-century song "A Hot Time in the Old Town Tonight" accompanies images of the bored inhabitants of Princess Jeannette's castle as they drag themselves through the day and we are made to understand immediately, without a word's being spoken by anyone, why she wants to escape from her boring life. In Clair's *Le million*, two obese and aging opera singers sing a love duet. Hidden in the scenery behind them are two quarreling young lovers, inadvertently trapped onstage when the curtain rises. The young lovers' gestures comedically contrast with the older couple's love song, but gradually the song's sentiments begin to work on them until at the end of the song they are reconciled in each other's arms. In another section Clair plays the sounds of a rambunctious rugby match over the chase and capture of an overcoat containing a winning lottery ticket as it is thrown from one end of the room to the other.

A related and more intricate device is used in the extended musical montage sequence that introduces and characterizes three of the film's main characters, Don, Cosmo, and Lina, in *Singin' in the Rain*. The montage also makes use of a device similar to the opening of *An American in Paris*, where the contrast between word, image, and music is used to make a cinematic joke. The actor Don Lockwood's inflated, pretentious—and patently false—voice-over account of his early career is juxtaposed with images and accompanied by music that reveal the truth about his humble origins. As Don (Gene Kelly) assures the audience that he received the finest of dramatic training, we see Don and Cosmo (Donald O'Connor) as children sneaking into a dilapidated theater to see a horror movie. While Don tells us that they studied in the greatest of musical conservatories, we see Cosmo playing honky-tonk piano in a smoke-filled pool hall. And when Don informs us that the two played in the most elegant of theaters and that "audiences everywhere adored us," we see the two shamelessly overplaying a corny vaudeville routine ("Fit as a Fiddle") superimposed over images of a succession of derelict small-town railroad stations ("Oatmeal, Nebraska," reads one sign). Finally we see the two bowing to boos and catcalls. The sequence concludes with an ever-accelerating series of images in which we hear Don proclaim his early triumphs in Hollywood at the same time that we see him working as a lowly stuntman, ignored by his fellow actors.

Another ironic juxtaposition of sound and image is used in the extended, brilliantly paced musical montage that takes us through *The Band Wagon*'s rehearsal period accompanied by the Arthur Schwartz and Howard Dietz song "That's Entertainment." This exuberant paean to the joys of show business is heard against images of harassed actors, quarreling writers, a failed audition, and special effects that don't work.

One of Minnelli's most hilarious musical montages uses a reprise of the Lerner and Loewe song "It's a Bore" in a musical adaptation of Colette's novella *Gigi*, about a young courtesan being trained for her future career in fin-de-siècle Paris. The song is initially sung as a musical conversation between the young millionaire bachelor Gaston (Louis Jourdan) and his uncle Honoré Lachaille (Maurice Chevalier), an old roué, to show Gaston's ennui and contrast it with his uncle's joie de vivre. As the lyrics tell us, everything in life is a "bore" to Gaston and a joy to his uncle. Later in the film, after being cuckolded by his mistress, Liane (Eva Gabor), Gaston, urged on by his uncle, attempts to save face and publicly demonstrate his happy new status as an unattached man-about-town. The montage presents a succession of parties and fêtes, each more elaborate and colorful than the last. In each scene the lively arrangement of the song and giddy, hyperactive crowds—orchestrated by Minnelli's sweeping boom camera—are pointedly contrasted with the bored and uncomfortable Gaston, to whom the camera sooner or later directs our attention. At the final party, it finds him peacefully asleep in the midst of the festivities.

THE FINALE

In Western music, a finale is the last movement or passage of a musical composition.[24] Often it is signaled by a heightening of musical activity: the finale of a nineteenth-century symphony is often characterized by intensified activity building to a climax in the last bars of the composition. Similarly, the finale of an opera or musical comedy may bring the whole cast onstage, and it may intensify the dialogue, song, and dance, raising the overall emotional temperature of the piece as it climaxes just before the curtain falls. Finales were incorporated into the very earliest of film musicals.

In the Busby Berkeley backstage musicals, the director provided a finale by means of a series of production numbers, ever grander in scale and more elaborate in visual effects and musical activity. But while a finale of this sort answered to some extent the formal demands of the musical film as a whole, it provided a satisfactory resolution to the drama itself only in the grossest sense. To be sure, the plot of most Berkeley backstage musicals led up to the staging of a successful show constituted by the production numbers. But the finale's connection with the film ended there. The numbers were essentially interchangeable from movie to movie; whatever happened onstage in the production number bore little resemblance to what had happened in earlier rehearsal sequences, and even less emotional relationship to the drama as enacted by the film's main characters. (Sometimes the protagonists themselves did not even perform.)

Interestingly, the formal relationship of the production number to the rest of the film was also tenuous. Berkeley films tend to have a lopsided feel. All the visual and musical excitement takes place at one end; the wait to get to the production numbers' effects is too long. Once there, Berkley's unrelieved piling up of effects tends to result in a kind of sensory overload, with the audience almost bludgeoned into a stupor, whereas earlier in the film they had been lulled into one.

The finales of the Astaire-Rogers films in the 1930s were extended song-and-dance sequences that were choreographically, musically, and dramatically satisfying in that they brought the courtship to a close with a celebratory dance for the two lovers, now definitively on their way to a happy life together. In *The Gay Divorcee* it is the extended dance sequence "The Continental"; in *Top Hat* it is "The Piccolino"; in *Shall We Dance* it is a show arranged to prove to Ginger Rogers that tap and ballet can coexist happily. In *Swing Time*, unusually, it is the emotionally excoriating "Never Gonna Dance" sequence, soon followed by an upbeat sung reprise of "A Fine Romance." The "Wedding Cake Walk" in *You'll Never Get Rich* is part of another show: this time it's a ruse used by the Astaire to "marry" his beloved, Rita Hayworth. In *Broadway Melody of 1940* Astaire and Eleanor Powell unite in the extraordinary "Begin the Beguine" number from the climactic show with a brief song-and-dance threesome to heal the friendship of Astaire and his buddy, George Murphy.

Kelly and Astaire continue to climax and conclude films with dance sequences. The most famous is the "American in Paris" ballet, which ends with the coming together of the couple whose love relationship has been explicated in the ballet; but there is also the "Girl Hunt ballet" (in which Charisse and Astaire dance together) followed by the reprise of "That's Entertainment" sung by the entire cast in *The Band Wagon*. *The Barkleys of Broadway* ends with Astaire and Rogers, as the quarreling show-business couple Josh and Dinah Barkley, reconciling and reuniting by dancing the "swing trot" before their new audience. Astaire and Hepburn symbolically unite in dance to Gershwin's "'S Wonderful" at the conclusion of *Funny Face*, ecstatically whirling through the churchyard where the fashion photographer Dick Avery (Astaire) had earlier photographed his reluctant Greenwich Village model (Audrey Hepburn) in a wedding dress and the two had quarreled.

Finales in Minnelli and Kelly-Donen musicals are the most difficult problems to solve because of the complexity of the task that Minnelli, Kelly, and Donen set themselves. The most successful are those in which the drama demands a festive, active, or grand setting that provides in its visual and musical elements the excitement that Hollywood film audiences demand of this moment. In *On the Town*, as in *Love Me Tonight*, this problem is solved with a chase sequence (a fight ups the ante too): the three sailors pursue their girls to Coney Island, and the taxi carrying them careens through the streets of New York out to the brilliant lights of Coney Island, to the music of Bernstein—here arranged and orchestrated by Saul Chaplin—and they finally end up back at the dockyard as the camera moves up and back and the opening theme of

"New York, New York" accompanies a new set of sailors on shore leave for their one day in New York City. *It's Always Fair Weather* has a similar ending: a fight sequence to an up-tempo arrangement of a song of friendship sung earlier in the film. Donen's *Seven Brides for Seven Brothers*, which is studded with musical chase and fight sequences (the abduction, the building and destruction of the barn), concludes with one of the most comic and at the same time exhilarating of musical finales as each brother tries to return his reluctant beloved to her family.

Models for dance-without-dancing finales again begin with Mamoulian's *Love Me Tonight* and Clair's *Le million*—and again, they employ some of the techniques later used in the establishing sequences of *Meet Me in St. Louis* and *On the Town*. In the ingenious "The Son of a Gun Is Nothing but a Tailor" in Mamoulian's *Love Me Tonight*, a traveling song resolves the plot and travels throughout the castle to the train in which the disgraced Chevalier is speeding back to Paris. Rhymed dialogue begins in whispers and gradually builds to a climax in which the characters burst into song. As Princess Jeanette (Jeanette MacDonald) follows the train on horseback, music and action speed up, the camera alternatingly frames the lover on horseback and the beloved on the train, and the film ends with a tremendous visual and musical punctuation point as MacDonald dismounts and places herself before the speeding train. In one of the most extraordinary shots in the film, the camera, placed below her, magnifies her height and thrillingly frames her as she stands fearlessly straddling the rails while we hear the film's love song played triumphantly.

THE DANCE-WITHOUT-DANCING FINALE: *GIGI*

However, it is the dance-without-dancing devices of the establishing-sequence musical montage that make up some of the most beautiful and dancelike of finales. In my final example, none of the performers are dancers, but Minnelli seems to have absorbed lessons he has learned from Mamoulian and from working with such dancer-choreographers as Balanchine, Astaire, and Kelly about the eloquence of the human body in motion and his own skills in the orchestration of camera movement, editing, color, and light. *Gigi*'s composers were Alan Jay Lerner and Frederick Loewe, but key musical roles were played by *Gigi*'s musical director André Previn and orchestrator Conrad Salinger, whose name, like Minnelli's, appears alone and on center screen in the credit sequence at the beginning of the movie. *Gigi*'s actors were not known for either singing or dancing, with two exceptions: Leslie Caron (who doesn't dance in this film) and the singer Maurice Chevalier, the star of *Love Me Tonight*—Minnelli's favorite musical. Chevalier was coming to the end of his career. Minnelli, Lerner, and Loewe were all aware of his contribution to the earliest through-composed musicals, and in *Gigi* Minnelli provided him with a vehicle that could match Mamoulian's achievements.

Like the establishing sequences of *Love Me Tonight, Meet Me in St. Louis*, and *On the Town, Gigi*'s finale is a song or songs and dance without dancers, but like the *American in Paris* ballet or Astaire's "Limehouse Blues" and "This Heart of Mine" from *Ziegfeld Follies*, the denouement of the plot is given to us in music and moving images.

In a now well-established tradition extending back to *Love Me Tonight*, the director accomplishes this by relying almost entirely on integrated music and moving image; dialogue plays an important but clearly secondary role. Drawing on and expanding techniques developed over more than a decade of experimentation and practice, Minnelli gives us in *Gigi* perhaps the most ingenious and impressive finale of the series.

Gaston's sung-chanted soliloquy, culminating with the song "Gigi," begins the final sequence. The soliloquy and song form a brilliant musical means through which Gaston comes to realize that Gigi is no longer a child, and that he does indeed love her. Lerner and Loewe had used such a device for a similar purpose in *My Fair Lady*, in the "I've Grown Accustomed to Her Face" sequence, to resolve Henry Higgins's agitation, and both sequences follow in the steps of the groundbreaking "My Boy Bill" in Rodgers and Hammerstein's *Carousel*. Like "It's a Bore" and "The Parisians," this is a traveling song—one of the most wide-ranging and beautiful in the Freed unit series. But there is a twist to it that recalls only one other traveling song among its predecessors. Like "Meet Me in St. Louis," it is circular: it ends where it begins. Here, however, the physical journey that Gaston takes through Paris as he sings becomes a metaphor for the mental journey charted by the song's lyrics. They outline the singer's debate with himself. Each of the musical sections finds him in a different location, starting at the stairs of Gigi's home as he defensively inveighs against her, continuing in the Luxembourg Gardens and on the Pont Alexandre as he begins to admit to his feelings for her, and climaxing in the small park in front of which he encountered her at the beginning of the film. There Gaston begins the song proper. Its lyrics, wedded to an expansive and romantic melody that contrasts with the agitated, staccato phrasing of the musical soliloquy that precedes it, express Gaston's wonder at the teenager's transformation. As he shifts from the soliloquy into the song, swans, symbolic of transformation (as in Hans Christian Andersen's "The Ugly Duckling") glide on the little lake before which he paces. One of them seems proudly to stretch out its neck to accent the harp glissando that builds to Gaston's beginning words ("Gigi, am I a fool without a mind / or have I merely been too blind"). The song's chorus travels with him as he retraces his steps. With its final chords, he has returned to the place where he started, ready to draw up the contracts with Madame Alvarez to make the liaison with Gigi official.

A brief dialogue sequence follows, backed by the song in which Gigi, appalled at the idea of leading the life of a courtesan, refuses Gaston. Gaston, confused and angry, goes for advice to Honoré, who comments musically on the situation with the song "I'm Glad I'm Not Young Anymore," a song that not only provides comic relief from the darker emotional scene that preceded it, but gives Chevalier a climactic song of his own. Lerner's lyrics, like those of "I Remember It Well" earlier in the movie, have a double meaning, referring simultaneously to Chevalier's real life and to the situation of the character he plays in the film. As in "I Remember It Well," the director surrounds Chevalier with an environment that visually reflects his song's sentiments. Thus, the elegiac sunset that parallels the pensive, bittersweet mood of the earlier song is replaced here by a fresh decor to frame this song's sprightly melody and genial, philosophical lyric.

Pressured by circumstance and by her feelings for Gaston, Gigi reconsiders and accepts Gaston's proposition. The scene is now set for Gigi's first evening as a courtesan, and the film, increasing its tempo and visual activity, moves swiftly to its conclusion. As in previous Minnelli films, *Gigi*'s finale is organized around a party. Gigi makes her debut at Maxim's amid one of Minnelli's most brilliantly arranged and festive crowd sequences. Two musical preparation sequences precede it. The song "The Night They Invented Champagne," played by orchestra alone, accompanies Gaston happily dressing for the evening ahead. In contrast, Gigi, alone in her little room, nervously prepares for her first night as Gaston's mistress. Her song "Say a Prayer for Me Tonight," framed, like Esther's in *Meet Me in St. Louis*, first by the mirror into which she peers anxiously and then by the window through which moonlight pours in to illuminate her face, alerts us to her fears about the evening ahead. The second verse, played by orchestra alone, carries us through time, accompanying Gigi as she emerges from her room dressed (symbolically in white) for the evening ahead. Played by orchestra alone, the song continues as she embraces her aunts and, paralleled by the floating camera, leaves the apartment for Maxim's on Gaston's arm.

At the restaurant, Gigi is introduced for the first time to the glittering, decadent world in which, up until this moment in the film, we have only seen Gaston. The girl's reaction to this society, and their astonished response to her, is ingeniously conveyed to us with one of Minnelli's (and Lerner and Loewe's) cleverest musical-visual devices: director, composer, and writer visually and musically reminisce about the film's first Maxim's sequence, in which we were introduced to Gaston and his first mistress. In that earlier sequence, the cynical attitude of the restaurant's patrons toward Gaston and his latest lover was conveyed in rhythmically chanted speech-song. As they entered the restaurant, moving from left to right across the Cinemascope screen, the backdrop of colorful, gesticulating patrons behind them suddenly froze in position, as if mesmerized, while they mouthed a none-too-complimentary lyric assessment of the couple.

Now, in the final Maxim's sequence, the prior image is repeated exactly when Gaston and Gigi enter. This time, however, the patrons simply freeze in position and the music stops suddenly for several beats as Gaston and Gigi (looking wonderingly around her) move in silence past the frieze of Minnelli's *tableaux vivants*. There is no need for a lyric; we already know, because of our memory of the earlier scene, what they are thinking. The silence, occurring so unexpectedly in the midst of the joyful music and the active, noisy crowd, serves to focus our attention on the film's central subject, to convey the crowd's astonished reaction to Gigi, and to pinpoint dramatically the contrast between the girl and her surroundings.

This almost dreamlike dramatic pantomime is repeated when Gigi and Gaston enter the main dining room of Maxim's. This time the music continues to play as the patrons rise from their seats and freeze again as she and Gaston thread their way through the room to their table. The camera remains at the room's entrance to capture the scope of the space; at the moment Gigi is seated, the movement of her white dress against the colorful crowd acts as a visual downbeat and sets the diners in motion as the action resumes. Accompanied by the song "She's Not Thinking of Me," ostensibly played by the restaurant's orchestra, with which Gaston, in the first Maxim's sequence, had inveighed against Liane, Gigi, like a dutiful student at her final exam, repeats the lessons taught to her by Aunt Alicia. As she gracefully pours his coffee, selects his cigars, and tries to make sophisticated conversation about the other diners, Gaston grows increasingly uncomfortable. At the climax of the scene he abruptly, without warning, pulls the bewildered girl from the restaurant and drags her, protesting, back home to her grandmother.

Now Gaston begins another musical-visual journey that, again, reminisces about an earlier sequence—paralleling the journey made in his earlier soliloquy. Again, it begins and ends in Gigi's grandmother's apartment, and again, it serves as a metaphor for a mental journey made by the character. This time, however, the trip is made at night, and as in the repeated Maxim's sequence, we need no lyric to tell us of the debate taking place in Gaston's mind as he retraces his steps through the Paris streets accompanied, as in the earlier sequence, first by the agitated orchestral music of the soliloquy and then, at the height of the journey, by the film's signature song, "Gigi." The song here accompanies one of the most beautiful images ever created by Minnelli and the cameraman Joseph Ruttenberg, an image designed to convey Gaston's moment of decision in a sequence of shots that, in concept and movement of the camera, relates closely to the climactic, decision-making scene in *Meet Me in St. Louis*. Gaston, his top-hatted head bowed, is silhouetted in full figure against the lit-up fountains of the Paris Observatory as they throw up shafts of white water against the blue-black sky. A hansom cab glides into the frame, pulling up immediately behind him. The horses, in silhouette (and paralleling their sculptural counterparts on the fountain), rear back slightly, and the driver pauses expectantly, but Gaston, completely involved in his thoughts, is oblivious to their presence. The cab moves out of the frame as, riding on the music, the camera, starting in long shot, begins to glide slowly toward the lights of the fountain—and toward Gaston, who, his head still bowed in concentration, paces in front of the fountain. As the song reaches its climax, Gaston suddenly straightens up and turns. The camera, confronting him, has now moved in close enough so we can see that his once hard and angry face, half illuminated by the light of the fountain, has softened.

As the song continues, a cut transfers us to a square near Gigi's home. For the next stage of the musical journey we are positioned at the top of the stairs leading to Gigi's apartment. We now view Gaston from above, his figure outlined in the light reflected from the wet cobblestones of the courtyard. His face, turned up toward us, is completely relaxed and smiling. With the song's final phrases, the camera floats with him up the stairs. His ringing of the doorbell punctuates its final chord. When Madame Alvarez opens the door, a cut transfers us to the warmly lit interior. Gigi, still dressed in her white satin gown, nervously flattens herself against the wall to the right side of the frame, while on the left Gaston confronts her grandmother. Paralleling this image come the last, and only, spoken words in the film's final minutes: Gaston gravely asks for "the honor of" Gigi's hand in marriage. The camera cuts to Gigi, whose expression changes from one of trepidation to relief and confidence. Tracked by the camera, she walks to Gaston and takes his arm as the music for the opening song of the film ("Thank Heaven for Little Girls") softly begins. The camera now cuts to Madame Alvarez. Her response to Gaston's request, spoken under her breath ("Thank Heaven!"), becomes the opening phrase of the song with which Chevalier completes the film—as he began it. A cut moves us immediately to the Bois de Boulogne in full daylight, where we reminisce about the film's opening images. As if to illustrate Uncle Honoré's words in the establishing sequence song, Gaston and Gigi, now the "married kind," stroll among the crowds that surround Chevalier, who, with a smile and a shrug to the audience, closes the movie.

Dance always follows music and the music changed in the 1950's . . . and wiped out the musical as we used to know it—as we used to do it. . . . The change was so distinct you could even see it in the popular dance. . . . The old style musicals died because the children of the 60's took over the box office, just as they took over the recording industry.
—GENE KELLY, interview by Howard Reich,
Chicago Tribune, August 7, 1983

11

LEGACY

THE SECOND HALF of the century saw the beginning of the demise of the dance-film musical as a popular form. As Kelly pointed out, a new generation with new musical interests began to take over, and the popular songs and dances that had once fed film-dance choreographers such as Astaire and Kelly changed radically. A new musical style, rock and roll, was in the ascendant. Its roots lay not in the urban jazz tradition and American musical theater, but more directly in the rhythm and blues and gospel music of the rural south. A new sound came along with it—a turn away from the rich harmonic language, color, and rhythmic intricacy that had emerged in big-band music and a return to smaller ensembles with the entirely different color and texture of a drum set and one or two guitars—increasingly electrified as the decades progressed. No choreographers arose from the younger generation to compete with or work alongside the groups that developed the genre—no dance equivalent of Elvis Presley or his colleagues. Some of the dance tradition held on with the great Motown groups such as the Temptations and Supremes, whose moves were choreographed—done with great style but relatively simple and straightforward compared to the great rhythm tappers of the Jazz Age. Their style too was a form of musical visualization, meant to parallel or punctuate their music rather than interacting with it.

In any case, the great songwriters, composers, and orchestrators who had originally inspired Astaire and Kelly were no longer writing hits. They and the choreographers who had been inspired by them were increasingly seen as old-fashioned.

Jazz music moved from the dance floor toward a listen-to-the-performer format. Its younger artists no longer wrote for dance, but for themselves, in new styles, such as bebop, that appealed increasingly to the cognoscenti of the beat generation. Nightclubs and coffeehouses increasingly took on the aura of the concert hall, in the sense that the newer jazz instrumentalists considered themselves artists. Their primary job was not to entertain and provide accompaniment to movement. Listening was serious business, and driving, pulsing dance rhythms were consciously abandoned for freer improvisatory forms that could change tempo and mood unexpectedly and in which audiences were meant to savor the color and texture by paying serious attention rather than moving to the music.

The demise of the dance-film musical was also intimately connected with the gradual collapse of the Hollywood studio system in the late 1950s and 1960s. As a studio, MGM had sponsored the development of, trained, maintained, and placed under the director's command a myriad of highly specialized technicians and the equipment necessary for the realization of this most complex art form. The studio had also created a protected environment in which these artists and craftsmen could function. The dancers and dance-film musical makers Astaire, Kelly, Donen, and Minnelli had been sheltered by the producer Arthur Freed from wasting their emotional and physical energies on financial matters.

In the new marketplace of the 1960s and '70s, however, the task of organizing the necessary resources and financing for each film fell to its directors, who were forced to become producers as well as creative artists. Minnelli and his colleagues, trained and nurtured within the studio walls, had never developed the skills necessary for survival when, as Minnelli says, "the studio contract system ended and we all had to fend for ourselves. . . . I was the world's oldest babe in the woods; I knew nothing about, and had no stomach for, the necessary infighting."[1]

After *Gigi* in 1958, Minnelli, although active as a director of film drama and comedy, made only two more musicals. These, however, focused on singers rather than dancers—*Bells Are Ringing* (1959) and *On a Clear Day You Can See Forever* (1969). From the 1960s on, American dancers, who had found work with relative ease in the first part of the century, had to look elsewhere, and the studio system that had housed, fed, and given a secure living wage to the creative artists and technicians necessary to the creation of film dance gradually fell apart. Films increasingly had to depend on independent producers to put together an appealing package. Many of them found employment in the new small-screen medium that gradually supplanted the movies in popularity.

Beginning in the 1950s, television gradually began to make inroads on the audiences that had once spent their leisure hours at the movies. Astaire, a pioneer of film dance and still an extraordinary dancer, continued on to the new medium of television, making a remarkable series of dance specials in 1959, 1960, and 1968 that he himself produced and to which he applied his experience in working with dance on film. He also helped pioneer other technical innovations.[2] Balanchine, who had stopped working in the musical theater and films to devote himself to the New York City Ballet, worked in the 1970s to document some of his stage ballet repertory in PBS's *Dance in America* series. In the movie ballets he had created, he had taken advantage of the film medium to choreograph the camera as well as the dance. On television, drawing on lessons he had learned from Greg Toland and Fred Astaire, he reconceived his choreography for the small screen and carefully supervised the filming of all his programs, working with the director Merrill Brockway.

Following the dissolution of the Kelly-Donen team in 1955, Kelly went on to direct six films, only one of which was a musical, *Hello, Dolly!* (1969). The star, Barbra Streisand, was a singer, but Kelly made sure she was surrounded by dancers. The choreographer listed in the credits was not Kelly but Michael Kidd, who had choreographed *Seven Brides for Seven Brothers* and *The Band Wagon* and had appeared as one of the three buddies in *It's Always Fair Weather*. One of Kelly's last appearances as a performer in a musical was in Jacques Demy's *Les demoiselles de Rochefort* (1968), a film by one of the young generation of French filmmakers whose works his own had influenced. Later in the century he would make a final appearance in *Xanadu* (1980), in which the techniques of filming dance he had developed over the years were largely ignored. He was, at his insistence, able to control the direction of one pas de deux with Olivia Newton-John; his choreographed camera and editing and dancer-centered framing made it one of the film's highlights.

Stanley Donen continued to direct movies, but starting in the 1960s and '70s he concentrated mainly on comedy and drama films, briefly returning to the musical genre in 1974 with *The Little Prince* (based on the book by Antoine de Saint-Exupéry) and affectionately satirizing Busby Berkeley (though not his own and Kelly's work) in *Movie Movie* (1978).

It was Donen who would direct the movie that gave the first starring role to the choreographer who would follow in Astaire's and Kelly's footsteps to become the next major force in film dance: Bob Fosse (1927–1987). Fosse began his career at MGM, appearing as a dancer in the chorus of *Kiss Me, Kate* (1953), but it was Donen's film *Give a Girl a Break* (1953) that would introduce Fosse to the world as a dancer, actor, and choreographer. His early dance persona and choreography drew heavily on Gene Kelly. (His courtship street dance with Debbie Reynolds in *Give a Girl a Break* is a Kelly clone.) He was also powerfully influenced by Astaire and Jack Cole. However, Fosse quickly evolved a distinctive new choreographic voice, which he would develop both on Broadway and in the movies. Donen, with George Abbott, also directed the film versions of the Broadway shows *Pajama Game* (1954) and *Damn Yankees* (1955), which were choreographed by Fosse. His film dances for *Pajama Game* (1957) and *Damn Yankees* (1958) reveal his own descent from the lineage of Astaire's no-limitations approach. Fosse's offbeat, witty, sexy style drew on Afro-Caribbean isolations of shoulders, hips, and torso. *Sweet Charity* (1969) demonstrates the mature Fosse, both as choreographer and film director. However, the most radical step in a new kind of choreography for dance and the camera came in Fosse's award-winning film *Cabaret* (1972), which used dance and music to examine the decadent political and artistic atmosphere of Berlin between the wars. In *Cabaret*, Fosse expanded but also drastically altered the editing techniques of his predecessors. He turns completely away from the full-body framing espoused by Astaire, jump-cutting from close shots of isolated portions of dancer's bodies for short periods and giving the editing a new, more vigorous pace. Both Balanchine and Kelly, while changing the angle of the camera and incorporating editing, had in the end put the focus on the dancer and the dance itself—cutting to close-ups and medium shots to make a dramatic point, but without interrupting the flow and shape of the dance itself. Kelly, Donen, and Minnelli, along with Astaire, had integrated their editing with the music and the flow of the dance: the choreography of the camera and editing was meant to be invisible, maintaining the centrality of the dancer and the full moving body. Fosse's fast-paced editing disrupted the flow of the dancer's body, returning in a different way to the principles that stood behind Berkeley's early filming of dance to create an exciting but essentially abstract series of images. Fosse's method would gradually become an accepted norm of dance filming. His new ways of filming dance—those jump-cuts to shots of isolated body parts combined with the influence of the street-dance genre developed largely by Kelly and Donen—began a new, powerful, and long life on television in music videos for the MTV generation.

Of all the dance video choreographers of the later twentieth century and the first part of the twenty-first, it was Michael Jackson and his choreographers and directors who built on the choreography, camera movement, and editing innovations of Astaire, Kelly, Donen, and Minnelli, adding to it new tools from the computer age. In Jackson's early videos, *Thriller* and *Beat It*, the choreographer Michael Peters, an admirer of Jerome Robbins, draws directly on Peters's own experience as a dancer in *West Side Story*, which is itself descended from Kelly's street dances. The gang dances in *Bad* (directed by Martin Scorsese and choreographed by Gregg Burge and Jeffrey Daniels) are not-too-distant relatives of the *West Side Story* dances—in particular "Cool," danced in an underground garage. In *Bad*, the dancers dance under the streets, in the New York subways.

Reflecting an urban culture where children carry Uzis and kill over designer clothing, Michael Jackson's street dances became progressively more surreal and frightening. Even love dances are scary. In *Thriller* (1983) a chorus of the dancing dead, led by a zombielike Jackson and captured by the moving camera of the director John Landis, transform an after-a-movie stroll into an unforgettable experience for Jackson's terrified date. In *The Way You Make Me Feel* (1987), choreographed by Vincent Paterson, Jackson dances through the streets singing of the same euphoric feelings as Kelly in *Singin' in the Rain*, but the streets through which he dances are rundown and graffiti-littered, as are the eerie, surrealistic cityscapes of his *Billie Jean* (1982). Urban poverty is brought up close and personal. And Kelly's childlike games and innocent enthusiasm are transformed into dancing with a real edge. Jackson aggressively taunts his would-be lover, and his openly erotic gestures have an undertone of anger. The finale of *The Way You Make Me Feel* resonates with the waterlogged ending of "Singin' in the Rain." This time a fire hydrant explodes in the heat of the summer: the arc of glimmering water is as beautiful as the backlit rain in Kelly's street dance. And the Place de la Concorde sequence in the ballet of *An American in Paris* is a direct ancestor of the moment when the girl finally succumbs to Jackson's wooing and we see them embrace in silhouette against a tapestry of vapor clouds. But the image is also a reminder, albeit unconscious, of those summer days when the poor spill into the streets to get relief from the heat and have to vandalize city property to do so. (Think of Spike Lee's *Do the Right Thing* [1989], which similarly evokes a hot summer night and in which kids open the city fire hydrants to cool off in the running water.)

In the street-dance section of Jackson's *Black or White* (1994), race issues are directly addressed—as they are in *West Side Story*—but this time on a global scale. Jackson dances with a classical Indian dancer on a busy highway and moves to various locations around the globe, Vincent Paterson's choreography reflecting a variety of folk forms. Both Kelly and Astaire are referenced in this video: in one street scene, Jackson combines an elegant hands-in-his-pocket nonchalance with intricate footwork that has its roots in Astaire's moves, although they are used along with crotch-grabbing gestures that Astaire wouldn't have considered.

Kelly's final window-smashing gesture in the "Alter Ego" sequence and Astaire's drunk dance in *The Sky's the Limit* (1943) are also in the background of this dance—but without the clear dramatic motivation. Jackson angrily vandalizes a car with hateful graffiti drawn in the dust on the window, resulting in an extended and violent glass-shattering sequence that concludes with the heaving of a barrel through a plate-glass window that duplicates the climactic gesture of the "Alter Ego" dance. He follows this with a very dark take on Kelly's ecstatic splashing at the end of the *Singin' in the Rain* street dance.

It is no secret that Jackson first and foremost idolized Astaire but also adored Kelly: he and his sister Janet grew up on the street-dance musicals of the first half of the century. Janet Jackson pays direct homage to these roots and to other of her African American dance predecessors in her video *Alright* (1989). And as in her brother's work, digital images are used to enhance the scope and drama of the dance. In *Alright*, the Nicholas Brothers, Cyd Charisse, and Cab Calloway appear with Janet Jackson and Heavy D as they dance through the busy city streets, captured by a choreographed and extremely mobile camera that sweeps over the streets on a level with the dancer and, at times, hovers in the air above them.

The popularity of the street dance has far outlasted Kelly and Astaire, and we can expect that there will be dancing in the streets far into the twenty-first century. The dance genre that grew up in the movies has now found a home on DVD and other digital devices. It seems likely to continue so long as we have streets to walk on and to dance through.

POSTMODERN DANCE

A chief aim of this book has been to set the film dances of Astaire, Kelly, and Balanchine firmly within the history of dance and to explore some of the mutually beneficial relationships of these men to the world of dance as a whole. At the outset, I argued for a new understanding of Astaire's outlaw style, one that drew on the many and disparate forms to be seen in the New York of the Jazz Age (much as with

Gershwin) and that fused with the new medium of sound cinema to create a new art form. Balanchine and Kelly, each in his own way, followed in Astaire's footsteps in creating film dance. I also argue that the artificial, socially constructed separation of art dance and popular dance has been the key culprit in preventing our recognition of these men's contributions. Nowhere has this been more evident than in fine-art dance. Earlier I talked about the profound influence of Astaire on Balanchine and modern ballet. Robbins too was powerfully influenced by Astaire and by Kelly and Donen (his film techniques for *West Side Story* in particular).

In postmodern dance, the influence of Astaire and Kelly is just as powerful and perhaps even more basic. Postmodern dancers of the 1960s grew up on the screen dances of Astaire and Kelly, and long before they were introduced to pioneer American modern dancers running, skipping, leaping, and processing across college lawns, they were going to the movies like everyone else: Twyla Tharp's father owned a drive-in theater in California. Tharp and others turned away from the histrionics and presentational ethos of modern dance to explore anew—as had Astaire and Kelly—everyday movement and other movement sources, such as sports and popular dances. They looked for new sites for dance and found them, like Astaire and Kelly, everywhere—indoors and outdoors, from the sidewalks, stoops, and street corners of New York to every kind of interior space in lofts and stores, gymnasiums and churches and museums, parks and playgrounds and swimming pools, fire escapes and building ledges. They turned what they found there—everyday objects—into materials to dance with and on. Astaire and Kelly had danced on and with chairs and tables and saw every kind of landscape—urban and rural, indoor and outdoor—as a place to dance, from domestic interiors to public spaces. They saw just about everything that came to hand, however mundane, as an inspiration or object to dance with and on. In the same way, David Gordon choreographed a dance for himself, his wife (Valda Setterfield), and two chairs, and Trisha Brown and other postmodern dancers explored the sidewalks, stoops, buildings, and rooftops of New York City.

Postmodern dancers also tried to abandon theatricality both in movement and in costumes and settings, dancing in casual clothes and shoes: sneakers and jeans, leg warmers over tights. The uniform slicked-back hair and dramatic makeup of both ballet and modern dance were abandoned. Most of all, dancers looked like people. They abandoned stage manners: the formal entrances and exits, the frozen expressions and heavily made-up eyes, and the shoulders-back, here-I-am positioning of both ballet and modern dance. Most of all, as Astaire and Kelly had done when walking and skipping down the street, they lessened the look of tension and visible effort in the body—though the look of ease was deceptive. The dances looked casual, almost improvised. And the impression was that this was something anyone could do. (They encouraged or brought bystanders into the dance, sometimes with an implied "let's all do it together" mentality.) But the performance still required the investment of time, thought, and great physical and mental effort for it to be worth looking at.

Kelly and Astaire too seemed to pull ordinary bystanders into their dances: the group of children who trail alongside him in *An American in Paris*'s "I Got Rhythm" sequence and the café owner and his overweight wife in the "By Strauss" sequence. Astaire and Rogers dance-walk an elderly crowd of stolid suburbanites through their country-club grounds in "The Yam" in *Carefree*. "Anybody can do it," these dances seem to imply. Surely these dances are an element in the roots of the strong twentieth- and twenty-first-century tendency to incorporate ordinary, everyday moves into the dance in some way, as when David Gordon counterpoints the formal processional of ballet dancers' bodies in the nineteenth-century ballet *La bayadère* with the ordinary people walking past the camera to the same music—or, in a darker, more expressionistic vein, when Pina Bausch began to place "ordinary people" and "ordinary bodies" front and center in her Surrealist stagescapes.

Then, too, there is the development of the use of street sports and games in post-modern dance. To be sure, ballet itself is related in many ways to the martial art of its day, fencing. But this tradition was highlighted, revivified, and carried forward by Kelly. In one of his earliest films, *Take Me Out to the Ball Game*, developed with Donen and partially directed by Busby Berkeley, Kelly drew for inspiration on Al Schact, "the clown prince of baseball," who, with the coach Nick Altrock, entertained baseball crowds with comic imitations of players. In the song and dance "O'Brien to Ryan to Goldberg," baseball throws and slides are a font of inspiration. In the "Baby, You Knock Me Out" sequence in *It's Always Fair Weather*, set in Stillman's Gym, he blends Cyd Charisse's dance with training moves and exercises derived from boxing. And as we have seen, he was influenced by his own experience with gymnastics and compared his own low-to-the-ground style with soccer and other streets sports. In his Emmy Award–winning television program *Dancing, A Man's Game*, Kelly made all this clear by demonstrating with the prominent sports figures Sugar Ray Robinson, Mickey Mantle, and others. Is it really too much of a stretch to compare this with the postmodernist Steve Paxton, who was fascinated with Asian martial arts and drew from his experiences in developing contact improvisation, a key postmodern dance technique? Postmodernists also find inspiration in and draw directly on the Brazilian martial art of *capoeira*, which originated in Africa and spread via the African diaspora to Latin America.

Finally, a willingness to draw from and blend a wide variety of popular and high-art sources is also distinctly postmodern and in many ways has more to do with the pluralist stance taken by both Astaire and Kelly in the development of their own outlaw styles than with modern matriarchs such as Graham and Humphrey, who on the whole took a more purist approach, stressing the development on their own techniques that were purged of the outside "contamination" not only of ballet but of popular styles.

However, unlike Astaire and Kelly, the postmodern dancers of New York did not, for the most part, dance to the popular songs of their generation. Instead, they began to distance themselves from music altogether. John Cage, for example, who as the partner of Merce Cunningham had a tremendous influence on postmodern dance, was a key figure in the beginnings of the separation of music and dance: the validation of silence as a kind of music, as well as the use of random street noises and the fascination with electronic music of all kinds, was for them the proper accompaniment for the new dance. Their new methods eliminated any close working relationship between choreographer and composer. Choreographers now choreographed to silence.

The separation of high from popular art has also led to the almost complete absence of Astaire, Kelly, and Balanchine (along with Minnelli and Donen) in accounts of the avant-garde world of film dance. A nod may be given to Busby Berkeley and his use of surrealistic effects and abstract compositions. Douglas Rosenberg's recent book *Screendance* devotes some space to Charlie Chaplin and Buster Keaton but completely ignores Astaire and Kelly. But filmmakers such as Maya Deren (a friend of Kelly's) and Yvonne Rainer would have had to have grown up blind and deaf to be unaware of Astaire's and Kelly's work. Just as Astaire's outlaw style, with its use of jazz movement and popular music, was on the whole ignored by or invisible to early modern-dance makers (with the possible exception of Helen Tamiris), current dance-film critics treat Astaire, Balanchine, and Kelly (along with Donen and Minnelli) as a completely different species from the avant-garde filmmakers who are their subjects.

The world of modern ballet between 1960 and the present has also been strongly affected by the pioneering work of Astaire, Donen, and Kelly. Just as the young George Balanchine was inspired by Astaire, so too were the Russian émigrés of a later generation who defected from the Soviet Union. Both Rudolph Nureyev and Mikhail Baryshnikov have expressed their profound admiration of Astaire and Kelly. Baryshnikov, dancing with Gregory Hines in *White Nights*, draws on the old tradition of bringing together tap and ballet movement, and Nureyev, in appearances on *The Muppet Show*, both tap dancing and in a parody of *Swan Lake* with Miss Piggy, continue Balanchine's tradition of affectionately lampooning early ballet forms while learning from jazz forms. Baryshnikov's tributes on the American Film Institute's Lifetime Achievement Awards to Astaire and Kelly were fervent.[3] British choreographers from Ashton to Christopher Wheeldon and Matthew Bourne are equally admiring—and their mixing and blending of the popular and classical forms continues in the tradition of Astaire's and Kelly's no-limitations style.

INFLUENCE ON CINEMA AS A WHOLE

If postmodern screendance has ignored Astaire, Minnelli, Kelly, and Donen, the international world of moviemaking has embraced them: they have become old masters to a new generation of directors. Betty Comden and Adolph Green, for example, make it clear how carefully one of the Kelly-Donen musicals was studied by the young directors of the French *nouvelle vague*:

A few years ago we were in Paris . . . at a party, and were rendered breathless and awestruck by the news that François Truffaut was right across the room from us. Suddenly, a small, lithe figure came sliding across at us like a hockey player zooming over the ice. It was Truffaut himself, and he was breathless and awestruck at meeting the authors of *Chantons sous la Pluie*. In total disbelief we heard him say, through his interpreter, that he had seen the film many times, knew every frame of it, felt it was a classic, said that he and Alain Resnais, among others, went to see it regularly at a little theater called the Pagode where it was even at the moment in the middle of a several-month run.[4]

Minnelli was equally idolized by young French filmmakers. When Henri Langlois arranged for a group of French directors to meet him, Minnelli was astonished at how closely they had studied his works:

It was one of the greatest eye openers of my life. The young men approached film with such furious dedication that I felt like a dilettante. They could quote chapter, verse, and rhyme about my work . . . the average length of my scenes, the recurring motifs, the camera angles I used. . . . They gave me back copies of their magazine [*Cahiers du cinéma*] in which several major articles had been devoted to my work. There was no doubt about it. To them I was a star.[5]

This went not only for French filmmakers like those that gathered around the Cinémathèque Française in Paris. There were also English directors and the British Film Institute in London. The publications they produced took Hollywood film seriously at a time when most artists and intellectuals disdained the form. Publications like *Cahiers du cinéma* and *Films and Filming* conducted valuable interviews of Minnelli, Kelly, and Donen, and published monographs on these artists long before Americans paid them any serious heed.

The influence of dance musicals, then, has had its strongest impact on the world of feature-length films. The dance-without-dancing devices—the musical establishing sequence, musical montage, and musical finale—influenced not only young French directors but young British directors too, such as Richard Lester, who successfully synergized the musical montage and jump-cut editing of *On the Town*'s establishing sequence with the music of the Beatles in *Help!* (1965). The American filmmaker Larry Kasdan (consciously or unconsciously) used the technique of the establishing sequence and the traveling song to introduce and link the characters of *The Big Chill* (1983) in disparate locations and to explicate, visually and musically, their reason for coming together (a classmate's suicide). "I Heard It through the Grapevine" is the first of the Motown songs of their college years in the late 1960s that Kasdan uses to provide both a commentary on their actions in the present and to recall their youthful relationships. The Rolling Stones' "You Can't Always Get What You Want" accompanies their former classmate's coffin as it is carried out by the mourners and travels with them to the burial ground. This use of music has since become commonplace in feature-length movies and television.

Although he does not make film musicals, Stephen Spielberg, in his partnership with John Williams, connects closely to classic dance-film musicals. Williams was powerfully influenced by Conrad Salinger's orchestrations—his ability to amass many and varied orchestral colors, textures, and leitmotifs to enhance and comment on the action. Spielberg is one of the most astute users of the devices linking sound and moving image and has even expanded many of these techniques in thrilling ways. Spielberg's choreography of the camera and musical editing is without equal, and many of his films use dance-without-dancing techniques developed by directors from Mamoulian to Minnelli. The musical chase sequences of the Kelly-Donen films are ancestrally related to the extraordinary melding of sound and moving image in *E.T.*'s (1982) breathtaking bicycle sequence at the end of the film as well as in its opening moments—an establishing sequence in which the story is told in music and movement alone.

BOLLYWOOD

Williams's music is not connected in vital ways to contemporary popular music and is not meant to be danced to. But there is one place where the no-limitations attitude of Astaire and Kelly and their distinctive blending of dance and popular song and cinematic technique remain a vital part of film and culture: the Bollywood films of South Asia. The huge film industry based in Mumbai turns out more films every year than did Hollywood in its heyday and regularly produces films with extensive dance sequences that combine South Asian music and dance influences with the popular music and dance styles of the West. The songs and dances created by blending these disparate sources are sung and danced to by young people not only in Asia and Africa, where the diaspora of Indian populations has spread, but also in Europe and the United States, where they are increasingly popular with young Westerners as well and where second-generation directors such as Gurinder Chada offer audiences their own distinctive take on the blend of East and West, as in his *Bride and Prejudice* (2004). Whether drama or comedy, most Bollywood films contain dances, and their most popular stars—both male and female—must be skillful dancers as well as actors. Bollywood dance references to *Singin' in the Rain* and even a resetting of *Seven Brides for Seven Brothers* (*Satte pe Satta*, 1982) are now Bollywood classics. Dance numbers in movies such as *Kaho Naa . . . Pyaar Hai* (Say . . . You Love Me, 2000), starring Hrithik Roshan and Amisha Patel, show influences from the courtship dances of Astaire, the street and location dances of Kelly, the spectacles of Busby Berkeley, and the dances of MTV stars like Michael and Janet Jackson. These are blended with movements from classical, folk, and popular Indian dance forms as well as Western popular dance from swing and disco to break dancing. Indian directors also employ and are expanding the repertoire of color and lighting effects, camera movement, and musical editing developed in Hollywood to add to the drama and excitement of film dance.

THE DEMISE OF THE DANCER-DIRECTOR AND THE DANCER AS STAR

Along with the demise of the film musical came the demise of the dancer as star. Astaire and Kelly were the first dancers (let alone film dancers) to be known by a worldwide audience of almost every class. They were the first dancing heroes of the movies and the only dancers to participate in the filmmaking process in order to take advantage of the new medium at their disposal. To be sure, John Travolta, beginning with *Saturday Night Fever*, the big hit of 1977, seemed on his way to becoming an exception to this rule. Like Maurice Chevalier in *Love Me Tonight* and Kelly in *On the Town*, he is introduced with a rhythmical walking tour of his urban neighborhood. His director, John Badham, employs a new variation for dance with his moving camera. It glides along the sidewalks level with Travolta's feet, pulling us along in tempo just ahead of the young dancer. Travolta's walk and the music of the Bee Gees captures the distinctive temper of this young character and his time, just as Rodgers's music did for Chevalier in *Love Me Tonight* and Gershwin and so many others did for Astaire's walking dances. *Saturday Night Fever* examined the alienation and restlessness of a young Brooklyn man who tries to see beyond the narrow world of his low-level job and teenage buddies. Reflecting and promoting the disco dance craze that swept the country in the 1970s and '80s, it became one of the most popular films of the second half of the twentieth century. It also created a new star: Travolta was the first screen idol since Astaire and Kelly to be identified as a dancer. *Saturday Night Fever* was followed by sequels and a spate of disco-dancing films, as well as choreographer Patricia Birch's rock and roll dance musical *Grease* (1978), which starred Travolta and Olivia Newton-John as high-school sweethearts in a mythical 1950s California, drawing heavily on the dance-filming techniques developed in the movies of Astaire through Kelly and Minnelli.

Another dance star was Patrick Swayze. *Dirty Dancing* (1987), set at the beginning of the 1960s, used dance to trace the coming of age of an upper-middle-class young woman (Jennifer Grey). Her worldview is challenged and forever changed by her relationship with a working-class dancer, played by Swayze, who, with the choreographer Kenny Ortega (an acknowledged Kelly fan), recreated the social, rock, jazz, and Latin American dances of the 1950s and '60s and who, like Astaire and Kelly, melded the moving camera into his own style. The film's director, Emile Ardolino, who had also worked with Balanchine on the *Dance in America* series for television in the 1970s, moved away from Fosse's breaking-up-of-the-body cutting and drew on techniques developed by Astaire and Kelly. Adrian Lyne's *Flashdance* (1983), on the other hand, focused on the quick-cutting techniques of the later Fosse but also used the musical montage and traveling song to examined the difficult life of a working-class welder (Jennifer Beals) trying to make it as a ballet dancer. In a reprise of a theme that we have followed throughout this book, *Flashdance* has the young dancer winning an audition at a ballet conservatory by combining classical and a then new popular dance form, breakdancing. *Billy Elliot* and *Center Stage* (both 2000) also drew on such a theme by tracing the professional journeys of aspiring young ballet dancers who are nonetheless connected in some way to the world of ordinary social, folk, or popular dance.

An explosion of interest in classical dance in the 1970s and '80s resulted in a number of films focusing on the world of ballet. This was partially jump-started, as it had been in the early 1930s, by a new (and much smaller) wave of Russian dancers who settled in the United States. New movies featured the talents and sensational arrival of the dancers who had defected from the Soviet Union, Rudolph Nureyev and Mikhail Baryshnikov. Nureyev appeared with Margot Fonteyn in Paul Zimmer's film of Kenneth MacMillan's ballet *Romeo and Juliet*, in his own 1973 production for the Australian ballet *Don Quixote* (after the nineteenth-century choreographer Marius Petipa), in a documentary titled *I Am a Dancer* (1973), and in the film biography of the silent-film star Rudolph Valentino. Herbert Ross (1927–2001) was another dominant presence in film dance in the second half of the century. Trained in both ballet and modern dance and also an actor and dancer on Broadway, Ross was briefly the resident choreographer of American Ballet Theatre. From 1959 on he collaborated with his wife, the American ballerina Nora Kaye, to bring dance subjects to film, including the story of the great Ballets Russes dancer Nijinsky and *The Turning Point* (1977), a portrait of life in a fictionalized American Ballet Theatre featuring the dancers Mikhail Baryshnikov and Leslie Browne. Baryshnikov also appeared with the jazz tap dancer Gregory Hines in the cold-war thriller *White Nights* (1985). George Balanchine's ballets *A Midsummer Night's Dream* (1967) and *The Nutcracker* (1993) were released as feature films. And the British choreographer Frederick Ashton choreographed *Peter Rabbit and the Tales of Beatrix Potter* (1971), in which he appears himself as Mrs. Tiggy-Winkle with members of the Royal Ballet in enacting the beloved children's stories.

If Astaire, in part, glamorized ballroom and social dance in films like *Swing Time*, a new wave has recurred in the movies. Set in Australia, Baz Luhrmann's *Strictly Ballroom* (1992) drew on the immensely popular culture of competition ballroom dancing, which has spread from the West all over the world. So too, did the Japanese film *Shall We Dance?* (1997), in which a Japanese businessman learns to dance (and to live) in his off hours. More recent ballroom-dance films include an American remake (in 2004) of the Japanese *Shall We Dance?* and a prequel to *Dirty Dancing* (*Dirty Dancing: Havana Nights*) as well as *Take the Lead* (2006). The documentary *Mad Hot Ballroom* (2005) has introduced new audiences to the form.

Although *Moulin Rouge* (2001) and *Chicago* (2002) have drawn influences from the dance musicals of Astaire and Kelly, their editing style owes more to Bob Fosse and to the MTV generation of directors, who have brought their own digital-age devices to expand and enhance screendance. The screendance of 3D in the world of film dance has been probably the most significant compositional device in feature filmmaking since fast-cut editing banished the body-centered framing and filming introduced by Astaire and continued (even with use of the moving camera) by Minnelli and by Kelly and Donen. The 3D technique was briefly used in dance film in the 1950s. *Kiss Me, Kate* is the major example, with movements "inserted" quite obviously into the choreography to take advantage of the medium (in the rooftop scenes, for example, dancers seem to swing out into the audience). But on the whole dances were not choreographed with this medium in mind. With the extraordinary success of James Cameron's *Avatar*, however, directors and choreographers are once again searching for innovative ways to exploit 3D in dance. Films like *Step Up 3D* (2010) have tried to move beyond simply exploiting the medium for shock effect, with moderate success. More recently the director Wim Wenders used 3D to extraordinary effect in *Pina* (2011), his tribute to the German postmodern choreographer-dancer Pina Bausch (1940–2009).

Even more significant as an influence on film dance of the twenty-first century has been the almost universal use of the Internet to post and download films. The easy access of cameras and sophisticated moviemaking software such as iMovie makes it possible for everyone to make their own dance films. If the advent of cinema first widened and democratized the audience for dance, the widespread ability for all to make and post their own films, making them instantly available, has created and will continue to create a change in what kinds of dances are made and how they are seen. From tiny tots in tutus at their first recital, to preprofessional student dancers posting their choreography to show to their teachers and potential audiences, to professional choreographers' Web pages, a never-before-available range of dance on film can be easily accessed by anyone with a computer and an Internet connection. YouTube and similar Internet sites also mean that an increasingly wide variety of dance from all over the world can be seen and studied—from dances of Australian aborigines to classical, social, and popular dance forms from virtually every country in the world. Historical performances too have been posted on the Web, from two seconds of Isadora Duncan to rare films of dancers of the Harlem Renaissance to films of Pavlova, and a whole new generation is rediscovering earlier dancer-choreographers from around the world. This amazing variety also includes interviews, examples, and rehearsal footage of all sorts of dance forms from around the world. (You can download at least two or three versions of the facial expressions for the nine rasas of Indian dance, for example.) This has already had a tremendous impact on dance and dancemakers worldwide, and it is bound in the future to result in an extraordinary new world of moving images of dance.

Kelly, Astaire, and the other dancers of this book are now being discovered by a new generation. The compilations of their dance sequences in the *That's Entertainment* series of films are easily available, but, much more important, most of their complete films are available to anyone now on DVD, Netflix, and the like. What is most remarkable is that their dance sequences are posted on the Internet—even their most obscure films. Young filmmakers have remixed their dances with a variety of new musics. Recent trawls on the Internet have shown Astaire and Rogers sequences and images set to a variety of contemporary popular songs, from Whitney Houston to hip-hop, as well as a mix of Elvis and bossa nova.

At the same time, the film-musical genre seems to have been especially in the ascendant on television, with the popularity of Disney's *High School Musical* series and Fox TV's *Glee*. While no dancer-choreographer-filmmaker has achieved prominence as yet, it is clear that Fred Astaire's no-limitations approach to dance and film is there for anyone to see and build on.

EPILOGUE: *LA LA LAND*

This book was essentially finished and in copyediting when Damien Chazelle's *La La Land* was released. Its relationship to the tradition described in this book is clear, and its popularity both with audiences and people in the industry couldn't have been predicted. Chazelle, born in 1985, grew up and was educated during the period when film musicals were pretty much disdained—well, okay for kids (Disney musicals, for example), but not for the adults who take them to the movies or pop in the DVD to amuse them. In the interviews he gave after *La La Land* was nominated for fourteen Academy Awards, Chazelle made clear the debt he owed to the tradition I discuss, the Astaire, Minnelli, Kelly and Donen films, as well as the films of young French filmmakers who were influenced by them, such as Jacques Demy. In *Les parapluies de Cherbourg* and *Les demoiselles de Rochefort* (in which Gene Kelly appeared), the dancing was to music of Michel Legrand. During Chazelle's years growing up, many of these films were available on video and then on DVD, and for his final project as a student at Harvard, he created a musical. Chazelle talks about how hard it was to sell his idea of a film musical to the industry. More important, he spoke of his psychological struggle— his struggle to turn from the idea, inculcated in him as a young man, of film musicals as basically frivolous forms to embracing his love for them. He rationalizes it by attributing to them the characteristics of avant-garde art. The idea of "musical comedy as a valid theatrical tradition," as Balanchine called it, had long since been pushed into the category of "lowbrow," or, even worse, "middlebrow," by American intellectuals— including film critics and historians who have championed as worthy of consideration directors of westerns (John Ford) and mysteries (Alfred Hitchcock). The championing of musicals had to come from European critics and directors, and it still hasn't really filtered into English-language film studies. When movie musicals are noticed at all, it is with apologies for how silly their conventions are—whereas the impossible feats of physical skill, endurance, and strength in westerns, war movies, and mysteries give no such cause for embarrassment. Like musicals and romantic comedies, these films of manliness are stylized and fantastic. Their audiences, though, aren't stereotyped and denigrated, as are the audiences for musicals (gay men and all women). It has been great progress that we can now recognize the greatness of the best westerns and mysteries, but the progress hasn't yet carried over to musicals.

Like Astaire, Balanchine, and Kelly, and like the directors Minnelli and Donen, Chazelle had to have the courage to not worry about labels. *La La Land* is filled with the dance genres and compositional devices, from the establishing sequence, filmed on a Los Angeles highway, to the courtship dance, danced by Ryan Gosling and Emma Stone, to the euphoria dance, when they suddenly float up to a starry sky in a Los Angeles observatory, to the street dance, in which Stone and her girlfriends walk-dance down California streets, to the wonderful and extended combination of musical montage and film ballet, filled with references to the films he admires. Chazelle does it, as do all of my subjects, in his own way, making his film modern for this generation; but his film musical's heritage is clear. His mastery of the basic concepts of the formal and dramatic synergy of music and moving image is obvious. Another key is the competing musical styles he uses. But now it is the performer's jazz of the bebop era that has become the new classic form, music meant for listening, not for dancing. Jazz stands against the popular music of the millennial generation, which calls for movement. For dance music, Chazelle's composer, Justin Hurwitz (living in a culture which no longer supports film musicals), had to reach back to older forms. The love theme of the courtship is a waltz, about as far away from contemporary tastes as it is possible to be and the anthesis of what popular dance now looks like.

The musicals of Astaire, Kelly and Donen, and Mamoulian constitute a key early tradition for film-dance musicals. As I said at the outset of this book, the traditions that most matter in the arts are the ones that guide artists themselves in their choices of what to emulate and develop in their own work. We historians of the arts have as our central task the tracing the development of the most significant artists' lineages and the analysis of the styles and genres to which this process of artistry, emulation, and invention gives rise. A chief goal of this book has been to demonstrate, through close visual and aural analysis, how repeated viewings and careful scrutiny of Astaire, Balanchine, Minnelli, and Kelly-Donen films can yield both information and inspiration. Choreographers, dancers, filmmakers, and composers of the younger generation to whom these works are now widely available and easily accessible are able to learn from the pioneers in a way that has never before in history been possible. Let's see what happens.

Appendix: Timeline

Unless otherwise noted, films are listed by their release dates when I have ascertained them. Birth dates are by year and sometimes month. Ages are rough in that they may be off by a year, and they are for the most part not given after age forty, except for deaths.

YEAR	FRED ASTAIRE	GENE KELLY	GEORGE BALANCHINE	OTHERS
1872–95				Marius Petipa b. March 1818
				Sergei Diaghilev b. March 1872
				Isadora Duncan b. May 1877
				Bill (Bojangles) Robinson b. May 1878
				Adeline Genée b. Jan. 1878
				George M. Cohan b. July 1878
				Ruth St. Denis b. Jan. 1879
				Anna Pavlova b. Feb. 1881
				Jerome Kern b. Nov. 1885
				Petipa: *Sleeping Beauty, Swan Lake, Nutcracker* (1890–95)
				Vernon Castle b. May 1887
				Irving Berlin b. May 1888
				Vaslav Nijinsky b. March 1889
				Cole Porter b. June 1891
				Ernst Lubitsch b. Jan. 1892
				Irene Castle b. April 1893
				Busby Berkeley b. Nov. 1895
1896	Adele Astaire (sister) b. Sept.			Ira Gershwin b. Dec.

(continued)

YEAR	FRED ASTAIRE	GENE KELLY	GEORGE BALANCHINE	OTHERS
1897				Rouben Mamoulian b. Oct.
1898				George Gershwin b. Sept. Ninette de Valois (Edris Stannus) b. June René Clair b. Nov. Isadora Duncan, 21, goes to London, embarks on European career
1899	b. May, Omaha			
1902				John W. Sublett (Bubbles) b. Feb.
1903				Vernon Duke (Dukelsky) b. Oct.
1904			Georgi Balanchivadze, b. Jan.	Vincente Minnelli b. Feb. George M. Cohan, 26: *Little Johnny Jones* ("The Yankee Doodle Boy") Frederick Ashton b. September
1905	7, with Adele, 9, moves to New York Claude Alvienne enrolls the siblings in his school			Ruth St. Denis, 26, first appearance as solo artist
1906	8, with Adele, 10, first vaudeville tour ("Wedding Cake"), 3 years			Josephine Baker b. June
1907	9, with Adele, 10, vaudeville			

1908	10, with Adele, 12, vaudeville; See Adeline Genée twenty-eight times in *The Soul Kiss*		Zangwill play *The Melting Pot*
1909	11, with Adele, 13, Orpheum Theatre, Omaha		Ballets Russes of Diaghilev, 37, opens, Paris; Fokine, 29, *Les sylphides*; Katherine Dunham b. June; Hermes Pan b. Dec.
1910	12, with Adele, 14, enrolls with Wayburn, who creates "Baseball Act"		Pavlova, 29, first appearance in U.S.; Diaghilev, 38, in London; Petipa 93, dies
1911	13, with Adele, 15, first New York appearance, Dec.		Irving Berlin, 23: "Alexander's Ragtime Band" (first big hit)
1912		b. Aug., Pittsburgh	Vernon and Irene Castle, 25, 19, success at Café de Paris, return to New York.
1913	With Adele, small-time vaudeville circuit; Aurelia Coccia creates new act	9, Enters ballet section of Imperial Theatre School	Nijinsky, 24, *Rite of Spring*, Paris
1914	16, with Adele, 18, begins touring with Coccia act		Castles, 27 and 21, in Berlin, "Watch Your Step," open dance school, tour U.S. World War I begins, Aug.

(continued)

YEAR	FRED ASTAIRE	GENE KELLY	GEORGE BALANCHINE	OTHERS
1915	17, with Adele, 19, Coccia act; vaudeville Meets Bill Robinson, 37, in vaudeville			Ruth St. Denis, 35, and Ted Shawn, 24, Denishawn School founded, Los Angeles
1916	18, with Adele, 20, Coccia act; vaudeville			Ballets Russes of Diaghilev in U.S. with Nijinsky, 27
1917	19, with Adele, 21, *Over the Top*, 44th St. Roof Theatre, Nov.		13, Imperial Theatre School closed in wake of revolution. Pianist for silent films	U.S. enters World War I, April October Revolution, Russia
1918	20, with Adele, 22, rehearsals for *The Passing Show*, June, New York; opens July, Winter Garden Theatre; produced by Shuberts (Lee and J. J.), book Harold Atteridge, mus. Sigmund Romberg and Jean Schwartz		14, resumes studies at renamed Petrograd Ballet School	Vernon Castle, 31, dies, Feb. James Reese Europe, 38, tours France with his regimental band, Feb. and March Jerome Robbins b. October World War I ends, Nov.
1919	21, with Adele, 23, *Apple Blossoms*; Oct., lyrics William Le Baron, mus. Victor Jacobi, Fritz Kreisler, and others		15, first choreography for Ballet School concerts; starts 3 years' study at Petrograd Conservatory of Music, focusing on piano and music theory; begins to compose music	George Gershwin, 21, publishes "Swanee"

1920	22, with Adele, 24: *Apple Blossoms*			
1921	23, with Adele, 25, *The Love Letter*, Globe Theatre, Oct.		17, graduates with honors from Petrograd Theatre (Ballet School); enters ballet company	*Shuffle Along* (Sissle and Blake) Josephine Baker, 15, joins show touring in Boston, then on Broadway *Krazy Kat*, jazz pantomime, Chicago, Adolph Bolm, 37
1922	24, sees Buck and Bubbles doing rhythm tap With Adele, 26, *For Goodness Sakes*, Feb. With Adele, *The Bunch and Judy*; Nov.–Jan. 1923, mus. Jerome Kern, lyrics Anne Caldwell		18, helps organize Young Ballet, an experimental company	St. Denis, last U.S. tour, ends 1923
1923	25, with Adele, 27, leaves New York for England With Adele, *For Goodness Sake* (now *Stop Flirting*) opens May 30, London, Shaftesbury		19, performs as pianist and dancer in caberets and cinemas Works with FEKS company	
1924	With Adele, *Stop Flirting*, London December 1: *Lady Be Good*, Liberty Theatre, New York	Stanley Donen b. April	20, leaves Russia, appears at Empire Theatre, London, with Geva, Danilova, Efimov, and Vladimirov. Engaged by Diaghilev's Ballets Russes as resident choreographer	George Gershwin, 26, *Rhapsody in Blue*, premiers at Paul Whiteman concert "An Experiment in Modern Music," Feb.

(continued)

YEAR	FRED ASTAIRE	GENE KELLY	GEORGE BALANCHINE	OTHERS
1925			21, *L'enfant et les sortilèges*, Ravel. Meets Vernon Duke	*Revue Nègre* in Paris starring Baker, 19. Ninette de Valois, 27, joins Diaghilev's Ballets Russes
1926	With Adele, leaves for London for British production of *Lady Be Good*. Jan. *Lady Be Good* opens April, Empire Theatre		Meets Josephine Baker. *Jack in the Box*, Satie. *La pastorale*, Auric. *Triumph of Neptune*, Berners	Gershwin, 28, in Paris. Martha Graham, 32, professional choreographic debut, April, 48th Street Theatre, New York. Martha Graham Dance Company founded
1927	*Lady Be Good* closes Jan. in London at Empire; Adeline Genée attends final night. *Lady Be Good* tours Scotland and Wales With Adele, returns to. U.S., June. November 22, *Funny Face*, Alvin Theatre; mus. and lyrics by George and Ira Gershwin		*La chatte*, Sauguet	Duncan, 50, dies, Sept. *The Jazz Singer*, Oct.
1928	30, *Funny Face* opens, Nov., Princess Theatre, London. Princess Theatre closes, Dec., due to gas explosion		24, *Apollo*, June. Sees *Funny Face*	*Blackbirds of 1928* (stage). Gershwin, 30, *An American in Paris*, Dec., Carnegie Hall, Damrosch conducting the New York Philharmonic

1929	*Funny Face* continues in London and tours UK	25, *Prodigal Son* / *Dark Red Roses*	Bill Robinson, 50, stair dance Ninette de Valois, 30, in West End Doris Humphrey, 33, and Charles Weidman, 27, found Humphrey-Weidman Studio and Company First Doris Humphrey–Charles Weidman concert, New York Diaghilev, 57, dies, Aug. Ernst Lubitsch, 37: *Love Parade* Stock market crash starts Great Depression
1930	32, with Adele, 34, returns to U.S., April *Smiles*, Nov, with Marilyn Miller, Ziegfeld Theatre, New York; mus. Kern	Charles B. Cochran revue	Heralded by John Martin in the *New York Times*, Graham, Humphrey, Weidman, Tamiris join forces in concert of "modern dance." Lubitsch, 38, *Monte Carlo* (film)
1931	*Smiles* closes, Jan. With Adele, vacations in Europe. With Adele, *The Band Wagon*, New Amsterdam Theatre, New York; mus. Arthur Schwartz, lyrics Howard Dietz	Another Cochran revue Contracts tuberculosis	Lubitsch, 39, *Smiling Lieutenant* (film) René Clair, 33, *Le million* (film)

(continued)

YEAR	FRED ASTAIRE	GENE KELLY	GEORGE BALANCHINE	OTHERS
1932	With Adele, final performance of *The Band Wagon*, Chicago, March. Adele, 36, marries Charles Cavendish, 2nd son of the Duke of Devonshire, May After visiting newlyweds, Fred leaves London for New York, Sept. Solo career begins. *The Gay Divorcee*, Nov., Barrymore Theatre, New York City; mus. and lyrics Cole Porter			Rouben Mamoulian, 35, *Love Me Tonight* (film), score by Rodgers, 30, and Hart, 37 Lubitsch, 40, *One Hour with You*
1933	January: Makes screen test for producer David O. Selznick and RKO Radio Pictures Signs contract with RKO to make *Flying Down to Rio*, May Marries Phyllis Livingston Potter, July Flies to California to begin screen work on *Dancing Lady* and *Flying Down to Rio*, July *The Gay Divorcee* opens, Nov. Palace, London *Dancing Lady* (film), Nov. *Flying Down to Rio* (film), Dec., dir. Thornton Freeland, music Vincent Youmans, lyrics Gus Kahn, launching team of Fred Astaire and Ginger Rogers	21, Graduates from University of Pittsburgh Sees Ballets Russe de Monte Carlo in Pittsburgh, during their first tour in America First studies with Berenice Holmes in Chicago that summer.	Les Ballets 1933 (company). Baker comes to rehearsals. Meets Lincoln Kirstein, who invites him to the U.S. Arrives in New York Oct.	Berkeley, 38, *42nd Street*, March Berkeley, *Gold Diggers of 1933*, May Martha Graham, 39, *Ekstasis*, mus. Lehman Engel, May

1934	Signs a seven-year contract with RKO *The Gay Divorcee* (film), Oct.	30, Starts School of American Ballet	Massine, 38, *Union Pacific*, Ballet Russe de Monte Carlo
1935	September: *Top Hat* (film), dir. Mark Sandrich, mus. and lyrics Berlin	31, with Kirstein, establishes The American Ballet, which becomes resident company at the Metropolitan Opera *Alma Mater* (stage), by Kay Swift; George Gershwin attends, as do Rodgers and Hart.	Gershwin, 37, *Porgy and Bess* Graham, 41, *Frontier*
1936	*Swing Time* (film), mus. Kern, lyrics Dorothy Fields *Follow the Fleet*, mus. and lyrics Berlin	*Ziegfeld Follies of 1936* (stage), Baker, mus. Duke, lyrics Ira Gershwin Choreographs *On Your Toes* (stage), April, mus. Richard Rodgers, lyrics Lorenz Hart	
1937	*Shall We Dance* (film), dir. Mark Sandrich, mus. George Gershwin, Lyrics Ira Gershwin *A Damsel in Distress* (film), dir. George Stevens, mus. and lyrics George and Ira Gershwin	April: Choreographs *Babes in Arms* (stage), mus. Richard Rodgers, lyrics Lorenz Hart	

(continued)

YEAR	FRED ASTAIRE	GENE KELLY	GEORGE BALANCHINE	OTHERS
1938	Carefree, dir. Mark Sandrich, mus. Berlin (songs)	Leave It to Me, Porter, specialty dancer / One for the Money	Goldwyn Follies (film), mus. George Gershwin, Duke, and Ray Golden, lyrics Ira Gershwin / I Married an Angel, mus. and lyrics Rodgers and Hart	Filling Station, Americana ballet, Lew Christensen, 29, mus. Virgil Thompson / Billy the Kid, Americana ballet, Eugene Loring, 27, mus. Aaron Copland, 38 / Frankie and Johnny, Americana ballet, Ruth Page, 39, mus. Jerome Moross, 25
1939	The Story of Vernon and Irene Castle (film)	The Time of Your Life / Pal Joey, Choreographs own dances, mus. and lyrics Rodgers and Hart	Choreographs "Slaughter on Tenth Avenue" in On Your Toes (film) / I Was an Adventuress (film)	Martha Graham, Every Soul is a Circus, Dec. / September 1: Hitler invades Poland and World War II begins in Europe
1940	Broadway Melody of 1940 (film), dir. Norman Taurog, mus. Porter and Roger Edens / Second Chorus (film), mus. Artie Shaw and Hal Borne, lyrics Mercer		Keep Off the Grass (musical revue), José Limón, Ray Bolger / Louisiana Purchase (stage), mus. Berlin / Cabin in the Sky (stage), mus. Duke, lyrics John Latouche, co-choreographer Katherine Dunham	Ballet Theatre (later American Ballet Theatre) first performance January

1941	*You'll Never Get Rich* (film), dir. Sidney Lanfield, mus. and lyrics Porter	Choreographs *Best Foot Forward*	*Concerto Barocco*	December 8: U.S. enters World War II one day after the Japanese attack Pearl Harbor
1942	*You Were Never Lovelier* (film) *Holiday Inn* (film), dir. Sandrich, mus. and lyrics Berlin	*For Me and My Gal* (film), screen debut, dir. Busby Berkeley, 47	*The Lady Comes Across* (stage), mus. Duke, lyrics John Latouche (flop) *Rosalinda* (operetta, revival of Strauss II, *Die Fledermaus*) *Star Spangled Rhythm*, film, "That Old Black Magic" helps develop camera techniques. Includes songs by Harold Arlen and Johnny Mercer, 33.	*Rodeo*, Agnes de Mille, 37, mus. Aaron Copland Weidman, *Flickers*
1943	*The Sky's the Limit* (film), dir. Edward H. Griffith, mus. Arlen, lyrics Mercer, 34	*DuBarry Was a Lady* (film), mus. and lyrics Porter, *Thousands Cheer* (film)	*The Merry Widow* (stage), mus. Franz Léhar, New Opera Company, Majestic Theatre, New York *What's Up?* (stage), mus. Alan J. Lerner, lyrics Frederick Loewe (two dream ballets)	*Cabin in the Sky* (film), dir. Vincente Minnelli, 39 *Oklahoma!* Choreography de Mille, mus. Rodgers, lyrics Oscar Hammerstein II. March

(continued)

YEAR	FRED ASTAIRE	GENE KELLY	GEORGE BALANCHINE	OTHERS
1944		Cover Girl (film)		Ballet, Fancy Free, Jerome Robbins, 26, mus. Leonard Bernstein. On the Town (stage), mus. Bernstein, choreography Robbins, lyrics Betty Comden and Adolph Green Meet Me in St. Louis (film), dir. Minnelli, mus. Ralph Blane, lyrics Hugh Martin Graham, Appalachian Spring, Oct., mus. Copland
1945	Yolanda and the Thief (film), dir. Minnelli, mus. Harry Warren, lyrics Fried	Anchors Aweigh (film) mus. Jule Styne, lyrics Sammy Cahn	Mr. Strauss Goes to Boston (stage), New York	Minnelli, The Clock (film) World War II ends
1946	Blue Skies (film) Ziegfeld Follies (film), dirs. Minnelli and others	Ziegfeld Follies (film)	Four Temperaments (stage), Organizes Ballet Society with Kirstein	
1947		Living in a Big Way (film)	The Chocolate Soldier (stage), revival, mus. Oscar Straus Le palais de crystal (later called Symphony in C), Bizet Theme and Variations	Graham, Errand into the Maze and Night Journey

1948	Easter Parade (film), mus. and lyrics Berlin	The Pirate (film), dir. Minnelli, mus. and lyrics Porter Three Musketeers (film), mus. Berlin	Where's Charley? (stage), mus. and lyrics Frank Loesser Founds New York City Ballet with Kirstein
1949	The Barkleys of Broadway (film), dir. Charles Walters, mus. Harry Warren, lyrics Ira Gershwin, script Comden and Green	Take Me Out to the Ball Game (film), mus. Edens, lyrics Comden and Green, with Frank Sinatra On the Town, film, dir. Kelly and Donen, mus. Bernstein, lyrics Comden and Green. Substitute mus. Edens	
1950	Let's Dance (film), mus. Loesser Three Little Words (film), dir. Richard Thorpe	Summer Stock (film), dir. Charles Walters, choreography and direction by Kelly for his own sequences, mus. and lyrics various	Courtin' Time (stage) House of Flowers, withdraws before opening
1951	Royal Wedding (film), dir. Donen, mus. Burton Lane, 39, lyrics Lerner, 38	An American in Paris (film), dir. Minnelli, mus. and lyrics George and Ira Gershwin	

(continued)

YEAR	FRED ASTAIRE	GENE KELLY	GEORGE BALANCHINE	OTHERS
1952	*The Belle of New York* (film)	*Singin' in the Rain* (film), dir. Kelly and Donen, mus. Nacio H. Brown, lyrics Arthur Freed, screenplay Comden and Green; *Invitation to the Dance* (film) made, released 1957		
1953	*The Band Wagon* (film), mus. Schwartz, lyrics Dietz, danced Cyd Charisse, James Mitchell, and corps de ballet			*Give a Girl a Break*, dir. Donen, mus. Lane, lyrics Ira Gershwin and Lane
1954		*Brigadoon* (film), dir. Minnelli, mus. Loewe, lyrics Lerner; *Deep in My Heart*, brief appearance with brother Fred, dir. Donen, mus. Sigmund Romberg		*Seven Brides for Seven Brothers*, dir. Donen, choreography Michael Kidd, mus. Gene de Paul, lyrics Mercer
1955		*It's Always Fair Weather* (film), dir. Kelly and Donen, mus. André Previn, lyrics Comden and Green		*Kismet* (film), dirs. Minnelli and Donen
1956	*Daddy Long Legs*, dir. Jean Negulesco		*Allegro Brillante*	

1957	Funny Face (film), dir. Donen, mus. and lyrics George and Ira Gershwin / Silk Stockings (film), dir. Mamoulian, mus. and lyrics Porter	Invitation to the Dance, filmed 1952, mus. Jacques Ibert, Previn, Rimsky Korsakov arr. Edens. / Les Girls (film), dir. George Cukor, mus. Porter	Agon (stage) / Stars and Stripes (stage) / Square Dance (stage)	Pajama Game, dir. Donen and George Abbott, mus. Richard Adler and Jerry Ross
1958				Gigi (film, non-dance), dir. Minnelli, mus. Loewe, lyrics Lerner / Damn Yankees, dir. Abbott and Donen, mus. Adler and Ross
1960		Choreographs Pas de dieux, June, Opéra de Paris		Bells Are Ringing (film, non-dance), dir. Minnelli, mus. Styne, lyrics Comden and Green
1961				West Side Story (film), mus. Bernstein, choreography Robbins, lyrics Sondheim
1969		Hello, Dolly!, dir.		
1970				On a Clear Day You Can See Forever (film, non-dance), dir. Minnelli, mus. Lane, lyrics Lerner

Some other works and choreographers are discussed in the "Legacy" chapter. Subsequent non-dance musicals are not included, apart from the three non-dance musicals, focused on singers, that Minnelli would go on to direct.

Notes

INTRODUCTION

1. More recently, to be sure, the technology for movies and videos changes to electronics, but in essence, what I say here about literal frames of film in the days of Astaire and Kelly applies to any way of joining moving image with music

2. Some of the material and language in this introduction also appeared in my "Dancin' in the Rain" and "Dance in Film."

3. For other approaches to screen dance, see Brannigan, *Dancefilm*; Dodds, *Dance on Screen*, and Rosenberg, *Screendance*. Each of these books treats screen dance as a whole, whereas my book has a narrower purview, stressing the synergy of moving image with sound (including among these elements music and camerawork) and focusing on a single important tradition of dance in movie musicals. Brannigan does devote a chapter to film musicals.

4. The term can be translated in various ways but literally means "complete [in the sense of united] artwork." Wagner wasn't the first to use the term, but he may have coined it independently. The term is widely applied to cinema, see, for example, Paulin, "Richard Wagner and the Fantasy of Cinematic Unity"; and Joe and Gilman, *Wagner and Cinema*, especially Joe, "Why Wagner and Cinema?"

5. Cinematographers were largely credited, but they had vital assistants, including those unnamed but highly skilled and essential people who were responsible for making the cameras move smoothly to a musical count. While head music and art directors and costume designers were usually named, the crediting of those who worked under them was haphazard. Members of the orchestras and bands that accompanied the films were usually not listed.

6. Other important assistants include Jeanne Coyne (who later became Donen's and then Kelly's wife), Carol Haney, and Gwen Verdon.

7. For an extensive accounting of Pan's work with Astaire and his subsequent career, see Franceschina, *Hermes Pan*.

8. Ries, "Sammy Lee." Both Harper and Lee were major forces in shaping the choreography of Balanchine's tap sequences, but there were others, too, who remained anonymous. Balanchine's co-choreography with Dunham in *Cabin in the Sky* is discussed in chapter 4.

9. On the development of the concept of art as opposed to mere craft, technique, and decoration, see Kristeller, "The Modern System of the Arts."

10. Prime examples of the model from art history that I work to generalize are found in Panofsky, "Style and Medium in the Motion Picture." Panofsky himself, in 1934, wrote the pioneering article bringing sound film into the history of art as a rebuttal to Rudolph Arnheim, who, in "Film as Art," held that film is adulterated by sound. For a discussion of Panofsky, see my *The Film Musicals*, viii–ix. Panofsky stresses the contrast between cinema and verbal narrative: "A moving picture, even when it has learned to talk, remains a picture that moves and does not convert itself into a piece of writing that is enacted" (248). In my treatment of Panofsky and of my methodology in *The Film Musicals*, I write, "Sound (both verbal and non-verbal) and moving picture, inseparably linked, work together to convey or, in Panofsky's words, 'coexpress' the film narrative" (ix).

11. The field of ethnomusicology is, in my view, an excellent model for how studies of the arts can be pursued in a way that is sensitive both to formal features and to culture. For an example, see Koskoff, *A Feminist Epistemology*, especially "Miriam Sings Her Song," 90–104. I am grateful to Susan Walton for helping me settle on what might serve as an exemplar of ethnomusicological method. My early involvement with Javanese music and dance and my contact with the ethnomusicologists Judith Becker and William Malm were of inestimable help in understanding this approach.

12. Jordan, *Moving Music*; and Smith, *Ballet and Opera in the Age of "Giselle."*

13. It would be impossible to list everyone who has written on this, but they range from Kallinak, *Settling the Score*, to, recently, Buhler, *Hearing the Movies*.

14. While I am far from an expert on dance notation and I do not include Labanotation in this book, I have benefited immensely from my discussions with Ann Hutchinson Guest and her close observation of how movement works, and also with Tina Curran. See, for example, Guest, *Dance Notation*.

15. Bales and Eliot, *Dance on Its Own Terms*, 5. This threatens, they say, "to erase from history the materiality and layers of meaning available through the examination of dance and its constitutive elements." Dance, they remind us, "is important because it is a rich human endeavor with a distinct identity that emanates from who we are and have been throughout history."

16. See Henrich and Gil-White, "The Evolution of Prestige," for an argument that this sort of emulation is a cultural universal.

17. Sondheim, "Sunday in the Park with George," act 2, in *Look, I Made a Hat*, 39.

18. Scorsese, "The Persisting Vision."

CHAPTER 1

1. Astaire describes his early career in his autobiography *Steps in Time*. Riley, *The Astaires: Fred and Adele*, details the siblings' career together in vaudeville and on Broadway.

2. Astaire, *Steps in Time*, 325 (emphasis added).

3. Stearns and Stearns, *Jazz Dance*, and Hill, *Tap Dancing America*, do note the multiple stylistic components of Astaire's style, but Hill and most others put Astaire (as well as Kelly) in the general overall category of tap dancer. The descendants of the rhythm tap community admire Astaire but don't see him as a true tap dancer. Decker, *Music Makes Me*, focuses on Astaire as a jazz rhythm tapper and links him primarily to that tradition. While I of course agree that Astaire incorporated tap into his work, a more precise definition of what he and Kelly did is needed. For tap dance, this book draws on Stearns and Stearns, *Jazz Dance*, and Hill, *Tap Dancing America*. Seibert's history of tap, *What the Eye Hears*, appeared too recently for this book to take proper notice of it.

4. Astaire, quoted in Billman, *Fred Astaire: A Bio-Bibliography*, 59.

5. Astaire underlines this sentence in the draft manuscript of *Steps in Time*; see Decker, *Music Makes Me*, 53. The draft manuscript is in the Cinematic Arts Library, University of Southern California.

6. "Musical Comedy's Contribution as Shown by the Astaires' Current Programs: The Dance on Broadway." Unidentified clipping, Adele Astaire Collection, Scrapbook, 1923–31, Box 7, Howard Gotlieb Collection, Boston University. The label is gone, but it is on the same page as other articles labeled January 23 and January 28, 1928.

7. *Philadelphia Inquirer*, September 1921, Adele Astaire Collection, Scrapbook, Howard Gotlieb Collection, Boston University.

8. Grein, "Criticisms in Cameo," London newspaper, 1923, Adele Astaire Collection, Scrapbook, 1923–31, Box 7, Howard Gotlieb Collection, Boston University.

9. Grein makes a start on identifying the elements, and in this chapter I elaborate on his list.

10. Adele was born on September 10, 1896, Fred on May 10, 1899.

11. See Martin, *A Nation of Immigrants*, especially chapter 7. In the 1900 census about 37 per-cent of New Yorkers were foreign-born; this figure rose to 41 percent in 1910 before falling to 36 percent in 1920 and 34 percent in 1930. In 1900 the largest foreign-born populations were Germans (9 percent of New Yorkers) and Irish (8 percent), followed by those from Russia and "Poland" (not a political entity at the time; the combined figure for both is 5 percent), Italy (4 percent), and Austria-Hungary (4 percent). By 1910 immigrants from Russia were by far the largest group, 10 percent of the city's population, followed by Italians with 7 percent; Germany was now the third most common birthplace of immigrants, at 6 percent, followed closely by Austria-Hungary at 6 percent and Ireland at 5 percent. In 1920 Russia was still the birthplace of 10 percent of New Yorkers and Italy, that of 7 percent; Austro-Hungarians had fallen to 5 percent, and Irish and Germans to 4 percent each (Martin, *A Nation of Immigrants*, 95). By the 1930 census, reported birthplaces of immigrants may have come to reflect changed political boundaries in Europe, but self-reported Russian-born immigrants had fallen to 6 percent, barely exceeding the number of Italian-born, also at 6 percent. Poland now was the reported birthplace of 3 percent, surpassing Germany and Ireland, also with 3 percent. Austria now accounted only for 2 percent of New Yorkers. Rosenwaike, *Population History of New York City*, 97.

Unlike information on place of birth, that regarding religion was not generally included in U.S. censuses, so the extent of Jewish population growth in early twentieth-century New York can only be surmised. For 1940 it has been estimated that Jewish immigrants were about 10 percent of the city's population, while Jews in total accounted for about a quarter of New Yorkers: specifically, Rosenwaike, *Population History of New York City*, 128–29, computes 752,470 foreign-born Jews in New York City in 1940, 10 percent of the total population of 7,454,995, and a total of 1,954,050 Jewish New Yorkers, or 26 percent of the population. These figures can be compared to earlier estimates of the city's Jewish population: 1,713,000 in 1925, "close to 1,050,000" in 1910, and "at least 510,000" in 1901. Of the 1901 and 1925 figures, Rosenwaike writes that "the Jewish population thus appears to have more than tripled in size in a very brief period, and much of the growth must be attributed to an outpouring from Russia and to a lesser extent from Austria-Hungary and Romania" (111). The 1901 estimate amounts to 15 percent of New York City's 1900 census population of 3,437,202.

12. See, for example, Horowitz, *Artists in Exile*.

13. See http://www.census.gov/population/www/documentation/twps0076/NYtab.pdf.

14. See Stearns and Stearns, *Jazz Dance*; Hill, *Tap Dancing America*; and Seibert, *What the Eye Hears*, for overviews of the development of tap dance and its multiple influences in the Americas.

15. Zangwill, *The Melting-Pot*, 184–85.

16. Ibid., 203 (emphasis added).

17. Levine, *The Opening of the American Mind*, 105–20.

18. "A great deal is being talked and written about changing the millions who have come to this country from foreign lands, or are the children of immigrants, into 100 percent Americans. So far as the advocacy of measures for this purpose is based on a sincere desire to bring home to everyone living under the national flag a knowledge of the essential principles for government and institutions, this is worthy of the encouragement and aid of all patriotic citizens. There is, however, another aspect of the Americanization movement that is not so admirable. This is the attack on ideas, manners, customs and amusements peculiar to certain foreign peoples, not because they are necessarily wrong, or antagonistic to genuine Americanism, but merely because they are different. According to some of these self-constituted authorities, the way to instill patriotism and love of country into the benighted aliens is to persuade them to abandon all that links them with the land of their ancestors, and become exactly like the prevailing type of Bangor, Maine, Augusta, Georgia, or Portland, Oregon. . . . Against the narrow ideas that would reject many things of great value because they are of foreign origin, there is need for a wise and discriminating selection of the best that all regions of the earth have to offer in the domain of science, literature, music, painting, the dance and other arts, and their combination with the results attained by American creative effort. . . . A foolish prejudice against foreign dances should not be allowed to prevent the incorporation of their best features into what will ultimately be the distinctive American school. . . . As the various races from other lands have mingled their several qualities and gifts, and have produced the highest civilization on a broad scale that the world has ever seen, so will the creators of new and more beautiful dance forms utilize the characteristic dances of all nations in achieving what will be the 100 percent American." Wayburn, *The Art of Stage Dancing*, 301–2.

19. "Only by blending all the splendors of the dance into one beautiful, harmonious unity can a master impart all that is of value to his students. Mr. Alvienne, accordingly, while conserving the best traditions of the past, is not bound by the fetters of custom and deadening routine. His soul reacts to the stimulus of life itself, to the ever-changing forms of the dance; Mr. Alvienne investigates the technique of all masters in all parts of the world, accepting, rejecting, improving, so that his technique is a marvel of progress and efficiency." *Alvienne School of Dance Arts Bulletin*, 1918, Jerome Robbins Dance Collection, New York Public Library for the Performing Arts.

20. Adele Astaire, interview by Helen Rayburn, 1979, transcript, Howard Gotlieb Collection, Boston University. Betsy Blair Reisz, interview by the author, London, May 10, 1999.

21. Clipping, undated review of vaudeville act at Perth Amboy, NJ, Adele Astaire Collection, Scrapbook, 1906–16, Box 1, Howard Gotlieb Collection, Boston University.

22. This description is taken from various clippings in ibid.; see in particular "Clever Young Stars at Bijou," signed JJ, February 1907: "In addition to figure dancing, they dance waltz, clogs, and execute a difficult routine of what is known in ballet circles as toe dancing. The finish of their act is one that has never been seen in this city before. They do a cakewalk and buck steps on their toes."

23. Gottschild, *Digging the Africanist Presence*; and Hill, *Tap Dancing America*, 79.

24. Garofalo, *"Austerlitz Sounded Too Much Like a Battle."* The author reveals Astaire's Jewish background in an extensive study of his family. This information was first presented by her at the Fred Astaire Conference, Oxford University, June 2008.

25. In a 1787 decree called *Das patent über die Judennamen*, Emperor Joseph II required Jews to adopt German surnames (instead of the traditional patronymics). Napoleon did the same in a decree of 1808. The site of one of Napoleon's greatest victories, the Battle of Austerlitz (1805), was the source of Astaire's father's surname and that of many other Jews as well. Astaire knew that his name originated with this battle, but whether he also knew of its association with Jews may be uncertain. (One of Fritz's brothers further disguised his Jewish origins by changing his surname to Artner.)

26. For the origins and significance of the highbrow/lowbrow distinction, see Levine, *Highbrow/Lowbrow*.

27. Prominent exceptions were Helen Tamiris and Charles Weidman.

28. Astaire, *Steps in Time*, 6–7. For a discussion of these historical distinctions, see Kristeller, "The Modern System of the Arts." As it applies to dance in the twentieth century, see my "Creating a Canon, Creating the 'Classics' in Twentieth-Century British Ballet."

29. Isaac Goldberg, "The Astaires: Early, Late and All the Way In Between." *Boston Evening Transcript*, January 23, 1932.

30. On the African roots of African American culture, including postures, see Gottschild, *Digging the Africanist Presence* and *The Black Dancing Body*.

31. Goldberg, *George Gershwin*, 139. According to Howard Pollack, "by *melting pot* Gershwin meant" the country's ethnic diversity, epitomized by the Manhattan of his youth and reflected in his work by a wide absorption of various musical styles, while by "national pep" he had in mind the nation's propensities for hard work and speed—a disposition that matched his own energetic personality and that found utterance in his music by way of vigorous rhythms, crisp accents, and dynamic chord progressions. " 'I'd like my compositions to be so vital that I'd be required by law to dispense sedatives with each score sold,' Gershwin once said." Pollack, *George Gershwin*, 704.

32. Woollcott, review of *Funny Face, New York World*, November 23, 1927.

33. Astaire, *Steps in Time*, 118–19 on Coward and 134 on Gershwin.

34. Hermes Pan, Astaire's assistant in Hollywood, regularly used the term "broken rhythm."

35. "Rhythm in Modern Musical Comedy," *London Morning Post*, November 12, 1928. The article is attributed to "our theatre correspondent."

36. See the excellent analysis of the music and lyrics of this song and their importance in Crawford, *The American Musical Landscape*, 213–36.

37. Ibid., 219; see also 336, n. 27. Crawford credits a letter from William Austin noting how often Gershwin uses the term "rhythm" and for suggesting that the Gershwins turned this

technical term into a commonplace. Crawford's own investigations confirm how uncommon the term was before that.

38. Woollcott, review of *Funny Face*.

39. The music and lyrics for "Crazy Rhythm" were written by Irving Caesar, Joseph Meyer, and Roger Wolfe Kahn for the 1928 Broadway show *Here's Howe*.

40. "Rhythm Is Our Business" was written by Sammy Cahn, Saul Chaplin, and Jimmy Lunceford.

41. Vitaphone film short, 1936, with Jimmie Lunceford's Dance Orchestra, tap dancers the Three Brown Jacks, and singer Myra Johnson; see http://www.30sjazz.com/videos/jimmie-lunceford-/1936-vitaphone-short.html#sthash.rCoomIUx.dpuf.

42. *New Orleans Times-Picayune*, June 20, 1918, quoted in Levine, *Highbrow/Lowbrow*, 221.

43. See Hill, *Tap Dancing America*, especially chapter 2.

44. Stearns and Stearns, *Jazz Dance*, 14; and Hill, *Tap Dancing America*, 5–8.

45. See Hill, *Tap Dancing America*, 83, for a discussion of when metal taps began to be used. No definitive dates can be given, nor for when metal taps came to be widely accepted; various sources put this between 1925 (the year of *No, No Nanette* and *Lady Be Good*) and 1928. For the Afro-Irish fusion that created tap dance, see ibid., chapters 1 and 2.

46. Billman, *Fred Astaire*, xiii and 5.

47. Astaire, *Steps in Time*, 49.

48. Armstrong provided the vocal equivalent of rhythm tap with his scat singing.

49. Stearns and Stearns, *Jazz Dance*, 215.

50. Honi Coles, quoted in Stearns and Stearns, *Jazz Dance*, 216–17.

51. "Another of his hobbies is to place the metal taps on dancer's shoes. He also repairs his own dancing shoes and often does the same service [for others]." Skolsky, in Adele Astaire Collection, Scrapbook, Howard Gotlieb Collection, Boston University.

52. "Musical Comedy's Contribution as Shown by the Astaires' Current Programs: The Dance on Broadway"; emphasis added. Clipping, Adele Astaire Collection, Scrapbook, 1923–31, Box 7, Howard Gotlieb Collection, Boston University. The label is gone, but it is on the same page as other articles labeled January 28 and January 23, 1928.

53. Wilder, *American Popular Song*, 304. Wilder's is a landmark work on this rich topic.

54. Astaire, *Steps in Time*, 134.

55. Ibid. See also Weber, *The Memory of All That*, 153; and Decker, *Music Makes Me*, 57ff., where he discusses Astaire's relationship with George Gershwin.

56. Astaire, *Steps in Time*, 134–35.

57. Ibid., 134.

58. Ibid.

59. *New York Herald Tribune*, quoted in ibid., 57.

60. Decker, *Music Makes Me*. 57. See also chapter 7, where Decker discusses the use of blues structure in Astaire's work.

61. Minnelli, *I Remember It Well*, 144.

62. See Stearns and Stearns, *Jazz Dance*, 14; and Hill, *Tap Dancing America*, 7.

63. Hill, *Tap Dancing America*, 12–13 and 345.

CHAPTER 2

1. See Smith, *Ballet and Opera in the Age of "Giselle."*

2. At the beginning of his film career, Astaire's main musical competitors were the team of Jeannette MacDonald and Maurice Chevalier in brilliant Ernst Lubitsch musical films

such as *The Merry Widow* and *The Love Parade*, as well as the extraordinary *Love Me Tonight*, directed by Rouben Mamoulian. There was also the waltz-clog, in which step dancing is performed to three-four time. Lubitsch directed a film version of *The Merry Widow* in 1938, its spectacular waltz scenes amplified by mirrors, and MGM paid tribute to the Johann Strauss family in *The Big Waltz*. Later Nelson Eddy would replace Maurice Chevalier in the American operettas *Rose Marie, Naughty Marietta,* and *Maytime*. On Broadway, Balanchine choreographed waltzes in revivals of *Die Fledermaus* (retitled *Rosalinda,* 1942) and *Song of Norway* (1944).

3. Although the song is attributed to Kern in the film credits, it was actually written by Hal Borne and Robert Russell Bennett. Croce, *The Fred Astaire and Ginger Rogers Book,* 112.

4. "Lady Will You Walk?," interview with Fred Astaire, London newspaper, November 18, 1928, Adele Astaire Collection, Scrapbook, Howard Gotlieb Archive, Boston University.

5. Fred Astaire, interview by Charles Higham, July 29, 1971, Beverly Hills, CA; transcript, Oral History Collection, Columbia University, 18.

6. Aurelia Coccia and his wife, headliners in vaudeville, were a powerful influence. They worked carefully with the Astaires to refine and smooth their act and to make the transition from a young person's novelty act to adult performance. One of their own specialties was the Apache Dance. An import from Paris, this was an intimate pas de deux form, related to the tango, with salacious overtones. It involved a highly theatricalized brutality as the male tosses the female around seemingly without regard to her safety. The dance was entirely unsuited to the Astaires, and it is clear that they never attempted it. But Coccia clearly was experienced with many other forms, and both Astaires remember him as being exceptionally helpful in bringing a new sophistication, stylishness, and maturity to their act.

7. There were exceptions to this general rule, however. Jessica Fogel, in a private communication, reminded me that the Renaissance dance "La Volta," a favorite of England's Elizabeth I, involves a brief close contact between the dancers' bodies.

8. "I knew Irene quite well. I actually staged a dance for her when she went off by herself—after her husband died some years before that." Astaire, interview by Higham, 18. An unlabeled newspaper clipping in one of the Adele Astaire Collection Scrapbooks, Howard Gotlieb Collection, Boston University, announced Irene Castle's return to vaudeville in November 1921: "Her dances and the rest of her act will be staged by Fred and Adele Astaire." Although Fred and Adele are both named here, it is likely that Fred provided the choreography, as that was his regular job. See also Billman, *Fred Astaire: A Bio-Bibliography,* 51.

9. Lovelace, *Betsy's Wedding*. The author bases the book closely on her own experiences and those of her friends during the period described.

10. "Its abolition is sought on the grounds that the Charleston is a 'glorified shimmy' and that the high kicking in this dance has resulted in injuries to a number of dancers who have been knocked on the shins by Charleston exponents. The Cricklewood Dancing Hall banned the Charleston, after having summoned an ambulance to take care of dancers hurt by couples performing, and the dance patrons of the Piccadilly Hotel were astonished to see printed cards with the request 'You are requested not to dance the Charleston' on the supper tables the other night. The Hammersmith Palais de Dance, a well-known London dance hall, has taken similar steps, as has the Savoy Hotel." Unlabeled clipping, Adele Astaire Collection, Scrapbook, 1923–31, Box 7, Howard Gotlieb Collection, Boston University.

11. Clipping, "The Charleston Dancer's Defense," *Melbourne Countryman* (Australia), July 2, 1926; Adele Astaire Collection, Scrapbook, 1923–31, Box 7, Howard Gotlieb Collection, Boston University.

12. See Decker, *Music Makes Me*, chapter 6, for a detailed examination of Astaire's dance and popular music interrelationships in this tradition.

13. Kelly, in American Film Institute, *AFI Life Achievement Award: A Tribute to Fred Astaire* [television movie], April 18, 1981, http://www.imdb.com/title/tt0262744/.

14. Astaire, *Steps in Time*, 26.

15. Ibid., 48. Astaire was careful not to name his favorite partner in public, but at the conference on Astaire at Oriel College, Oxford, organized by Kathleen Riley and Chris Bamberger, June 2008, Astaire's daughter, Ava Astaire McKenzie, and her husband, Richard, told me that it was indeed Hayworth.

16. Adele Astaire, interview by Rayburn.

17. Ibid. See also Goldberg, "The Astaires": "He admires good ballet work, for example, and all other types of the dance behind which there is a more or less artistic purpose."

18. The Astaires arrived in New York in January 1905, and in November 1905 they premiered an act designed for them by Alvienne, so the longest they could have studied was nine months. In 1906 they took their vaudeville act on a three-year tour, after which they left vaudeville for two years to enroll in public school. They enrolled in Wayburn's school in 1910 and by December 11 had their first vaudeville booking. Beginning in 1912 they toured a vaudeville circuit for two years. Billman, *Fred Astaire: A Bio-Bibliography*, 29.

19. Zeller, "Luigi Albertieri"; see also her *Shapes of American Ballet*, in which she includes Astaire as one of Albertieri's pupils. "Cheri," according to Adele, maintained a troupe to appear in the ballet sequences in opera. Adele Astaire, interview by Rayburn.

20. See Wayburn, *Home Study Course in Stage Dancing*, reprinted in Stratyner, *Ned Wayburn and the Dance Routine*, 91. To be sure, Claude Alvienne did identify himself as a ballet master. His wife, known as La Neva, claimed to be a former star of the Russian Imperial Ballet.

21. In the article, he described the way one American stage dancer used it, predicting that it would be as popular as the "skirt" dancing that dominated the stage at the end of the nineteenth century. For Astaire's first act, Alvienne would have the six-year-old duplicate it. Although dancing on pointe (Americans called it "toe dancing") was something that signaled "ballet" to the general public (and still does), pointe work was a fairly recent phenomenon in ballet—and unlike Astaire, other males never did it at all on the stage. Well into the nineteenth century female dancers danced, for the most part, on the balls of the feet (*demi-pointe* or half-toe), rising only occasionally to the tips of their toes. Continual and sustained pointe work came in only gradually in the second half of the century, promoted by choreographers like the Russian Imperial Ballet master Marius Petipa in his ballets such as *Sleeping Beauty*. The famous "Rose Adagio," in which the female ballerina demonstrates her ability to maintain long balances on pointe, was created in 1890—less than a decade before Astaire was born and Alvienne wrote his article.

22. Adele Astaire, interview by Rayburn. In Adele's childhood notebook, also in the Gotlieb Collection, she gives careful attention to dancers' turnout, another indication of Albertieri's rigorous, Cecchetti-based system of training.

23. Wayburn, *The Art of Stage Dancing*.

24. Adele Astaire Collection, Scrapbook, 1923–31, Box 7, Howard Gotlieb Collection, Boston University.

25. Frederick Franklin, interview by the author, New York City, June 6, 2012.

26. Fred Astaire, interview by the arts reporter for the *Brooklyn Daily Eagle*, 1927; Adele Astaire Collection, Howard Gotlieb Collection, Boston University.

27. For the parallels between practitioners of this art and Astaire, see Riley, "A Pylades for the Twentieth Century."

28. Adele Astaire, interview by Rayburn.

29. Ibid.

30. See Pritchard, "Dancing at the Alhambra and Empire."

31. Guest, *Adeline Genée*, 64.

32. Adele Astaire, interview by Rayburn.

33. J. Crawford Flitch, quoted in Guest, *Ballet in Leicester Square*, 103.

34. Letter from Adeline Genée to Adele Astaire, June 23, 1927; Adele Astaire Collection, Scrapbook, 1923–31, Box 7, Howard Gotlieb Collection, Boston University.

35. The attitude pose is said to derive from Giovanni da Bologna's sculpture of Mercury (1580).

36. Adele Astaire, interview by Rayburn.

37. Anton Dolin, private communication, London, 1980.

38. Astaire, *Steps in Time*.

39. Astaire was not as averse to using pointed feet as he was to turnout—as one can see when he does his own versions of cabrioles and entrechats. Leslie Caron says that Astaire hated it when she walked with ballet turnout.

40. For another view of Astaire's walking into dance, see Brannigan, *Dancefilm*, chapter 6, especially 166.

CHAPTER 3

1. Balanchine's admiration throughout his career for Fred Astaire has been reported in many sources. For "the most elegant dancer of our era," see Balanchine, *By George*, a pamphlet put out shortly after Balanchine's death. "Concentration of Genius," *Horizon* 3, no. 3 (January 1961): 48. See also Carmichael and Nabokov, "Balanchine: An Interview."

2. Bolger, in Mason, *I Remember Balanchine*, 158; and Lerner, *The Musical Theater*, 138.

3. Printed in a "Tribute to George Balanchine" program, Huntington Hartford Theatre, Los Angeles, June 2, 1983.

4. Russell, "He Brought Ballet to Broadway." Astaire had already left for Hollywood, and he and Ginger Rogers were about to break box-office records in their newest hit, *Top Hat*, released a few days after the press conference on August 29.

5. Balanchine, "Dance Will Assert Its Importance" (emphasis added).

6. Balanchine, "Ballet in Films," 8.

7. Abbott, *Mr. Abbott*. Lerner says that Rodgers and Hart were "inspired [by] or envious" of George Gershwin's serious work when they conceived of *On Your Toes* (Lerner, *The Musical Theater*, 138). Rodgers and Hart had attended the first performance of Balanchine's company American Ballet in 1935 at the Adelphi Theater (which included a ballet called *Alma Mater* on American college life, with the score written by Gershwin's close friend Kay Swift.) "Once Larry and I had seen his work, Balanchine was the man we wanted." Rodgers, *Musical Stages*, 175.

8. Ibid.

9. *On Your Toes* and its jazz ballet "Slaughter on Tenth Avenue," choreographed by Balanchine and composed by Rodgers, became almost as popular as *Rhapsody in Blue*. But "Slaughter on Tenth Avenue" was not an isolated *ballet d'action*, part of a revue—as was Astaire's dream ballet in *The Band Wagon*. It was part of a show, in which dance became as important as or more important than song in conveying the story. The dénouement of the show takes place

within the ballet toward which the show builds. However, it wasn't just the ballet at the end of the musical that was important. Ray Bolger recounts that Balanchine taught him about dancing with the whole body—not just the feet. "As you've probably noticed, in all of Mr. Balanchine's works, his hands are terribly important. He uses the whole body. This is what I learned from him: the humor, from the top of my head to the tip of my toes to the soles of my feet, to the turnout, to the turn-in, the strength of the turnout. And he paid attention to the music. He taught . . . that in the American musical you don't have to do kick, stomp, thump, turn, jump, turn kick. You can *dance*." Mason, *I Remember Balanchine*, 158.

10. Edith Isaacs, "Spring Dances in." On Astaire's declining the role, see Abbott, *Mr. Abbott*, 177.

11. She was married to the Russian pianist and composer Dimitri Tiomkin.

12. Eventually the Ballets Russe de Monte Carlo would split and breakaway companies were formed, each insisting that they and they alone carried forward the banner of Russian ballet and of the great Diaghilev in his glory days. For the many names that de Basil and others used for these companies, see Walker, *De Basil's Ballets Russes*, x–xi, and García-Márquez, *The Ballets Russes*, xvi–xvii. At first de Basil was not the sole director, running the company with René Blum, but the two had a falling out. On these companies, see also Anderson, *The One and Only*; see also Chazin-Bennahum, *René Blum and the Ballets Russes*.

13. "Euro-Russian" is of course a strange term for Western Europe plus Russia, since of course a major part of Russia, with the bulk of the Russian population and the most important Russian cities, including St. Petersburg and Moscow, is, according to the customary division, in Europe. But by "Euro-Russian," I, like many other authors, mean the joining of French, Italian, and other Western European traditions to traditions of Russia.

14. See Banes, "Balanchine and Black Dance," and Gottschild, *Digging the Africanist Presence*, 59–79.

15. Banes, "Balanchine and Black Dance," 56. In a ballet called *Die Puppenfee* that Balanchine remembered seeing as a "young boy," there was "a dance of two dolls in black face wearing American trousers . . . they were doing tap and the music was Gottschalk." Reynolds, "Listening to Balanchine," 153.

16. On Dotson's "quiver," see Stearns and Stearns, *Jazz Dance*, 233.

17. The premiere was October 2, 1925, at the Théâtre des Champs-Élysées.

18. For a more extensive treatment and evidence concerning the personal and professional relationship between Baker and Balanchine, see my "Glorifying the American Woman."

19. Volta, *Satie et la danse*, 155. I am grateful to Steven Whiting for pointing out this source to me.

20. See, for example, Balanchine's pas de deux "La nuit," first performed ca. 1920 in Petrograd (St. Petersburg), later sometimes called "Romance," in which the female dancer is lifted onto the shoulders of her male partner, leaning back with one leg extended and the other crooked. A picture can be found in Danilova, *Choura*, 44.

21. Beaumont, *The Diaghilev Ballet in London*, 269. Banes, "Balanchine and Black Dance," also cites Beaumont's description and points out that although the "negro" (Snowball) in the original Sitwell libretto was modeled after a lame black man who sold flowers on the Scarborough streets during Sitwell's childhood, Balanchine transformed him: "Of course, black men in nineteenth century England—whether in real life or as represented by whites on the pantomime stage—did not dance twenties-style jazz steps. But historical authenticity was not what he had in mind" (65). My own feeling is that "Snowball" might have been created not only in response to this, but in response to Balanchine's seeing of Will (Marion) Cook in the

Revue Nègre. André Levinson's description of Cook is reminiscent of Beaumont's: "To see him beating time with one foot whilst the other slides, or hangs loose, numbed, one is seized by an irresistible gaiety, then using unexpected side-steps and sham falls saved at the last moment, he fluidly breaks up the uniform rhythm of the 'step' hidden under his mask of burnt cork with white-painted lips [he] is one of the most inventive dancers I know." Levinson, quoted in O'Connor and Hammond, *Josephine Baker*, 30. Balanchine's makeup is derived from minstrelsy.

22. Quoted in Duberman, *The Worlds of Lincoln Kirstein*, 179.

23. Dunning, *"But First a School,"* 17, reprints excerpts from Kirstein's letter.

24. Dolin spoke of his *The Rhapsody in Blue* as "the best ballet I created at that time." It was, he said, "successful not only at the Théâtre des Champs-Élysées, where it had its first performance, but all over England and Italy, where I danced it with Nemchinova hundreds of times" in 1928. *Autobiography*, 42. Back in New York, the Russian pianist and composer Dimitri Tiomkin and his wife, the choreographer Albertina Rasch, had also created a ballet to Gershwin's *Rhapsody in Blue* (1927).

25. Biographical information on Duke is drawn largely from his autobiography: see Duke, *Passport to Paris*. For Balanchine's biography, see Taper, *Balanchine: A Biography*. Although he was raised in the Caucasus, Duke's grandparents and uncles lived in St. Petersburg, whereas Balanchine had been brought up in the cultured atmosphere provided by his father, a composer and collector of Georgian folk music. Both Duke and Balanchine were slated for military school but were diverted to the arts.

26. Duke studied music at the Kiev Conservatory; Balanchine, in addition to his ballet training, studied music at the St. Petersburg Conservatory. Duke himself had loved Sergei Prokofiev's work ever since he had heard the young conservatory graduate perform his First Piano Concerto in Kiev. He was especially thrilled with this approbation from Diaghilev's "second son." After *Zéphire*, Prokofiev became Duke's mentor and was the only composer, according to Duke, to rival Gershwin in his affections.

27. For a full account of Balanchine's experiences with jazz in Russia, see Banes, "Balanchine and Black Dance," 59–77. See also Gottschild, *Digging the Africanist Presence*, 59–79, for a discussion of how Balanchine incorporated jazz movements into *Apollo* and other of his neoclassical concert dance works and for the overall influence of Africanist dance in his work.

28. Duke, "Gershwin, Schillinger, and Dukelsky," 105. See also Duke, *Passport*, 88.

29. See Duke, *Passport*, chapters 2 and 3, on Duke's musical training.

30. Ibid., 96.

31. Ibid., 90.

32. Ibid.

33. Ibid.

34. Duke, "Gershwin, Schillinger, and Dukelsky," 109.

35. Personal communication with the author. See Kernfeld, *New Grove Dictionary of Jazz*, 1117, for a discussion of the beginnings of this trend toward "symphonic jazz" (the term that Paul Whiteman coined for this kind of music). Whiteman commissioned not only Gershwin's *Rhapsody* (1924) but George Antheil's *Jazz Symphony* (1925), Duke Ellington's *Blue Belles of Harlem* (1942), and (curiously) Stravinsky's *Scherzo à la russe* (1944).

36. Duke, *Passport*, 98.

37. Ibid., 103.

38. Ibid., 124.

39. Ibid., 149. Nothing further is known about the "interesting proposition." The secretary referred to was Duke's friend Boris Kochno, who wrote the scenario for *Zéphire et Flore*.

40. Duke, *Passport*, 149.

41. Poulenc reviewed both performances, and Duke quotes from his reviews in *Passport*, 142–52. Prokofiev, far from being jealous, loved the ballet.

42. Ibid., 175.

43. Ibid., 179. Diaghilev hated autumn, and so the seasons were winter, spring, and summer.

44. Ibid., 178.

45. Taylor, "La musique pour tout le monde."

46. Duke, *Passport*, 209.

47. "It was wonderful to see George again," remembers Duke (ibid., 295). He immediately approached Balanchine's sponsor, Edward Warburg, for a commission but was rejected. It seems Warburg already had his cousin's wife, Kay Swift, in mind for Balanchine's first American ballet, *Alma Mater*, which premiered in 1935. Swift says it was George Gershwin who recommended her for the commission. Weber, *The Memory of All That*, 197.

48. This was Ira's second *Follies* collaboration with Duke. George was preoccupied with *Porgy and Bess*, and Duke, so close to him, was someone Ira knew and respected. And indeed, the *Follies* were a high-level operation. The creative team included not only Duke and Gershwin, but John Murray Anderson and Vincente Minnelli. Josephine Baker, Balanchine's old friend and colleague, came from Paris to star along with Fannie Brice. The supporting cast included Bob Hope, Harriet Hoctor, and Eve Arden, and the Nicholas Brothers, making their Broadway debut. Duke had given Balanchine an introduction into the circle of the young movers and shakers of Broadway.

49. Correspondence with Ira and Leonore Gershwin now archived in the Harvard Theatre Collection makes this clear. The earliest is a telegram from Lee and Ira Gershwin dated December 31, 1934. "Dear George Happiest of New Years and Much Love, Lee and Ira." There were other, longer letters from Ira, who always signed his letters to Balanchine "with much love."

50. *George Gershwin's Song Book* (1932) consists of transcriptions for piano of his own songs. The book is autographed to Balanchine by the illustrator, Constantin Alajalov, and can be found at the Harvard Theatre Collection. The order of songs follows closely that of *Who Cares?*, which was originally choreographed to Gershwin's piano arrangement and later orchestrated by Hershy Kay.

51. See Duke, *Passport*, 178. Under Duke and Gershwin's influence, Balanchine wrote several popular songs, which are archived in the Harvard Theatre Collection. Jacques d'Amboise tells us that Balanchine wrote several songs for his National Dance Institute. D'Amboise, *I Was a Dancer*, 370.

52. Bonita Borne, interview by the author, San Francisco, April 19, 2012.

53. Duke, *Passport*, 109. Gershwin, Duke tells us, "was still under the sway of the Wagnerian formula which I held . . . to be completely anti-theatrical. I insisted on the old Italian approach with separate numbers, duets, trios and ensembles." Eager to bring everything he could to his most ambitious project to date, Gershwin had taken lessons from Joseph Schillinger, and he made it a point to show off his newly developed skills to Duke. "One day he played the ingenious crap game fugue from *Porgy*, his face beaming," remembers Duke. "Get this! Gershwin writing fugues. What will the boys say now?" Ibid., 312.

54. Ibid., 308. While Duke and Ira Gershwin were collaborating on *The Ziegfeld Follies*, George was on Folly Island, South Carolina, from mid-June to mid-July. He also visited other islands in the area, where he heard the music of the Gullahs, who, isolated as they were, retained many

more traces of their ancestral home than did African Americans on the mainland. Gershwin himself participated in their singing and rhythmic clapping during the church services he attended while staying there.

55. Ibid., 110.

56. Duke, "Gershwin, Schillinger, and Dukelsky," 10.

57. As examples, the funeral scene with its central lament "My Man's Gone Now" and the call-and-response techniques that Sportin' Life uses in "It Ain't Necessarily So."

58. This was not as far-fetched as it might seem. Baker had already successfully performed in Offenbach's operetta *La créole* in Paris—and Duke, though worried about her projection, praises her virtuoso singing of his songs from the *Follies*. Baker's wish was chronicled in O'Connor, *Josephine Baker*, 101.

59. A photograph taken by George Gershwin at a rehearsal of one of Baker's dance sequences in *The Ziegfeld Follies* is held in the Ira and Leonore Gershwin Trust archive in San Francisco. I thank the curator, Mark Trent Goldberg, for alerting me to this source.

60. Minnelli, *I Remember It Well*, 78, and my interview of Minnelli, London, July 22, 1980. Balanchine was credited on the program for the ballets "Five A.M.," "Words without Music," and "Night Flight." We do know, however, that he choreographed the Conga Line in Baker's West Indies number (without credit) and a number dropped from the show on the road, "The Great McGinty." For an exploration the use of the term "choreographer" as opposed to "dance director" and its relation to race, gender, and intellectual property rights—all beyond my purview in this book—see Kraut, *Choreographing Copyright*.

61. To be sure, this was not the first time a "serious" choreographer had created a sequence for *The Ziegfeld Follies*: Doris Humphrey and Charles Weidman had done one, but using the modern movement technique that Humphrey had developed. (Robert Alton, who choreographed the rest of the show, was identified with the more usual job description "dance director" and was not singled out and given credit for each of his numbers.)

62. "Ballerinas Won't Tap with Chorus," *New York Herald Tribune*, December 15, 1935: "Rehearsals of the forthcoming Ziegfeld Follies were completely disrupted last week by a ballerina strike. The dancers are to appear in several terpsichorean interludes of the revue being arranged by George Balanchine and have been practicing entrechats and fouettés since childhood. Following a Broadway custom, it was decided that they should also double in the regular chorus line, learning a few tap routines for the occasion, but they thought differently. An ultimatum was drawn up by the girls, stating that they were ballet dancers, not hoofers, and they quit work. Their strike was completely successful. They will do no "hoofing'" in "Ziegfeld Follies" which opens in Boston Christmas Night and comes to the Winter Garden next month."

63. I would like to thank Christian Matjias Mecca, who participated with me on a presentation of this material at the University of Michigan and the subsequent paper for the Sound Moves conference at Roehampton University. Matjias Mecca contributed to the analysis of the music of these ballets, and each of his contributions is acknowledged in a note. I include Ira Gershwin with the composer and choreographer because, if evidence from his later practices with Balanchine and Duke in *The Goldwyn Follies* is any indication, it is possible that Ira had a hand in the scenario or "libretto" for each ballet.

64. Thanks to Kay Duke Ingalls and the Vernon Duke Trust.

65. *Vol de nuit* was first published in 1931, when Balanchine was still in Europe.

66. *New York American*, January 31, 1936.

67. The sources are the unpublished *Follies* script, the critics' descriptions, and Duke's unpublished scores, for which I thank the Vernon Duke Trust and the Ira and Lenore Gershwin Trust.

68. Genné, "Glorifying the American Woman."

69. Baker's colleague Maude Russell's description is quoted in Baker and Chase, *Josephine: The Hungry Heart*, 205.

70. This analysis has benefited from the insights of Christian Matjias Mecca.

71. Christian Matjias Mecca was the first to point out the musical indications of each dream figure as they entered.

72. Duke, *Passport*, 379 and 299. Duke had been accustomed to working with Massine (*Zéphire et Flore, Jardin publique*), who, as he explains, "had no musical intuition; he [Massine] didn't know or feel why a certain passage was right, another wrong. He never guided me the way Diaghilev did, by talking, or the Balanchine way, by sitting down at the piano and improvising the sort of music he needed."

73. It is clear that Balanchine and Duke functioned pretty much as equals. In contrast, Stravinsky, almost a generation older than Balanchine and with a well-established reputation when they first met, was a figure to be venerated. Balanchine's attitude to Stravinsky was "bordering on filial idolatry," as Lincoln Kirstein once described it. Jacques d'Amboise's description of Balanchine and Stravinsky's relationship confirms this: "I never saw Balanchine intimated by anyone except Stravinsky. He became almost like a little boy in his presence." Although Balanchine would play an increasingly equal role in later collaborations, he never quite lost the filial attitude that Kirstein describes.

74. Newspaper clipping, Josephine Baker Clipping File, New York Public Library for the Performing Arts, Schomburg Collection.

75. Brooks Atkinson, *New York Times*, January 31, 1936.

76. *Time*, February 10, 1936.

77. *Chicago Defender*, February 1936.

78. Baker's voice was delicate and lyrical, but there were complaints about its small size. With her distinctive, birdlike vibrato, Baker sounded more like Adele Astaire than Fanny Brice. And the Winter Garden theater was larger than most. Patrick O'Connor suggests that the public perception of Baker's voice resulted from the introduction of the microphone and resulting audience expectations for a more powerful sound. Yet, in Paris Baker had made herself heard in French operetta; indeed, she was lauded by such experts as Reynaldo Hahn for her mastery of Offenbach. Her recordings were great successes in Paris and continued to be after her return. Vernon Duke, confusingly, notes the "smallness" of her voice and says that it was almost "inaudible" in the Winter Garden, but at the same time calls it "exquisite" and praised Baker as a virtuoso singer for whom he wrote an especially difficult part: "We gave her fioriture that would have frightened the daylights out of Lily Pons. Baker went through it all like a trouper, mastering the difficult intervals" (*Passport*, 311). These fioriture or "vocalises" (as they were as called in the score) were a sort of elaborate descant sung above the basic melody. It is instructive to note that Baker's vocalises were eliminated in the recent Encore series production and subsequent CD of the *Ziegfeld Follies of 1936* because the singer's limited range kept her from mastering it.

79. Balanchine, quoted in Joseph, *Stravinsky and Balanchine*, 135. Joseph suggests that this remark hints that "his collaboration with Baker had heightened his sensitivity to the parochial and sometimes bigoted attitudes of the Broadway public." I agree.

80. This is not the ending in the *Ziegfeld Follies* script, which has Baker answering the door to the shadow of another admirer. It could be that the ending was changed—or it could be that after the shadows carry herb offstage, she returns under cover of darkness to resume her sleeping position on the sofa.

81. Wyatt, interview by Jean-Claude Baker, quoted in Baker and Chase, *Josephine: The Hungry Heart*, 203.

82. Fayard Nicholas, interview by Jean-Claude Baker, quoted in ibid., 198. Nicholas said that he found Josephine crying in the lobby during rehearsals. She was talking about her number called "Maharanee," choreographed by Robert Alton, in which, as Nicholas describes, "she dances with white men in top hats and tails and masks, but they never touch her. She said, 'They're trying to make me act like the people in those movies, like a maid or something.'"

83. George Church, unpublished autobiography, "*Dancing Amongst the Stars*," chapter 6, "George Balanchine." Included in the Popular Balanchine archives, Boxes 15–16, New York Public Library for the Performing Arts.

84. Two decades later, Balanchine cast Arthur Mitchell, who is African American, in his ballet *Agon* with Diana Adams, who is European American.

85. Baral, quoted in O'Connor and Hammond, *Josephine Baker: Compilation*, 100.

86. Review of *Ziegfeld Follies, Variety*, February 5, 1936.

87. Russell, quoted in Baker and Chase, *Josephine: The Hungry Heart*, 205. Russell tells of being approached during the run of the *Follies* to replace Baker by the Shubert organization: "All those people were saying, 'She's black, trying to be white, why don't she go on and be her original self like she was in *Shuffle Along*, when she was stickin' her fanny out and looking ugly.'" Though a replacement was discussed, it never happened.

88. Tamara Geva said in an oral symposium that Balanchine created a number for her, pre-dating the *Ziegfeld Follies*, that was the first to integrate black and white dancers: the "Two-Faced Woman" number in *Flying Colors*, with music by Arthur Schwartz and Howard Dietz. "George was the first and I was the first to integrate black and white dancers. I sang a song: "Can't help being a two faced woman—a little bit of white a little bit of black." George choreographed and I danced. I chose five black girls and five white girls—they danced in back of me. The song was about how I had a little bit of white and a little bit of black in me—and as I did it very classically towards the white girls and then move toward the black girls and get cooler danced towards the white girls I'd be a little cooler and then the black girls I'd get a little hotter and everything was in flesh color and black. Norman Bel Geddes did the stage de-sign: when I got very hot I went and flipped a switch and the whole stage went into magenta. That was the first time black and white danced together on stage. Except in Philadelphia they wouldn't let them dance—refused to do the number there. That was the first time black and white people danced together on stage: black and white chorus girls. We were not allowed to mix races on stage in Philadelphia—so I refused to do the number. Then in NY we reinstated it." (Interview of Tamara Geva by Hill, *Rethinking the Balanchine Legacy: Balanchine, Jazz, and Popular Dance*, symposium at the New York Public Library, 1993. Cassette 1 of 7. https://beta. worldcat.org/archivegrid/collection/data/80649927, accessed March 15, 2017.)

The problem with this account is that Balanchine did not arrive in NYC until 1933, after the show (which did indeed include a number called "Two-Faced Woman") had opened. It is true, however, that Balanchine choreographed numbers for Geva for her appearance in the Chauve Souris review, which began in Europe and then came to America.

89. Constance Valis Hill, *Babes in Arms*: Notes on the Major Dance Numbers. Popular Balanchine Project Dossiers, 2002. Dance Collection, New York Public Library for the Performing Arts at Lincoln Center.

90. April 11, 1936, New York City.

91. René Blum and Colonel de Basil's Ballet Russe brought together some of the Diaghilev troupe after his death in 1929 and attempted to keep the repertory alive, as well as commissioning new works, while capitalizing on the by now legendary name and glamour of the Ballets Russes. Balanchine had been resident choreographer for their first year but quit and was replaced by Massine. To maintain the association with Russian ballet and the Diaghilev company, all members had to adopt Russian names. Both Markova and Dolin were English and had indeed danced with Diaghilev's Ballets Russes. Mark Platoff was an American.

92. For a description of the "black and white" number he did for Geva, see my "Glorifying the American Woman," 46.

93. Gottschild, *Digging the Africanist Presence*, has pointed out this combination in Balanchine's ballets, as has Banes. I argue further that Balanchine also did it in creating the form of jazz dance that would eventually become standard in other Broadway shows and musical films of the 1940s and '50s; Gene Kelly, Jerome Robbins, and others are the prime beneficiaries here. Kelly and Robbins would also give the ballets their own shapes and create their own styles.

94. Stearns and Stearns, *Jazz Dance*, 169. My description of "Slaughter on Tenth Avenue" is based on the film *On Your Toes*, which Balanchine choreographed two years later. While not the same in every respect, it was substantially similar. The ballerina is Vera Zorina, who had appeared in the London production of *On Your Toes* and later became Balanchine's wife.

95. See Beaumont, *Complete Book of Ballets*, 955–56 for a fuller description. The theme of this ballet is the contest for supremacy between jazz and classical music. Jazz, temporarily vanquished by classical music, eventually triumphs because it is an expression of modern life.

96. Isaacs, "Spring Dances in."

CHAPTER 4

1. According to Gershwin's biographer, Gershwin was trying at this time to write for ballet. Jablonski and Stewart, *The Gershwin Years*, 282.

2. For a complete discussion of the precursor companies to Balanchine's New York City Ballet and their repertory, see Reynolds, *Repertory in Review*.

3. Jablonski and Stewart, *The Gershwin Years*, 282, say that Eddie Warburg "so appreciated news of George's initial attempt in this genre that in early June he urged the brothers to think about creating a ballet for his company." If that had happened, Balanchine would probably have done the choreography.

4. Pollack, *George Gershwin*, 685.

5. The scenario is published in Kimball, *Complete Lyrics*.

6. Balanchine, quoted in Kimball, *Complete Lyrics*, 278. Balanchine's account indicates that he and Gershwin must have discussed the reordering of certain musical sequences to fit the action. I believe the ballet Gershwin referred to as "our ballet" was another projected ballet, an original one for which Gershwin had not yet written music. Two or three ballet sequences had been projected for the Balanchine-Gershwin collaboration. (Scenarios exist in the Goldwyn

Collection at the Margaret Herrick Library of the Academy of Motion Picture Arts and Sciences in Los Angeles, though whether they were written before or after Gershwin's death is uncertain. For these ballets, Duke would take Gershwin's place.) Balanchine remembered that George (unlike Ira) would often communicate to him in baby talk in response to his heavy Russian accent—even though Balanchine's English comprehension was by this time very good.

7. I would like to thank George Gibbard for translating Balanchine's remarks in the score. He notes that the letters i (with the sound i) and ѣ (with the sound (y)e) had been abolished after the Revolution, replaced by the already more common и and е.

8. Balanchine, quoted in Kimball, *Complete Lyrics*, 278.

9. Ibid.

10. Kendall, *Balanchine and the Lost Muse*, 133.

11. On FEKS, see Clark, *Petersburg: Crucible of Cultural Revolution*, 179–81; the group is mentioned in Taper, *Balanchine*. On the young Balanchivadze (Balanchine), see Souritz, *Soviet Choreographers in the 1920s*, 73–78. See also Yuri Slonimsky in Mason, *I Remember Balanchine*, 19–78, and Kendall, *Balanchine and the Lost Muse*, 207.

12. Balanchine, "Ballet in Films."

13. Ibid.; emphasis added.

14. Zorina, *Zorina*, 173.

15. Ibid.

16. Duke, *Passport*, 352.

17. The choreographer Sammy Lee served as tap consultant, helping Balanchine with the tap sequence.

18. Zorina, *Zorina*, 173. Born Brigitta Hartwig in Norway, Vera Zorina took a Russian name, as did so many in the first third of the century. She studied with Legat and danced with de Basil's Ballet Russe before being hired to play the egomaniacal Vera Barnova in the London company of *On Your Toes*. The success of that performance led to a seven-year contract with Sam Goldwyn, which Zorina signed only when she was assured that her first film would be choreographed by Balanchine. Studio memos tell us that it was at Zorina's insistence that Balanchine was hired for the film *The Goldwyn Follies*—and for all the rest of her films. The world of ballet and dance in film is small: Massine was Zorina's mentor and lover before she and Balanchine got together. See Zorina, *Zorina*, 90 and much of chapter 4.

19. These two images are used in Cooper, "The Body Censored," to discuss this attitude devant position; she considers its meaning (97) and compares the images (109) to discuss Hollywood censorship of dance.

20. In the "Swan Lake" sequence of his film *I Was an Adventuress*, Balanchine would pioneer the effect of varying the camera speed slightly to give the impression of Zorina hovering in the air when she jumps. This was later used by Powell and Pressburger for Massine as the shoemaker in the ballet of *The Red Shoes*, which both Ian Christie and Martin Scorsese single out as an innovation. The experience that Balanchine gained would later be applied successfully to the *Dance in America* television series, the most invaluable record of his dance in the twentieth century.

21. For a full account of how this was made and its relationship to Balanchine, see Aloff, *Hippo in a Tutu*, 118–23.

22. Again from the press release: "The studio signed two black swans, rare birds from Australia, for the ballet scenes. Aged 10 and 12, they bore the prosaic names of Mike and Ike.

Each wore diamond studded crowns which cost 400 dollars each." They played alongside Zorina as the Swan Queen, Lew Christensen as the "knight," and Charles Laskey as the "evil one"— along with eighteen dancers and Balanchine himself as the conductor, Mr. Bonaventura. Balanchine is credited with the choreography for four films with Zorina, but my research has shown that he also choreographed a dance sequence for a fifth: Zorina's last picture, *Follow the Boys* (1944), another wartime cavalcade of musical numbers to entertain the troops. It is all held together with a rather thin plot involving the vicissitudes of a romance between Zorina and, in her words, "an aging overweight George Raft"—a man better known for his gangster roles (Scarface), although he was actually once considered a pretty nifty Charleston dancer. Balanchine's solution was to use Raft as a prop around which Zorina twirls and to activate the camera to suggest a sensuality that Raft himself lacked. During one beautifully lit sequence involving a fluidly moving camera and beginning with a very sensual close-up of their hands meeting, Raft lifts and whirls Zorina, but he couldn't manage the sustained movement Balanchine wanted as a chorus of dancers conceals and then reveals the dancers. A raising and lowering of hands serves to disguise the cut between the two takes it took to complete the sequence.

23. Barbara Horgan, Balanchine's friend and personal assistant who went to *Star Wars* with him, told me he loved the scene of the Wookies in the bar.

24. Tallchief and Kaplan, *Maria Tallchief*, 84.

25. Shown in the Balanchine Interpreter's Archive.

26. Suki Schorer, private communication.

27. All attributions to Dunleavy are from my interview with her, June 19, 2002.

28. Paul Bos, interview by the author, New York City, January 18, 2016.

29. See Gottschild, *Digging the Africanist Presence*; Genné, "Glorifying the American Woman"; Banes, "Balanchine and Black Dance"; and Hill, *Brotherhood in Rhythm*.

30. This or variants of it are widely attributed to Balanchine; the wording here is from Alastair Macaulay in the *New York Times*, August 4, 2010.

31. Maria Tallchief, interview with Nancy Goldner, Balanchine Foundation Video Archive for *Swan Lake*, May 31–June 1, 1997, Fort Worth, TX.

32. Arthur Mitchell, interview by Anna Kisselgoff, Balanchine Foundation Video Archive on the pas de deux from *Agon*, January 7, 2002. He confirmed this in an interview; Arthur Mitchell, interview by the author, 2012.

33. I have heard this from a number of Balanchine dancers, including Suki Schorer and Arthur Mitchell.

34. Taper, *Balanchine*, 195.

35. For biographical background on Dunham, see Aschenbrunner, *Katherine Dunham*.

36. Dunham, interview with Constance Valis Hill, January 15, 2000, New York. Included in a dossier entitled "Cabin in the Sky (1940): A Musical Play in Two Acts and Nine Scenes," compiled by Hill, June 2002 (amended January 2003) for *The Popular Balanchine Dossiers 1927–2004*, Series III, Box 20 (part of the Popular Balanchine Project sponsored by the George Balanchine Foundation, Jerome Robbins Dance Division, New York Public Library for the Performing Arts). Hill says that "Balanchine inhaled Dunham's lexicon of hip motions to reconceptualize American ballet style" ("Cabin in the Sky").

37. Interview with Hill, "Cabin in the Sky (1940)," Popular Balanchine Project.

38. Hill, "Cabin in the Sky."

CHAPTER 5

1. Kelly told this to Helen Marlowe, a close friend during his early years in New York, who would spend hours watching him practice and listening to him discuss his theories of dance (Hirschhorn, *Gene Kelly*, 70), and he repeated it to Marilyn Hunt. Kelly, interview by Hunt, March 10–14, 1975, transcript, Oral History Archive, Jerome Robbins Dance Division, New York Public Library for the Performing Arts. Where information and quotations from Kelly are not otherwise attributed, they are from this interview.

2. Unpublished script for "Dancing Is a Man's Game," 2, Gene Kelly Scrapbook, No. 1, Gene Kelly Box 1, Howard Gotlieb Collection, Boston University.

3. Hirschhorn, *Gene Kelly*, 37. He took lessons from Frank Harrington in Pittsburgh and went to see Dancing Dotson perform several times at Loew's Penn Theater.

4. Clover, "Dancin' in the Rain," 742, charges that *Singin' in the Rain* "denies, by whiting out, knowledge of black dance" and crosses a vague line that separates homage from theft. What the movie "doesn't-but-does know," she says, is "*that the real art of the film musical is dance, that a crucial talent source for that art is African-American performance, and that relative to that contribution, this talent source is undercredited and underpaid*" (emphasis added). I strongly agree with this assertion, and I'm confident that Kelly and Astaire would too. I'm not convinced, though, that the movie is feigning ignorance of this, as opposed to drawing on dance traditions that crucially include African Americans, and doing so without lecturing us on the history of what it is doing. Kelly's waterlogged tapping on the beat in *Singin' in the Rain* has more in common with the clog and step dancing of his Irish ancestry—a group that was also discriminated against. Tap dancing was a result of a fusion of these forms. We must understand the complexity of dance itself and distinguish between various styles of movement and their sources.

5. Kelly, interview by Hunt: "I was in college and I had been teaching and learning and going to classes in New York and Chicago in the summertime to improve my dancing because I was, along with the rest of my family, teaching dance and also by appearing in little night clubs."

6. For a description of *La concurrence*, see García-Márquez, *The Ballets Russes*, 21–27. The dancer quoted is Yurek Lazowski, 25.

7. Kelly, interview by Hunt.

8. Ibid.

9. Cyd Charisse, in *Gene Kelly: Anatomy of a Dancer*.

10. Kelly, interview by Hunt. During the 1930s Chicago was a vital center for dance training, drawing students from all over the country. Kelly's Cecchetti-method teacher was a Sr. Gambelli.

11. Betsy Blair Reisz, interview by the author, London, May 10, 1999.

12. As others have pointed out, these taps were dubbed by his assistant Carol Haney. This was standard practice in Hollywood films; nonetheless, it was Kelly who conceived them, and he certainly could have done them himself.

13. Hirschhorn, *Gene Kelly*, 267–69. Kelly was awarded the French Legion of Honor immediately afterward. The 2014 revival was for the Ballet de Nice.

14. Igor Youskevitch, interview in Hirschhorn, *Gene Kelly*, 233. He qualifies: "It is true, Gene is not an ideal classical dancer. He does not have the proper training. His technique is not good enough. But in dancing that calls for a freer, less restricted technique than classical roles—and I'm talking about the stage—he could have been outstanding."

15. Hirschhorn, *Gene Kelly*, 60.

16. Hill, *Tap Dancing America*, 156–57, brilliantly breaks down Kelly's influences in this sequence, "drawn from the lexicon of jazz and tap dance," and talks about Kelly's "re-imagining of jazz tap." To this I would add that Kelly's choreography in "Slaughter on Tenth Avenue" could not have come into being without the incorporation of the devices of ballet technique and narrative devices in the mix, which Astaire had started and Balanchine had developed in his own ballet "Slaughter on Tenth Avenue." Kelly's dance draws on these elements as well.

17. Blair, interview by the author.

18. Saroyan, *The Time of your Life*, 17. Kelly and Betsy Blair became close to Saroyan, who would write a play for her. Saroyan was the son of Armenian immigrants whose parents were part of the generation that grew up under the cloud of the Armenian genocide by the Turks during World War I.

19. See Billman, *Film Choreographers and Dance Directors*, 204, as well as the Kelly interview by Hunt. Alton had been in the Mikhail Mordkins ballet troupe.

20. Donen discusses his early years in two interviews: Clark, "Interview with Stanley Donen," 7–8; and Tavernier and Palas, "Entretien avec Stanley Donen." See also Casper, *Stanley Donen*. The information that follows is drawn from these sources.

21. Clark, "Interview with Stanley Donen," 7.

22. Donen, interview in Casper, *Stanley Donen*, 3–4.

23. Donen, referred to in Harmetz, *The Making of "The Wizard of Oz*," 85. Donen repeated his admiration of Mamoulian's *Love Me Tonight*—and of the Clair, Lubitsch, and Astaire-Rogers musicals—in my interview of him, Chicago, April 19, 1986.

24. In Tavernier and Palas, "Entretien avec Stanley Donen," 7, Donen makes clear that from the first, cinema held more fascination for him than theater. He decided to go to New York after he finished high school because it was closer than California to his home in South Carolina. See also Casper, *Stanley Donen*.

25. The other was Alex Romero, who would continue to work with Kelly. Donen himself refers to his role on *Cover Girl* as Kelly's assistant (Clark, "Interview with Stanley Donen," 7). Hirschhorn also says that Donen was Kelly's assistant on this film (*Gene Kelly*, 131), and Kelly describes at least one of the things Donen did on the "Alter Ego" dance in *Cover Girl*: "With this situation, I had to invent two dances that could be synchronized, and the main problem was rehearsing the cameraman. We had to use a fixed-head camera in order to get the precision, and Stanley Donen—without whom the piece couldn't have been done—would call out the timings for the cameraman, like "one, two, three, stop." We worked for about a month on that dance, then shot it in four days with a lot more time spent editing all this double-printed footage." (Thomas, *Films of Gene Kelly*, 53)

26. Chaplin, *The Golden Age of Movie Musicals*, 58. Chaplin feels that

"Stanley Donen . . . owes his entire career as a director to Gene. As Gene became more influential, many opportunities opened up for him, and when he was given his first picture to direct, *On the Town*, he insisted that Stanley be his co-director. As co-choreographers and co-directors, they revolutionized and reshaped the American film musical. In every case, Gene was the prime mover and Stanley an eager and talented pupil."

Chaplin did not receive screen credit for his work as assistant musical director on *Cover Girl* (ibid., 60).

27. Clark, "Interview with Stanley Donen," 7. A revisionist view of Kelly and Donen's work, promoted by Silverman in *Dancing on the Ceiling*, has put forth the idea that Kelly was responsible only for the choreography, whereas Donen controlled the camerawork and was therefore the real director of the films. However, Saul Chaplin, Betsy Blair Reisz, and Vincente Minnelli provide evidence that refutes this view. For a more extensive discussion of this issue, see my "Dancin' in the Rain," 76–77, n. 7.

28. In addition to the sources cited above and the interviews cited throughout this chapter, dance sequences in Kelly and Donen's films have been discussed in two scholarly works: Charness, "Hollywood Cine-Dance," and Delameter, *Dance in the Hollywood Musical*, which includes a chapter on Kelly and reprints a series of invaluable interviews conducted by Delameter and Paddy Whannel with the dancer and other members of the Freed unit, including Minnelli. Charness describes twenty-nine Kelly-Donen dance sequences, including one of the dances discussed in this chapter, the "Alter Ego." Analyses of all dance sequences in this book are, however, my own, and are the result of my observation of them using a Steenbeck viewer.

29. On *Showboat*, see Bordman, *Jerome Kern*.

30. *On the Town*, and with Kelly alone in *An American in Paris*.

31. Most notably *An American in Paris* (with Kelly) and *Give a Girl a Break* (with Donen). He was already a good friend of Minnelli, Freed, and Garland, and his home was a legendary meeting place for the great composers and lyricists of this era, who admired his and his brother's work.

32. In several sources Kelly indicates that the "Make Way for Tomorrow" and "Alter Ego" sequences in *Cover Girl* were his and Donen's in conception and direction, although screen credit for the overall dance direction of *Cover Girl* was given to Felix Seymour and Jack Cole (Hirschhorn, *Gene Kelly*, 131–32; Kelly, interview by Hunt; and Thomas, *Films of Gene Kelly*, 52–53). Unfortunately, in Hollywood full credit was not automatically given to all those who contributed to a film, even though their contributions, as in the case of Kelly and Donen on *Cover Girl*, might have been major. Donen in particular was a victim of this system. He did not receive complete credit for his collaboration with Kelly until *Take Me Out to the Ball Game* (1948).

33. Chaplin, *The Golden Age of Movie Musicals*, 52.

34. Ibid., chapters 5 and 6. Donen presents the sequence of activity: "We developed the idea of the sequence, arranged the transitions in and out, and mapped out the camerawork and lighting. Very rarely did I tell him about dance steps. We next arranged the music in such a way that it would help to organize the staging and camera movement. During the actual filming Gene worked in front of the camera, I behind. There was no director on the set except us. Then we checked to see if it was photographed properly and supervised the editing. A curious thing about the photographing and editing in those days was that you never shot more than exactly what ended up on the screen." (Casper, *Stanley Donen*, 10) That is, they cut in the camera.

35. The "buddies" in subsequent Kelly-Donen films are:

    Anchors Aweigh: the two sailors—Clarence and Joe

        Take Me Out to the Ball Game: the three baseball players—Ryan, O'Brien, and Goldberg

> *On The Town*: the three sailors—Gabey, Ozzie, and Chip
> *An American in Paris*: Gerry and Adam
> *Singin' in the Rain*: Don, Cosmo, and Kathy
> *It's Always Fair Weather*: the three soldiers—Ted, Doug, and Angie

The dance clowning of *Cover Girl*'s three buddies in "Make Way For Tomorrow" has at least one precedent in film musicals of the 1930s in "Follow in my Footsteps," where three pals—played by Eleanor Powell, Buddy Ebsen, and George Murphy—in *Broadway Melody of 1938* are motivated by a general feeling of camaraderie and use some of the playing-around gestures seen in "Make Way for Tomorrow." Astaire, George Burns, and Gracie Allen also perform a type of "buddy" dance, "Stiff Upper Lip," in *Damsel in Distress*. The closest parallel to the two-boys-and-a-girl relationship in *Cover Girl* is the central trio in *Singin' in the Rain*, with Kelly and Reynolds as the romantic couple (paralleling Kelly-Hayworth) and Donald O'Connor (paralleling Genius) as their comic friend.

36. The enthusiasm, camaraderie, and enthusiasm for their careers is a standard trope in musicals, expressed vividly by the words. For the full lyrics, see Kimball, *Complete Lyrics of Ira Gershwin*, 310.

37. The piccolo embroidery recalls the penultimate section of "The Stars and Stripes Forever."

38. Four-four time, with a strong stress on the first beat.

39. Ira Gershwin has said that his brother's music for the "Walking the Dog" sequence of *Shall We Dance* was inspired by Astaire's walk. "The Fred Astaire Story," script by Benny Green, British Broadcasting System, broadcast March 1975.

40. Clark, "Interview with Stanley Donen," 7.

41. Kelly, interview by John Russell Taylor, May 20, 1980, transcript, National Film Theater of the British Film Institute, London.

42. Kelly, "Dialogue on Film," 43.

43. Kelly, interview by Hunt.

44. Most of Astaire's strictly followed the "180-degree rule" used by cinematographers in the "classical Hollywood style." The dance in *Damsel in Distress* breaks both the spirit and the letter of this rule. See Bordwell, Staiger, and Thompson, *The Classical Hollywood Cinema*, 56.

45. Though the street dance in *Cover Girl* was not filmed outdoors, it does simulate a "real" street in length: to create a great enough expanse for filming, a wall between two adjacent sound stages was broken down. Hirschhorn, *Gene Kelly*, 132.

46. Kelly would often insist that the dance sections of his films be shot in softer, darker, or brighter shades to reflect the mood of the dance (ibid., 76). Like Minnelli, he understood how color could be used for dramatic effect.

47. Saul Chaplin has said that some of the music for the *Cover Girl*'s dance sequence had to be composed after the filming, during the postproduction phase of work on the picture, because Kelly had altered his choreography during the shooting. Though Chaplin doesn't specify the section, I believe it to be the "Alter Ego" sequence, because of the particularly dance-determined nature of the music. See Chaplin, *The Golden Age of Hollywood Musicals*, 61.

48. Kelly, in Thomas, *Gene Kelly*, 52. Donen has said the initial idea for the "Alter Ego" sequence was his: "I can remember the goose bumps when I got the idea. It occurred to me straightaway that a dance with two people was more powerful and fun to watch than a solo." Casper, *Stanley Donen*, 12.

49. Hillier, "Interview with Stanley Donen." Before what I have quoted in the text, he says: "Astaire, funnily enough, had these ideas for numbers despite his lack of knowledge of cinema. It was Fred Astaire who did the number with the fun house mirrors, and who did the number in the rain, "Isn't it a Lovely Day to be Caught in the Rain"; it was Fred Astaire who did the golf number; it was Fred Astaire who did the rear-projection number— this was all before Kelly and I came on the scene. All these were cinematic innovations of Fred Astaire."

And after the passage I quote in the text, he continues: "While he himself literally doesn't know anything about a camera, he knows about movies as something quite different from dancing on stage. Even the number he did on the stage in *Top Hat* is an unbelievable piece of movie, a sensational idea."

Charness ("Hollywood Cine-Dance," 42) says that Kelly and Donen "each . . . had to approach the collaboration with nothing more than intuition and a dancers' instincts." But Donen's clear acknowledgment of Astaire's influence undermines any claim that Kelly and Donen worked without precedent or model.

50. The camera stops only to highlight a new choreographic idea: a brilliant musical and dramatic joke when the Alter Ego, satisfied with his power, suddenly stops dancing and, leaning against a lamppost, watches in amusement as Danny continues to dance wildly while a phrase from "Make Way for Tomorrow" interrupts the flow of "Long Ago" ("Don't let the clouds get you down! Show us a smile not a frown!").

51. Kelly, "Dialogue on Film," 40.

52. The aspect ratios of the new, wide-screen processes that came to dominate the film industry from the late 1950s on (Cinemascope was introduced in 1953) varied according to the process (Cinemascope, Superscope, Technirama, Techniscope, Ultra-Panavision, etc.), going from 2.55:1 (Cinemascope with stereo sound) to 2.7:1 (Ultra-Panavision). Kelly's last films— *Brigadoon*, *It's Always Fair Weather*, and *Les Girls*—were all in Cinemascope. (Other wide-screen processes—Todd AO and VistaVision—also had different aspect ratios: Todd AO's was 2.2:1, and VistaVision's was 1.85:1. All, however, were much wider than they were high.)

53. See Croce, *The Fred Astaire and Ginger Rogers Book*, 126–27, for a description of Astaire's single-take system. See also Mueller's more detailed discussion, *Astaire Dancing*, pp. 26ff. It should be stressed here that Astaire's camera is rarely completely static: Astaire's camera (sometimes cameras) move, paralleling the dancers' movements to keep the full bodies of the dancers within the frame. The "Astaire dolly," a camera on wheels, was invented for this purpose. (On occasion it takes on a life of its own.) In Astaire's films, however, the dancers' movement always remains the primary movement on the screen.

54. Kelly, quoted in Knox, *Magic Factory*, 170. Minnelli also valued Fazan for exactly the same reason, and his remarks indicate that "musical cutting" was of great concern to him: "The one [editor] I worked with most was Adrienne Fazan, and she was especially good. She was the best musical cutter there was. She could cut right on the notes." Minnelli, quoted in Delameter, *Dance in the Hollywood Musical*, 274.

55. It should be noted here that Kelly and Donen always "cut in the camera," meaning that their shots and angles were carefully planned in detail in advance. Only what was necessary was actually photographed—there were never any alternate shots. This ensured that even if the finished film were given to someone else to edit, they would be forced (for lack of alternatives) to cut it the way Kelly and Donen had planned.

56. Kelly, quoted in Knox, *Magic Factory*, 47.

57. Johnson, "The Tenth Muse," 47.

58. Of this Kelly said, "The more you go into the camera, the more *force* you'll get, the more impression of a third dimension you'll get. You won't make it three dimensional, but you'll get force." Kelly, in Delameter, *Dance in the Hollywood Musical*, 212.

59. Kelly, quoted in Hirschhorn, *Gene Kelly*, 122.

60. The Astaires had some of their first major successes in London, where they appeared for extended periods during the 1920s. The Astaires' connections with the British aristocracy were strong: Fred became a friend of, among others, Edward, Prince of Wales, whom he greatly admired and whose appearance he consciously emulated, and Adele eventually married into the British peerage. See Astaire, *Steps in Time*, chapters 2 and 3.

CHAPTER 6

1. Croce has described this dance (as she has all of the Astaire-Rogers dances of the 1930s) in her *Fred Astaire and Ginger Rogers Book* (1972). She seems to have been the first to identify in detail the process of seduction traced out in Astaire-Rogers dances of this type. My description of "Night and Day," though expanded with my own observations, is based on hers, and, to a lesser extent, on her description of "Isn't It a Lovely Day," as well as my own analysis of the dances and camerawork themselves. Delameter has also described some of Astaire's and other Hollywood dances as "rituals of courtship and love making" (*Dance in the Hollywood Musical*, 114). Most of the material contained in this section, and the description and analysis of other "courtship dances" of Astaire, Kelly, other Kelly-Donen, Donen, and Minnelli films first appeared in my *Film Musicals of Vincente Minnelli*. Mueller expands Croce's descriptions to include Astaire's entire dance career in his meticulously detailed *Astaire Dancing*. All other dance descriptions and analyses in this chapter and others are my own. My analyses of the films themselves are made on the basis of frame-by-frame viewing on the Steenbeck viewers at the British Film Institute and the Museum of Modern Art as well as watching the films in their entirety in movie theaters and on videos and DVDs. Altman, *The American Film Musical*, sees one category of the American musical as organized around courtship but does not analyze the music or dance. Gallafent, *Astaire and Rodgers*, looks at all the films of Astaire and Rogers from *Flying Down to Rio* (1933) to *The Barkleys of Broadway* (1949), considering the romantic relationship played out in their films, but neither examines the music and dance in depth to support his argument nor treats the film musicals of the other choreographers I discuss.

2. Letter from Fred to Adele Astaire, Adele Astaire Collection, Howard Gotlieb Collection, Boston University,

3. Astaire, *Steps in Time*, 176.

4. Negri, *Le gratie d'amore*, 12 (emphasis added). Earlier, in 1589, Thoinot Arbeau said similar things in his *Orchesography*.

5. Ibid.

6. Ibid (emphasis added).

7. For the scenario, see Cohen, *Dance as a Theatre Art*, 19.

8. For an example of this dance see Sutton, "Il ballarino (The Dancing Master)." The dances are introduced and reconstructed by Sutton from dance manuals published by Negri and Fabritio Caroso.

9. For an account of dance at the court of Louis XIV and its relationship to the art of the time, see Cohen, *Art, Dance and the Body*, especially chapters 5 and 6.

10. Banes uses the term "marriage plot" in *Dancing Women*.

11. I am grateful to Marian Smith, Ivor Guest, and Selma Jeanne Cohen, with whom I have discussed this concept as it applies to nineteenth-century ballet. Smith tells me that the pursuit-rebuff tactics of the first-act pas de deux of *Giselle* is written into the 1842 Antoine Titus score on which she drew for the reconstruction that she and Doug Fullington did for the Pacific Northwest Ballet. She has found that it was a common convention in ballet that when a man asks a woman to dance, her initial refusal to dance confirms her modesty. On the reconstruction, see the Pacific Northwest Ballet webpage, https://www.pnb.org/repertorylist/giselle/, accessed March 19, 2017.

12. Ann Astaire, Diary, February 8, 1926.

13. The lyrics to the 1933 stage musical that included this Jerome Kern song are said to be by Otto Harbach, but IMDB attributes them to Bernard Dougall.

14. For more on this tradition, see Smith, *Ballet and Opera in the Age of "Giselle,"* and Schwartz-Bishir, "Musical Expression in the Bournonville-Løvenskjold *La sylphide* Variation."

15. Sondheim, "The Musical Theater," 12. Sondheim, who writes both lyrics and music for his works, has written, if briefly, on the role of the orchestrator in musical theater and musical films. It should be noted, though, that he is writing only about the role of the orchestrator in the musical theater, where, according to him, there seems to be a clear distinction between the person who arranges the song (determines the chord structure, tempo, and dynamics) and the person who orchestrates it (determines its instrumentation). Sondheim says that in the theater, the composer is in effect the arranger of the song, and the orchestrator merely sets it for an instrumental ensemble. That distinction, however, does not seem to have been made in the Freed unit: both tasks—orchestrating and arranging—were seen as part of the same job, and that job was carried out by the musical director and orchestrator, who, working with the melodic line given them by the composer, arranged and orchestrated it for a specific segment of film. Alexander Courage, interview by the author, Los Angeles, August 20, 1981; and Saul Chaplin, interview by the author, Los Angeles, August 24, 1996.

16. Croce, *The Fred Astaire and Ginger Rogers Book*, 126. The "Astaire dolly" was invented for this purpose.

17. In 1937 Astaire also does an early predecessor of the "male dazzles watching female" theme in *Carefree*, when he tries to impress Rogers by hitting a series of golf balls in tempo to music while she watches scornfully from a hill overlooking the green.

18. Miller, *The Mating Mind*; Burling, *The Talking Ape*; and Brown, Cronk, Grochow, Jacobson, Liu, Popović, and Trivers, "Dance Reveals Symmetry."

19. Tennov, *Love and Limerence*. I am grateful to Jon Elster and Gustavo Munevar for suggesting the social scientific and anthropological literature on this topic that I draw on.

20. Fisher, *Why We Love*.

CHAPTER 7

1. De Beauvoir, *The Prime of Life*, 3:11. "Pour moi, dans le laisser-aller des jeunes Américans, c'était la liberté même qui s'incarnait; la nôtre et celle—nous n'en doutions pas—qu'ils allaient répandre sur le monde." De Beauvoir, *La force des choses*, 14. (Emphases added.)

2. For example, Minnelli's first non-musical film, *The Clock* (1945), was a romance in which a soldier on leave meets a girl in New York, falls in love, loses her, finds her again, marries her, and then leaves for the war, all in the space of forty-eight hours.

3. For biographies of Jerome Robbins with treatments of his dance work, see Jowitt, *Jerome Robbins*; Conrad, *That Broadway Man, That Ballet Man*; and Vaill, *Somewhere*. Balanchine choreographed *Great Lady*, although, for contractual reasons, William Dollar got the formal credit; Jowitt, *Jerome Robbins*, 39.

4. Tobias, "Bringing Back Robbins's *Fancy*," 6.

5. *Billy the Kid* was created for Ballet Caravan but entered the repertory of the American Ballet Theatre in 1940.

6. Tobias, "Bringing Back Robbins's *Fancy*," 69.

7. Edwin Denby, review of *Fancy Free, New Herald Tribune*, April 19, 1944; reprinted in Denby, *Dance Writings*, 218; emphasis added.

8. In the 1940s it was not unusual—in fact, in many towns it was the norm, if not the only way—for those who wanted to learn to dance to be taught what was then called "tap, toe, acrobatics, and interpretive dance," often by the same teacher and within one class. The separation of dance genres was by no means always followed. Betsy Blair Reisz, interview by the author, London, May 10, 1999. Reisz was a young dancer on Broadway in the late 1930s. As the wife of Gene Kelly and a dancer in her own right who knew many other dancers and went to a variety of teachers, she was well equipped to comment on the dance training and practices of the time. Robbins also talks about this eclectic kind of American training in Tobias, "Bringing Back Robbins's *Fancy*," 71. Flash tap is also quoted in *Fancy Free*. Robbins gave Harold Lang an air turn ending in the splits, which was a specialty of such acts as the Nicholas Brothers and the Berry Brothers.

9. Harold Lang, quoted in Tobias, "Bringing Back Robbin's *Fancy*," 69. For an example, see the full-page photograph of three sailors on leave in *Newsweek*, April 2, 1945, 14.

10. Kelly, interview by Hunt.

11. However, examples of military dances abound in, for example, Hungary, Russia, and Eastern Europe. I would like to thank David Slade for pointing this out to me.

12. Prototypes for musical dancing sailors are given in Kirstein, *Movement and Metaphor*, though he omits John Durang.

13. *Anchors Aweigh* was made in 1944, and the stage musical *On the Town* opened on December 28 of that year. Based on *Fancy Free* and choreographed by Robbins, it also concerned sailor buddies on shore leave. It would be made into a movie by Kelly and Donen, discussed in chapter 10. Betty Comden and Adolph Green wrote the books and lyrics of both the stage and screen versions of *On the Town*.

14. Comden, in Dramatists' Guild, "Symposium on *On the Town*," 20.

15. Muriel Bentley, quoted in Tobias, "Bringing Back Robbins's *Fancy*," 72–73.

16. Robbins, "The Libretto for *Fancy Free*," 180.

17. Music by Jule Styne, lyrics by Sammy Cahn.

18. Jerome Robbins, interviewed in Tobias, "Bringing Back Robbins's *Fancy*," 69.

19. I am grateful to Hubert Cohen for information he provided me on this matter.

20. D'Emilio, *Sexual Politics, Sexual Communities*, chapter 2.

21. Deborah Jowitt, who has access to Robbins's letters, confirmed this in a personal communication.

22. Among the many examples of such images are those in *Life*, May 29, 1944, 22; August 28, 1944, 17; and December 6, 1943, 23; and in *Newsweek*, March 3, 1945, 31.

23. See, for example, images in *Newsweek*, February 19, 1945 (cover photograph), and March 3, 1945, 31; and photographs distributed to French, British, and American news services published in Boivin and Cobrion, *La manche libérée*. Other photographs of this type can be found in the archives of the Bibliothèque du Mémorial at the Caen-Normandy Memorial Centre for History and Peace.

24. See, for example, photographs in Boivin and Corbrion, *La manche libérée*, 76, 86, and 96.

25. Examples of non-musical movies in which this boy citizen-soldier appears include *The Human Comedy* (1943), *A Guy Named Joe* (1943), *See Here, Private Hargrove* (1944), *Since You Went Away* (1944), *Thirty Seconds over Tokyo* (1944), *The Clock* (1944), and *What Next, Corporal Hargrove* (1945).

26. We cannot be completely sure whether the invasion took place while the "Worry Song" section in *Anchors Aweigh* was being planned, while it was being filmed, or later. *Anchors Aweigh* was filmed in the middle of 1944. An educated guess is that the "Worry Song" was devised before the invasion, because dance sections—especially those as complex as this—were planned and choreographed long before a film went into production.

27. Stoppard, *Dirty Linen and New-Found Land*, 61. This is part of a monologue about America recited by Arthur (described as a very junior Home Office official), in *New-Found Land*.

28. One exception is Astaire's "By Myself" song in *The Band Wagon*, which is similar in tone but was not written for the film.

29. "Once I Had a Friend," music by André Previn, lyrics by Betty Comden and Adolph Green.

30. This chapter is based on my article "Freedom Incarnate," published in honor of Ivor Guest, which in turn was based in part on material from my "Film Musicals" and on research done subsequently during 1998–99 as an Honorary Senior Research Fellow at Roehampton Institute (University of Surrey) and at the Bibliothèque du Mémorial, Caen-Normandy Memorial Centre for History and Peace, where I was helped by the archivists Carole Lechartier and Franck Moulin. I would also like to thank Frederick Grossman for his invaluable research assistance and Deborah Jowitt and Ramsay Burt for reading and commenting on earlier versions of the article from which this chapter is drawn. Most important, I would like to thank those veterans of World War II, American, British, and French, who talked to me about their experiences and perceptions of American servicemen: Ivor Guest, David Newton, James Robertson, Robbins Burling, Joseph Genné, and others who wished to remain anonymous. Oja's more recent book *Bernstein Meets Broadway* also discusses *Fancy Free*.

CHAPTER 8

1. Rogers and Hammerstein, "I'm in Love with a Wonderful Guy," *South Pacific*.

2. See Genné, "Film Musicals," 234–62.

3. Quoted in Knox, *Magic Factory*, 109.

4. See Genné, "Film Musicals," 375.

5. In the tradition of Astaire, Kelly, and Balanchine, Robbins wanted very much to be in control of the filming and editing of his dance sequences, and originally he was hired to do just that. However, his perfectionist approach to the material and the length of time he took to set up the sequences and edit them was not supported by the changing film economy. Without the resources of the old studio system at hand and a producer like Arthur Freed to protect him, he was forced to leave after the filming of the opening sequence. There is some suggestion that he did direct the "Cool" sequence, but the rest of the film was directed by Robert Wise.

6. Music by Burton Lane, lyrics by Alan Jay Lerner. In this euphoria dance Astaire also uses a device he has used before: he sings and dances to a picture of his beloved, as he had to a picture of Eleanor Powell in *Broadway Melody of 1940* ("I've Got My Eyes on You").

7. Sondheim used this phrase during the course of a program on musical theater produced by the British Broadcasting Corporation and broadcast in London on May 20, 1980.

CHAPTER 9

1. This chapter expands and draws on material from earlier articles of mine, including "Vincente Minnelli and the Film Ballet."

2. Minnelli, interview by John Russell Taylor, July 20, 1980, National Film Theatre of the British Film Institute, London.

3. For a discussion of Astaire's first attempt at retirement as well as his account of his years at MGM, see Astaire, *Steps in Time*.

4. Croce, *The Fred Astaire and Ginger Rogers Book*, was the first to analyze these dances, and her analysis remains, to my mind, the best.

5. Nureyev, in Heeley, "Fred Astaire." It should be noted that Robert Alton has been credited with participating in the staging of this sequence, but his exact contribution is unknown. As this documentary demonstrates, Astaire often worked with other choreographers, but his was the dominant and controlling influence. In style, the sequence clearly belongs to Astaire.

6. Minnelli and Arce, *I Remember It Well*, 142–43, suggests the relationship to Griffith's *Broken Blossoms*. The song "Limehouse Blues" may have been chosen as the basis for an extended dance sequence because Astaire liked it so much. One of the main reasons he signed a contract with MGM to perform in the *Ziegfeld Follies*, he writes, was "to get an opportunity to put on some kind of number to Philip Braham's 'Limehouse Blues,' which had always been a favorite song of mine. When I told Arthur Freed the thought, he immediately approved and asked Vincente Minnelli . . . to get busy on a production idea" (*Steps in Time*, 264).

7. Astaire, *Steps in Time*, 264–65. Robert Alton helped with the choreography.

8. Pennell and Pennell, *The Life and Times of James McNeill Whistler*.

9. Minnelli and Arce, *I Remember It Well*, 50.

10. Ibid.

11. This same color is also seen in a number of the films Kelly and Donen made together.

12. Minnelli, in Minnelli and Arce, *I Remember It Well*, 143. The mezzotint was a method of engraving popular in the seventeenth, eighteenth, and early nineteenth centuries, especially in England.

13. Minnelli indicates these visual sources in ibid. It will be seen in the analysis that follows that the sets and costumes of the dream sequence are clearly derived from chinoiserie. The influence of "an old English mezzotint" is more difficult to establish. I have been unable to locate any English mezzotints of any period that correspond to the vision of Limehouse that Minnelli presents in this sequence. Minnelli suggests, however, that it may have been only the overall color scheme of the "Limehouse Blues" sequence that was meant to be evocative of the quality of the mezzotint medium: he "limited the colors of the costumes and set to black, brown, and shades of yellow, filled the stage with fog, and lit it with yellow light" (ibid.). Minnelli's description still does not correspond with what we see onscreen—the colors are more varied and high key than he suggests, although smoky yellows and browns are predominant in the sequence's first few minutes.

14. For examples of black-and-white films that illustrate this point, see *Dr. Jekyll and Mr. Hyde* (1941, directed by Victor Fleming, cinematography by Joseph Ruttenberg); *Gaslight* (1944, directed by George Cukor, cinematography by Joseph Ruttenberg), and *The Picture of Dorian Gray* (1944, directed by Albert Lewin, cinematography by Harry Stradling).

15. Minnelli and Arce, *I Remember It Well*, 143.

16. Ibid.

17. The singer distinctly resembles, in dress, makeup, and manner, this character as portrayed in Albert Lewin's film version of Oscar Wilde's *The Picture of Dorian Gray*. In the film, Dorian Gray first encounters Sibyl Vane singing in a pub in the Limehouse district of London.

18. The rise and proliferation of "dream ballet" sequences, as they were often called, in Broadway musicals has yet to be investigated, but this phenomenon can be traced in Bordman, *The American Musical Theater*, in which capsule summaries of all musicals produced on Broadway between 1866 and 1977 are given.

19. Like the "put on a show" sequences at the end of the 1930s "backstage" musicals, the dream sequence could be used as a catch-all for a wide variety of often disparate performances and special effects while retaining—in line with the ideals of the integrated musical—a coherent dramatic structure. Alfred Hitchcock's study of neurosis in *Spellbound* (1945, the same year as *Yolanda*), for example, incorporated a dream sequence designed by Dalí. In both the stage (1941) and film (1943) versions of the Kurt Weill–Ira Gershwin–Moss Hart musical *Lady in the Dark*, the dreams of a woman undergoing psychoanalysis are visually and musically "explicated" in a series of elaborate production numbers.

20. In *Carefree* (1938), as in *Lady in the Dark*, the heroine's dreams provide the occasion for a dance sequence in which she expresses her innermost feelings about her doctor. Although not specifically concerned with psychoanalysis, Laurey's dream sequence "Out of My Dreams" in *Oklahoma!* (1943), like that in *Yolanda*, uses the central female character's dream to present, in condensed and surrealistic form, her complex and conflicted feelings about a man with whom she is involved.

21. Minnelli and Arce, *I Remember It Well*, 51. For Minnelli, as for many, the discovery of Freudian thought and Surrealist art were linked events, part of the same general phenomenon. In Chicago, he wrote, "the world of art was already one step beyond, and even we in the provinces were taken up with the surreal. Freud was starting to penetrate the consciousness of the world. . . . Suddenly we were all interpreting dreams, and the talents of Duchamps, Ernst, and Dalí burst wide open."

22. A chronology (compiled by Irene Gordon) tracing important events in the introduction and dissemination of Surrealist art and thought in the United States can be found in Rubin, *Dada, Surrealism, and Their Heritage*, 197–216. Gordon lists this show, titled "Newer Super-Realism," which originated at the Wadsworth Athenaeum (Hartford, Connecticut) in November 1931 and then traveled to the Julien Levy Gallery in New York, where it could be seen between January 9 and 29, 1932, as the "first important Surrealist exhibition in the United States" (209).

23. Minnelli and Arce, *I Remember It Well*, 77. For a reproduction of the sketch, see Casper, *Vincente Minnelli and the Film Musical*, 17. The caption for this sketch (17), however, appears to have been mistakenly switched with the caption for a different picture (18). The sketch for what must surely be the ballet for "Words without Music" is captioned "A sketch for the 'Death in the Afternoon' Ballet, At Home Abroad." This sketch, however, fits Minnelli's description of the "Words without Music" ballet. On the next page (18) is what must surely be the right caption for the sketch on p. 17: *"One of the surrealistic designs, Ziegfeld Follies of 1936."* The

picture on p. 18 is right for the caption on p. 17; it is full of bull-fighting motifs that fit "Death in the Afternoon."

24. Minnelli's arcade relates, for example, to that found in the right foreground of de Chirico's *The Melancholy and Mystery of a Street* (1914; private collection; Arnason, *History of Modern Art*, plate 124). Minnelli's use of cast shadows in the sketch may also derive from this or similar sources. The disembodied head in Minnelli's sketch suggests that found in de Chirico's *The Song of Love* (1914; private collection). I do not mean to imply, however, that these are direct sources of Minnelli's work, because we do not know which of them the director saw before 1935.

25. See, for example, Salvador Dalí, *The Persistence of Memory* (1931; Museum of Modern Art). This was one of the works exhibited in the major Surrealist exhibition ("Fantastic Art, Dada, and Surrealism"), curated by Alfred Barr, held at the Museum of Modern Art from December 9, 1936, to January 17, 1937, and was illustrated in the catalog that accompanied the show (Barr, *Fantastic Art, Dada, and Surrealism*). It is probable that Minnelli saw this show, considering his interest in Surrealism and the fact that he says that he lived "next to the Museum of Modern Art" at this time (Minnelli and Arce, *I Remember It Well*, 70). For an example of a work of de Chirico that displays a space comparable to the one Minnelli offers, see de Chirico's *Mystery and Melancholy of a Street*. This painting appears in Barr's catalog as no. 194.

26. See, for example, Dalí's *Persistence of Memory* and Yves Tanguy's *A Large Painting Which Is a Landscape* (1927; Mr. and Mrs. William Mazer, New York) and *Indefinite Divisibility* (1942; Albright Knox Art Gallery). I have no proof that Minnelli knew of these particular paintings, but his involvement with Surrealist art makes it clear that he might have known these or similar ones.

27. René Magritte, *The Lovers* (1928; Richard Zeisler, New York), and Paul Delvaux, *Hands* (1941; Richard Zeisler, New York).

28. "I wanted to suggest South American Baroque without actual architectural forms, and used a series of rock formations in fantastic shapes. These were on rollers and would be grouped in different compositions for each shot." Minnelli and Arce, *I Remember It Well*, 156.

29. Minnelli, in ibid., 187.

30. Kelly, interview by Hunt.

31. Vincente Minnelli, interview by the author, London, July 22, 1980. That Minnelli's and Kelly's working relationship was important to Minnelli is indicated not only by these words, but by the manner in which he said them, which clearly conveyed his deep affection and re-spect for his colleague.

32. Minnelli and Arce, *I Remember It Well*, 184. Siegel, "*The Pirate*," traces the work's theatrical history to 1911, citing as its initial source *Der Seerauber* by the German playwright Ludwig Fulda. S. N. Behrman used Fulda's play, Siegel says, as the basis for a play, *The Pirate*, that he wrote for Alfred Lunt and Lynn Fontanne. Behrman's *The Pirate*, a nonmusical comedy, was produced by the Theatre Guild in 1943, and Arthur Freed probably bought the screen rights at that time. However, as Siegel points out, the script was completely rewritten for the film by screenwriters Francis Goodrich and Albert Hackett ("*The Pirate*," 23). As with every script written for him, Minnelli closely supervised and participated in the writing of *The Pirate*'s screenplay before production began and further altered it (probably working with Kelly) during the course of the filming. What emerged, then, was basically Minnelli's and Kelly's conception.

33. Kelly, interview by Hunt.

34. Minnelli and Arce, *I Remember It Well*, 114.

35. It is interesting to note that one of the first (and most famous in its time) color films was a swashbuckler, *The Black Pirate* (1926), produced by Douglas Fairbanks. Four of only eleven Technicolor cameras then in existence were employed on this film. The color process used in 1926, however, was a primitive version of that employed by Minnelli on *The Pirate*, and the range of colors it was able to reproduce was limited.

36. Originally created for Borodin's opera *Prince Igor*, these dances were performed separately by Diaghilev's Ballets Russes as a ballet.

37. Hirschhorn, *Gene Kelly*, 163. The device was nicknamed the "Ubangi" for the facial decoration of women from the French Congo who were exhibited in circus sideshows in the late nineteenth and early twentieth centuries with plates extending their lower lips. They were said to be of the "Ubangi" tribe, but in fact this name was not of a tribe but of a river in the northern Belgian Congo, taken arbitrarily from a map. Nickell, *Secrets of the Sideshows*, 189. (Facial decorations such as these are found in many parts of the world.)

38. Knox, *Magic Factory*, 44. Besides influencing American film ballets, the ballet section of *The Red Shoes* may, to some extent, have been influenced by American films—in particular by Minnelli's work on the films *Ziegfeld Follies* and *Yolanda and the Thief*, which started the tradition that climaxed in the "American in Paris" ballet. For a further discussion of the impact of *The Red Shoes* on American audiences, see also my *"The Red Shoes*," 11–12.

39. Freed, quoted in Fordin, *The World of Entertainment*, 262.

40. Knox, *Magic Factory*, 125.

41. Quoted in ibid., 140.

42. Ibid., 90.

43. Ibid., 88–89.

44. Freed, quoted in Knox, *Magic Factory*, 38.

45. See Minnelli's discussion of this subject in ibid., 162, and Strohm, *Gene Kelly*; and Preston Ames's description of Alton's work in Knox, *Magic Factory*, 162–63. For more on Alton, see his *Painting with Light*, where he describes his techniques of lighting. Alton apparently was willing, as Kelly puts it, to try anything. "We'd say, 'Can you do this?' He'd say, 'Yeah, that's easy, yeah.' And, for the first few days, we were sort of worried because we'd been used to a lot of cameramen saying 'You guys are nuts, you can't do that.' It seemed that about every picture we'd try something new and the person with whom we'd be working would say 'No, you can't do that' because they had never done it before."

46. Sharaff, quoted in Knox, *Magic Factory*, 142.

47. Ibid., 142 and 150.

48. Quoted in Hirschhorn, *Gene Kelly*, 201.

49. Sharaff has detailed some of the pictorial sources to which she referred for her costumes for certain sections of the ballet: "The Rousseau section I definitely based on *The Sleeping Gypsy*, and the Carnival came from his *Notre Dame*. With Renoir, I used his painting of the *Pont Neuf*. The Van Gogh section which was placed in the Place de l'Opéra found its style from the pattern of his *Cypresses* painted at Arles—all the yellows and sunflowers. There I tried to get the Van Gogh palette. With Toulouse-Lautrec, I used lucite figures of actual characters that he painted, like Chocolat at the Achilles Bar." (Sharaff, quoted in Knox, *Magic Factory*, 144)

In her autobiography Sharaff is more specific about the Rousseau section. She says that the striped costumes of Caron and the corps of dancers are taken from the striped robes of *The Sleeping Gypsy* (Museum of Modern Art) and goes on to cite other sources, saying that the second section "was set in a flower market with an atmosphere suggested by paintings of Manet. The stalls were filled with fresh flowers in the colors of his palette, and the costumes were based on figures in his paintings. The set was the simplest to design, for the flowers conveyed the idea sufficiently, although the brilliance of some of the California flowers had to be sprayed to soften the tone." (Sharaff, *Broadway and Hollywood*, 73)

Sharaff's remark that "the set was the simplest to design" indicates that she was involved with the design of the sets as well as costumes. Her involvement is also made clear by Kelly: "Sharaff, Minnelli, and I met for several days at Vincente's office to try to 'lay out' the theme of the ballet . . . . Two of the scenes of the ballet, the Dufy opening and the Van Gogh colors of the Paris Opera, were done completely by Irene Sharaff. I'm afraid Vincente and I just threw those at her and said 'flood us with costumes and we'll make it work.'" Kelly, quoted in Knox, *Magic Factory*, 142.

50. For Sharaff, "color, more than anything else, was the important factor" in evoking a painter's style (Sharaff, *Broadway and Hollywood*, 74). "Each one of the painters that I used had a palette that was very much his own . . . his own sense of color and his own sense of light. I love color and I understood color" (Sharaff, quoted in Knox, *Magic Factory*, 151). Preston Ames, MGM's art director, says that Sharaff gave him "a color key that was invaluable and that ran through the whole ballet" (Ames, quoted in Knox, *Magic Factory*, 152). Sharaff felt that, in the print of *An American in Paris* that she saw, the part that most successfully captured a painter's "palette" was the "Van Gogh" sequence: "For both the set and the costumes the colors of his . . . sunflower painting(s) were used, the background had a pale yellow moon and stars of a creamy white in an orange sky. When I eventually saw the movie some time after it had been released, the colors in this section in that particular print of the film turned out best of the entire ballet; the range and tones of yellow, orange, green, gray, and brown came out exactly." (Sharaff, *Broadway and Hollywood*, 73)

51. See chapter 4. Delameter, "A Critical and Historical Analysis," 186, also discusses the use of this contrast to symbolize the difference between two groups of people.

52. Kelly, quoted in Knox, *Magic Factory*, 142.

53. Ibid, 158. Kelly's inclusion of Rousseau among the French impressionists reflected a broad use of that label at the time, which included painters whom we now label post-impressionists and early twentieth-century artists (not only Rousseau, but also Van Gogh and Toulouse-Lautrec).

54. For another view on the meanings of the ballet in *An American in Paris* for Minnelli and the role of painting and the painter as he presents it, see Dalle Vacche, "A Painter in Hollywood."

55. *Broadway Melody of 1929* was followed by *Broadway Melody* movies of 1936, 1938, and 1940. The Freed-Brown song "Broadway Rhythm" was not used in *Broadway Melody of 1929* but was sung in the *Broadway Melody* films of 1936, 1938, and 1940, and the Berkeley backyard film musical *Babes in Arms* (1939). The major theme of all these films was that of the neophyte performer who struggles and eventually becomes successful in the musical theater in New York.

56. Betty Comden makes this clear: "We were very nervous about Fred's character because it was based in so many ways on his actual position in life" (quoted in Fordin, *The World of*

Entertainment, 400). For another interpretation of the subject of *The Band Wagon*, see Feuer, "The Self-Reflexive Musical."

57. The fictional scriptwriters are played by the real-life scriptwriters Betty Comden and Adolph Green, and Cordova is played by Jack Buchanan.

58. Kelly had, for example, found Leslie Caron (cast for the role of Lise in *An American In Paris*) performing with Roland Petit's company, Ballets des Champs Elysées. For Kelly and Caron's account of this, see Knox, *Magic Factory*, 6. Comden and Green indicate that the role of Cordova was modeled on certain "avant garde" directors who strove to give artistic stature to the musical, singling out José Ferrer as typical. Comden said: "It was also the period where there were people like José Ferrer, who put on four or five different kinds of shows at the same time. The idea came to us of an actor of the "old school" falling into the hands of a director of the avant garde who wants to overload or "overwork" a simple musical." (Hauduroy, "L'écriture musicale," 47)

The film's satire, Green notes, was on target, because "in the two years that followed *The Band Wagon* there were seven shows that used the theme of Faust in one way or another." Hauduroy, "L'écriture musicale," 47.

59. For a discussion of this new style, "modern jazz dance," see Hill, *Tap Dancing America*, chapter 2, especially 158–59.

CHAPTER 10

1. Panofsky, "Style and Medium in the Motion Picture."

2. Minnelli, interview by the author, July 22, 1980, London.

3. Kelly, quoted in Knox, *Magic Factory*, 41.

4. The music is by Leonard Bernstein and the lyrics by Betty Comden and Adolph Green. *On the Town*'s connections with *Fancy Free* are perhaps most evident in these opening moments. The mood of the three buddies exactly conforms to Robbins's description of his sailor heroes and their initial onstage activities in his scenario for *Fancy Free*: "Three sailors explode onto the stage. They are out on shore leave, looking for excitement, women, drink, any kind of fun they can stir up. Right now they are fresh, full of animal exuberance and boisterous spirits, searching for something to do. They walk down the street with typical sailor movements—the brassy walk, the inoffensive vulgarity, the quality of being all steamed up and ready to go. They boldly strut, swagger, and kid each other along. . . . One should feel immediately that the three are good friends, used to bumming around together, used to each other's guff . . . that they are in the habit of spending their time as a trio, and that, under all their rough and tumble exterior, there is a real affection for each other, a kind of 'my buddy' feeling." (Jerome Robbins, libretto for *Fancy Free*, in Amberg, *Ballet in America*; reprinted in Cohen, *Dance as a Theater Art*, 180)

5. Like St. Louis in *Meet Me in St. Louis* and later Paris in *An American in Paris* and *Gigi*, New York is a major character in *On the Town*. The sequence on top of Rockefeller Center in which Gabey, Ozzie, and Chip sing the city's praises is probably also an accurate visual and musical metaphor for the nation's feelings about New York in the postwar years. Oliver Smith, the set designer for the stage musical *On the Town*, made this clear during a symposium involving himself, Comden, Green, Robbins, and Bernstein. Smith here refers to the stage production, but his words apply equally well to the film and its makers: "One thing we all shared was the feeling of what the show was really about. . . . It was about the enormous love each of us felt

for New York City. It was a valentine to New York. We each adored New York in our own way, and that became a unifying theme" (Smith, quoted in Dramatists' Guild, "Symposium on *On the Town*," 20). Arlene Croce has described similar feelings and, interestingly, uses an image from *On the Town*: "New York had a tremendous glamour in the post-war years; I certainly felt it in *On the Town*, and every time the Twentieth Century Fox orchestra played 'Street Scene' behind a New York stock shot. . . . I would be paralyzed with desire" (Croce, *The Fred Astaire and Ginger Rogers Book*, 171).

6. Donen, interview by Hugh Fordin, tapes PAC 19:126–28, Hugh Fordin Collection, Special Collections (Cinema), Doheny Library, University of Southern California.

7. Kobal, *Gotta Sing, Gotta Dance*, 220. See also Genné, "Vincente Minnelli's Style." Feuer calls such songs "passed-along" (both in her dissertation, "The Hollywood Musical," 84, and in her book, *The Hollywood Musical*, 16). In the dissertation she defines it as "a device whereby a diegetically performed song is started by one person and then taken up and 'passed along' by others" (84). By "traveling song" I mean any song that travels by means of camerawork through space and/or time. Thus, I refer not only to songs passed along directly from one person to another (as in the opening of *Meet Me in St. Louis* and *Love Me Tonight*), but also those that, for example, are sung by the same person (or persons) in successive locations and time periods (as in the opening of *On the Town*, or Gaston's soliloquy in *Gigi*), or those played by orchestra alone to parallel series of images that are disparate in space and time (such as the painting sequence of *An American in Paris*). According to Feuer's dissertation (84), the passed-along song spreads "a sense of community given through entertainment."

8. Quoted in Hirschhorn, *Gene Kelly*, 269.

9. Minnelli, quoted in Kobal, *Gotta Sing, Gotta Dance*, 220.

10. Donen, interview by the author.

11. Exceptions include my dissertation, "The Film Musicals"; and Horowitz, *On My Way*.

12. The work of the orchestrator/arranger is described in Previn, *No Minor Chords*, and Chaplin, *The Golden Age of Movie Musicals and Me*. Both men were key orchestrators and arrangers, and eventually music directors, at MGM when the movies I'm discussing were made. See also my dissertation, "The Film Musicals," and Decker, *Music Makes Me*, which concentrates on Astaire's orchestrators.

13. Knox, *Magic Factory*, 93.

14. Salinger clearly deserves a book of his own. His background is briefly mentioned in Knox, *Magic Factory*, 91, and Fordin, *The World of Entertainment*. Suskin, *The Sound of Broadway Music*, has scattered references to him throughout the book but does not give him a section of his own as a Hollywood orchestrator. Fordin says that Salinger "had started his career on Broadway. Returning to New York after seven years in Paris, he met Adolph Deutsch, who at that time was musical director of Paramount-Publix Theaters. Deutsch engaged Salinger as his chief orchestrator. A short time later, Deutsch moved over to the legitimate theater and the two worked together on several Broadway shows. Salinger came to Hollywood in 1938 to work for Alfred Newman at Twentieth Century Fox. It was only a short stay, however, because his first impression of Hollywood was not a pleasant one. He returned to New York and the Broadway theater, but came back in 1939 when MGM offered him a long-term contract he could not resist. Roger Edens, who was well aware of Salinger's work and had met him in New York, saw to it that he immediately joined the Freed Unit." (Fordin, *The World of Entertainment*, 101–2)

15. André Previn, interview by Hugh Fordin, Hugh Fordin Collection, tape PAC 19: 83–84.

16. Alexander Courage, interview by the author, Los Angeles, August 20, 1981.

17. Quoted in Knox, *Magic Factory*, 91.

18. Chaplin, *The Golden Age of Movie Musicals*, 88. He repeated this sentiment later in Chaplin, interview by the author.

19. Chaplin, interview by the author. John Green, a member of the MGM music department, says that Salinger began working at Paramount Studios in 1929: "He was miles ahead of me in academic training. He had just come back from his years with André Gedalge in Paris; he's one of the few people who didn't study with Nadia Boulanger, but he studied with Gedalge, who was no slouch" (Knox, *Magic Factory*, 91). Fordin, on the other hand, asserts that Salinger did study with "Nadja" Boulanger "and had had some lessons with Ravel," but cites no sources for this information.

20. Wilder, *American Song*, xxxvi.

21. Chaplin, interview by the author.

22. Minnelli and Arce, *I Remember It Well*, 134.

23. For a definition of montage, see Bawden, *Oxford Companion to Film*, 477. The "conventional montage" I refer to is "designed to compress background information or provide atmosphere by combining a number of images in quick succession. Much used in Hollywood features until the early sixties . . . montages are characterized by newspaper headlines spiraling into view, falling calendar leaves, clock faces, train wheels, place names flashing by, and a profusion of 'wipes' and 'dissolves.'"

This type of montage appears frequently in musicals from the 1930s. A conventional montage sequence appears in the Berkeley and Kelly-Donen film *Take Me Out to the Ball Game*, and also in *On The Town*, when the sailors travel through a series of museums looking for Ivy.

24. Apel, *Harvard Dictionary of Music*, 315.

CHAPTER 11

1. Minnelli and Arce, *I Remember It Well*, 124.

2. For an account of Astaire's television work in relation to jazz, see Decker, *Music Makes Me*.

3. American Film Institute, *AFI Life Achievement Award: A Tribute to Fred Astaire* [television movie], April 18, 1981, http://www.imdb.com/title/tt0262744/, accessed March 27, 2017; American Film Institute, *AFI Life Achievement Award: A Tribute to Gene Kelly* [television special], May 7, 1985, http://www.imdb.com/title/tt0268602/, accessed March 27, 2017.

4. Betty Comden and Adolph Green, "How the Kids Made Movie Musical History," *Saturday Review*, April 22, 1972, 63.

5. Minnelli and Arce, *I Remember It Well*, 296.

References

BRITISH FILM INSTITUTE

Howard Gotlieb Collection, Howard Gotlieb Archival Research Center, Mugar Memorial Library, Boston University. This includes the Adele Astaire Collection Scrapbooks. A scrapbook for 1923–31 is in Box 7.

Jerome Robbins Dance Collection, New York Public Library for the Performing Arts.

Cinematic Arts Library, University of Southern California.

Margaret Herrick Library, Academy of Motion Picture Arts and Sciences.

Abbott, George. *Mr. Abbott*. New York: Random House, 1963.

Aloff, Mindy. *Hippo in a Tutu: Dancing in Disney Animation*. New York: Disney Editions, 2008.

Alton, John. *Painting with Light*. Berkeley and Los Angeles: University of California Press, 1995.

Altman, Rick. *The American Film Musical*. Bloomington: Indiana University Press, 1987.

Alvienne School of Dance Arts Bulletin. Jerome Robbins Dance Collection, New York Public Library for the Performing Arts, 1918.

Amberg, George. *Ballet in America*. New York: Duell, Sloan & Pearce, 1949.

Amboise, Jacques. *I Was a Dancer: A Memoir*. New York: Knopf, 2011.

Arbeau, Thoinot. *Orchesography*. First published 1589. Translated by Mary Stewart Evans. New York: Dover, 1967.

Apel, Willi, ed. *The Harvard Dictionary of Music*. Cambridge, MA: Harvard University Press, 1950.

Arnason, H. H. *History of Modern Art: Painting, Sculpture, Architecture*. Revised and enlarged ed. New York: Harry N. Abrams, 1977.

Arnheim, Rudolph. *Film als Kunst*. Berlin: Ernst Rowohlt Verlag, 1932.

Aschenbrunner, Joyce. *Katherine Dunham*. Urbana: University of Illinois Press, 2002.

Astaire, Ann. Diary, 1923–26. Howard Gotlieb Collection, Howard Gotlieb Archival Research Center, Mugar Memorial Library, Boston University.

Astaire, Fred. *Steps in Time*. London: Heinemann, 1959.

Baker, Jean-Claude, and Chris Chase. *Josephine: The Hungry Heart*. New York: Cooper, 2001.

Balanchine, George. "Dance Will Assert Its Importance." *Dance*, April 1939.

Balanchine, George. "Ballet in Films." *Dance News*, December 1944, 8.

Balanchine, George. *By George*. New York: San Carlo Press, 1984.

Bales, Melanie, and Karen Eliot. *Dance on Its Own Terms: Histories and Methodologies*. Oxford: Oxford University Press, 2013.

Banes, Sally. "Balanchine and Black Dance." *Choreography and Dance* 3, no. 3 (1993): 59–77.

Banes, Sally. *Dancing Women: Female Bodies on Stage*. London: Routledge, 1998.

Barr, Alfred H. *Fantastic Art, Dada, and Surrealism* [exhibition catalog]. New York: Museum of Modern Art, 1936.

Bawden, Liz-Anne, ed. *The Oxford Companion to Film*. New York: Oxford University Press, 1976.

Beaumont, Cyril W. *Complete Book of Ballets*. London: Putnum, 1937.

Beaumont, Cyril W. *The Diaghilev Ballet in London*. London: Black, 1951.

Beauvoir, Simone de. *The Prime of Life*. Translated by Peter Green. London: Andre Deutsch, 1962.

Beauvoir, Simone de. *La force des choses*. Paris: Gallimard, 1963.

Bennahum, Judith Chazin, ed. *The Living Dance: Anthology of Essays on Movement and Culture*. Dubuque, IA: Kendall Hunt, 2003.

Billman, Larry. *Fred Astaire: A Bio-Bibliography*. Westport, CT: Greenwood Press, 1997.

Boivin, Michel, and Vincent Corbrion. *La manche libérée*. Condé-sur-Vire: Corbrion, 1994.

Bordman, Gerald. *The American Musical Theater: A Chronicle*. New York: Oxford University Press, 1978.

Bordman, Gerald. *Jerome Kern: His Life and Music*. Oxford: Oxford University Press, 1980.

Bordwell, David, Janet Staiger, and Kristin Thompson. *The Classical Hollywood Cinema: Film Style and Mode of Production to 1960*. New York: Columbia University Press, 1985.

Brannigan, Erin. *Dancefilm: Choreography and the Moving Image*. New York: Oxford University Press, 2011.

Brooks, Virginia. "Dance and Film." *Ballett International* 2 (1993): 23–25.

Brown, William M., Lee Cronk, Keith Grochow, Amy Jacobson, C. Karen Liu, Zoran Popović, and Robert Trivers. "Dance Reveals Symmetry Especially in Young Men." *Nature* 438 (2005): 1148–50.

Buhler, James. *Hearing the Movies: Music and Sound in Film History*. 2nd ed. New York: Oxford University Press, 2016.

Buhler, James, Caryl Flinn, and David Neumeyer, eds. *Music and Cinema*. Hanover, NH: University Press of New England, 2000.

Burling, Robbins. *The Talking Ape*. Oxford: Oxford University Press, 2005.

Carmichael, Elizabeth, and Ivan Nabokov. "Balanchine: An Interview." *Horizon*, January 1961, 44–56.

Casper, Joseph Andrew. *Vincente Minnelli and the Film Musical*. New York: A. S. Barnes, 1977.

Casper, Joseph Andrew. *Stanley Donen*. Metuchen, NJ: Scarecrow Press, 1983.

Chaplin, Saul. *The Golden Age of Movie Musicals and Me*. Norman: University of Oklahoma Press, 1994.

Charness, Casey. "Hollywood Cine-Dance: A Description of the Interrelationship of Camera Work and Choreography in the Films of Stanley Donen and Gene Kelly." Ph.D. diss., New York University, 1977.

Clark, James. "Interview with Stanley Donen." *Films and Filming* 4 (July 1958): 7–32.

Clark, Katerina. *Petersburg: Crucible of Cultural Revolution*. Cambridge, MA: Harvard University Press, 1995.

Clover, Carol J. "Dancin' in the Rain." *Critical Inquiry* 21 (Summer 1995): 722–47.

Cohen, Sarah R. *Art, Dance, and the Body in French Culture of the Ancien Régime*. Cambridge: Cambridge University Press, 2000.

Cohen, Selma Jeanne, ed. *Dance as a Theatre Art: Source Readings in Dance History from 1581 to the Present*. New York: Harper & Row, 1974.

Cohen, Selma Jeanne, ed. *International Encyclopedia of Dance*. Oxford: Oxford University Press, 2000.

Colette, Sidonie-Gabrielle. *Gigi*. Lausanne: La Guilde du livre, 1944.

Comden, Betty, and Adolph Green. "How the Kids Made Movie Musical History." *Saturday Review*, April 22, 1972, 60–63.

Conrad, Christine. *Jerome Robbins: That Broadway Man, That Ballet Man*. London: Booth-Clibborn Editions, 2000.

Cooper, Betsy. "The Body Censored: Dance, Morality, and the Production Code During the Golden Age or the Film Musical." In Bales and Eliot, *Dance on Its Own Terms*, 97–126.

Crawford, Richard. *The American Musical Landscape*. Berkeley and Los Angeles: University of California Press, 1993.

Crawford, Richard. *America's Musical Life: A History*. 2nd ed. New York: W. W. Norton, 2013.

Crawford, Richard, and Larry Hamberlin. *An Introduction to America's Music*. 2nd ed. New York: W. W. Norton, 2013.

Croce, Arlene. *The Fred Astaire and Ginger Rogers Book*. New York: Outerbridge & Lazard, 1972.

Dalle Vacche, Angela. "A Painter in Hollywood: Vincente Minnelli's *An American in Paris*." *Cinema Journal* 32, no. 1 (1992): 63–83.

Danilova, Alexandra. *Choura: The Autobiography of Alexandra Danilova*. New York: Knopf, 1986.

Decker, Todd. *Music Makes Me: Fred Astaire and Jazz*. Berkeley and Los Angeles: University of California Press, 2011.

Delamater, Jerome. "A Critical and Historical Analysis of Dance as a Code in the Hollywood Musical." Ph.D. diss., Northwestern University, 1978.

Delamater, Jerome. *Dance in the Hollywood Musical*. Ann Arbor: UMI Research Press, 1983.

D'Emilio, John. *Sexual Politics, Sexual Communities: The Making of a Homosexual Minority in the United States, 1940–1970*. Chicago: University of Chicago Press, 1983.

Denby, Edwin. *Dance Writings*. New York: Knopf, 1986.

Dodds, Sherril. *Dance on Screen: Genres and Media from Hollywood to Experimental Art*, New York: Palgrave, 2001.

Donen, Stanley. Interview by Hugh Fordin. Tapes PAC 19:126–28. Hugh Fordin Collection, Special Collections (Cinema), Doheny Library, University of Southern California.

Dramatists' Guild. "Symposium on *On the Town*." *Dramatists' Guild Quarterly* (Summer 1981): 11–24.

Duberman, Martin. *The Worlds of Lincoln Kirstein*. New York: Knopf, 2007.

Duke, Vernon. "Gershwin, Schillinger, and Dukelsky: Some Reminiscences." *Musical Quarterly* 33, no. 1 (1947): 102–15.

Duke, Vernon. *Passport to Paris*. 1st ed. Boston: Little, Brown, 1955.

Dunning, Jennifer. *"But First a School": The First Fifty Years of the School of American Ballet*. New York: Viking, 1985.

Feuer, Jane. "The Hollywood Musical: The Aesthetics of Spectator Involvement in an Entertainment Form." Ph.D. diss., University of Iowa, 1978.

Feuer, Jane. "The Self-Reflexive Musical and the Myth of Entertainment." *Quarterly Review of Film Studies* 2, no. 3 (1977): 313–26.

Feuer, Jane. *The Hollywood Musical*. Bloomington: Indiana University Press, 1982.

Fisher, Helen. *Why We Love: The Nature and Chemistry of Romantic Love*. New York: Henry Holt, 2004.

Fordin, Hugh. *The World of Entertainment*. New York: Doubleday, 1975.

Franceschina, John Charles. *Hermes Pan: The Man Who Danced with Fred Astaire*. Oxford: Oxford University Press, 2012.

Gallafent, Edward. *Astaire and Rodgers*. New York: Columbia University Press, 2002.

García-Márquez, Vicente. *The Ballets Russes: Colonel de Basil's Ballets Russes de Monte Carlo, 1932–1952*. New York: Knopf, 1990.

Garofalo, Alessandra. *"Austerlitz Sounded Too Much Like a Battle": The Roots of Fred Astaire's Family in Europe*. Trento: Editrice UNI Service, 2009.

Gene Kelly: Anatomy of a Dancer. DVD, Warner Bros. Home Video, 2002.

Genné, Beth. "The Film Musicals of Vincente Minnelli and the Team of Gene Kelly and Stanley Donen, 1944–1958." Ph.D. diss., University of Michigan, 1984.

Genné, Beth. "*The Red Shoes*: Choices between Life and Art." *Thousand Eyes Magazine* 7, February 1976, 11–12.

Genné, Beth. "Vincente Minnelli's Style in Microcosm: The Establishing Sequence of *Meet Me in St. Louis*." *Art Journal* 43, no. 3 (1983): 247–54.

Genné, Beth. "'Freedom Incarnate': Jerome Robbins, Gene Kelly and the Dancing Sailor as an Icon of American Values in World War II." *Dance Chronicle* 24, no. 1 (2001): 83–103.

Genné, Beth. "Creating a Canon, Creating the 'Classics' in Twentieth-Century British Ballet." *Dance Research* 18, no. 2 (2000): 132–62.

Genné, Beth. "Dancin' in the Rain: Gene Kelly's Musical Films." In *Envisioning Dance on Film and Video.*, Edited by Judy Mitoma, 71–77. London and New York: Routledge, 2002.

Genné, Beth. "Dance in Film." In *The Living Dance: An Anthology of Essays on Movement and Culture*, edited by Judith Chazin-Bennahum and Ninotchka Bennahum. Dubuque, IA: Kendall Hunt, 2003.

Genné, Beth. "Glorifying the American Woman: Josephine Baker and George Balanchine." *Discourses in Dance* 3, no. 1 (2005): 31–57.

Genné, Beth. "Vincente Minnelli and the Film Ballet." In *Vincente Minnelli: The Art of Entertainment*. Edited by Joe McElhaney, 229–51. Detroit: Wayne State University Press, 2009.

Gershwin, George. *George Gershwin's Song Book*. New York: New World Music, 1932.

Goldberg, Isaac. *George Gershwin: A Study in American Music*. New York: Frederick Ungar, 1931.

Goldberg, Isaac. "The Astaires: Early, Late and All the Way in Between." *Boston Evening Transcript*, January 23, 1932.

Gottschild, Brenda Dixon. *The Black Dancing Body: A Geography from Coon to Cool*. New York: Palgrave Macmillan, 2003.

Gottschild, Brenda Dixon. *Digging the Africanist Presence in American Performance: Dance and Other Contexts*. Westport, CT: Greenwood Press, 1996.

Grein, J. T. "Criticisms in Cameo: 'Stop Flirting' at the Shaftesbury." London newspaper, 1923. Adele Astaire Scrapbooks, 1923–31, Box 7. Howard Gotlieb Collection, Howard Gotlieb Archival Research Center, Mugar Memorial Library, Boston University.

Guest, Ann Hutchinson. *Dance Notation: The Process of Recording Movement on Paper*. London: Dance Books, 1984.

Guest, Ivor. *Adeline Genée: A Lifetime of Ballet under Six Reigns: Based on the Personal Reminiscences of Dame Adeline Genée-Isitt, D.B.E.* London: A. & C. Black, 1958.

Guest, Ivor. *Ballet in Leicester Square: The Alhambra and the Empire, 1860–1915.* London: Dance Books, 1992.

Harmetz, Aljean. *The Making of "The Wizard of Oz."* New York: Knopf, 1977.

Hauduroy, Jean-François. "L'écriture musicale: Entretien avec Betty Comden et Adolph Green." *Cahiers du cinéma* 174 (January 1966): 43–50.

Henrich, Joseph, and Francisco Gil-White. "The Evolution of Prestige: Freely Conferred Status as a Mechanism for Enhancing the Benefits of Cultural Transmission." *Evolution and Human Behavior* 22, no. 3 (2001): 1–32.

Herskovits, Melville J. *The Myth of the Negro Past.* With a new introduction by Sidney W. Mintz. 2nd ed. Boston: Beacon Books, 1990.

Hill, Constance Valis. *Brotherhood in Rhythm: The Jazz Tap Dancing of the Nicholas Brothers.* New York: Oxford University Press, 2000.

Hill, Constance Valis. *Tap Dancing America: A Cultural History.* Oxford and New York: Oxford University Press, 2010.

Hill, Constance Valis. "*Cabin in the Sky*: Dunham's and Balanchine's Ballet (Afro) Americana." *Discourses in Dance* 3, no. 1 (2005): 59–71.

Hillier, Jim. "Interview with Stanley Donen." *Movie* 24 (Spring 1977): 26–35.

Hirschhorn, Clive. *Gene Kelly: A Biography.* Chicago: Regnery, 1975.

"'Hi Yaller' Girls No Longer Wanted." *Variety*, January 19, 1927.

Horowitz, Joseph. *Artists in Exile: How Refugees from Twentieth-Century War and Revolution Transformed the American Performing Arts.* New York: Harper, 2008.

Horowitz, Joseph. *On My Way: The Untold Story of Rouben Mamoulian, George Gershwin, and "Porgy and Bess."* New York: Norton, 2013.

Hungerford, Mary Jane. *Dancing in Commercial Motion Pictures.* New York: Columbia University Press, 1946.

Isaacs, Edith. "Spring Dances In: On Your Toes and the Ziegfeld Follies of 1936." *Theatre Arts Monthly* (June 1936): 413–417.

Jablonski, Edward, and Lawrence Stewart. *The Gershwin Years.* New York: Doubleday, 1973.

Joe, Jeongwon, and Sander Gilman, eds. *Wagner and Cinema.* Bloomington: Indiana University Press, 2010.

Johnson, Albert. "The Tenth Muse in San Francisco." *Sight and Sound* 26 (Summer 1956): 49–60.

Jordan, Stephanie. *Moving Music: Dialogues with Music in Twentieth-Century Ballet.* London: Dance Books, 2000.

Joseph, Charles M. *Stravinsky and Balanchine: A Journey of Invention.* New Haven, CT: Yale University Press, 2011.

Jowitt, Deborah. *Jerome Robbins: His Life, His Theater, His Dance.* New York: Simon & Schuster, 2004.

Kalinak, Kathryn. *Settling the Score: Music and the Classical Hollywood Film.* Madison: University of Wisconsin Press, 1992.

Kendall, Elizabeth. *Balanchine and the Lost Muse: Revolution and the Making of a Choreographer.* Oxford: Oxford University Press, 2013.

Kendall, Gustavia Yvonne. "*Le gratie d'amore*, 1602, by Cesare Negri: Translation and Commentary." D.M.A. thesis, Stanford University, 1985.

Kernfeld, Barry Dean. *New Grove Dictionary of Jazz.* New York: Macmillan, 2001.

Kimball, Robert, ed. *The Complete Lyrics of Ira Gershwin.* New York: Knopf, 1993.

Kirstein, Lincoln. *Movement and Metaphor: Four Centuries of Ballet*. New York: Praeger, 1970.

Knox, Donald. *The Magic Factory: How MGM Made "An American in Paris."* New York: Praeger, 1973.

Kobal, John. *Gotta Sing, Gotta Dance: A Pictorial History of Film Musicals*. London: Hamlyn, 1972.

Koskoff, Ellen. *A Feminist Epistemology: Writings on Music and Gender*. Champaign: University of Illinois Press, 2014.

Kraut, Anthea. *Choreographing Copyright: Race, Gender, and Intellectual Property Rights in American Dance*. New York: Oxford University Press, 2016.

Kristeller, Paul Oskar. "The Modern System of the Arts: A Study in the History of Aesthetics." In *Renaissance Thought and the Arts: Collected Essays by Paul Oskar Kristeller*, 163–227. Princeton, NJ: Princeton University Press, 1990.

Lerner, Alan Jay. *The Musical Theater: A Celebration*. London: Collins, 1986.

Levine, Lawrence, *Highbrow/Lowbrow: The Emergence of Cultural Hierarchy in America*. Cambridge, MA: Harvard University Press, 1988.

Levine, Lawrence. *The Opening of the American Mind: Canons, Culture, and History*. Boston: Beacon Press, 1996.

Lovelace, Maud Hart. *Betsy's Wedding*. New York: Thomas Y. Crowell, 1955.

Malcolm, Norman. *Ludwig Wittgenstein: A Memoir*. Oxford: Oxford University Press, 1958.

Martin, Susan F., *A Nation of Immigrants*. Cambridge: Cambridge University Press, 2011.

Mason, Francis, ed. *I Remember Balanchine*. New York: Doubleday, 1991.

Miller, Geoffrey. *The Mating Mind: How Sexual Choice Shaped the Evolution of Human Nature*. New York: Doubleday, 2000.

Minnelli, Vincente, with Hector Arce. *I Remember It Well*. New York: Doubleday, 1974.

Mueller, John. *Astaire Dancing: The Musical Films*. New York: Knopf, 1985.

Neumeyer, David. *Meaning and Interpretation of Music in Cinema*. Bloomington: Indiana University Press, 2015.

Nickell, Joe. *Secrets of the Sideshows*. Lexington: University Press of Kentucky, 2005.

O'Connor, Patrick, and Hammond, Bryan. *Josephine Baker: Compilation by Bryan Hammond Based on His Personal Collection; Theatrical Biography by Patrick O'Connor*. London: Cape, 1988.

Oja, Carol. *Bernstein Meets Broadway: Collaborative Art in a Time of War*. New York: Oxford University Press, 2014.

Panofsky, Erwin. "Style and Medium in the Motion Picture." In *Film Theory and Criticism*. Edited by Gerald Mast, 234–63. New York: Oxford University Press, 1974.

Pennell, Joseph, and Elizabeth R. Pennell. *The Life and Times of James McNeill Whistler*. 5th ed. Philadelphia: Lippincott, 1911.

Pollack, Howard. *George Gershwin: His Life and Work*. Berkeley and Los Angeles: University of California Press, 2007.

Previn, André. *No Minor Chords: My Days in Hollywood*. New York: Doubleday, 1991.

Pritchard, Jane. "Dancing at the Alhambra and Empire: Dance and Dancers in the Victorian and Edwardian Music Hall Ballet." *Dance Chronicle* 30, no. 1 (2007): 107–15.

Reynolds, Nancy. *Repertory in Review: Forty Years of the New York City Ballet*. New York: Dial, 1977.

Reynolds, Nancy. "Listening to Balanchine." In *Dance for a City : Fifty Years of the New York City Ballet*. Edited by Lynn Garafola with Eric Foner, 153–68. New York: Columbia University Press, 1999.

"Rhythm in Modern Musical Comedy." *London Morning Post*, November 12, 1928.

Ries, Frank W. D. "Sammy Lee: The Broadway Career." *Dance Chronicle* 9, no. 1 (1985): 1–95.

Riley, Kathleen. *The Astaires: Fred and Adele*. New York: Oxford University Press, 2012.

Riley, Kathleen. "A Pylades for the Twentieth Century: Fred Astaire and the Aesthetic of Bodily Eloquence." In *The Ancient Dancer in the Modern World: Responses to Greek and Roman Dance.* Edited by Fiona Macintosh, 99–119. Oxford: Oxford University Press, 2010.

Rodgers, Richard. *Musical Stages.* New York: Random House, 1975.

Rosenberg, Douglas. *Screendance: Inscribing the Ephemeral Image.* Oxford: Oxford University Press, 2012.

Rosenwaike, Ira. *Population History of New York City.* Syracuse, NY: Syracuse University Press, 1972.

Rubin, William. *Dada, Surrealism, and Their Heritage.* New York: Museum of Modern Art, 1968.

Russell, Frederick. "He Brought Ballet to Broadway." *American Dancer,* April 1939.

Saroyan, William. *The Time of Your Life.* New York: Harcourt, Brace, 1940.

Schorer, Suki, with Russell Lee. *Suki Schorer on Balanchine Technique.* Gainesville: University Press of Florida, 1999.

Schwartz-Bishir, Rebecca. "Musical Expression in the Bournonville-Løvenskjold *La sylphide* Variation." In Bales and Eliot, *Dance on Its Own Terms,* 341–62.

Scorsese, Martin. "The Persisting Vision: Reading the Language of Cinema." *New York Review of Books,* August 15, 2013, 25–27.

Seibert, Brian. *What the Eye Hears: A History of Tap Dancing.* New York: Farrar, Straus & Giroux, 2015.

Sharaff, Irene. *Broadway and Hollywood: Costumes Designed by Irene Sharaff.* New York: Van Nostrand Reinhold, 1976.

Siegel, Joel. "The Pirate." *Film Heritage* 7, no. 1 (1971): 21–30.

Silverman, Stephen M. *Dancing on the Ceiling: Stanley Donen and His Movies.* New York: Knopf, 1996.

Smith, Marian. *Ballet and Opera in the Age of "Giselle."* Princeton, NJ: Princeton University Press, 2010.

Sondheim, Stephen. *Look, I Made a Hat: Collected Lyrics (1981–2011) with Attendant Comments, Amplifications, Dogmas, Harangues, Digressions, Anecdotes and Miscellany.* New York: Knopf, 2011.

Sondheim, Stephen. "The Musical Theater." *Dramatists Guild Quarterly* 15, no. 3 (Autumn 1978): 6–29.

Souritz, Elizabeth. *Soviet Choreographers in the 1920s.* Translated by Lynn Visson. Edited, with additional translation, by Sally Banes. Durham, NC: Duke University Press, 1990.

Stearns, Jean, and Marshall Stearns. *Jazz Dance.* New York: Macmillan, 1968.

Stoppard, Tom. *Dirty Linen and New-Found-Land.* London: Faber & Faber, 1976.

Straytner, Barbara. *Ned Wayburn and the Dance Routine: From Vaudeville to the Ziegfeld Follies.* Society of Dance History Scholars Studies in Dance History 13. Madison, WI: A-R Editions, 1996.

Suskin, Steve. *The Sound of Broadway Music.* Oxford: Oxford University Press, 2009.

Sutton, Julia, introducer and reconstructer. "Il ballarino (The Dancing Master)." In *The Art of Renaissance Dance.* Dance Horizons Video. Princeton, NJ: Princeton Book Company, 1990.

Tallchief, Maria, and Larry Kaplan. *Maria Tallchief: America's Prima Ballerina.* New York: Henry Holt, 1997.

Taper, Bernard. *Balanchine: A Biography.* New York: Macmillan, 1960.

Tavernier, Bernard, and Daniel Palas. "Entretien avec Stanley Donen." *Cahiers du cinéma* 143 (May 1963): 1–18.

Taylor, Deems. *"An American in Paris"*: A Narrative Guide. 1928. Reprinted in Wyatt and Johnson, *The George Gershwin Reader*.

Taylor, Denise Pilmer. *"La musique pour tout le monde*: Jean Wiéner and French Jazz between the Wars." Ph.D. diss., University of Michigan, 1998.

Tennov, Dorothy. *Love and Limerence: The Experience of Being in Love.* New York: Scarborough House, 1979.

Thomas, Tony. *Films of Gene Kelly: Song and Dance Man.* New York: Citadel Press, 1977.

Thompson, Robert Farris. *Flash of the Spirit: African and Afro-American Art and Philosophy.* New York: Random House, 1983.

Tobias, Tobi. "Bringing Back Robbins's *Fancy." Dance Magazine* 54, no. 1 (January 1980): 60–77.

Vaill, Amanda. *Somewhere : The Life of Jerome Robbins.* New York : Broadway Books, 2006.

Volta, Ornella. *Satie et la danse.* Paris: Éditions Plume, 1992.

Wayburn, Ned. *The Art of Stage Dancing.* New York: Belvedere, 1925.

Weber, Katherine. *The Memory of All That: George Gershwin, Kay Swift, and My Family's Legacy of Infidelities.* New York: Crown, 2011.

Wilder, Alec. *American Popular Song: The Great Innovators, 1900–1950.* New York: Oxford University Press, 1972.

Woollcott, Alexander. Review of *Funny Face. New York World*, November 23, 1927.

Wyatt, Robert, and John Andrew Johnson, *The George Gershwin Reader*. New York: Oxford University Press, 2004.

Zangwill, Israel. *The Melting Pot: Drama in Four Acts.* New York: Macmillan, 1909.

Zeller, Jessica. "Luigi Albertieri: Bringing Italian Traditions to American Ballet." *Dance Chronicle* 8, no. 1 (2015): 55–80.

Zeller, Jessica. *Shapes of American Ballet: Teachers and Training before Balanchine.* New York: Oxford University Press, 2016.

Zorina, Vera. *Zorina.* New York: Farrar, Straus & Giroux, 1986.

Index

Page numbers followed by *f* indicate figures. Numbers followed by n indicate notes.

Aaronson, Boris, 112–13
Abbott, George, 124, 257, 285
Abie's Irish Rose, 20
Académie Royale de la Danse, 147–48
Academy ratio, 138
acrobatics, 42–43
adagio dancing, 98
Adam, Adolphe, 80, 154
Adams, Diana, 120, 301n84
Adelphi Theater, 295n7
Adler, Richard, 285
Aeolian Hall, 24, 72
African Americans, 2, 5–6, 18, 18*f*, 27, 38, 113, 291n30
Africanism, 9, 18, 109, 297n27
Afro-Caribbean dance, 112
Afternoon of a Faun, 117
Agon, 33, 108, 110–11, 285, 301n84, 304n32
Alajalov, Constantin, 298n50
Albert, Eddie, 102–3
Albertieri, Luigi, 44–45, 118, 294n19
Alex, Joe, 68
"Alexander's Ragtime Band," 273

Alhambra (London, England), 42
Allegro Brillante, 108, 109*f*, 110, 284
Allen, Gracie, 308n35
Allen, Woody, 163
Alma Mater, 66, 74, 279, 295n7, 298n47
"Almost like Being in Love," 186
Alright, 259
"Alter Ego" dance, 4, 134–40, 136*f*, 189, 259, 306n25, 307n28, 307n32, 308nn47–48, 309n50
Alton, John, 217
Alton, Robert, 76–77, 123, 299n61, 301n82, 314n5, 317n45
Altrock, Nick, 261
Alvienne, Claude, 20, 44, 272, 290n19, 294n18, 294nn20–21
Alvin Theatre (New York, NY), 75, 276
Americana, 113
American Ballet (company), 67, 115, 279, 295n7
American Ballet Theatre, 52*f*, 115, 169, 176, 211–12, 266, 280, 312n5
American Cinematographer, 104

American Document, 169–70
An American in Paris (Gershwin tone poem),
  56, 90–91
  opening, 56, 78
  score marked by Balanchine, 91–95,
    92f–94f, 241
An American in Paris (film), 6–7, 120–26,
  197, 276, 297n24, 307nn30–31, 308n35,
  318n50, 319n58, 320n7
  "By Strauss," 260–61
  "Cohan walk," 116
  dance sequences, 126, 173f, 175–76, 179
  dream sequence, 4–5, 202
  finale, 248
  "How Long Has This Been Going On," 238
  "I Got Rhythm," 120, 173f, 260–61
  "I've Got a Crush on You," 191
  opening, 122, 238
  "Our Love Is Here to Stay," 157, 245–46
  painting sequence, 243–46, 244f–45f
  "'S Wonderful," 4–5, 179–92, 182f
  tableaux vivants, 204
  timeline, 283
  "Tra-la-la-la," 191, 245–46
"An American in Paris" (film ballet), 91, 116,
  204, 212–20, 241, 248, 258
Americanization, 290n18
Ames, Preston, 157, 216, 317n45, 318n50
Anchors Aweigh, 5, 140, 170–75, 173f, 282,
  307n35, 312n13, 313n26
  "La Cumparsita," 158, 159f–60f
  Olvera Street dance, 173f, 175
  "Worry Song," 173f, 176, 313n26
Anderson, John Murray, 80–81, 122, 298n48
Andrews, Julie, 186
animal dances, 38–40, 39f
Antheil, George, 297n35
Apache Dance, 293n6
Apollo, 68, 118, 276, 297n27
Appalachians, 27
Appalachian Spring, 59, 122, 282
Apple Blossoms, 36, 274
"Araby" (Gershwin), 72
Arbeau, Thoinot, 310n4
Arden, Eve, 298n48
Ardolino, Emile, 265
Arlen, Harold, 104, 281
Armstrong, Louis, 28, 292n48

Arnheim, Rudolph, 288n10
arrangers, 7, 127, 185–86, 238–41, 320n12
art, 8, 288n9
art deco, 47–48, 47f
Arthur, Jean, 151
"Ascot Gavotte," 215
Ashton, Frederick, 262, 266, 272
aspect ratio, 138, 309n52
Astaire, Adele, 25, 29, 36, 51, 53, 293n8, 294n22
  connections with British aristocracy,
    310n60
  dance studies and training, 17, 20, 28,
    44–45, 48–49
  dance style, 15–17
  defense of the Charleston, 40–41
  timeline, 272–77, 289n10
  vaudeville circuit, 20–21, 42–43, 294n18
Astaire, Fred, 1, 64–66, 295n4, 308n35, 311n17,
  314nn5–6. see also specific productions
  ballroom-dance schools, 41
  The Band Wagon satire of the film ballet,
    99f, 222–26, 224f
  birth, 289n10
  "Bojangles" dance sequence, 137
  camera positioning, 138–39
  choreography, 3–5, 203
  collaborations, 70, 80, 190
  connections with British aristocracy,
    310n60
  courtship dances, 147–53, 157–65, 163f,
    310n1
  dance studies and training, 17, 20, 28,
    44–45, 48–49
  dance style, 2–9, 15–33, 30f, 32f, 35–61, 37f,
    39f, 49f, 52f, 58f, 60f, 70, 99, 133, 143–44,
    192–226, 259–60, 264–65, 289n3, 295n39,
    309n49
  dream dance sequences, 202, 295n9
  Donen and, 7, 159–60
  early career, 42–43, 288n1
  euphoria dances, 188–89
  favorite partner, 42, 294n15, 294n17
  film debut, 26
  film musicals, 89, 229, 248
  "Fred Astaire step" or "pose," 108, 109f
  Gershwin and, 29–30
  golf dance, 157–58, 159f
  "I Can't Be Bothered Now" dance, 131, 131f

influence and legacy, 131, 255–69
influence on Balanchine, 63, 107–11, 109f, 295n1
influence on Donen, 124
influence on Gershwin, 131
influence on Kelly, 124
inspirations, 153–54
"Isn't It a Lovely Day" dance, 30f, 31, 149–50, 150f
Jewish background, 291nn24–25
last Broadway effort, 16
"Let's Kiss and Make Up" dance, 159–60, 162f
"Limehouse Blues" dance, 197–201, 198f
Minnelli and, 6–7, 99f, 192, 194–96, 222–26, 224f
musical competitors, 292n2
"Night and Day" dance, 144–47, 146f
off-balance dancing, 54–59, 55f, 57f, 58f
props, 133
retirement, 314n3
rhythm dances, 26–28
seduction dances, 143–44
Silk Stockings dances, 162–63, 163f
single-take system, 309n53
street dances, 133–34, 188
television work, 321n2
"Things Are Looking Up" dance, 131, 132f
"This Heart of Mine" dance, 195–96
timeline, 271–85
vaudeville circuit, 20–21, 42–43, 294n18
"Wedding Cake Walk," 272
whole-body dancing, 45–48, 46f–47f
Yolanda and the Thief dance, 201–4
Astaire dolly, 309n53
"Astaire" pose, 108, 109f
As Thousands Cheer, 171
At Home Abroad, 76
Atkinson, Brooks, 81
Atteridge, Harold, 274
Atys, 201
aural literacy, 10
Auric, Georges, 117, 171, 276
Austerlitz, Battle of, 291n25
Austerlitz, Frederic ("Fritz"), 21
Austin, William, 291n37
Autumn Bacchanal, 53
avant-garde, 262, 268
Avatar, 266

"The Babbitt and the Bromide," 31
Babes in Arms, 74, 84, 121, 279, 318n55
"Baby, You Knock Me Out," 261
"Bacchanal Rag," 53
Bach. J. S., 63
backstage musicals, 143, 315n19
Bad, 258
Badham, John, 265
Baker, Jean-Claude, 301nn81–82
Baker, Josephine, 8, 28, 40, 68, 69f, 74–82, 79f, 109, 298n48, 299nn58–59, 300nn78–79, 301n82, 301n87
timeline, 272, 275–76, 278–79
Le bal, 105
Balanchine, George (Georgi Balanchivadze), 1–2, 6–7, 33, 42, 47, 53, 63–87, 211, 240, 260, 266, 293n2, 299n65, 302n91, 304n22, 312n3
Astaire and, 190
Astaire's influence on, 63, 107–11, 109f, 295n1
on ballet in films, 96
Baker and, 40, 68, 82–84, 300n79
Berkeley and, 96–97, 102–03
black dance and 9, 66–69, 76, 109, 111–13
on Broadway, 63–87, 111–113, 123
camera work, 180
choreography, 3–5, 77, 82–87, 91, 95–99, 98f, 99f, 102–9, 109f, 123, 167–70, 191–92, 256–57. *see also specific works*
cinematography, 102–3
dance studies and training, 86
dance style, 8–9, 69f, 296n9, 302n93
as director-choreographer, 3–4, 96–97, 102–4. *see also specific works*
Duke and, 70–74, 80, 111–13, 167–68, 202, 300n73
Dunham and, 112–13
Gershwins and, 63, 90–91, 302–3n6
Geva and, 70, 86, 301n88, 302n92
Goldwin and 91, 97, 101, 104–05, 107, 303n18
in Hollywood, 89–113
jazz experiences, 63–64, 297n27
Kelly and, 120
legacy or influence, 255–69
love for *Star Wars,* 107, 304n23
love of popular songs, 74–5, 298n51

Balanchine, George (Georgi
    Balanchivadze) (*cont.*)
    Minnelli and, 193, 202
    music studies, 297n26
    on musical comedy, 65
    Polito and, 102–03, 121, 220, 225
    piano score for *An American in Paris*, 91–95,
        92f–94f
    Robbins and, 190
    Rodgers and Hart and, 63, 66, 74–75, 84, 89,
        121, 117, 193, 222, 275, 295n7
    as silent-film accompanist, 95
    Stravinsky and, 300n73
    on tap dance, 65
    technical innovation, 106–7
    as "Tiflis pixie," 98
    timeline, 271–85, 297n25
    Toland and, 91, 96–98, 106, 256–7
    Zorina and, 104–7
Bales, Melanie, 9
ballerina strikes, 299n62
ballet, 9, 64–65, 193, 265–66. *see also specific*
    performances
    American style or Americanized, 44,
        304n36
    Astaire's roots, 35–61, 55f
    British invasion, 211–13
    on Broadway, 74–84
    "ciné ballet," 193
    cinematic, 95–99
    dream sequences, 52, 78–80, 79f, 201–4,
        203f, 315n18
    jazz, 4–5, 86, 89–113
Ballet Caravan, 312n5
Ballet comique de la reine (de Beaujoyeulx), 147
ballet d'action, 6–7, 48–51, 86–87, 91, 119, 193,
        201–2
Ballet de Nice, 305n13
Ballets des Champs Elysées, 319n58
Ballet Russe de Monte Carlo, 67, 117, 121,
        273–75, 279, 296n12, 302n91
Ballets Russes (Diaghilev), 44, 51–53, 73–74,
        317n36
Ballet Society, 282
Ballet Theatre (later American Ballet Theatre),
        115, 211–12, 280
Ballets Suédois, 70
ballroom dance, 35–61, 120, 266

The Band Wagon (Broadway), 48, 66, 74, 277
    "The Beggar and the Ballerina," 52, 52f
The Band Wagon (film), 3, 6–7, 99f, 194, 219,
        222–26, 318–19n56, 319n58
    "By Myself," 313n28
    central plot, 143
    "Damnation Scene" ballet, 223, 224f
    "Dancing in the Dark," 1, 60f, 189
    Dream Ballet, 295n9
    "The Girl Hunt Ballet," 48, 106, 223–25,
        224f, 248
    musical montages, 243, 247
    "That's Entertainment," 248
    timeline, 277, 284
Banes, Sally, 9
Baral, Robert, 83
Barber, Samuel, 59
The Barkleys of Broadway, 48, 58, 248, 283, 310n1
Baronova, Irina, 85
Barr, Alfred, 316n25
Barrymore Theatre (New York City,
        New York), 277
Baryshnikov, Mikhail, 262, 266
baseball, 261
"Baseball Act," 273
Bausch, Pina, 261, 266
BBC, 74
Beals, Jennifer, 265
beating, 53
Beat It, 258
Beatles, 263
Beaton, Cecil, 215
Beat the Band, 124
Beaumont, Cyril, 68, 119
"Beauty," 202–4
bebop, 22, 225
Beck, Hans, 49f
Bee Gees, 265
"Begin the Beguine," 36, 248
Behrman, S. N., 316n32
Belcher, Ernest, 106
Bel Geddes, Norman, 301n88
The Belle of New York, 31, 33, 188, 284
Bells Are Ringing, 256, 285
Bender, "Doc," 74
Bennett, Robert Russell, 293n3
Bentley, Muriel, 168f, 170, 172
Berg, Alban, 59

Berkeley, Busby, 4, 97, 102–3, 123, 194, 229, 257, 261–62
  finales, 247–48
  timeline, 271, 278, 281
Berlin, Irving, 5, 21, 165, 271, 273, 279–80, 283
  songs, 30, 153, 273. *see also specific works*
Bernstein, Leonard, 169, 186, 248–49, 282, 285, 319n4
Berry Brothers, 312n8
Bessy, Claude, 120
Best Foot Forward, 122, 124–25, 281
"Bewitched, Bothered and Bewildered," 180
bharata natyam, 225
big apple, 41
The Big Chill, 263
The Big Waltz, 293n2
Billie Jean, 258
Billman, Larry, 123
Billy Elliot, 265
Billy Rose's Diamond Horseshoe, 122
Billy the Kid, 90, 169–70, 280, 312n5
Birch, Patricia, 265
Bizet, Georges 108, 282
black-and-white films, 315n14
Blackbirds, 28
Blackbirds of 1928, 276
black bottom, 41
black dance, 9, 305n4
blackface, 69f, 83, 296n15, 296–97n21
black musicals, 28
Black or White, 259
The Black Pirate, 317n35
Blair, Betsy (Betsy Boger, Betsy Reisz), 20, 119–20, 122, 306n18
Blake, Eubie, 27–28, 275
Blane, Ralph, 241–42, 282
Blasis, Carlo, 44, 119
"Bless Your Beautiful Hide," 238
Blue Belles of Harlem (Ellington), 297n35
Blue Skies, 282
Blum, Léon, 85
Blum, René, 296n12, 302n91
Boger, Betsy, *see* Blair, Betsy
"Bojangles," 137
"Bojangles of Harlem," 27, 30
Bolger, Ray, 64, 66, 86, 103, 280, 296n9
Bollywood, 264
Bolm, Adolph, 66–67, 118–19, 159, 207, 275

"Bonjour Paris," 188
boom camerawork, 180–83, 194, 203–9
Boos, Paul, 109
Borchsenius, Valborg, 49f
Borel, Henri, 238
Börlin, Jean, 70
Borne, Bonita (Bonny), 75
Borne, Elyse, 75
Borne, Hal, 30, 75, 154, 293n3
Boulanger, Nadia ("Nadja"), 240, 321n19
Bourne, Matthew, 262
Bournonville, Auguste, 50–51
Bournonville style or tradition, 49f, 50–51, 118
boy next door, 132–34
"The Boy Next Door," 242
The Boys from Syracuse, 74–75, 121
Bradley, Buddy, 28
Braham, Philip, 197, 314n6
Brandard, John, 46f
Bremer, Lucille, 37f, 51, 195–204, 198f
Brice, Fannie, 53, 81, 298n48
Bride and Prejudice, 264
Brigadoon, 125, 186, 225–26, 284, 309n52
British aristocracy, 310n60
British ballet, 211–13
British Film Institute, 263
British Isles clog dancing, 18, 27
Broadway, 8, 63–87, 123
Broadway Melody, 143
"Broadway Melody" (Freed and Brown), 113, 219–20
Broadway Melody of 1929, 26, 185, 318n55
Broadway Melody of 1936, 318n55
Broadway Melody of 1938, 130–31, 308n35, 318n55
Broadway Melody of 1940, 30f, 31, 32f, 51, 280, 318n55
"Begin the Beguine," 36, 248
"I've Got My Eyes on You," 314n6
"Jukebox Dance," 49f
"Broadway Rhythm" (Freed and Brown), 26, 113, 219–20, 318n55
Brockway, Merrill, 256–57
Broken Blossoms, 197, 314n6
"broken rhythm" (term), 291n34
Brown, Nacio Herb, 26, 113, 284
Brown, Trisha, 260
Browne, Leslie, 266

Bubbles, John W. (John W. Sublett), 16, 28, 30*f*, 31, 32*f*, 33, 116–17, 272, 275
Buchanan, Jack, 319n57
"buck and wing" dancing, 27
"buck" dancing, 27
buddy dances, 5, 127, 172–74, 307–8n35. *see also* dancing sailors
The Bunch and Judy, 275
Burge, Gregg, 258
burlesque, 225
Burling, Robbins, 164
Burns, George, 308n35
"Butter and Egg Man," 28
"By Myself," 313n28
"By Strauss," 260–61

Cabaret, 238, 257–58
Cabin in the Sky, 32*f*, 33, 76, 111–13, 169–70, 280–81
Cadmus, Paul, 174
Caesar, Irving, 292n39
Café de Paris, 38, 273
Cage, John, 261–62
Cagney, James, 133
Cahiers du cinéma, 263
Caldwell, Anne, 275
call and response, 30*f*, 31–33
Calloway, Cab, 259
camerawork, 134, 137–38, 155, 194–95, 229
    angles and framing, 138–40, 257–58
    boom shots, 180–81, 183, 194, 203–9
    choreography, 242
    musical establishing sequence, 230–31
Cameron, James, 266
Cansino, Angel, 42, 120, 126
Cansino, Eduardo, 42, 43*f*, 120
Cansino, Elisa, 42, 43*f*
Cansino, Margarita Carmen (Rita Hayworth), 42, 43*f*
capoeira, 261
Capra, Frank, 173
Carefree, 137, 157–58, 159*f*, 280, 311n17, 315n20
    "I Used to be Colorblind," 202, 203*f*
    "The Yam," 41, 148, 261
"The Carioca," 41
Carnegie Hall (New York, NY), 42, 276
Caron, Leslie, 99, 106, 113, 226, 249, 295n39, 319n58
    "American in Paris" dance, 213–14, 214*f*–15*f*
    "Our Love Is Here to Stay" dance, 157

Carousel, 250
Carpenter, John Alden, 67, 119
Casino de Paris, 69*f*
Castle, Irene, 37–40, 39*f*, 271, 273, 293n8
Castle, Vernon, 37–40, 39*f*, 271, 273–74
Castle Walk, 38, 39*f*
Cavendish, Charles, 278
Cecchetti, Enrico, 44–45, 53
Cecchetti method, 305n10
ceiling dance, 190–91
censorship, 303n19
Center Stage, 265
Chabelska, Marie, 54*f*
Chada, Gurinder, 264
challenge dance, 30*f*, 31, 36–37
Champion, Gower, 106, 144
Champion, Marge, 106, 144
Chanel, Coco, 53
Chaplin, Charlie, 187, 262
Chaplin, Saul, 125–27, 135, 186, 212, 216, 239–40, 248–49, 307nn26–28, 308n47, 320n12
"Chaplin walk," 42, 43*f*
Charisse, Cyd, 58, 60*f*, 99, 106, 113, 119, 259, 284
    The Band Wagon dances, 1, 99*f*, 224–25, 224*f*, 225*f*
    "Gotta Dance" ballet, 220–22, 221*f*
    in *Silk Stockings,* 162–63, 163*f*, 189
    Singin' in the Rain ballet, 99*f*
Charleston, 40–41, 293n10
Charlot's Revue, 197
chase sequences, 264. *see also specific dances*
La chatte, 276
Chauve Souris, 301n88
Chazelle, Damien, 267–69
"Cheek to Cheek," 165
Chéri, Albert. *see* Albertieri, Luigi
Chevalier, Maurice, 130–31, 247–49, 252–53, 292n2
    in *Love Me Tonight,* 236*f*–37*f*, 237, 265
Chicago, 266
Chicago, Illinois, 66, 76, 118–19, 305n10
Chicago Defender, 81–82
Chicago National Association of Dance Masters, 118
children: dances with, 173*f*, 175
chinoiserie, 314nn12–13
chivalry, 157, 158*f*
The Chocolate Soldier (stage), 282

choreographers, 76–77. *see also specific individuals*
choreography
  camera, 242
  dance, 1–11, 197–201, 198f, 229–53, 256–57, 299n60
  small screen, 256–57
choreomusicology, 8
Christensen, Lew, 90, 280, 304n22
Christie, Ian, 303n20
Chu Chin Chow, 25
chugging, chugs, 33, 110
Church, George, 82–83
cigarettes, 145–47
"ciné ballet," 193. *see also* ballet
Cinemascope, 138, 177, 177f, 309n52
Cinémathèque Française, 263
cinematic ballet, 95–99. *see also* ballet
cinematic dance, 193–226. *see also* dance
cinematography, 96–97, 102, 157, 206, 308n44
Citizen Kane, 97
Clair, René, 11, 124, 237, 246, 249, 272, 277
classical dance, 265–66
The Clock, 282, 312n2, 313n25
clog dance, 27, 33, 293n2
Coccia, Aurelia, 38, 273, 293n6
Cochran, Charles B., 73, 277
Cochran revues, 74
"Coffee Time," 51
Cohan, George M., 116, 218, 271–72
Cohan strut, 116, 218
Cojocaru, Alina, 149f
Cole, Jack, 113, 115, 225, 257, 307n32
Coles, Honi, 28
Colette, 247
collaboration, 6–10
color, 308n46, 314n11, 317n35, 318n50
  "American in Paris," 213–17, 214f–15f
  "Limehouse Blues," 197–201, 198f
  Minnelli yellow, 199
  The Pirate, 206, 317n35
  "Colorblind, I Used to be" 202, 203f
Comden, Betty, 122, 171, 176, 187, 222–26, 262–63, 282–84, 312n13, 318–19n4, 319nn56–58
comedy, 65, 268. *see also* satire
composition, 229–53
Concerto Barocco, 281
contact improvisation, 261
"The Continental," 36, 41, 248
contrapposto, 55f, 56

Cook, Will (Marion), 296–97n21
"Cool," 258, 313n5
Cooper, Gary, 104
Copland, Aaron, 59–60, 90, 132, 169–70, 280–82
Coppélia, 49–50, 52, 148
Coracaju, Alina, 46f
Cornejo, Herman, 52f
Le corsaire, 207
costume design, 204, 206, 317–18nn49–50
counterbalance, 109
couple dancing, 35–39, 37f, 39f, 46f, 109–10, 119, 147
Courage, Alexander, 239
Courtin' Time, 283
courtship dance, 7–8, 143–65, 146f, 163f, 191–92, 207, 257, 264, 268–69, 310n1
Cover Girl, 4, 42, 124–27, 206, 211, 282, 306n25, 308n45, 308n47
  "Alter Ego," 4, 134–40, 136f, 189, 259, 306n25, 307n28, 307n32, 308nn47–48, 309n50
  dance sequences, 126, 134–38, 189, 307n32
  "Make Way for Tomorrow," 126–32, 128f–29f, 133–34, 307n32, 308n35
Coward, Noel, 24
Coyne, Jeanne, 7, 211, 287n6
crane camera. *see* boom camera
Crawford, Joan, 26
Crawford, Richard, 25–26
"Crazy Rhythm," 26, 292n39
Cricklewood Dancing Hall, 293n10
Croce, Arlene, 144–45, 310n1, 319–20n5
Cronjager, Edward, 106–7
Crystal, Billy, 163
Cukor, George, 285, 315n14
Cunningham, Merce, 261–62
Curran, Tina, 288n14
cutting, film, 139, 309n54

Daddy Longlegs, 41, 226, 284
Dagonova, Ella, 119
Dalí, Salvador, 202, 204, 315n19, 316n25–316n26
d'Amboise, Jacques, 300n73
"Damnation Scene" ballet, 223, 224f
Damn Yankees, 257, 285
A Damsel in Distress, 31, 131, 279, 308n44
  "A Foggy Day," 188
  "Funhouse" dance ("Stiff Upper Lip") 137, 308n35
  "I Can't Be Bothered Now," 131, 133
  "Things Are Looking Up," 131, 132f

dance, 288n15. *see also specific dances and
    forms*
  adagio dancing, 98
  aesthetic, 43
  African American, 18
  Afro-Caribbean, 112
  American, 44, 123–24
  Astaire's roots, 35–61
  ballroom, 35–37
  buddy dances, 5, 127, 172–74, 307–8n35
  with camera, 115–40
  with children, 173f, 175
  cinematic, 193–226
  citizen-soldier dances, 173f, 175–76
  classical, 265–66
  clog dance, 27, 33, 293n2
  for common man, 132–34
  couple or partner dancing, 35–39, 37f, 39f,
    46f, 109–10, 119, 147
  courtship dances, 7–8, 143–65, 146f, 150–65,
    163f, 191–92, 207, 257, 264, 268–69, 310n1
  dream dances or sequences, 4–5, 52, 78–80,
    79f, 137, 193–226, 203f, 224f, 315nn18–20
  film dance, 2–3, 141–226
  "flag-waving" steps, 117
  "Fred Astaire step," 108
  genres, 312n8
  golf dances, 157–58, 159f, 311n17
  history of, 147–50
  integration with music, 28–33
  modern, 16–17, 53, 59–61, 60f, 113, 115, 210,
    225, 277, 319n59
  musical establishing sequence for, 230–35,
    263–64
  named dances, 41
  notation for, 288n14
  off-balance dancing, 54–59, 55f, 57f, 58f
  onstage, 7–8
  outlaw style, 6, 15–33, 56–57, 61, 259–60
  postmodern, 259–62
  pure, 48
  rhythm dances, 26–28
  roller-skate dances, 187–88
  storytelling in, 48–51
  street dances, 4, 133–34, 140, 179–92, 258–59,
    264, 268–69, 308n45
  whole-body, 45–48, 46f–47f
  without dancing, 238–41, 243–47, 249–53

Dance Magazine, 65
dance centers, 5–6
dance directors, 76–77, 104, 299n61
dance drama, 209–11. *see also specific
    productions*
dance-film, 3. *see also specific films*
Dance in America (PBS), 256–57, 265, 303n20
Dance Magazine, 43
dance-mime sequences, 58–59
dance musicals, 255–69. *see also specific
    musicals*
dancers, 3–5, 264–67. *see also specific
    individuals*
dance schools, 20, 41
dance videos, 258–59
Dancing, A Man's Game, 133, 261
"Dancing in the Dark," 1, 60f, 189
Dancing Lady, 26, 278
dancing sailors, 167–78, 168f, 173f, 209–11,
    210f, 312n9, 312nn12–13
Daniels, Jeffrey, 258
Danilova, Alexandra, 68, 275
Danzas mexicanas, 122
Dark Red Roses, 95–96, 277
Day, Richard, 107
"A Day for Love," 237–38
"A Day in New York" film ballet, 209–11, 210f
Day on Earth, 59
de Basil, Wassily, 85, 296n12, 302n91
de Beaujoyeulx, Balthasar, 147
de Beauvoir, Simone, 167
de Becque, Émile, 179
Debussy, Claude, 59, 240
de Chirico, Giorgio, 77, 202, 204, 316nn24–25
Decker, Todd, 30, 289n3, 292n55, n60, 294n12,
    320n12, 321n2
decor, 207–9, 217. *see also* set design
Deep in My Heart, 284
Delibes, Léo, 49–50, 154
Delsarte, François, 59
Delvaux, Paul, 204, 316n27
D'Emilio, John, 174
de Mille, Agnes, 113, 115, 169–70, 201, 281
demi-pointe (half-toe), 294n21
Les demoiselles de Rochefort, 257, 268
Demy, Jacques, 257, 268
Denby, Edwin, 170
Denishawn School (Los Angeles, CA), 43, 274

de Paul, Gene, 284
Derain, André, 69f, 117
Deren, Maya, 8, 262
de Saint-Exupéry, Antoine, 77, 257
Deutsch, Adolph, 320n14
de Valois, Ninette (Edris Stannus), 49, 120,
    212, 272, 276–77
Diaghilev, Sergei, 42, 44, 66–70, 85, 171,
    298n43, 300n72, 317n36, *see also* Ballets
    Russes (Diaghilev)
    and Balanchine 49, 64, 67, 70–74
    and Duke, 73–74
    timeline, 271–73, 275–77
Diaghilev diaspora, 66–70
Die Fledermaus, 281, 293n2
Dietrich, Marlene, 104
Dietz, Howard, 16, 76, 247, 277, 284, 301n88
directors, 1–11, 96–97, 264–67. *see also specific*
    individuals
Dirty Dancing, 265
Dirty Dancing: Havana Nights, 266
Dirty Linen, 177
disco-dancing films, 265
Disney, Walt, 105–6, 105f, 267
diversity. *see* pluralism
Dixon-Gottschild, Brenda, 9
Dolin, Anton (Patrick Healy-Kay), 53, 54f, 70,
    95–96, 302n91
Dollar, William, 98–99, 99f, 105, 312n3
Donen, Stanley, 115–40, 161, 193–226, 260,
    306n20, 306–7nn23–27, 307n31
    Astaire and, 7, 159–60
    as director, 7, 125, 138, 188, 190–91, 257–58
    film work, 125, 234–35, 246–49. *see also*
        specific films
    Kelly and, 5, 7, 124–26, 134, 137–38, 176–77,
        205, 209–11, 225–26, 243, 248–49, 307n28,
        307n32, 307nn34–35, 308–9nn48–49,
        309n55, 310n1, 312n13, 314n11
    timeline, 275, 283–85
Don Quixote, 157, 266
Do the Right Thing, 259
Dotson, Clarence "Dancing," 49, 67, 116–17,
    305n3
Doucet, Clément, 74
Dougall, Bernard, 311n13
Dr. Jekyll and Mr. Hyde, 315n14
Dragon, Carmen, 126

drags, 110
Draper, Paul, 91–93, 297n24
Dream Ballet, 295n9
dream sequences, 4–5, 137, 193–226, 224f,
    315nn18–20. *see also specific dances*
    ballet, 52, 78–80, 79f, 201–4, 203f, 315n18
Drigo, Riccardo, 154
drum dance, 31
drumming, 26–27
DuBarry Was a Lady, 281
dubbing, 305n12
Duke, Vernon (Vladimir Dukelsky), 2, 63–87,
    90, 98, 240, 297nn25–26, 298nn47–48,
    299n58, 300n78. *see also specific works*
    Balanchine and, 70–74, 80, 111–13, 167–68,
        202, 300n73
    Gershwins and, 70–84, 298n48
    Minnelli and, 202
    timeline, 272, 276, 279–81
The Dumb Girl of Portici, 53
Duncan, Isadora, 42–43, 53, 59, 60f, 267,
    271–72, 276
Duncan, Todd, 112
Dunham, Katherine, 8, 112–13, 169–70, 225,
    273, 280
Dunleavy, Rosemary, 108–9
Durang, John, 171, 312n12
DVD, 259, 267
Dwenger, Dick, 122
The Dying Swan, 49, 51–53

Earhart, Amelia, 77
Easter Parade, 31, 188, 283
Ebsen, Buddy, 308n35
eclecticism, 21
Eddy, Nelson, 293n2
Edens, Roger, 185, 280, 283, 285, 320n14
editing, 266
Edward, Prince of Wales, 310n60
Eisenstein, Sergei, 95
Ekstasis, 122, 278
Eliot, Karen, 9
Elizabeth I, 148, 293n7
Ellington, Duke, 297n35
embroidery, 37
Empire Theatre (London, England), 49, 51, 275
L'enfant et les sortilèges, 276
Engel, Lehman, 278

Ernst, Max, 202
Errand into the Maze, 282
Escuela Bolera, 42
Establishing sequence, 204, 230–38, 241
E.T., 264
ethnomusicology, 288n11
euphoria dance, 179–92, 187f, 268–69
Europe, James Reese, 38, 274
"Euro- Russian" (term), 296n13
everyday movement, 23–25, 57–59, 58f,
   260–61
Everyone Says I Love You, 163
Every Soul is a Circus, 122, 280
"An Experiment in Modern Music"
   (Whiteman), 275
"Exposition," 90
Expressionism, 59

Fairbanks, Douglas, 120–21, 158–59, 317n35
Fancy Free, 167–76, 168f, 282, 312n13, 319n4
Fanfare for the Common Man, 132
Fantasia, 105–6, 105f
Farrell, Suzanne, 79f
"Fascinating Rhythm," 25–26, 29–30
Faust, 319n58
Fazan, Adrienne, 139, 309n54
FEKS (Factory of the Eccentric Actor), 95, 275,
   303n11
Ferrer, José, 319n58
Feuer, Jane, 319n56–57, 320n7
Fields, Dorothy, 279
Fiennes, Joseph, 148
Filling Station, 90, 169–70, 280
film(s). see also specific films
   black-and-white films, 315n14
   early, 42–43
   synergy with music, 1–11
film cutting, 139, 309n54
film dance, 2–3, 7–9, 115–40
   ballet, 1, 192
   genres, 141–226
   jazz ballet, 89–113
film-dance drama, 193
film musicals
   establishing sequence for dance, 230–35,
      263–64
   Golden Age, 1
   legacy, 255–69
   production, 256

satire, 85, 222–26, 257, 319n58
   through-composed, through-choreographed
      musicals, 229–53
Films and Filming, 263
film speed, 103
finale(s), 247–53, 258–59
"A Fine Romance," 248
Finian's Rainbow, 180
Firebird, 240
Fire Island, 75
"Fit as a Fiddle," 238, 246–47
Fitzgerald, F. Scott, 22
"Five A.M.," 77, 79f, 80, 82, 113, 202, 299n60
"flag-waving" steps, 117
Flashdance, 265
Flash tap, 312n8
The Fleet's In (Cadmus), 174
Fleming, Victor, 315n14
Flickers, 122, 281
Flitch, J. Crawford, 50
flow, 109. see also streamlining
Flower Festival in Genzano, 50
Flying Colors, 301n88
Flying Down to Rio, 41, 97, 124, 278, 310n1
"A Foggy Day," 188
Fokine, Mikhail, 49, 51–52, 66, 117–19, 207, 273
folk dance, 37, 37f, 122
"Follow in my Footsteps," 308n35
Follow the Boys, 304n22
Follow the Fleet, 41, 170, 279
   "I'd Rather Lead a Band," 30f, 31
   "Let's Face the Music and Dance," 47f,
      58–59
Folly Island, South Carolina, 298n54
Folsey, George, 194–95, 199, 242
Fonda, Henry, 23–24
Fontaine, Joan, 132f
Fontanne, Lynn, 316n32
Fonteyn, Margot, 266
Forbush, Nelly, 179
Ford, John, 268
foreign dance, 290n18
Forget Paris, 163
For Goodness Sake, 275
Forman, Milos, 178
For Me and My Gal, 123–24, 281
42nd Street, 102, 278
48th Street Theatre (New York, NY), 276
Fosse, Bob, 144, 257–58

The Four Temperaments, 107–8, 111, 282
fox trot, 38
Fox TV, 267
framing, 96–97, 138–40, 257–58
Frankie and Johnny, 90, 169–70, 280
Franklin, Frederick, 45
"Fred Astaire step," 108
Freed, Arthur, 26, 113, 124–25, 195, 213, 216–17, 256, 284, 307n31, 313n5, 314n6, 316n32
Freeland, Thornton, 278
French impressionism, 318n53
French Legion of Honor, 305n13
Freud, Sigmund, 59, 201–4, 315n21
Frontier, 279
fugues, 298n53
Fulda, Ludwig, 316n32
Fullington, Doug, 311n11
"Funhouse," 137
Funny Face, 7, 16, 25, 31, 70, 125, 276, 285
  "Bonjour Paris," 188
  "How Long Has This Been Going On?," 180
  "Let's Kiss and Make Up," 159–60, 162f
  "'S Wonderful," 179, 248

Gabor, Eva, 247
Gambelli (teacher), 305n10
Garland, Judy, 123, 159, 185, 207, 208f, 307n31
Gaslight, 315n14
Gauthier, Eva, 71
The Gay Divorcee, 45, 52f, 143–45, 278–79
  "The Continental," 36, 41, 248
  "A Needle in a Haystack," 31, 42, 43f, 57f, 58f, 60f
  "Night and Day," 144–48, 146f, 149f
Gaynor, Mitzi, 179
Gedalge, André, 321n19, 240
Gelius, Joanna, 21
Genée, Adeline, 8, 48–51, 49f, 53, 118, 271, 273, 276
Genée, Alexandre, 50
Genet, Jean, 167
George Gershwin's Song Book (Gershwin), 74, 298n50
German Expressionism, 59
Gershwin, George, 15–16, 19–21, 24–26, 63–87, 291n31, 292n55, 298n47, 299n59, 302n1
  Astaire and, 29–30
  Balanchine and, 63, 89–91, 302–3n6
  Duke and, 70–75

George Gershwin's Song Book, 74, 298n50
  in the Gullahs, 75, 298n54
  health, 90–91
  inspirations, 131
  music and songs, 2, 5, 8, 153. *see also specific works*
  Piano Concerto in F, 74
  terminology, 291n34
  timeline, 272, 275–76, 279–80
  tributes to, 216
Gershwin, Ira, 5, 16, 21, 24–26, 63–87, 113, 126, 180, 216, 240, 315n19
  Balanchine and, 74–75, 90, 98, 298n49, 302–3n6
  Duke and, 72, 74–84, 298n48
  songs, 153. *see also specific works*
  timeline, 271, 276, 279–80, 283–84
Gershwin, Leonore (Lee), 298n49
Geva, Tamara, 70, 86–87, 275, 301n88
ghostwriting, 41, 72
Gigi, 204, 239, 243, 247, 249–53, 285, 320n7
  "Gigi," 250, 252–53
  "I'm Glad I'm Not Young Anymore," 250–51
  "I Remember It Well," 250
  "The Night They Invented Champagne," 251
  "Say a Prayer for Me Tonight," 251
"Gigi," 250, 252–53
Gilks, Alfred, 217
"Girl Hunt Ballet," 48, 106, 223–25, 224f, 248
Giselle, 36, 46–47, 46f, 52, 52f, 53, 80, 148, 149f, 195, 311n11
Give a Girl a Break, 257, 284, 307n31
Glee, 267
glides, 33
Glière, Reinhold, 71
Globe Theatre (London, England), 275
gobos, 200–201
Godard, Jean-Luc, 235
Goddard, Paulette, 33
Gold Diggers, 97, 102–3, 143, 278
Golddiggers in Paris, 89–90
Golden, Ray, 280
Golden Age, 1
Goldwyn, Francis, 107
Goldwyn, Sam, 97, 104, 303n18
The Goldwyn Follies, 90, 96–99, 98f, 99f, 101, 280, 299n63, 303n18
golf dances, 157–58, 159f, 311n17
Goodrich, Francis, 316n32

Gordon, David, 260–61
Gordon, Irene, 315n22
Gosling, Ryan, 268–69
"Gotta Dance," see Singin' in the Rain, Broadway ballet
Graham, Martha, 8, 17, 43, 113, 122, 169–70, 276–82
Grayson, Kathryn, 159f–60f, 172
Grease, 265
Great American Song Book, 74
Great Depression, 277
Great Lady, 167–68, 312n3
"The Great McGinty" (Balanchine), 299n60
Greek archetypes, 59
Green, Adolph, 122, 176, 187, 262–63, 312n13, 319n4, 319nn57–58
    in The Band Wagon, 222–26
    timeline, 282–84
Green, John, 216, 239, 321n19
Grein, J. T., 17
Grey, Jennifer, 265
Griffith, D. W., 59, 95, 197
Griffith, Edward H., 281, 314n6
Grisi, Carlotta, 46, 46f
Guest, Ann Hutchinson, 288n14
Guétary, Georges, 179, 181
Guildhall School of Music, 24
Gullahs, 75, 298n54
A Guy Named Joe, 313n25

Hackett, Albert, 316n32
Hahn, Reynaldo, 300n78
Hair, 178
Hairspray, 238
"The Half of It Dearie Blues," 30
half-toe (demi-pointe), 294n21
Halprin, Anna, 191
Hammersmith Palais de Dance (London, England), 293n10
Hammerstein, Oscar II, 21, 179, 281
Haney, Carol, 7, 211, 287n6, 305n12
Hans Christian Andersen, 107
Harbach, Otto, 311n13
Harburg, E. Y. "Yip," 180
Harlem Renaissance, 22, 267
Harper, Herbie, 7, 86, 103, 288n8
Harrington, Frank, 116–17, 305n3
Hart, Lorenz (Larry), 21, 63–87, 235, 279. see also specific works

Hart, Moss, 315n19
Hartvig, Brigitta (Vera Zorina), 303n18
Hashimoto, Zenzo, 42
Haskell, Arnold, 119
Hays Production Code, 172–73
Hayworth, Rita (Margarita Carmen Cansino), 36–37, 51, 126, 294n15
    dance style, 42, 43f, 57f
    "Make Way for Tomorrow" dance, 127–30, 128f–29f
Hayworth, Volga, 42
Healy-Kay, Patrick (Anton Dolin), 53, 54f
"Heaven, I'm in heaven," 165
Heavy D, 259
Hello, Dolly!, 257, 285
Help!, 263
Helpmann, Robert, 212
Hepburn, Audrey, 159–60, 162f, 179–80, 248
Hepburn, Katherine, 151
Here's Howe, 292n39
highbrow, 21–23, 26, 42, 63, 262
High School Musical series, 267
Hill, Constance Valis, 18, 113, 304n36
Hines, Gregory, 262, 266
Hirschhorn, 306n25
history, dance, 147–50
Hitchcock, Alfred, 268, 315n19
H.M.S. Pinafore, 171
Hoctor, Harriet, 77–78, 89, 298n48
Holiday Inn, 281
Hollywood, 5–8, 13–140, 303n19, 307n32
Hollywood style, 308n44
Holm, Hanya, 113
Holmes, Berenice, 118–19, 207, 278
homoerotic subtetxts, 174
homosexuality, 174
Honneger, Arthur, 71
Hoofers Club, 8, 28
Hope, Bob, 298n48
Horgan, Barbara, 304n23
House of Flowers, 283
Houston, Whitney, 267
Howe, James Wong, 102
"How Long Has This Been Going On?," 180, 238
The Human Comedy, 313n25
Humphrey, Doris, 17, 43, 59, 113, 122, 277, 299n61
Humphrey-Weidman Studio and Company, 277
Hungary, 312n11

Hunt, Marilyn, 305n1
Hunter, Mary, 174
Hurwitz, Justin, 268–69

"I Ain't Hep to That Step," 33
I Am a Dancer, 266
"I Begged Her," 172–73
Ibert, Jacques, 285
"I Can't Be Bothered Now," 131, 131*f*, 133
"I'd Rather Charleston," 40
"I'd Rather Lead a Band," 30*f*, 31
Idzikowski, Stanislas, 68
"I Got Plenty of Nothin'," 75
"I Got Rhythm," 5, 26, 120, 173*f*, 260–61
"I Heard It through the Grapevine," 263
"I Like Myself," 186–87, 187*f*
"I'll Be Hard to Handle," 31, 33, 39*f*, 40, 58, 58*f*,
    151–53, 152*f*
I Married an Angel, 74–75, 121, 280
"I'm Glad I'm Not Young Anymore," 250–51
"I'm in Love with a Wonderful Guy," 179
immigrants, 5–6, 17–21, 18*f*, 21
    Diaghilev diaspora, 66–70
    New Yorkers, 17–19, 18*f*, 289–90n11
"I'm Not Complaining," 98
"I'm Old Fashioned," 36, 51
iMovie, 267
Imperial Theatre School, 273
impressionism, 217, 318n53
improvisation, contact, 261
Ingram, Rex, 112
innovation, technical, 106–7
integration, 301n88
intellectual property rights, 299nn60–61
Internet, 267
Intolerance, 59, 95
Invitation to the Dance, 120, 171, 175,
    235, 285
"I Remember It Well," 250
Irish step dancing, 27, 116
Isaacs, Edith, 66, 87
"Isn't It a Lovely Day," 30*f*, 31, 58, 149–51,
    150*f*, 310n1, 309n49
"It Ain't Necessarily So" (Gershwin), 75,
    299n57
"It's a Bore," 247, 250
It's Always Fair Weather, 4–5, 171, 177–78, 177*f*,
    225–26, 308n35, 309n52
    "Baby, You Knock Me Out," 261

central plot, 143
dance sequences, 5, 126, 189
finale, 249
"I Like Myself," 186–87, 187*f*
"March," 238
musical montages, 243
"Once I Had a Friend," 177, 177*f*
street dance, 189
timeline, 284
Ivanova, Lida, 95
"I've Got a Crush on You," 191
"I've Got My Eyes on You," 314n6
"I've Grown Accustomed to Her Face," 250
"I Want to Be a Dancing Man," 31
I Was an Adventuress, 106–7, 280, 303n20

Jack in the Box, 68, 69*f*, 117, 276
Jackson, Janet, 259, 264
Jackson, Michael, 8, 140, 258–59, 264
Jackson and Johnson, 67
Jacobi, Victor, 36, 274
Jardin publique, 300n72
jazz, 18, 22–23, 38, 71, 224–25, 255–56, 297n27,
    297n35
"jazz" (word), 26
Jazz Age, 25–26
jazz ballet, 4–5, 86, 89–113
jazz dance, 18, 223, 302n93
jazz generation, 21–23, 40, 61
The Jazz Singer, 276
jazz tap, 6
Jennings, Edward, 104
Jerry the Mouse, 173*f*, 176
Jews, 17, 21, 289–90n11, 291n25
Jimmie Lunceford's Dance Orchestra, 292n41
Jocasta, 59
Johansson, Christian, 50
Johnson, Myra, 292n41
Jordan, Stephanie, 8
Joseph II, 291n25
Jourdan, Louis, 247
Judson Theatre Group, 191
"Jukebox Dance," 49*f*
Julien Levy Gallery (New York, NY), 202, 315n22
June, Ray, 157
Jung, Carl, 59

Kahn, Gus, 278
Kahn, Roger Wolfe, 292n39

Kaho Naa... Pyaar Hai (Say ... You Love Me), 264
Kasdan, Larry, 263
Kay, Hershy, 298n50
Kaye, Nora, 266
kazatski, 21
Keaton, Buster, 262
Keep Off the Grass, 167–68, 280
Kelly, Fred, 2, 116, 284, 306n25
Kelly, Gene, 67, 113, 115–40, 260, 302n93,
    306n18, 306–7nn26–27, 307nn31–32,
    319n58
    "Alter Ego" dance, 4, 134–40, 136f, 189, 259,
        306n25, 307n28, 307n32, 308nn47–48,
        309n50
    "American in Paris" dance, 212–19, 214f–15f
    in *Anchors Aweigh*, 170–71, 173f, 175
    The Band Wagon satire of film ballet, 222–26
    Balanchine and, 64, 120–21
    camera work, 310n58
    choreography, 3–5, 120–25, 132, 137, 183–85,
        207–13, 210f, 219, 222–26, 308n47
    ciné ballet, 193
    citizen-soldier dances, 173f, 176
    collaborations, 41, 80
    courtship dances, 154–65, 207, 310n1
    "La Cumparsita" dance, 158, 159f–60f
    dance studies and training, 42, 49, 116–19
    dance style, 5–8, 99, 115–20, 123–24, 133,
        144, 193–226, 255, 264–65, 305n5, 305n14
    dances with children, 173f, 175
    "Dancing, A Man's Game," 133
    "A Day in New York" ballet, 209–11, 210f
    as director, 3–4, 121, 124, 138, 222–26, 257
    Donen and, 3, 5, 7, 124–26, 134, 137–38,
        176–77, 192, 205, 209–11, 225–26, 243,
        248–49, 307n28, 307n32, 307nn34–35,
        308–9nn48–49, 309n55, 310n1, 312n13,
        314n11
    euphoria dances, 180
    favorite musicals, 230
    on film, 96
    film ballets, 193. *see also specific productions*
    finales, 248–49
    "flag-waving" steps, 117
    French Legion of Honor, 305n13
    "Gotta Dance" ballet, 219–22, 221f
    "I Like Myself" dance, 186–87, 187f
    last appearances as performer, 257
    legacy, 255–69
    Minnelli and, 6–7, 106, 125, 180, 192, 204–9,
        213–19, 225–26, 316nn31–32, 317–18n49
    "Make Way for Tomorrow" dance, 127–30,
        128f–29f
    musical montages, 246
    on musicals, 255
    Olvera Street dance, 173f, 175
    "Our Love Is Here to Stay" dance, 157
    Pas de dieux, 120
    The Pirate dance, 204–9, 208f
    political involvement, 132–33
    roller-skate dance, 187–88
    sailor dances, 170, 173, 173f
    seduction dance, 144
    "Singin' in the Rain" ballet, 1–2, 4, , 99f,
        113, 179, 183–86, 184f
    street dances, 132–34, 140, 189, 207
    "'S Wonderful" dance, 4–5, 179–92, 182f
    timeline, 271–85
    in *On the Town*, 176–77, 231–34, 232f–33f, 265
    use of color, 308n46
    "You Were Meant for Me" dance, 155–57,
        156f
    in *Ziegfeld Follies*, 31
Kelly, Kerry, 187
Kern, Jerome, 5, 16, 21, 36, 126, 153, 271
    "Bojangles of Harlem," 30
    "Long Ago and Far Away," 135
    timeline, 275, 277, 279
Kidd, Michael, 7, 106, 113, 115, 161, 211–12,
    224–25, 257, 284
Kiev Conservatory, 297n26
Kirstein, Lincoln, 68–69, 76, 90, 278–79, 282
Kismet, 284
Kiss Me, Kate, 257, 266
Kita Banzai Japs, 42
knee slides, 210, 222
Kobborg, Johann, 46f, 149f
Kochetovsky, Alexander, 119
Kochno, Boris, 297n39
Kosloff, Theodore, 66
Krazy Kat, 67, 119, 275
Kreisler, Fritz, 36, 274
Kriza, John, 168f, 173–74

Laban, Rudolf, 59
Labanotation, 288n14

La bayadère, 201, 261
La pastorale, 68, 276
labor strikes, 299n62
La caccia d'amore (The Hunt of Love) (Negri), 147
La concurrence, 117
La création du monde, 70
La créole, 299n58
"La Cumparsita," 158, 159f–60f
Lady Be Good, 1, 16, 24–26, 29–30, 51, 70, 73, 275–76, 292n45
   "Fascinating Rhythm," 25–26
   "The Half of It Dearie Blues," 30
   "I'd Rather Charleston," 40
The Lady Comes Across, 281
Lady in the Dark, 315n19
"Lake of the Swans," 106–7
La La Land, 11, 267–69
La manche liberée, 168f
Landis, John, 258
Ländler, 36
Lane, Burton, 283–85
Lanfield, Sidney, 281
Lang, Harold, 168f, 170, 174, 312n8
Langlois, Henri, 263
La nuit, 53
"La nuit" ("Romance"), 296n20
Laskey, Charles, 304n22
Latin American dance, 38
Latouche, John, 280–81
Lawrence, Gertrude, 197
Lazowski, Yurek, 305n6
Leave It to Me, 122, 280
Le bal, 68
Le Baron, William, 274
Lee, Sammy, 7, 288n8, 303n17
Lee, Spike, 259
Léger, Fernand, 70
Legrand, Michel, 268
Léhar, Franz, 36, 281
Le million, 11, 188, 246, 249, 277
Lerner, Alan Jay, 64, 230, 247, 249, 281, 283–85.
   see also specific works
Les Ballets 1933 (company), 278
Les Girls, 285, 309n52
Leslie, Lew, 28
Les matelots, 171
Lester, Richard, 263

"Let's Call the Whole Thing Off," 187
Let's Dance, 56, 283
"Let's Face the Music and Dance," 47f, 58–59
Levant, Oscar, 182f, 191, 216
Levinson, André, 40
Lewin, Albert, 315n14, 315n17
Liberty Theatre (New York, NY), 275
Life magazine, 312n22
lifts, 119
lighting, 157, 242, 317n45
   "American in Paris," 217
   "Limehouse Blues," 197–201, 198f
   The Pirate, 206–9
"Limehouse Blues," 48, 194, 197–201, 198f, 314n6, 314n13
limerence, 164–65
Limón, José, 122, 280
Lindbergh, Charles, 77
Lindy hop, 41
literacy, 10
Little Johnny Jones ("The Yankee Doodle Boy"), 272
Little Nellie Kelly, 116, 185
The Little Prince, 257
Living in a Big Way, 122, 175, 282
location dance, 264
Loesser, Frank, 283
Loewe, Frederick, 247, 249
Loew's Penn Theater, 305n3
"Long Ago and Far Away" (Kern), 135
Lopokova, Lydia, 95–96
Loring, Eugene, 90, 203, 280
Losch, Tilly, 52, 52f, 66
Louisiana Purchase, 280
Louis XIV, 44, 147–48, 311n9
love, romantic, 164–65
Lovelace, Maud Hart, 40
The Love Letter, 275
Love Me Tonight, 11, 124, 188, 235–38, 265, 293n2, 306n23, 320n7
   central plot, 143
   establishing sequence, 236f–37f, 237
   finale, 248–50
   musical montages, 246
   opening, 130–31
   "The Son of a Gun Is Nothing but a Tailor," 249
   timeline, 278

The Love Parade, 237, 277, 293n2
lowbrow, 21–23, 26, 42, 63, 71–72, 268
Loewe, Frederick, 281, 284–85
Loy, Myrna, 151
Lubitsch, Ernst, 7, 11, 124, 162, 237,
　　292–93n2
　musical montages, 246
　timeline, 271, 277
Lucas, George, 107
Luce, Clare, 145
Luhrmnn, Baz, 266
Lunceford, Jimmie, 26
Lunt, Alfred, 316n32
Lyne, Adrian, 265
lyrics, 5

MacDonald, Jeannette, 236f–37f, 249, 292n2
Macmanus, Sharon, 173f
MacMillan, Kenneth, 266
"Mac the Black" (Porter), 207
Mad Hot Ballroom, 266
Magritte, René, 204, 316n27
"Maharanee" (Alton), 301n82
Maher, James T., 240
Majestic Theatre (New York, NY), 281
"Make Way for Tomorrow," 126–32, 128f–29f,
　　133–34, 307n32, 308n35
"male dazzles watching female" theme, 311n17
male friendship, 5, 174. see also buddy dances
Mamoulian, Rouben, 7, 11, 124, 162, 188,
　　235–38, 246, 249, 293n2, 306n23. see also
　　specific works
　legacy, 269
　timeline, 271, 278, 285
Mantle, Mickey, 261
"March," 238
Maria Theresa, 148
Marie Antoinette, 148
Marlowe, Helen, 305n1
marriage plots, 311n10
Martha Graham Dance Company, 276
martial arts, 261
Martin, Hugh, 241–42, 282
Martin, John, 277
Martin, Mary, 179
Massine, Léonide, 53, 67, 70, 85, 117, 169–71,
　　212, 279, 300n72, 302n91
Masson, André, 202

maxixe, 38
Maytime, 293n2
McKenzie, Ava and Richard, 42
Medea, 59
Meet Me in St. Louis, 125, 134, 194, 234–35,
　　237–39, 320n7
　"The Boy Next Door," 242
　central plot, 143
　costume design, 197
　gaslight sequence, 241–42
　opening, 230
　"Over the Bannister," 242
　timeline, 282
"Meet Me in St. Louis," 250
melismatic singing, 27
"melting pot" (term), 19–20, 291n31
The Melting Pot, 19, 273
Menjou, Adolph, 31
Mercer, Johnny, 36, 104, 180, 281, 284
The Merry Widow, 36, 281, 293n2
metal taps, 28, 292n45, 292n51
Metro-Goldwyn-Mayer. see MGM
Metropolitan Opera, 64, 115, 279
Meyer, Joseph, 292n39
mezzotint, 314nn12–13
MGM (Metro-Goldwyn-Mayer), 113, 173, 256,
　　293n2, 314n3, 314n6, 320n12. see also
　　specific film productions
　art department, 186
　film ballets, 194
　Freed unit, 123, 138, 185–86, 219, 250,
　　307n28, 311n15, 320n14
　music department, 7, 239
MGM orchestra, 241
middlebrow, 268
A Midsummer Night's Dream, 266
military dance(s), 312n11
Miller, Geoffrey, 164
Miller, Marilyn, 53, 277
Mills, Florence, 28
mime, 48, 53, 58–59, 195
Minnelli, Vincente, 6–7, 64, 124, 157, 240,
　　298n48, 307nn27–28, 307n31, 309n54,
　　310n1, 312n2, 314n6, 314n13, 315n21,
　　315–16nn23–24, 316n32
　Astaire and, 6–7, 99f, 192, 194–96, 222–26,
　　224f
　Balanchine and, 106, 202

The Band Wagon satire of the film ballet,
222–26, 224*f*
cameravork, 180–81, 183, 203–4, 206,
208–9, 229
choreography, 191–92
as director, 113, 138, 222–26, 241–42, 256
dream ballet, 201–4
Duke and, 202
favorite musical, 249
film ballets, 193–94. *see also specific*
productions
film or cinematic dance, 134, 193–226
finales, 248–49
interest in Surrealism, 316nn25–26
Kelly and, 6–7, 106, 117, 125, 180, 204–9,
213–19, 222–26, 316nn31–32, 317–18n49
legacy, 255–69
on *Love Me Tonight*, 235, 249
musical montages, 243–7, 265–8
as producer, 256
Sharaff and, 197, 206
timeline, 272, 281–85
use of color, 308n46
Minnellium, 76
Minnelli yellow, 199
Miró, Joan, 202
"Miss Turnstiles," 210
Mitchell, Arthur, 79*f*, 111, 224*f*, 301n84,
304n33
Mitchell, James, 284
modern dance, 16–17, 53, 59–61, 60*f*, 113, 115,
210, 225, 277, 319n59
modernism, 53, 111, 117, 122
modern woman, 150–53
montages, 243–47, 265, 321n22
Monte Carlo, 277
Monte Carlo Ballet Russe. *see* Ballet Russe de
Monte Carlo
Mordkin, Mikhail, 53
Moross, Jerome, 90, 280
Motown, 255, 263
Moulin Rouge, 266
Mouse, Jerry the, 173*f*, 176
movement. *see also* dance
everyday American, 23–25, 57–59, 58*f*
naturalistic, 35
movie dance. *see* film dance
Movie Movie, 257

moving image. *see also specific films*
synergy with music, 1–11
Mr. Strauss Goes to Boston, 282
MTV, 258
Mueller, John, 144, 310n1
multiculturalism, 19
Munshin, Jules, 177, 231–34, 232*f*–33*f*
The Muppet Show, 262
Murphy, George, 130–31, 308n35
Murphy, Gerald, 70
Museum of Modern Art, 76, 316n25
music, 5
integration with dance, 28–33, 207–9
synergy with moving image, 1–11
musical comedy, 65, 268
musical cutting, 139, 309n54
musical montage, 243–47, 265–8, 321n22
musicals. *see also* film musicals; *specific works*
backstage, 143, 315n19
black, 28
dance, 143–65
establishing sequences, 230–35, 263–64
finales, 247–49
through-composed, through-choreographed,
229–53
musical theater
Golden Age, 1
musical-theater dance
Astaire's outlaw style, 6, 15–33, 56–57, 61,
259–60
music videos, 258–59
"My Boy Bill," 250
My Fair Lady, 215, 250
"My Man's Gone Now," 299n57

Nabokov, Nicholas, 107
named dances, 41
Napoleon, 291n25
Napoli, 49*f*, 51, 148
National Dance Institute, 298n51
national pep, 291n31
naturalistic movement, 35
Naughty Marietta, 293n2
"A Needle in a Haystack," 31, 42, 43*f*, 57*f*,
58*f*, 60*f*
Needle Trades High School, 122
Negri, Cesare, 147–48
Negulesco, Jean, 284

Nemchinova, Vera, 70, 297n24
Netflix, 267
La Neva (Mrs. Claude Alvienne), 294n20
"Never Gonna Dance," 248
New Amsterdam Theatre (New York, NY), 277
"Newer Super-Realism," 315n22
New-Found Land, 177, 313n27
Newman, Alfred, 320n14
New Opera Company, 281
Newsweek, 173f, 312–13nn22–23
Newton-John, Olivia, 257, 265
New York City Ballet, 8, 64, 107–9, 121, 190, 211, 302n2
New Yorkers, 17–19, 18f, 289–90n11
New York Philharmonic, 276
New York Times, 81
"Nice Work If You Can Get It," 238
Nicholas, Fayard, 301n82
Nicholas Brothers, 8, 81, 84, 259, 298n48, 312n8
"Night and Day," 57–58, 144–48, 146f, 149f, 153–54, 165, 310n1
"Night Flight (Aero Ballet)," 77–78, 113, 299n60
Night Journey, 282
"The Night They Invented Champagne," 251
Nijinska, Bronislava, 53, 67, 117, 224–25
Nijinsky, Vaslav, 118, 266, 271, 273
Ninotchka, 162
No, No Nanette, 292n45
"No Strings," 31, 32f, 33, 58f, 131
notation, 3–4, 288n14
Nouvel, Valitchka (Walter), 73
nouvelle vague, 235, 262–63
Noverre, Jean-Georges, 6–7, 48, 119
Nureyev, Rudolf, 196, 262, 266
The Nutcracker, 107, 266, 271

"O'Brien to Ryan to Goldberg," 261
O'Connor, Donald, 144, 246–47, 308n35
O'Connor, Patrick, 300n78
October, 95
off-balance dancing, 54–59, 55f, 57f, 58f
Offenbach, 299n58
Oklahoma!, 113, 115, 235–237, 281
    "Out of My Dreams," 79, 201–2, 315n20
Olvera Street dance, 173f, 175
On a Clear Day You Can See Forever, 256, 285

"Once I Had a Friend," 177–78, 177f
180-degree rule, 308n44
One for the Money, 122, 280
"One for the Road," 4
One Hour with You, 237, 278
On the Town, 125, 140, 171, 237–38, 265, 282, 308n35, 312n13, 319–20nn4–7, 321n22
    dance sequences, 5, 126, 189
    "A Day in New York" ballet, 209–11, 210f
    film adaptation, 176–77, 283, 306n26, 307n30, 312n13
    finale, 248–49
    musical arrangement, 186
    musical establishing sequence, 230–35, 232f–33f
    sailor buddies, 168f
    screenplay, 122
On Your Toes, 65–66, 74, 84–87, 97, 99–104, 121, 169–70, 295n7, 295n9
    costume design, 197
    "The Princess Zenobia Ballet," 85–86
    "Slaughter on Tenth Avenue," 66, 84–87, 100f–101f, 121, 225, 225f, 280, 302n94
    timeline, 279
"Oops," 188–89
Opéra de Paris, 285
operettas, 36
orchestration, 155–57, 185, 239–40
orchestrators, 7, 127, 238–41, 320n12
Orpheum Theatre (Omaha), 273
Orpheus (Stravinsky), 108
Ortega, Kenny, 265
"Our Love Is Here to Stay," 157, 245–46
outlaw style, 6, 15–33, 56–57, 61, 259–60
"Out of My Dreams," 79, 201–2, 315n20
"Over the Bannister," 242

Pacific Northwest Ballet, 311n11
Page, Ruth, 90, 280, 297n24
painting(s), 317–18nn49–50, 318n53
Pajama Game, 257, 285
Palace theater (London, England), 278
Le palais de crystal (later called Symphony in C), 282
Pal Joey, 122–24, 170, 180, 280
Paltrow, Gwyneth, 148
Pan, Hermes, 7, 36, 153, 239, 273, 288n7, 291n34

Panofsky, 288n10

Parade, 53, 54f, 70

Paramount-Publix Theaters, 320n14

Paramount Studios, 321n19

Les parapluies de Cherbourg, 268

Paris, France, 213

Paris en joie, 69f

"The Parisians," 250

Paris Opéra Ballet, 120, 148

parody, *see* satire

partner dance, 35–39, 37f, 39f, 46f, 109–10, 119, 147

Pas de dieux (Kelly), 120, 285

passed-along song(s), 320n7

The Passing Show, 274

The Passing Show of 1912, 53

Patel, Amisha, 264

Paterson, Vincent, 258–59

patriotism, 290n18

Pavlova, Anna, 42, 49, 51–53, 107, 267, 271, 273

Paxton, Steve, 261

PBS, 256–57

Pennell, Joseph and Elizabeth, 197

percussion, 26–27

The Perils of Pauline, 53

Peter Rabbit and the Tales of Beatrix Potter, 266

Peters, Michael, 258

Petipa, Marius, 157, 266, 271, 273, 294n21

Petit, Roland, 107, 226, 319n58

Petrograd Ballet School, 275

Petrograd Conservatory of Music, 274

Petrouchka, 240

Phaedra, 59

Piccadilly Hotel, 293n10

"The Piccolino," 36–37, 37f, 41, 248

"Pick Yourself Up," 148

The Picture of Dorian Gray, 199, 315n14, 315n17

Pina, 266

The Pirate, 5–7, 125, 140, 197, 204–9, 208f

   central plot, 143

   color process, 206, 317n35

   courtship dance, 158–59

   "Damnation Scene" ballet parody, 223, 224f

   screenplay, 316n32

   timeline, 283

placement, 54–59

Platoff, Mark, 302n91

plot, 143, 311n10

pluralism, 212

   Astaire's outlaw style, 6, 15–33, 56–57, 61, 259–60

   Balanchine's approach, 112

   Cole's style, 225

   Hollywood, 5–8, 13–140

   Kelly's style, 116, 121–22

poetry, 5

pointe (toe dancing), 21, 44, 104, 291n22, 294n21

Polito, Sal, 102–3, 121, 220, 225

polka, 36

Pollack, Howard, 291n31

Polovtsian Dances, 118, 159, 207

polyrhythms, 27

Pons, Lily, 300n78

Pontipee, Adam, 238

popular song, 23–25

populism, 61

Porgy and Bess, 66, 74–84, 112, 235–237, 279, 298n48, 298n53

Porter, Cole, 5, 16, 36, 70, 122, 165

   songs, 153. *see also specific works*

   timeline, 271, 278, 280–81, 283, 285

post-impressionism, 318n53

postmodernism, 191, 259–62

Potter, Phyllis Livingston, 144, 278

Powell, Eleanor, 30f, 31, 32f, 42, 49f, 51, 130–31, 308n35, 314n6

Powell, Michael, 201, 212

Pressburger, Emeric, 201, 212

Presley, Elvis, 267

Previn, André, 7, 239, 249, 284, 320n12. *see also specific works*

Prince Igor, 317n36

Princess Theatre (London, England), 276

"The Princess Zenobia Ballet," 85–86

Prodigal Son (1929), 277

Prokofiev, Sergei, 73–74, 297n26, 298n41

props, 31–33, 42, 58, 131, 131f, 132f, 133, 190–91, 196

Pugni, Cesare, 154

Die Puppenfee, 296n15

"Puttin' on the Ritz," 30–33

racial integration, 301n88

racism, 2, 81–84, 112

Raft, George, 304n22

ragtime, 18
Rainer, Yvonnne, 8, 262
Rasch, Albertina, 66–67, 297n24
Ravel, Maurice, 240, 276, 321n19
Ray, Man, 68
Raymonda, 157
The Red Shoes, 201, 211–13, 303n20, 317n38
Reed, Janet, 168f
Reisz, Betsy Blair, 307n27, 312n8
Renaissance, 147–48, 157
Resnais, Alain, 263
Revue Nègre, 40, 68, 275, 296–97n21
Reynolds, Debbie, 1, 144, 257, 308n35
    "You Were Meant for Me" dance, 155–57, 156f
Rhapsody in Blue (Gershwin), 24, 56, 70–74,
    275, 295n9, 297n24, 297n35
Rhodes, Erik, 45
rhythm as a term, 25–27, 291n34
    as a code word, 26
    fascinating rhythm, 25–26
rhythm instruments, 31–33. *see also* props
"The Rhythm of the Day" (Rodgers and
    Hart), 26
rhythm tap, 28, 30f, 31
Rimsky-Korsakov, Nikolai, 285
The Rink, 187
The Rite of Spring, 240, 273
"The Ritz Roll and Rock," 41
RKO Radio Pictures, 278
Robbins, Jerome, 113, 115, 119, 140, 170, 212,
    260, 302n93, 312n3, 312n13, 313n5
    choreography, 189–90
    dance studies and training, 167–68, 312n8
    Fancy Free, 167–69, 168f
    homosexuality, 174
    timeline, 274, 282, 285
Roberta, 97
    "I'll Be Hard to Handle," 31, 33, 39f, 40, 58,
    58f, 151–53, 152f
    "Smoke Gets in Your Eyes," 47f
Robinson, Bill "Bojangles," 16, 27–28, 31,
    116–17, 271, 274, 277
Robinson, Sugar Ray, 261
Rodeo, 169–70, 281
Rodgers, Richard, 5, 21, 63–87, 103, 179, 235,
    278, 279, 281. *see also specific works*
Rogers, Ginger, 26, 37f, 39, 39f, 40–41, 46–47,
    46f, 47f, 58–59, 144, 229, 278, 295n4
    in *Carefree*, 159f

"I'll Be Hard to Handle" dance, 58, 58f, 151, 152f
"Isn't It a Lovely Day" dance, 30f, 31,
    149–50, 150f
"Night and Day" dance, 144–47, 146f
    off-balance dancing, 57f
    in *Shall We Dance*, 89
roller-skate dance, 187–88
The Rolling Stones, 263
"Romance" ("La nuit"), 296n20
romantic love, 164–65
Romberg, Sigmund, 274, 285
Romeo and Juliet, Prokofiev-MacMillan, 266
"Romeo and Juliet" ballet, *Goldwyn Follies*,
    98–99, 99f
Romero, Alex, 124, 211, 306n25
Roosevelt, Theodore, 19
Rosalinda, 281, 293n2
"Rose Adagio," 294n21
Rose Marie, 293n2
Rosenberg, Douglas, 262, 287n3
Roshan, Hrithik, 264
Rosher, Charles, 203–4
Ross, Herbert, 266
Ross, Jerry, 285
Rousseau, Henri, 218, 318n53
Royal Ballet, 149f, 212, 266
Royal Wedding, 7, 125, 190–91, 283
Rubies, 33, 110
Runnin' Wild, 28, 40
Russell, Maude, 84, 300n69
Russell, Rosalind, 151
Russia
    Diaghilev diaspora, 66–70
    military dance, 312n11
    October Revolution, 17, 274
Russian Imperial Ballet, 51–53, 118–19
Russian State Ballet, 42, 67
Russian tap, 21
Russian tradition, 118–19
Ruttenberg, Joseph, 315n14

Sadler's Wells (later Royal Ballet), 212
sailors, 167–78, 168f, 173f, 209–11, 210f, 312n9,
    312nn12–13
sailor's hornpipe, 171
Saint-Léon, Arthur, 49–50
Salinger, Conrad (Connie), 37, 64, 157, 195,
    216, 238–41, 245–46, 249, 263–64,
    320n14, 321n19

sand dance, 31, 33
Sandrich, Mark, 279–80
Saroyan, William, 123, 306n18
Satie, 70, 275
satire, 85, 222–26, 257, 262, 319n58
Satte pe Satta, 264
Saturday Night Fever, 265
Sauguet, 276
Savoy Ballroom (Harlem), 8, 39f, 40
Savoy Hotel (London, England), 293n10
"Say a Prayer for Me Tonight," 251
Sayer, Leo, 179
Scandals, 72
scat, 28
Schact, Al, 261
Scheherazade, 85, 96, 207
Scherzo à la russe (Stravinsky), 297n35
Schillinger, Joseph, 240, 298n53
Schoenberg, Arnold, 59
School of American Ballet, 67, 107, 279
Schorer, Suki, 304n33
schuhplattler dance, 31
Schwartz, Arthur, 16, 74, 76, 247, 277, 284, 301n88
Schwartz, Jean, 274
scores, 241
Scorsese, Martin, 10, 258, 303n20
Scott, Lee, 211
Seay, Deanna, 109f
Second Chorus, 33, 280
seduction dance, 143–49, 146f. see also
    courtship dance
See Here, Private Hargrove, 313n25
Der Seerauber (Fulda), 316n32
Seitz, John, 104
Selznick, David O., 123, 278
set design, 77, 217–18, 317–18n49. see also decor
Setterfield, Valda, 260
Seven Brides for Seven Brothers, 7, 125, 143, 161,
    211, 249, 284
    barn-raising sequence and courtship
        dance, 249
    "Bless Your Beautiful Hide" (establishing
        sequence), 238
    Bollywood version, 264
    courtship dance, 161
Seymour, Felix, 307n32
Shakespeare in Love, 148
Shall We Dance, 26, 45, 89, 131, 187–88,
    248, 266

"Let's Call the Whole Thing Off," 187
"Slap That Bass," 56
"They All Laughed," 57f
"Walking the Dog," 56, 308n39
"Shall We Dance," 30, 89
Sharaff, Irene, 197, 204, 206, 217,
    317–18nn49–50
Shawn, Ted, 43, 60f, 225, 274
Shearer, Moira, 212
"Shoes with Wings," 48
"Shorty George," 57f
Showboat, 20, 307n29
Shubert, J. J., 274
Shubert, Lee, 274
Shuffle Along, 27–28, 275, 301n87
Silk Stockings, 58, 144, 162–63, 163f,
    188–89, 285
    "The Ritz Roll and Rock," 41
    "Stereophonic Sound," 56
Silvers, Phil, 127–30, 128f–29f
Sims, Sandman, 31
Sinatra, Frank, 170–73, 176–77, 283
    in Anchors Aweigh, 176–177
    in On the Town, 231–34, 232f–33f
Since You Went Away, 313n25
Singin' in the Rain, 3, 26, 106, 120–22, 125–26,
    140, 143, 238, 259, 284, 305n4, 308n35
    Broadway ballet, 99f, 219–22, 221f
    "Broadway Rhythm," 219
    "Fit as a Fiddle," 238, 246–47
    "Gotta Dance," 219–22, 221f
    "Singin' in the Rain," 1–2, 4, 113, 179,
        183–86, 184f
    "You Were Meant for Me," 155–57, 156f
"Singin' in the Rain," 1–2, 4, 113, 179,
    183–86, 184f
Sissle, Noble, 27–28, 275
site dance, 191
"Skip to My Lou," 194
The Sky's the Limit, 4, 259, 281
"Slap That Bass," 56
"Slaughter on Tenth Avenue," 66, 84–87,
    100f–101f, 102–3, 106, 121–22, 225, 225f,
    280, 295n9, 302n94, 306n16
Sleeping Beauty, 52f, 271, 294n21
slides, 110
Slonimsky, Yuri, 303n11
Small's Paradise, 28
Smiles, 277

The Smiling Lieutenant, 237, 277

Smith, Marian, 8, 311n11

Smith, Oliver, 319–20n5

"Smoke Gets in Your Eyes," 47f

"Snowball," 296–97n21

soccer, 133

social dance, 38, 40–41

soldiers, 167–68, 168f

Sombert, Claire, 120

"Somebody Loves Me," 72

Sondheim, Stephen, 9, 285, 311n15, 314n7

"So Near and Yet So Far" (Porter), 42

song(s). *see also specific titles*

    courtship song and dance, 143–65

    melismatic singing, 27

    popular, 23–25

Song of Norway, 293n2

"The Son of a Gun Is Nothing but a Tailor," 249

The Soul Kiss, 49, 49f, 50, 273

The Sound of Music, 186, 238

South American Baroque, 316n28

South Carolina, 75, 298n54

Spanish dance, 42, 120–21

Spellbound, 315n19

Speranzeva, Lumilla, 112

Spessivtseva, Olga, 52, 52f, 148

Spielberg, Stephen, 263–64

Spillane, Mickey, 223

Square Dance, 285

St. Denis, Ruth, 35, 42–43, 59, 60f, 225, 271–74

St. Petersburg Conservatory, 297n26

stage dance, 7–8, 290n18

Stannus, Edris (Ninette de Valois), 49, 120, 212, 272, 275–76

Stars and Stripes, 285

"The Stars and Stripes Forever," 308n37

Star Spangled Rhythm, 103–4, 180, 281

Star Wars, 107, 304n23

step dance, 27, 33, 116

Step Up 3D, 266

"Stereophonic Sound," 193

Stevens, George, 279

Stewart, Jimmy, 23–24

"Stiff Upper Lip," 308n35

Stoll, Oswald, 74

Stone, Dorothy, 145

Stone, Emma, 268–69

Stone, Fred, 145

Stop Flirting, 275

Stoppard, Tom, 177

The Story of Vernon and Irene Castle, 39, 39f, 280

storytelling, 48–51

Stradling, Harry, 206, 315n14

Strauss, Johann, 293n2

Strauss, Oscar, 281–82

Stravinsky, Igor, 59, 240, 297n35, 300n73

streamlining, 47–48, 47f, 108, 109f

street dance, 4, 133–34, 140, 258–59, 264, 268–69, 308n45. *see also specific dances*

    euphoric, 179–92

    prototypes, 131–32

Streisand, Barbra, 257

Strictly Ballroom, 266

Strike, 95

Strohm, Walter, 181

Sublett, John W. (Bubbles), 16, 28, 30f, 31, 32f, 33, 116–17, 272, 275

Summer Stock, 283

"Summertime" (Gershwin), 75

Superscope, 309n52

Supremes, 255

Surrealism, 201–4, 220, 261, 315n21–315n22, 316nn25–26

"Swanee," 71, 274

Swan Lake, 51–52, 106–7, 148, 157, 271

"Swan Lake" (Balanchine), 303n20

Swayze, Patrick, 265

Sweet Charity, 257

Swift, Kay, 66, 76, 279, 295n7, 298n47

swing, 18, 22, 115

"Swing Symphony," 90

Swing Time, 30–31, 36, 97, 143, 279

    "Bojangles," 137

    "Never Gonna Dance," 135, 248

    "Pick Yourself Up," 148

    "Waltz in Swing Time," 46–47, 46f

    "'S Wonderful," 4–5, 179–92, 182f, 248

La sylphide, 52

Les sylphides, 117, 273

symphonic jazz, 297n35

Symphony in C, 108, 111, 282

syncopation, 25, 31–33

tableaux vivants, 204, 218–20, 221f, 223, 251

taboos, 82–83

Take Me Out to the Ball Game, 261, 283, 307n32, 307n35, 321n22
Take the Lead, 266
Tales of the Jazz Age (Fitzgerald), 22
Tallchief, Maria, 47, 107–8, 109*f*, 111
Tamiris, Helen, 262, 277, 291n27
tango, 38
Tanguy, Yves, 204
tap dance, 7, 33, 65, 113, 218, 289n3, 292n45, 305n4
  Flash tap, 312n8
  jazz tap, 6
  Kelly's approach to, 116–17
  rhythm tap, 28, 30*f*, 31
  Russian, 21
taps, metal, 28, 292n45, 292n51
tassle kicks, 157
Taurog, Norman, 280
Taylor, Deems, 90
Tchaikovsky, 80, 108, 154
Tchelitchev, Pavel, 73
technical innovation, 106–7
Technicolor, 97–98, 199, 317n35
Technirama, 309n52
Techniscope, 309n52
television, 256–57, 303n20
Temptations, 255
Tharp, Twyla, 8, 178, 260
"That Old Black Magic," 104, 180
"That Old Devil Moon," 180
That's Entertainment, 267
"That's Entertainment," 247–48
Théâtre des Champs- Élysées (Paris, France), 296n17, 297n24
Theatre Guild, 316n32
Theme and Variations, 111, 279
"They All Laughed," 57*f*
"They Can't Take That Away from Me," 89
"Things Are Looking Up," 131, 132*f*
Thirty Seconds over Tokyo, 313n25
"This Heart of Mine," 36, 37*f*, 48, 194–95, 203
Thompson, Virgil, 90, 280
Thorpe, Richard, 283
Thousands Cheer, 281
3D technique, 266
"Three Blind Mice," 103
Three Brown Jacks, 292n41
Three Little Words, 283

Three Musketeers, 283
The Three Seasons, 73
Thriller, 258–59
through-composed, through-choreographed musicals, 229–53
"Tiger Rag," 56
Tiller girls, 72
Time magazine, 81
The Time of Your Life, 122–23, 170, 280
Tiomkin, Dimitri, 296n11, 297n24
Titus, Antoine, 311n11
Todd AO, 309n52
toe dancing *(pointe)*, 21, 44, 104, 291n22, 294n21
Toland, Gregg, 91, 96–97, 256–57
Top Hat, 55*f*, 57*f*, 97, 279, 295n4, 309n49
  dance-mime sequences, 58–59
  finale, 248
  "Isn't It a Lovely Day," 30*f*, 31, 58, 149–50, 150*f*
  "No Strings," 31, 32*f*, 33, 58*f*, 131
  "The Piccolino," 36–37, 37*f*, 41, 51, 248
  "Top Hat, White Tie, and Tails," 30–33
Toumanova, Tamara, 107, 120
Le train bleu, 53, 54*f*
"Tra-la-la-la," 191, 245–46
traveling song(s), 237, 250, 265, 320n7
Travolta, John, 265
Triumph of Neptune, 53, 68, 69*f*, 275
trucking, 45
Truffaut, François, 262–63
turkey trot, 38
The Turning Point, 266
Twentieth Century Fox, 320n14
"Two-Faced Woman" (Balanchine), 301n88

"Ubangi" (device), 317n37
Ultra-Panavision, 309n52
Union Pacific, 117, 169–70, 279
University of Pittsburgh, 278

Valentino, Rudolph, 266
Van Gogh, Vincent, 318n53
Variety, 83
variety revues, 74
Varsity Show, 32*f*, 33
vaudeville, 20–21, 35, 42–43, 74, 272–73, 293n8, 294n18

Vera-Ellen, 99, 113, 144
Verdon, Gwen, 7, 287n6
vernacular movement, 57–59, 58f, 211
Versailles, 148
Vestris, Auguste, 50
video, 258–59
Vidor, Charles, 126
vision sequences, 201–2
VistaVision, 309n52
visual literacy, 10
Vitaphone, 26
Vladimirov, 275
vocalises, 300n78
Vol de nuit, 299n65
Volta, Ornella, 68
"La Volta," 148, 293n7

Wadsworth Athenaeum (Hartford, CT),
    315n22
Wagner, Richard, 287n4, 298n53
Walbrook, Anton, 212
"Walking the Dog," 56, 308n39
Wallace, Henry, 132
Walters, Charles, 113, 115, 188, 283
waltz, 36, 37f, 268–69, 293n2
waltz-clog, 293n2
Warburg, Edward (Eddie), 64, 76, 90, 298n47,
    302n3
Warren, Harry, 195, 283
"Watch Your Step" (Castle), 273
"Water Nymph," 98, 104–7, 105f
Wayburn, Ned, 20, 44, 273, 294n18
The Way You Make Me Feel, 258–59
Weamer, Ted, 104
Webb, Chick, 68–69
Webern, Anton, 59
"Wedding Cake" (Astaire), 272
"The Wedding Cake Walk," 36, 248
Weidman, Charles, 17, 122, 277, 281, 291n27,
    299n61
Weill, Kurt, 315n19
Welles, Orson, 97
Wenders, Wim, 266
West Africa, 26
Westport Country Playhouse, 122
West Side Story, 20, 126, 140, 189–90, 238, 285
    "Cool," 258, 313n5
Whannel, Paddy, 307n27

What Next, Corporal Hargrove, 313n25
What's Up?, 281
Wheeldon, Christopher, 262
Where's Charley?, 283
Whistler, James McNeill, 197–99
White, George, 72, 116
Whiteman, Paul, 24, 72, 275, 297n35
White Nights, 262, 266
Who Cares?, 33, 74, 110, 298n50
whole-body dancing, 45–48, 46f, 47f
wide-screen processes, 309n52
Wiéner, Jean, 74
Wigman, Mary, 59
Wilder, Alec, 29
Williams, John, 263–64
Winter Garden Theatre (New York, NY),
    75–76, 274, 300n78
Wise, Robert, 186, 313n5
Within the Quota, 70
Woollcott, Alexander, 24
Words and Music, 106
"Words without Music," 77, 113, 202, 299n60,
    315–16n23
World War I, 22, 273–74
World War II, 280–82
    dancing sailor icon, 167–78
"Worry Song," 173f, 176, 313n26
Wright, Joseph C., 107
Wuthering Heights, 97
Wyatt, Donald, 82–83
Wyler, William, 97

Xanadu, 257

"The Yam," 41, 148, 261
Yankee Clipper, 21
"The Yankee Doodle Boy" (*Little Johnny
    Jones*), 272
Yolanda and the Thief, 134, 193–94, 197, 240,
    282, 315n19
    "Coffee Time," 51
    "A Day for Love," 237–38
    dream sequences, 5, 201–4, 203f
"You Can't Always Get What You Want"
    (The Rolling Stones), 263
You'll Never Get Rich, 248, 281
    "So Near and Yet So Far," 42
    "The Wedding Cake Walk," 36, 248

Youmans, Vincent, 278
Young Ballet, 275
"You're All the World to Me," 190–91
Youskevitch, Igor, 107, 120
YouTube, 267
"You Were Meant for Me," 155–57
You Were Never Lovelier, 31–33, 36–37, 240, 281
　"I'm Old Fashioned," 51
　"Shorty George," 57f

Zangwill, Israel, 19–20, 273
Zéphire et Flore, 70, 73, 297n26, 297n39,
　300n72
Ziegfeld Follies, 31, 53, 134, 193–96, 282,
　314n6
　"Beauty," 202–4
　"Limehouse Blues," 48, 194, 197–201, 198f
　"This Heart of Mine," 36, 37f, 48, 194–95, 203
　"Water Nymph," 98, 104–7, 105f
Ziegfeld Follies of 1915, 42
Ziegfeld Follies of 1916, 53

Ziegfeld Follies of 1936, 74–84, 79f, 298n48,
　299nn59–62, 301n82
　CD, 300n78
　choreography, 123
　ending, 301n80
　"Five A.M.," 77, 79f, 80, 82, 113, 202,
　　299n60
　orchestration, 240
　rehearsals, 75, 80–81, 299n62
　timeline, 279
　"Words without Music," 77, 113, 202,
　　299n60, 315–16n23
Ziegfeld Theatre (New York, NY), 277
Ziegfield, Florenz, 78
Zimmer, Paul, 266
Zorina, Vera (Brigitta Hartvig), 91, 94–95,
　104–7, 302n94, 303n18, 303n20, 304n22
　in *The Goldwyn Follies*, 97–99, 99f
　"Slaughter on Tenth Avenue" dance,
　　100f–101f, 102–3, 225, 225f
　"Water Nymph" ballet, 98, 104–7, 105f